Three Ri

Three Rivers

A Kentucky Folk History

DAN LEE

McFarland & Company, Inc., Publishers
Jefferson, North Carolina

ISBN (print) 978-1-4766-9190-9
ISBN (ebook) 978-1-4766-4936-8

LIBRARY OF CONGRESS AND BRITISH LIBRARY
CATALOGUING DATA ARE AVAILABLE

Library of Congress Control Number 2023001710

Front cover image: Abandoned mill at Falls of Rough, Kentucky
(image by the author); *background* © Cryptographer/Shutterstock

Printed in the United States of America

*McFarland & Company, Inc., Publishers
Box 611, Jefferson, North Carolina 28640
www.mcfarlandpub.com*

Table of Contents

Table of Contents

Acknowledgments

Among the many who helped with this project, the author wishes to thank John Lay, Steven L. Wright, Sherrill Williams, Mike Sisk, Carolyn Wimp, Helen A. McKeown, Carly Smith, Rick Gardner, Stephen Lee, Christina Snyder, and Jacob Fielding Lee. The author is especially grateful to his wife, Linda Akins Lee.

Finally, the author owes a lifelong debt of gratitude to Harvey Edward Copelin, Jr., a fine man, a great farmer, and a storyteller without equal. This book is dedicated to his memory.

Rivers know this: there is no hurry.
We shall get there someday.
—A.A. Milne

Preface

What a hold the rivers have on us! Rivers of blood course through our bodies, floods of sweet and sad memories rise in us until our eyes overflow with tears, and streams of consciousness pour from our mouths. Rivers are very deep in our collective memory. Human life took root along the rivers, and faith tells us that when life is done, it is a river we will cross to find our final rest.

No other object in nature is so commonly compared to the individual human life as the river. The life as sky? It makes no sense. As earth? No. As a rainbow? Ridiculous. The life as a cave? God forbid. It is the river whose winding, sometimes tranquil and sometimes troubled journey most closely conforms to the human experience. In our myth and metaphor, in our hearts and our history, it is always the rivers to which we return.

The James and the Potomac; the Ohio, Mississippi, and Missouri; the Platte, Sweetwater, and the Columbia: these are the chapters of our national saga. They pointed the way west and sustained us until we arrived. There are mountains, deserts, and plains to admire, but they do not resonate in our imagination like the rivers.

Kentucky is richly blessed with rivers. This book tells the story of only three of them: the Rolling Fork, the Nolin, and the Rough. It is the tale of a fractious force of nature flowing through a land that varied in its quality but which, rocky or rich, always had to be won. It is the story of people who made out with what they had and often it was not much. Sometimes they were wasteful and violent and vain; at other times, they were inventive and graceful and kind. What they all had in common was that the rivers called them.

The rivers were life itself to our ancestors, but time has worked a cruel reversal. Now, the continuing life of these historic streams depends on *us*. The recreational lakes of their impounded waters are safe; they are among the economic engines of the region and their value is readily apparent, but the once wild places that the day trippers never see have been misused as dumps and sewers and, in these days of legislative retrenchment, they continue to be in peril. Unless they are protected from the depletion of filtering vegetation; from agricultural, industrial, and urban runoff; from accidents such as the summer 2018 spill of tens of thousands of gallons of whiskey from a warehouse near Bardstown; and from the sheer accumulation of daily litter, they may finally be unknown to our children except as sluggish channels lined with refuse and running thick with poison, not life givers but stinking beds of toxicity, dangerous, repulsive, and always to be avoided.

The rivers are our natural inheritance, and it is simple common sense to preserve and defend them. But what will be necessary to launch that twenty-first-century campaign of enlightened legislation and individual action required to protect our rivers? First is acknowledging the fundamental morality of it and taking mature responsibility for our own actions. However, to drive it deep where it will live to guide us, we must turn to a means of inspiration as old as the Greeks. To remind themselves of their proud traditions and present obligations as citizens, they told the stories.

With that same purpose in mind, here are some of our stories.

Part One
The Rolling Fork

The Rolling Fork River Valley

Map by Sasha Jovanovic.

Introduction

If there is a region of Kentucky that truly does deserve to be called "dark and bloody ground," it is the valley of the Rolling Fork. This is a land that has been struggled over and the struggles have been brutal. Ancient Indians built elaborate forts to defend their claims to the resources of the river and the land. Much later, the pioneers endured galling attacks from the Shawnee and other tribes. After that, the blue fought the gray, and the farmer and the storekeeper fought them both to try to save what they had earned from becoming plunder dangling from some trooper's saddle horn or jingling away in his haversack. It has always been and, in modern times, is still a land of war. One who forgets that is soon reminded by the pounding thunder of the Fort Knox artillery ranges.

The struggle, though, has not just been between people of different races or of competing beliefs. The land and the river have been an unmerciful adversary to man. The land itself seems to brood—it *is* dark in the narrow corridors of the Knobs. It is not a comforting shade; it is a *shadow* and one in which the traveler becomes wary. Suddenly, the traveler emerges from the twisting Knobs into a flat sunny valley where the roads are as straight as the cornrows. How welcome the sight of these wide, sunlit valleys must have been to those who came to settle here, but it was an enticing trap. The pioneers who were encouraged to settle in the valleys where the soil was deep and the shade gave way did not yet know of the river's uniquely unstable temperament. The Rolling Fork has an extreme tendency to flood. In these broad valleys between the knobs the river can rise with surprising speed and spread over hundreds of acres with no impediment and thus drown the farmers' corn and tobacco along with his hopes.

It is as if the land and the river have a malevolent spirit that consciously schemes against the people who strive to live there. Perhaps that is why the Catholic Church found such a welcoming sanctuary in the valley of the Rolling Fork. Other churches were also established there, but they were only a patch to the Catholics. The people needed divine help and the Church of Rome, the original Christian faith, had the experience and power to battle against the evil spirits in a land so dark and bloody.

And yet, it is a beautiful land to see, the rugged Knobs and the flat farmland with the river winding through. It is a land worth having, though never easily won, and for fifteen thousand years, people have undertaken to conquer the dark spirit of the Rolling Fork Valley and make it serve them. There have been notable successes, but the struggle has always been hard.

This is the story of that struggle.

ONE

The Struggle Begins

The Rolling Fork was born of a struggle, a contest between the continental masses for position on the face of the earth. Between five hundred and three hundred million years ago, the free-floating African-Eurasian-South American continent tried to shoulder the North American continent to one side. The crushing impact of this collision created the Appalachian Mountains, the oldest on the continent. Geologists believe they were as high as the Himalayas or the Alps. Locally, the force of the blow thrust up what came to be known as Muldraugh Hill and the Knobs. Millions of years of erosion followed and carved them into the familiar shapes which are seen today. The lands along the Appalachian's western flank rose from the shallow sea that covered them and tilted so that a slow draining began.[1]

The westward flowing waters found their channels and improved them, scouring them into proper riverbeds. The new rivers ran through a strange world. Ferns thirty meters tall and other weird plants sprouted to cover the drying land. Dragonflies as big as buzzards hovered over the feeding salamanders and toads. No evidence of dinosaurs has yet been found in Kentucky, though many believe it will be. If these great masters of the land did somehow miss Kentucky, the mammals certainly did not. The first tiny fur-bearers appeared about sixty-five million years ago, and they thrived. Then, about one million years ago the giants appeared. Mastodons, mammoths, huge bison, and even rhinos grazed on the grasses along the riverside. The end of the last Ice Age made many of these creatures extinct, but the hardiest survived to attract the first people into the valley, their way opened by the retreating glaciers.[2]

To speak of spans of time like those mentioned above is nearly meaningless. However, with the arrival of man in the Rolling Fork Valley, we begin to approach a time near enough to the present and a way of life near enough to our own that we can understand it. The climate was colder and wetter, but the land began to resemble the land we see today, and the people who lived on it were ennobled by the same virtues and crippled by the same frailties that we ourselves have.

Even so, there are many mysteries about the pre–Columbians that can never be solved. The little we know about the earliest settlers of the Rolling Fork has been pieced together from the physical clues of stone, bone, and ceramic that have been discovered in their hunting grounds, camps, burial sites, and towns. Scholars, though they are not always in perfect agreement, have done an admirable job of detective work in piecing together the clues.

The first Kentuckians were nomadic hunters of woolly mammoths, traveling always behind the herds, trying to bring down one of the elephant-sized mammals with their spears. No one knows what they called themselves; modern man calls them the Paleo Indians. The flint points they used were beautifully crafted and were also the deadliest weapon that they would have for a long time to come. These Clovis points, as they are called, are the first ones known to have been used in North America, and they have been found in plowed fields and at the river's edge all along the Rolling Fork. Later times brought refinements and changes to the spear points, but the Clovis was classic in both beauty and function.

Hunting such large animals as mammoths and giant buffalos required a group effort and some planning, so the Paleo Indians must have had a spoken language. After a mammoth was brought down, the small band camped around the body, butchering meat off the carcass as it was needed and working the hide into clothes, moccasins, and shelter. When the mammoth was used up, the next hunt began. Authors Greg J. Maggard and Kary L. Stackelbeck speak of a "notable concentration" of Paleo sites in the valley of the Rolling Fork. The Paleo Indians found something pleasing about the area, but, as the climate warmed, they found that they must adapt to new conditions. The large game that had sustained them grew more scarce, partly as a consequence of overhunting and partly because the herds followed the receding glaciers north. What remained behind was small game such as deer and the woodland buffalo, and plant life developed and diversified. Nuts and berries became a staple of everyday diet. Eventually, the shift to smaller game and a foraging way of life became so complete that a new cultural phase is considered to have commenced, the Archaic.[3]

The Archaic Indians hunted small game and the size of their projectile points diminished accordingly. They gathered hickory nuts, grapes, persimmons, and blackberries. More significant than all of this, they eventually began to cultivate small garden plots where they grew squash and sunflowers, as well as goosefoot, little barley, and sumpweed.

Evidence shows that the Indians cultivated them as early as 5,000 years ago. With the advent of cultivation, the Archaic people began roaming less in order to be near their gardens. They harvested mussels from the rivers, and the shells they discarded grew into tall mounds. At some point, the Indians began to bury their dead in the shell mounds, customarily in the side facing the river, and what had been a habitation site originally chosen on the practical basis of good soil and reliable water assumed an emotional and spiritual significance as the resting place of their ancestors. In the late Archaic period, textiles appeared. Weavers made baskets, and some clothing and moccasins, too, began to be made of textiles. Burials became more elaborate and sometimes the graves contained items fashioned from materials that were traded into the valley of the Rolling Fork.[4]

Trade was a benefit of a more sedentary way of life, and as it increased in importance the third pre–Columbian culture of Kentucky emerged, the Woodland Culture. The Woodland Indians occupied the valley of the Rolling Fork for two thousand years, roughly 1000 BCE to 1000 CE, and most of that time is considered to be the golden age of Kentucky's pre–Columbians. The climate was ideal and the food supply was stable. The people still hunted and gathered, but cultivated crops began to be increasingly relied upon, especially corn. Corn, also called maize, appeared during this period as a ceremonial crop and continued to increase in importance until it became a staple. It produced a greater yield than goosefoot and the lesser crops of earlier times. Near the villages, there were sacred or ceremonial places where the people buried their dead in large earthen mounds. Interments occurred over a period of time, just as is the case in modern cemeteries. As each body was placed and covered with a layer of earth, the burial mound grew to impressive dimensions. One Kentucky mound (this one not in the Rolling Fork Valley, however) was about twenty feet high, 130 feet across, and contained eighty-nine burials. Furthermore, the mounds were maintained with the addition of more dirt as it was needed.[5]

The Native villagers may have been preoccupied with matters pertaining to death, but life was burgeoning. The population was growing and the influx of trade goods enriched the lives of the people. They traded as far west as the Rocky Mountains for grizzly bear claws and obsidian and as far north as the Great Lakes for copper. Bennett Young found copper spools in one of the many mounds near Lebanon in Marion County. The Indians traded south to the Gulf Coast and east to the Chesapeake Bay for shells and sharks' teeth. They probably traded with the Indians of Mexico. More than one bust showing a definite Meso-American influence has been found in the upper reaches of the

Rolling Fork. Life for the Woodland Indians was rich and interesting, what with the regular arrival of trade goods and new ideas from the outside. They enjoyed a long period of relative tranquility, but it did not last.[6]

The Indians who populated the Rolling Fork Valley in the last pre-contact period (1000 CE to about 1600), were primarily of a group called the Mississippians, and they lived in fear of their enemies. By 700 CE., the bow and arrow made what one scholar calls "a sudden dramatic appearance throughout most of the Eastern Woodlands." Significant numbers of skeletons from burial sites of this time display bones pierced by arrowheads and other wounds that plainly indicate a violent death. Warfare seems to have been sporadic rather than constant. The people in outlying farm villages tended their gardens in times of peace, and when danger threatened, they retreated to the safety of towns that were surrounded by a defensive palisade. These large communities were built around a plaza and a platform mound—a tall, flat topped mound that served as the base for the priest's or ruler's house.[7]

If still more evidence is needed of violent intertribal or interregional conflict, there are the remains of two Indian forts near the Rolling Fork. The researchers Lewis Collins, of the nineteenth century, and Bennett Young of the twentieth documented them. Both men mentioned the fort that was found six miles east of Hodgenville in LaRue County. Young described it in 1910:

> This fort included an area of three and three-fourths acres. It is now covered with heavy forest. In its shattered and broken condition it yet gives evidence of advancement among these prehistoric people in the art of fort building. It was situated on a bluff 300 feet high, either perpendicular or partially overhanging the river below. Its elevation gave it a position from which a splendid lookout could be maintained for miles away ... the rock wall, which was the real protection of this fort, had no gateway or entrance. Behind the wall was a ditch. The remains of the wall ... show a structure four and one-half feet high, with a base of 15 feet.... The length of the main wall across the neck of the fortification is 363 feet ... all in all there is no stone fort in Kentucky that presents more painstaking preparation or more careful construction for efficiency in defense.[8]

On Ritchie's Run several miles south of Bardstown was another stone fortification that Young called "probably the most remarkable of all the stone remains in Kentucky." This fort was in the shape of two half-squares, one inside the other, sixteen feet apart; the north-south walls ran 225 feet and the east-west walls ran 225 feet, both were six feet high. Foundations four feet thick and extending three and one-half feet down to bedrock supported the walls. Some of the foundation stones were estimated to weigh one thousand pounds. Above grade, the walls were made of slabs of rock, some of them three feet wide and nine feet long, topped by a course of irregularly shaped stones fitted tightly together. The fort stood between two fine springs of water and there was Ritchie's Run below.[9]

The ancient fort became a well-known landmark after white settlement. People continually pestered the elderly owner to sell the stone from the ancient fort for chimneys, garden walls, and the like, but he refused. He recognized the structure as the wondrous (and as yet unexplained) curiosity that it was. The son who inherited the ruins, however, lived by different values. When the Louisville and Nashville Turnpike was under construction, the directors approached him to sell the stone, and he agreed. For $350 and a lifetime pass for himself and his family to travel the turnpike, he sold away one of Kentucky's greatest early treasures. Uncounted wagonloads of stone from the fortification were hauled away, right down to the foundation. The turnpike was built and the fort was gone.[10]

The early Natives undertook extraordinary feats of labor to defend their rights to the valley of the Rolling Fork, but in the last years, they abandoned the region. It probably happened about the year 1600 and no one knows why. In later years, even the Indians themselves could not explain why their ancestors had left the land where they had lived for so long. The Indians would come back in the 1770s, after the settlers had begun to stake their claims. Once again it would be in a time of war, and this time they would be carrying British muskets and scalping knives.

Two

Trailblazers

The Rolling Fork is shaped like a dowser's switch. The business end points west, bending toward the Salt River, and the "V" is in the East. The north branch of the "V" comes out of Boyle County. The southern branch flows out of Casey County. They meet in Marion County, just west of Bradfordsville and there the Rolling Fork starts to become a legitimate river. Some claim the Rolling Fork takes its name from the roiling action of its waters as it merges with the Salt River at Pitts Point. Others believe the name Rolling Fork is a corruption of the name Rawlings' Fork, named for the family of Edward Rawlings who lived near the river's end in Hardin County in the 1780s and 1790s. Sometimes, in the old records, the family name is spelled "Rolling."

Edward Rawlings came to Hardin County in the company of his father-in-law Jacob Van Meter, Sr., in 1780. Their party drifted down the Ohio River on twenty-seven flatboats from Fort Pitt in the fall of 1779. They wintered at the Falls and in the spring crossed overland into Severns Valley. Rawlings took up land east of there, on the present Rolling Fork. In between times of clearing his land and building his cabin, he served with General George Rogers Clark. He fought in the Shawnee campaigns of 1780 and 1782, and in the 1790s he became a deputy sheriff in a vast region which included today's Hardin, Meade, Breckinridge, Daviess, and Ohio Counties and parts of Hart, Grayson, and Edmonson.

Rawlings was described as a "slender, tall man ... nearly all muscle, very active." He was illiterate, but he took pride in his manliness and stood ready to defend his honor when challenged. The best known example of his sense of fair play is related by Samuel Haycraft, Jr., in his *History of Elizabethtown, Kentucky, and Its Surroundings*.[1]

Rawlings had a warrant for the arrest of an offender named William Smothers, who lived in that distant part of Hardin County, which is now Daviess County, 130 miles away from Elizabethtown. Rawlings's capture of Smothers was uneventful. The bad man was tied on his horse and the deputy led him as they began the long ride back to the jail in Elizabethtown. Haycraft says that between Hartford and Hardinsburg, Smothers started taunting Deputy Sheriff Rawlings, "Ned, I have heard of you, and that you boast yourself to be much of a man. Is it fair if you are a better man than me?" Finally, Smothers proposed a wrestling match; if Rawlings won then Smothers would ride back to Elizabethtown willingly, but if he won, Rawlings must let him go. Rawlings accepted the challenge. He untied the prisoner and the two wrestled until the outlaw bested the deputy. True to his word, Rawlings set Smothers free. Rawlings had lost both his prisoner and his fee of three shillings in tobacco.[2]

It may have been this sense of chivalric honor and willingness to gamble everything on his physical abilities that cost Rawlings his life. He is said to have died in the line of duty in 1796, possibly the earliest lawman in Kentucky to be killed trying to maintain order.

By the time of his death, Edward Rawlings had already had a foretaste of the kind of trouble that could come to those who came to settle in the wilderness around the Rolling Fork. In 1791 Indians from the North carried away his married daughter Elizabeth and her children. Elizabeth Rawlings was married to Miles Hart whose skill with a rifle had won him the nickname "Sharp Eye." In a recent fight with a war party of Shawnee or Wyandots, Hart had killed the chief. The other braves plotted revenge. One morning in May 1791, Hart opened the door of his cabin, which stood not far from the Rolling Fork, and a shot dropped him dead at his threshold. The Indians had surrounded the cabin in the night. The oldest son Joe leaped to the door and tried with his father's rifle and tomahawk to keep the war party out of the cabin, but they burst in, gathered up what household plunder they wanted, and hurried north with the family: Elizabeth the mother, who was heavily pregnant; Miles Jr., age seven or eight; a daughter whose name is unknown, age nine; and Joe, age twelve. The Indians killed the little girl on the trail because she cried and Miles Jr., because he had a sore foot and could not keep up. Only Elizabeth and Joe were left alive when they reached the Ohio River. Mrs. Hart tore pieces of her undergarments and dropped them on the path for her rescuers to follow, but none came.

Arriving at their villages, the Indians took Joe to live with another band. Mrs. Hart was used as a slave by the Indians, made to water and firewood until the day she gave birth to the child she had been carrying, a son. After the baby was born, the village women brought her turkey broth and a blanket for the newborn. Her chores continued, though, and she went about them with the baby strapped to her back. It was a hard life. The baby died in the next winter, only six months old. After it died,

Mrs. Hart took her baby to the woods and buried it. She had seen her husband, her daughter, and her son murdered by her captors. Her other son had been taken from her, perhaps never to be seen again, and now her infant, the last reminder of the contented life she had once known, had died and was buried in the snow.

The next morning as Mrs. Hart walked down to the river for water, she saw something on the trail ahead of her. It was her baby's body. The Indians, for a lark, had dug it up and placed it in the trail to torment their white slave woman. Mrs. Hart laid her kettles down and reburied the tiny corpse. The next morning she again noticed an object on the trail in front of her, a smaller one this time. It was her baby's head, which the Indians had cut from the body. Once again, she performed a crude burial in the woods, but the next morning it was there again. Elizabeth Rawlings Hart realized that this cruelty would continue as long as she showed it was affecting her, so on this third morning she took her foot and pushed the baby's severed head aside and went on about her chore. When she came back with the kettles full of water, the head was gone and she never saw it again.

Her life as a slave among the Indians continued for the next five years, at least. The record is incomplete, but about 1796 (the year her father was killed) the Indians made the mistake of taking Mrs. Hart with them to Detroit to visit with their British friends. There, Mrs. Hart spoke hurriedly to a French fur trader down from Canada and explained to him her predicament. He purchased Mrs. Hart from the Indians for a keg of wine and returned her to her family in Hardin County.[3]

Back among her loved ones, Mrs. Hart learned that an attempt had been made to save her. Her brother-in-law Josiah Hart, brother of her slain husband, had undertaken to "redeem Mrs. Hart from the Savages" and had been paid for his effort £15:5:0 out of Miles Hart's estate. Josiah Hart failed to find Mrs. Hart, but his search may explain how Joe had returned to Kentucky. Joe married briefly, but when his young wife of only a few months died, he moved to Missouri and spent the rest of his life there.[4]

Women who had been Indian captives often found that they were outcasts once they returned to the white world, but that was not the case with Mrs. Hart. She remarried in 1797 to Peter Gunterman, a widower who lived with his small children on the Bullitt County side of the Rolling Fork. With Gunterman, she had a new family of three daughters. She lived long enough that her grandchildren remembered her well. At night, she sat in a rocking chair by the fire and told them tales of her Indian captivity, and they passed the stories down through the generations, along with the beads and moccasins she was wearing when she returned home to Kentucky. Elizabeth Rawlings Hart Gunterman died in 1844, having outlived her husband and all but one of their children. Near the end of her life she suffered from rheumatism and was confined to her bed, a woman surrounded by death who had survived to be one of the last of her generation. The Rolling Fork was not kind to the family who may have given the river its name.

The killing of Elizabeth Rawlings Hart's family and her captivity in the Northwest was one of the later episodes in the long contest between the whites and the Indians in the valley of the Rolling Fork. It was a two-decade-long struggle that began with the arrival of the explorers in 1776 and intensified as the settlers followed. In the spring of 1778, British Colonel Henry Hamilton at Detroit was able to inform his superiors, "The people of the frontiers have been increasingly harassed by parties of Indians. They have not been able to sow grain in Kentucky and will not have a morsel of bread by the middle of June. Cloathing is not to be had, nor do they expect any relief from Congress." The war with the Indians was fought along no battle lines and honored no rules of combat. All ages and both sexes were liable to find themselves fighting for their lives in their churchyards, barnyards, and front yards, and inside the very walls of their homes. Still, the settlers poured into the basin of the Rolling Fork, 1,443 square miles of howling wilderness, where any shadow might conceal an enemy.[5]

John Muldraugh was with the first party of white men to visit the Rolling Fork. Muldraugh and the others arrived in the valley in 1776, sent out by William McAfee at Harrodsburg to explore and to claim vast tracts of untouched forest and prairie. Muldraugh marked the corners to one thousand acres lying on both banks of the river, but he and his companions did not stay any longer than it took to build the cabin and plant the corn crop that secured their right to claim the land. They went back to Harrodsburg with an imperfect knowledge of what they had seen. No one would discover for some time the Rolling Fork's course or that it was a tributary of the Salt River.

Muldraugh was living near Danville in 1780, but he kept returning to the Rolling Fork to hunt around Cedar Lick where, he later said, he sometimes saw as many as one hundred buffalo at a time. At last, in 1784, Muldraugh moved to his claim with his wife Margaret McElroy. He spent the rest of his life there. The records show that he was a captain in the Nelson County militia, a slave owner, and the father of nine children. He was a trustee for the Presbyterian Church on Hardin's Creek. He owned a ferryboat on the Rolling Fork to carry across travelers on the Lexington-Nashville Road. Muldraugh is best remembered now by the seventy-five-mile-long escarpment that bears his name and which bounds the valley of the Rolling Fork from Calvary in Marion County to West Point in Hardin County.[6]

Samuel Pottinger was another of the early pioneers. In 1778, he wandered into the region east of Muldraugh Hill with his friend James Harrod, founder of Kentucky's first settlement. Pottinger was a twenty-four-year-old native of Prince George's County, Maryland, who had only recently returned to Kentucky from the east where he had been fighting the British. Now he was in Harrod's militia company, but when they could spare the time from defending the Bluegrass settlements, the two explored the land further west. At a spot where a smaller stream entered the Rolling Fork, Pottinger saw land that attracted him. He later said that the cane "was rank and plentiful ... generally as high as a man's head, and a great many as high as a man's head on horseback," a sure sign of fertility. The creek bank was laced with buffalo and deer tracks, along with those of wild turkey and smaller game. Blackberries and persimmons, pecans, walnuts, hickory nuts, and chestnuts grew all around. Harrod named the creek Pottinger's for his young friend who marked four hundred acres on the south bank and erected a small cabin to secure his claim.[7]

Pottinger returned in 1781 to build his station, a log stockade with a blockhouse on each corner. Pottinger's Station was a popular site. The extended Pottinger family came to join Samuel, as did the Mastersons from Pennsylvania. Other newcomers to the Rolling Fork found shelter with Pottinger until they were able to locate their own claims, and refugees from Indian trouble sometimes sought protection there. In 1782 Pottinger and his men joined George Rogers Clark's campaign to chastise the troublesome Shawnee and returned safely home to prosper in a more peaceable Kentucky. With the Indians at least somewhat subdued, the settlers at Pottinger's began to scatter farther out, away from the sanctuary of the fort.

Pottinger moved in 1788 two miles west of his station to build one of the first brick houses in Nelson County. The house resembled the brick homes Pottinger had known while growing up in Prince George's County. The interior woodwork was crafted primarily from black walnut, and there were wainscoting and chair rails and a mantle with fluted panels, all carved by hand. It was a gem of elegance in a raw setting that was still vulnerable to occasional Indians raids—Mrs. Hart's ordeal was still three years in the future. Just to be safe, Pottinger put up a log stockade around his mansion, but he need not have worried that violent death was stalking him. He enjoyed a long life at Walnut Hill. He died in January 1831 while visiting his daughter Betsey (the first child who was born in his station, long ago) and was buried in the Cox's Creek Baptist

Church Cemetery. Pottinger was dead but his settlement lived on and eventually acquired another name, New Haven.[8]

Simply surviving in Kentucky's frontier stations presented no end of practical complications for the settlers, but when moral complications were layered on, life took on challenges of a whole different sort. Samuel Goodin's life was testimony to that. Goodin was a Pennsylvania Quaker, that sect of plain and thoughtful people who have so often been the moral compass of our nation. As a Quaker, he was a man of peace, but his Nelson County fort was more than once the scene of bloody fighting. And, as a Quaker, he was an anti-slavery man, but, in the dowry of his second wife, he became the master of a slave named General Braddock who became one of the best-known Indian fighters in central Kentucky. The hard necessities of frontier life sometimes forced a man into moral contradictions.

Goodin came down the Ohio River in 1779 and, the next year, made his claim on land close to where Beech Fork enters the Rolling Fork. He claimed four thousand acres and built a stockade of split lumber. Goodin's Fort became kind of a crossroads in later years. It was on the path from the Falls of the Ohio to Pottinger's Station and was on the way, also, to Lynn's Station and Cox's Station. A road to the salt works at Bullitt's Lick was made from Goodin's in 1785 and one to Hodgen's Mill in 1793.

Like most able-bodied men, Goodin and his sons served in the militia, William Harrod's company, and son Isaac was a soldier under General George Rogers Clark during the 1782 Shawnee Campaign. They felt at Goodin's Fort that they had reason to make war against the Indians. One year before, in 1781, the settler John Bosman was killed in an Indian raid at Goodin's. That same year a party of men from Goodin's fell into an ambush that resulted in the death of five settlers and the capture of Peter Kennedy.[9]

A war party had been plaguing the area. They had killed twelve settlers, and some men from Goodin's and the surrounding neighborhood went in pursuit. They pushed hard, trying to catch the Indians before they reached the mouth of Salt River where they would cross the Ohio. Within a mile of the river, they came under fire; the Indians had stopped to wait for the whites to catch up. Five of the frontiersmen died immediately in the fight that followed, and Peter Kennedy was captured after his right hip was pierced by a musket ball. Young Kennedy struggled through the pain of his wounded hip, kept pace with the Indians, and survived to reach their village on the Wabash.

For two years, Kennedy lived among the Indians. Gradually he again became sound of limb and on a day when the Indians' watchfulness relaxed, Kennedy made his escape south. Once across the Ohio River, he began to feel that he had opened up enough distance between himself and the Indians that he could shoot some supper. He brought down a deer and cooked a steak. Just as he was finishing, an Indian musket cracked, and he jumped up and ran in the direction of Goodin's, thirty miles away.

The gap between Kennedy and his pursuers had barely widened when, hours later, he reached a hill (probably Miller Knob) overlooking the Rolling Fork and Goodin's Fort below. He stumbled down the hill and, with the Indians still close behind him, sprinted across the flat land toward the fort. Near there, the Indians gave up the chase. But now it was the white men's turn. The men of the fort grabbed their rifles and chased the warriors, who were exhausted from their long pursuit. They could not outrace the frontiersmen. All the Indians were killed, it is said, and that night Goodin's Fort celebrated the return of Peter Kennedy.[10]

Samuel Goodin was a widower even before he left Pennsylvania. In 1782, he took as his second wife Elizabeth Van Meter, the widow of Abraham Van Meter who had died of a battle wound at Squire Boone's Painted Stone Fort. She brought four daughters and a good deal of property into the marriage: pitchforks, plowshares, spades, harrow teeth, and grubbing hoes. Also, hammers, chisels, axes, augurs, saws, drawing knives, a flax hackle, spinning wheel, an iron pot and pot racks, griddles, tea kettles, and pewter dishes. And she brought livestock: eleven head of cattle, one bull, and three horses, and probably some hogs, too. The Widow Van Meter also brought a slave, General Braddock, who was appraised at a value of £100. We shall hear more of General Braddock later.

Goodin did not have the luck or the skill of Samuel Pottinger at keeping his land. Like so many of Kentucky's early settlers, he was the victim of murky land titles. In 1799 he lost his Nelson County station and the land surrounding it to Benedict Swope. Goodin's Fort disappeared and the site became tilled fields, without a trace to suggest the struggles of earlier times. Goodin did keep about two thousand acres in LaRue County and that is where he died in 1807. Sharpe Spencer built Goodin's coffin and charged the estate $3. It was a fine coffin, but Samuel Goodin lies somewhere in a forgotten grave.[11]

These years of Muldraugh, Pottinger, and Goodin, say 1778 to 1784, were the years when western civilization was planted in the rich soil of the Rolling Fork. Bardstown (originally Salem) was laid out in 1780, subdividing David Baird's one thousand acre claim into thirty-three parcels to be sold by lottery. Colonel Isaac Cox built his station a few miles southeast of Bardstown that same year, and Peter Bradford the hunter was killing deer in the forests where the town named for him, Bradfordsville, would soon sprout up. Other men were taking out claims of a thousand acres, two thousand, four thousand all along the Rolling Fork. These old frontiersmen were all of an adventurous spirit, but they were not hewn from the same log. Some were rough and tumble Virginians on the run from something bad back home; some were veterans looking for a fresh start with their military land warrants; some were speculators only in it for the profit; and some were true settlers whose interest was not only in what they could take from the land but also what they could make of it. James Rogers was one of these last. He was a force for civilization.[12]

Rogers was a thirty-eight-year-old Pennsylvania Irishman. He was a veteran of Lord Dunmore's War in 1774 and a patriot of the Revolution when, in 1780, he filed his claim for one thousand acres and built his station. It was made of cedar posts and was well situated near a spring and two deer licks. In his new Nelson County home Rogers helped start Cedar Creek Baptist Church. He was a lieutenant-colonel of the Nelson County militia and a justice of the peace whose appointment came from Governor Patrick Henry himself. He also attended two of Kentucky's enabling conventions in Danville, in May 1785, and again in August of that same year. These conventions and the ones that followed would finally accomplish Kentucky's separation from Virginia. Back in Nelson County, when he was not busy with religious, military, or political duties, Rogers directed young settlers to choice lands for their claims. Atkinson Hill was one who got off to a good start in Kentucky because of Rogers. Hill was married to Samuel Goodin's daughter, but for reasons now forgotten, he made his early home not in his father-in-law's colony but at Rogers Station. Rogers helped Hill locate the land he wanted and likely advised him when he marked the corners of his initial 325-acre claim. From this modest beginning, Hill went on to become a prominent mill owner, lawyer, and one of Nelson County's first gentleman justices.[13]

A religious disagreement eventually drove a wedge between Rogers and Hill, and others became caught up in the controversy as well. The issue was slavery. Hill was a slave owner (he bequeathed at least seven slaves to his family in his 1824 will), and Rogers was an opponent of human bondage. Atkinson Hill left Rogers Station to relocate at Goodin's, but the controversy stirred up by discussions of slavery spread beyond the settlement. Their church, Cedar Creek Baptist, also split over the issue. Hill had helped Rogers start Cedar Creek Baptist Church, but when slavery was introduced as a moral question, the congregation found itself pulled apart, attracted toward two opposite poles: Hill, who accepted slavery among Christian people and Rogers, who did not. The majority of the Cedar Creek congregation sided with Hill. He stayed with them, and Rogers left to "raise up" another church, Lick Creek Baptist. It was the sort of split that was becoming more common among the frontier congregations. J.H. Spencer said that even this early, well before the days of the grand estates, "Slavery was by far the most fruitful of mischief of all the questions that agitated the Baptist churches of Kentucky." It seems that on this issue there was no room for compromise. Rogers and Hill, were both civic minded men, and each accomplished much toward the bringing of justice and religion to the valley of the Rolling Fork, yet they finally found themselves unable to work in harmony because of the question that would divide the whole nation in the years to come.[14]

There was one more settlement that should concern us here, not because it grew into a thriving town like Bardstown or New Haven, but because it was the starting place of one of the Rolling Fork's signature industries. Benjamin Lynn was a Baptist preacher, a scout and soldier for George Rogers Clark, and a Kentucky explorer almost without peer. He found and followed Kentucky's interior rivers like the Green and the Elk Garden beginning in the middle 1770s. Lynn knew the Rolling Fork, as well, and decided to build his own station there. In 1779, he led a party from his home in the Bluegrass down the Licking River to the Ohio, past Louisville to the Salt River, up the Salt River to the Rolling Fork, thence to the Beech Fork, thence to Landing Run, about five miles from Bardstown. It was heavy paddling in the last part of their journey. They were moving upstream in five poplar log canoes sixty feet long and five feet wide.[15]

It must have been tricky. The Rolling Fork is full of tight bends, and although the current is only two to five miles per hour, there are logjams and other obstructions that require the skills of an expert waterman to negotiate. In his excellent book *A Canoeing and Kayaking Guide to Kentucky*, Bob Sehlinger warns that the Rolling Fork is an international class one plus river, which means that it can run to medium difficulty. This is in modern boats made of fiberglass or aluminum; one can imagine how much harder it was to maneuver around the hazards in a long canoe crudely fashioned from a rough poplar log. However, along with their other skills, Lynn's party were good canoeists, and they arrived safely. From Landing Run, the settlers tramped three miles overland to a plateau where they built Lynn's Station.[16]

Among the settlers with Lynn were John Ritchie and his wife Jemima. Ritchie was a twenty-seven-year-old Scotsman. The smell of freshly notched logs had scarcely faded from the cabins in Lynn's Station when Ritchie and his wife moved to a 650-acre claim two miles away on the south bank of the Beech Fork. There, Ritchie built a two-story log house with a stone chimney containing an upturned rock he inscribed with the characters "J. R., 1780." Ritchie cleared a field and planted his corn. Nearby was a never failing spring of cold limestone water, which gave him an idea about what to do with all that grain. Near his cabin, Ritchie built a one-story distillery, eighteen feet square, with a puncheon floor and walls of cedar logs. Here, John Ritchie made the first sour mash whiskey ever distilled in Kentucky.[17]

It was the start of something big. Today, Kentucky produces ninety-five percent of the world's bourbon and most of that comes from the valley of the Rolling Fork.

THREE

Whiskey and Salt

Ritchie's distillery became the center of an interconnecting web that gave rise to other pioneer industries and generated income for the settlers of the Rolling Fork. The essential ingredient was corn, so Ritchie began buying significant amounts of the grain from his neighbors. The whiskey from Ritchie's still had to be kegged, so some frontier cooper was given the work of making barrels bound with wooden hoops. The whiskey had to be transported to market, so men like Jesse Ice on the Beech Fork and Martin Everhart at New Market built flatboats to carry the liquor to New Orleans.

New Orleans was the main market for the tobacco, furs, and whiskey of Kentucky. It was much easier to move goods down the river than to transport them over rough trails across Knobs and mountains to Virginia. The Spanish in New Orleans paid good prices, too. After John Ritchie delivered his first cargo of whiskey to the Crescent City, he walked home up the Natchez Trace with a heavy load of New Orleans goods on his back. Others followed Ritchie's example, and for those who survived the trip, the profits were terrific, so the men kept flatboating south and then walking north, bringing wonderful things up the Trace to their wives and children.

Other distilleries sprang up in the years after Ritchie's original, but the free and easy days of whiskey making soon came to an end. The treasury department under Secretary Alexander Hamilton imposed a twenty-five percent excise tax on distilled spirits in 1791. In western Pennsylvania the protests erupted into actual rebellion against the government. The protests in Kentucky were milder; the distillers just refused to pay the tax. However, the government was serious about tax collection, and indicted, convicted, and fined those who resisted. In the end, they paid their taxes or went out of business, or, a third option, moved their stills far up the head of some hollow where they ran their untaxed whiskey illegally and kept their guns and their ears cocked for government agents. The brands had colorful names: Maple Grove,

Widow McBee, Old Grand-Dad, and Rolling Fork. The champion was Maker's Mark, first produced by Charles Banks, who built an 1805 gristmill and distillery about three miles south of Loretto.[1]

The landing and warehouse that Samuel Pottinger built near the mouth of his creek, where it flowed into the Rolling Fork, became a major shipping point for the "Orleans boats" heading down the Mississippi, and there were other changes because of whiskey. Industry necessitated better roads and a population of workers, some of whom had to be lettered in order to keep the accounts. Educated workers desired schools for their children, and a more educated population expected to live in homes finer than the rustic cabins, so carpenters and brick masons were soon in demand and cabinet makers to fill the houses with good furniture. More sawmills were needed, as well as a supply of iron to be blasted and forged into nails and hinges and the long iron rods that held the brick walls tight and true. The architectural stars we see threaded onto the ends of these iron rods are an identifying detail of the oldest mansions in the valley of the Rolling Fork.

Another major pioneer industry was the making of salt. It was a labor-intensive process. Kentucky's first commercial salt works was started at Bullitt's Lick, on the Salt River, in 1779. It took eight hundred gallons of water boiled down to produce one bushel of salt and from five hundred to one thousand men on site to keep the troughs filled and the fires burning. Salt making was slow, laborious work, but there was money to be made, and the markets grew. In 1796, the geographer Jedediah Morse wrote, "Bullitt's Lick ... has supplied this country and Cumberland with salt at 20 shillings per bushel, Virginia currency ... and some exported to the Illinois country. The method of procuring salt from the licks is by sinking wells 30 to 40 feet deep; the water thus obtained is more strongly impregnated with salt than water from the sea."[2]

To the Indians, the industries of frontier Kentucky were worse than the forts. They watched even more white people coming onto their land, using up more of their resources, changing nature to satisfy their needs. The Indians waited and watched outside the salt works at Bullitt's Lick, hoping to pick off the men who came out to hunt meat or cut firewood. Their most determined attempt against the salt making occurred in 1788 and is remembered as the Battle of Pitts Point.

Henry Crist was described by one who knew him as "a small man, almost tiny in stature, but with an unquenchable drive, vigorous, colorful, autocratic, and contentious." He settled at the Falls of the Ohio in 1780. He was soon speculating in land and other ventures. The salt works at Bullitt's Lick looked like a sure moneymaker to him. In May

1788, with ten other men and one woman, he planned to pole a flatboat filled with iron kettles up the Salt River to Bullitt's Lick. Kettles were a necessary item to have in salt making and they would bring a good profit there.[3]

Early in the morning of their first full day on Salt River, the men on the flatboat heard a flock of turkeys gobbling on shore, near where the Rolling Fork enters the Salt, and they secured their boat to the bank and went to hunt them. They soon found that it was not turkeys they had heard; it was Indians. They chased the whites back toward the river. The boat was made fast to the shore by a stout log chain, but a back current had caught the stern of the boat and turned it perpendicular to the riverbank. The gunfire of the Indians ran the length of the boat. Amidst flying lead, the white men loosened the chain and the boat began drifting downstream. The running battle between boat and shore lasted an hour. The whites were outnumbered twelve to one, and despite their barricade of iron kettles, they were getting the worst of it. The Indians crossed the river to the opposite bank and caught the flatboat in a withering crossfire. Finally, the boat lodged on the opposite shore from where it began. The men were all down, killed or wounded, except for Crist, a man named Moore, and another man named Christian Crepps. Crist, Moore and Crepps decided to charge the Indians and save themselves and the woman by this show of bravado. As Lewis Collins related it, the men "offered to assist [the woman] to shore, that she might take her chance of escape in the woods; but the danger of her position, and the scenes of blood and death around her, had overpowered her senses, and no entreaty or remonstrance could prevail with her to move. She sat with her face buried in her hands, and no effort could make her sensible that there was any hope of escape." The three men left her behind.[4]

In the brief fight that followed, Moore burst through the attackers' line and escaped. Crepps and Crist were both wounded. Crepps got into the trees, but later died of his wounds at the salt works. Crist had suffered a shattered heel from a musket ball. Luckily for him, the Indians did not follow his trail, but returned to the boat. In a few minutes, Crist heard the woman scream.[5]

Crist floated on a log over to the far bank to get away from the side where the drifting boat had become stuck. The woods were full of Indians; he could see their campfires that night. All the next day and into the second night he crawled toward the salt works, but the way was rocky and the moccasins he had tied to his knees and the hat and vest he had wrapped around his hands gave poor protection. On the third night, weak from starvation, his hands and knees torn and bleeding, his broken heel throbbing and fevered, Crist decided that he could go no farther. He could see in the distance the glow of the fires at the salt works, but they were still too far away. He was going to die alone within sight of a thousand men.[6]

Lying there waiting for the end, he heard a horse and rider approaching through the trees. Crist tried to hail the rider, but the man turned and galloped away. In a while, Crist heard more riders coming. It was the slave General Braddock leading a rescue party back to the spot where a few minutes earlier he had heard a man call out. How it was that Braddock, who lived at Goodin's Fort, happened to be at Bullitt's Lick is not known. Maybe he had been sent to buy salt for the fort. Maybe he had been hired out by Goodin as an armed guard for the workers. Braddock was a fierce wilderness fighter who was said to have killed and scalped nine Indians in his life. For whatever reason, Braddock was there; he had earned his keep this night. He and the others carried the wounded Crist down to the salt works.[7]

Henry Crist's recovery took a year, but his "unquenchable drive" never failed. He was elected to the Kentucky House of Representatives in 1795. In 1798 he was appointed to be one of the commissioners to survey the boundary line between Bullitt and Nelson Counties. He was elected a state senator from Bullitt County in 1800. He was a state representative from 1806 to 1807, and in 1809 was sent as a Whig to the U.S. House of Representatives. In 1811, he was given a commission as general in the Kentucky state militia. His was a long and useful life. In 1844, Henry Crist died at age eighty in Shepherdsville and was buried on his Bullitt County farm. He was disinterred in 1869 and buried beneath an impressive monument in Frankfort.[8]

Crist's rescuer, General Braddock, continued to be listed as a tithable in the household of Samuel Goodin for the years 1789, 1790, and 1791. His next appearance in the records is March 1797, when he was emancipated. Braddock was the first free black man in Hardin County. Within three weeks of gaining his freedom, General Braddock married Becky Swan. Their marriage, on April 9, 1797, was the only non-white marriage in Hardin County's Marriage Book A. They lived on a small farm on the Hardin County side of the Rolling Fork near the Bardstown Road. The land had once belonged to Edward Rawlings. Becky Swan Braddock died, and on August 15, 1825, General Braddock married as his second wife Cassander Dorsey. The clerk made a notation of the couples' emancipated status and also of the advanced age of the newlyweds. Braddock seems to have survived his second wife as well, for there is no mention of her in the sketchy accounts of his last years. He lived to be nearly one hundred years old. He was a familiar sight on the sidewalks of Elizabethtown even into the 1830s, but, in the end, he went to

Meade County to live on the Otter Creek farm of Jacob Van Meter, Jr., the brother of Abraham Van Meter, who had owned him so long ago. General Braddock died at Van Meter's and was buried there.[9]

The old Indian fighter had lived well beyond the days of the tomahawk and the scalping knife in the valley of the Rolling Fork. Such dangers had ended forty years before. One of the last killings on the Rolling Fork was that of Ignatius Buckman in April 1794. An immigrant to Marion County from Maryland, Buckman had settled near the mouth of Cloyd's Creek. One morning he went out to feed his horses and was attacked by a party of six Indians. His wife and children heard the commotion but stayed inside their cabin until it became quiet outside. When they came out, they saw the Indians and the family's horses disappearing in the woods and found Buckman "pierced by four bullets and his scalp gone." They arranged for Buckman's burial in the Holy Name of Mary Cemetery near Calvary.[10]

Buckman was a Catholic, and by the time of his killing, those of the Catholic faith were becoming a new and powerful presence in the dark, violent valley of the Rolling Fork.

FOUR

The Catholics Arrive

The habit of deadly violence was hard for the citizens of the Rolling Fork to give up. Now that the Indian threat was ended, they began turning their guns on each other.

On January 29, 1801, John Rowan, a young lawyer and business partner of Atkinson Hill, sat in the Duncan McLean Tavern in Bardstown. He was playing cards with Dr. James Chambers, and they were drinking. They began to argue over who was the better student of classical languages. Arguing led to cursing and cursing led to a fistfight. Rowan threw an awkward punch and dislodged his thumb. Their fight interrupted by Rowan's injury, the doctor challenged the lawyer to a duel; Rowan accepted and chose pistols at a distance of ten paces. Their seconds could not obtain an apology from either man. They met on February 3 on the Beech Fork about two miles south of Bardstown. The combatants checked the loads in their pistols, marched off the distance, and fired. Both missed. They stood motionless for a long moment; their friends asked them if they were wounded. "I'm not," said Rowan. "I'm sorry for it," replied Chambers.

Rowan and Chambers reloaded for another round. The question of classical scholarship was at stake. It must be settled. On the second fire, Chambers fell with a fatal wound beneath his left arm. Rowan was arrested, but because the duel had been conducted according to the *code duello* the grand jury ruled that there was no evidence of a crime and refused to indict. There was no trial.[1]

Religion is supposed to change people's behavior for the better. The Baptists had been in the valley of the Rolling Fork since at least 1781 when Cedar Creek Baptist Church was organized. Yet, men still met in saloons to drink whiskey and play cards. The Presbyterians began arriving sometime before 1788 when they founded the first Presbyterian church in the valley at Springfield. But men pounded each other with their fists over who spoke Greek better. The valley's Methodists organized in 1792 under Joseph Ferguson at Poplar Flat in Nelson County.

Still, men calmly shot at each other with deadly results across a "field of honor" and it was so accepted that they were not even held legally accountable for the resulting murders. There was a dark spirit that brooded over the valleys and hollows of the Rolling Fork that the Baptists and Presbyterians and Methodists had not exorcised. Beginning in 1794, the Catholics got their chance to try.[2]

Actually, Catholics had first arrived in the valley of the Rolling Fork in 1785. In that year, a colony of twenty-five families from St. Mary's County, Maryland, came to Goodin's Fort where the old Quaker gave them refuge. The leader was Basil Hayden and the names of the families he led became important in the history of the Rolling Fork: Spalding, Hill, Mattingly, and Cissell, among others. They lived at Goodin's while they located their claims. They finally decided on land over near Pottinger's, and that's where they settled. This was the beginning of the Louisville Archdiocese, the oldest inland Catholic diocese in America. Eventually, thirty other dioceses would be struck from the original. A lot of Catholics were needed to fill up this empire for God.[3]

They were on their way. The good news from Hayden's party inspired others to follow in the late 1780s and early 1790s. Groups congregated at Hardin's Creek, Poplar Neck, Cartwright's Creek, and Cox's Creek. They had no influence, though. They were loosely organized, widely spread over eight hundred square miles. Whether or not there would even be a priest to say Mass was always an open question. An early priest who was shared by the various settlements was Father Charles Whelan. He was an Irish Franciscan who had been educated in France. He came to America as a chaplain aboard a French ship-of-the-line during the War for Independence, and arrived in Kentucky in 1787. His personality was markedly contentious. He complained so bitterly about the people whom he led in worship that he was once successfully sued for slander. He was not the man to serve these frontier Catholics and he left in 1790.[4]

Whelan was followed by William de Rohan. He was never officially assigned to the parish, but he was a man who wandered wherever he pleased. The Catholics of the Rolling Fork were glad to see him. It was de Rohan who built the first Catholic church in Kentucky, Holy Cross, at Pottinger's Creek in 1792. With Holy Cross, the Rolling Fork Catholics began to be organized, but what they needed was a priest who was actually assigned to guide them. They wrote an appeal to Bishop John Carroll in Baltimore.[5]

The answer to their plea arrived on horseback in late 1794. He was Stephen Theodore Badin, a small man with large, sad eyes; a long nose; and a mouth down turned at the corners, as if he was mourning the sins of a selfish world. He was twenty-seven years old, an exile from the French Revolution. He was ordained in May 1793, the first man to become a priest in the United States. At Baltimore, Bishop Carroll wanted immediately to send him to Kentucky, but the young priest pleaded inexperience and an imperfect mastery of English. Badin studied English at Georgetown College and, later, when Carroll approached him again, saying he believed it was God's will that Badin should serve in Kentucky, Badin answered with an unenthusiastic "I will go, then."[6]

He came downriver to Limestone (Maysville) in 1793 and stayed a year before coming to Pottinger's. He built a cabin three miles from Holy Cross and named it St. Stephen's. From there, he directed the destiny of 1,500 Kentucky Catholics. It was a mission of almost unimaginable demands on Badin's time and physical reserves. Lewis Collins said of Father Badin, "Wherever there was sickness or spiritual destitution; wherever error or vice was to be eradicated; wherever youth was to be instructed and trained to religious observances; wherever, in a word, his spiritual ministrations were most needed, there he was sure to be found laboring with all his native energy.... Difficulties and dangers, which would have appalled a heart less stout and resolute, were set at naught by this untiring man." Badin himself later estimated that the sum of his travels on Kentucky's turnpikes and back trails amounted to 100,000 miles, but such exertions were expected. "Dainty service is not pleasing to our Divine Lord," Badin said.[7]

Despite the cold, the hunger, and the endless miles on horseback, Badin was always courteous when met with courtesy. When met with rudeness, he could be sharp tongued.

Once, as he trudged down the road carrying a saddle, Badin met a Presbyterian minister. The minister asked, "Where's your horse, Father Badin?"

"He was taken sick and died on the road."

The smirking Presbyterian asked, "Did you give him absolution before he died?"

"Oh, no, it would have been useless," Badin answered, "the silly animal turned Presbyterian in *articulo mortis* and went straight to hell."[8]

Father Badin led Kentucky's Catholics until Benedict Flaget became Kentucky's first Bishop in 1811. Badin stayed in Kentucky another eight years after that and then returned briefly to France. When he came back to America, he became a missionary among the Pottawatomi Indians and to the Irish workers digging the Wabash Canal in Indiana. The land he bought in Indiana became the campus of University of Notre Dame. He was buried there when he died on April 19, 1853.[9]

Father Charles Nerinckx arrived to help Theodore Badin in 1805.

Like Badin, he was a refugee from the French Revolution, and like Badin, he studied English at Georgetown College before coming west. He was forty-four years old, a square-jawed man with long wavy hair and a look of determination in his eye. He might have been a stonemason or a rollicking keelboatman—he exuded an aura of physical power. He was strong in spirit, too. Collins wrote of Nerinckx, "Strong, healthy, robust, and full of faith and religious zeal, he was admirably suited to endure the hardships necessarily connected with our early missions. He shrank from no labor, and was disheartened by no difficulties."[10]

Badin at first assigned Nerinckx to an area which included the congregations at Cartwright's Creek, Hardin's Creek, and Rolling Fork, but his sphere of responsibility eventually grew to be much larger than that. It took his horse Printer six weeks to carry Nerinckx on his soul-seeking circuit. The day's riding often began before 4:00 a.m. He sometimes rode sixty miles in a single day, into the dark of night, braving treacherous rivers, ugly weather, and all manner of other dangers. Another man would have considered this constellation of widely spaced churches to be enough, but Nerinckx was not satisfied. More churches were needed and he sat about building them, as many as fourteen during his career in Kentucky. When Father Nerinckx built a church, he asked each parishioner to donate two logs, already prepared. That way, the erection of the church took no more than one or two days. Nerinckx was able to lift his end of the log alone, while two men were needed to muscle the other end into place. His physical strength was legendary. Splitting rails, he could drive a wedge half its length into a log with one blow of the maul, without starting it with a series of taps as was usually done to prevent a possibly crippling rebound. Yet, there was a gentleness about him. Accosted once by a bully who wanted to give him a thrashing for some remarks he had made about the young man's rowdy behavior, the good Father avoided his blows until he could subdue him with a bear hug and lay him flat on the ground.[11]

Nerinckx took pleasure in working with children. Sometimes there were as many as ninety preparing for their first Communion. It may have been this love of the younger generation that inspired him to help begin that society of frontier teachers, the Sisters of Loretto. Nerinckx and Badin had attempted once before to create a sisterhood, but a fire destroyed the building intended for the nuns' use, and with that, the plans for the sisterhood turned to ashes, too. Then, in 1811, Mary Rhodes came to Nelson County from Maryland to visit her cousin James Dant and her brother Bennett Rhodes and their families. She was astounded to discover that their children could neither read nor write. She began teaching them. Soon neighbor children were attending her classes. A school was organized and two other teachers were recruited, Christine Stuart and Ann Havern. There was wide interest in a school for Catholic children. The common schools were looked down upon; boys and girls learned bad habits there. Soon the three teachers had thirty or forty pupils attending their classes. The women appealed to Father Nerinckx to help them begin an educational sisterhood. The result was the Friends of Mary at the Foot of the Cross, organized in April 1812. The order came to be called by the more familiar name Sisters of Loretto at the Foot of the Cross.[12]

The order's first home was fifty acres of land, for which Sister Ann paid $75. It is revealing of the painful contradictions in antebellum Kentucky that, in order to raise the money for the land and for other expenses at the genesis of their mission, she turned to a time-honored Southern practice—she sold a slave. The first curriculum at the Sisters of Loretto school was "reading, writing, needlework, etc. sound morality and Christian politeness." Orphans were accepted, and the poor of any faith if they proved otherwise qualified to be scholars. The women endeavored to become a self-sustaining community with a garden, cows, pigs, and poultry. In 1824, they moved from their original site to St. Stephen's farm. From there, the Sisters organized forty Kentucky schools and expanded their class offerings to include history, science, language, philosophy, art, and music. Student by student, they were transforming Kentucky. It would be hard to think of a more enduring and useful legacy than these schools begun by the pioneer Catholics in the valley of the Rolling Fork.[13]

The same year that Mary Rhodes came to visit her relatives on the Rolling Fork, there arrived in Kentucky the first Bishop of the West, Benedict Joseph Flaget. He had come to America in 1792, but it was not until 1807 that Pope Pius VII assigned Flaget to be the first Bishop of the West. A subscription was taken up in Baltimore to pay the cost of Flaget's journey to the frontier, for Kentucky's Catholics were too poor to pay his way. Flaget commissioned a flatboat and arrived at Louisville in June 1811. Father Nerinckx came to Louisville to meet Bishop Flaget. It was his first look at the man with whom he labored and quarreled over the next thirteen years. Flaget was a well-proportioned man, almost six feet tall. He was described by some as having a "sweetness of character," but his eyes were shrewd and his mouth curled up in a little smile at the corners. He knew well that it took shrewdness and humor to battle the Devil in the wilderness. He brushed his long mane of hair back from an aristocratic forehead. Four wagons hauled Bishop Flaget's books and vestments from Louisville. The priests rode horseback to Bardstown and on to St. Stephen's, where the bishop lived with Badin.[14]

Seeing the poverty of the parish, Flaget immediately began soliciting funds from France. He described the pitiable situation in Kentucky to his European superiors in the church hierarchy: "I was compelled to borrow nearly two thousand francs [about $380] in order to reach my destination. Thus, without money, without a house, without property, almost without any acquaintance, I found myself in the midst of a Diocese, two or three times larger than all France, containing five large states and two immense territories, and myself speaking the language ... very imperfectly. Add to all this that almost all the Catholics were emigrants, but newly settled, and poorly furnished."[15]

Flaget stayed at Badin's only a short time before relocating to St. Thomas. He moved into a two-story cabin with pine floors. It dated back to 1795 and was built by a devout but childless couple, Thomas and Ann Howard. The little brick church Flaget built nearby (in 1816) was probably the first brick church erected in Kentucky, but the bishop had his mind on grander things.[16]

In June 1816, the dimensions of a great cathedral, St. Joseph in Bardstown, were staked out and a foundation excavated. On July 16 of that year, Flaget blessed the cornerstone in a public ceremony. He was dressed in full bishop's regalia. Father John B. David (Dah-veed) explained the proceedings to the Baptists and Presbyterians in the watching crowd. Flaget had always gotten along well with his Protestant neighbors and they had an undisguised interest in seeing him and speaking to him. In fact, the Protestants were solidly behind Bishop Flaget's efforts to build a cathedral, and promised to contribute liberally to it, as long as it was a "good, large substantial church."[17]

On the committee to oversee construction of the cathedral were three Catholics, two Protestants, and one atheist, and every hand must have stayed busy, for the "good, large substantial church" was finished in only three years. J. Herman Schauinger writes that St. Joseph, the first cathedral west of the Alleghenies, was "built of materials at hand, the great pillars were trees of the surrounding forest, shaped and polished for their place, the bricks were made by hand on the spot." It was consecrated on August 8, 1819, before an "immense crowd." St. Joseph still stands straight and true today, a classically beautiful edifice in Bardstown, a city rich with architectural beauty, the prettiest town in the valley of the Rolling Fork.[18]

Bishop Flaget moved to Bardstown once St. Joseph was completed. It was regrettable that his relations with his priests did not receive the same attention as he gave the construction of his cathedral. Both Father Badin and Father Nerinckx left Kentucky after quarreling with Flaget. Badin quit Kentucky in 1819. Nerinckx went to Missouri in 1824 and died at St. Genevieve on August 12 of that year. His body was brought back to the Loretto motherhouse, where he was buried.[19]

Flaget removed to Louisville in 1841 when the pope made that city the headquarters of the diocese. He died there in February 1850 and was buried at the Cathedral of the Assumption. By the time of his death, the number of Catholics in Kentucky, the convents, and the schools and colleges gave the church in Kentucky an importance unimaginable in 1785. The hard work of the faithful had amounted to something. Not every group could claim the same.[20]

In 1794, a company of English investors planned a town on the banks of the Rolling Fork, between Salt Lick and Otter Creek. It would be the most beautiful city in the world, they boasted. Its name would be Lystra. They purchased fifteen thousand acres of land and drew a city plan showing five large squares, each containing at its center a park. A larger park, in the shape of a huge circle, made a hub in the center of the plan. The streets were laid out at practical ninety-degree angles. They would be one hundred feet wide, and there would be 188 lots fronting the streets, including spaces for churches, colleges, places of amusement, and a dignified city hall.[21]

To populate Lystra with the brightest and the best, a generous offer was made by the investors. Free town lots would be given to the college president, the state senator, the judge, and the other professionals who came there to live. The commercial district was to be strictly regulated. Each lot would be restricted as to type of business. Lystra was a model of city planning before that phrase ever became common, and it would become an urban paradise shining in Kentucky's verdant natural Eden.[22]

And it would never exist except on paper. The hardest work that was ever done on Lystra was the scratching of a pencil at the draftsman's table.

The creation of good works on the Rolling Fork frontier, and in the dark frontier of men's hearts and minds as well, required more than dreams and plans on paper. It required the work of men who abandoned the comfortable east and came west on horseback and on flatboats one by one, who rode over a wilderness kingdom larger than France to minister to the needs of those whose bodies and souls suffered and cried out in the night. It required men who dreamed the dreams, but then rolled up their sleeves and did the building themselves. It required men like that trinity of frontier priests in the valley of the Rolling Fork—Badin, Nerinckx, and Flaget.

FIVE

The Struggles
of Thomas Lincoln

On April 10, 1794, the Jefferson County Court assigned Benjamin Lynn, James Davis, Samuel Pottinger, and Samuel McAdams to lay out a road between Bardstown and Pottinger's Landing. The route they selected became the local section of the Louisville and Nashville Turnpike, a major highway of pioneer times. One could sit and watch a whole parade of interesting humanity pass by. A fisherman sitting on the bank of, let us say, Knob Creek near the Turnpike in May of 1797 would have seen the unusual sight of a party of four Frenchman passing by on horseback. They were Louis-Philippe, future King of France, and his entourage, and they had just left Hodgenville. Louis-Philippe, an enthusiastic diarist, left us his impression of the land through which he was passing:

> Beyond Hodgin's the traveler continues sharply downhill for a long time, for the Barrens are a very high plateau. In the valleys now we began to note the renowned rich soil of Kentucky. It is truly very rich and excellent. The valley lowlands (what they call here *Bottom land*) are a black soil equal in quality to any of our good European soil. With these goodly lands we also saw thick forests again, and trees enormous in both circumference and height. In crossing the creeks we noticed that here as in the Cumberland the bed was of flat, smooth rock. At times we were even able to see the depth of the rock beneath the water, and so to see clearly the depth of the soil above the hardpan.
>
> We had dinner in a log-house belonging to a man named Hazel, where we were astounded by a very tolerable meal, with fresh venison, coffee, etc.
>
> That night we reached Beardstown after considerable more downhill travel.... We reached Beardstown after dark. There we lodged at Captain Been's. Good people and a good inn.
>
> Beardstown is already a fairly large town for Kentucky. They say there are almost 150 houses. It is on a plateau surrounded by dense forests of tall trees. Its population is, like that of all American towns, merchants or innkeepers or laborers.[1]

34

Louis-Philippe and his well-dressed dandies would hardly have taken notice of a humble fisherman, but he would certainly have noticed them. Such sights were not common on the L. and N. Turnpike. Watching the traffic from the creek bank, the fisherman would see instead rough handed and rough talking teamsters hauling a load of black walnut timber to Pottinger's Landing for shipment to New Orleans. And here was an open-sided stagecoach picking up speed for the long pull up Muldraugh Hill, full of passengers headed for Nashville. Near the top, those passengers might have to get out and walk. Now came a coffle of slaves, chains clanking, trudging to the auction block, a grim slave driver on horseback watching over them. Militiamen, traders, emigrants, and priests; year after year the fisherman watched them hurrying up and down the hot turnpike while he sat in the shade and fished.

Going to his spot on the creek bank on a morning in 1815, our fisherman might have met a young girl and her younger brother walking up the road to Zachariah Riney's school. It was a one-roomed, one-doored, dirt-floored school, windowless and bookless. Walking home at mid-day, cane pole over his shoulder, he might hear the school before he saw it, for it was a "blab school" where the children spoke their lessons out loud until it was time to recite individually for their teacher.

Zachariah Riney, the teacher, came to Holy Cross as part of the Catholic migration from St. Mary's County, Maryland, about 1785. In 1811, he moved from Holy Cross to a place two miles north of the Rolling Fork, near Pottinger's Landing. The same year, a dark-haired family named Lincoln moved to a new cabin an equal distance south of the Rolling Fork. They were Thomas, a stout and slightly stoop-shouldered cabinetmaker, millwright, and farmer; his pregnant wife Nancy; their four-year-old daughter Sarah; and their two-year-old son Abraham. In a way, moving to the valley of the Rolling Fork was coming home for Thomas and Nancy Lincoln, for they had both been young people there, in the Beechland neighborhood of Washington County.[2]

Nancy Hanks was raised in the home of her cousin Francis Berry. She had been a ward of his parents, Richard and Rachel Berry, who were her uncle and aunt. Another cousin, Sarah Mitchell, lived in the Berry household, too. She had been half-orphaned on the way to Kentucky when the Indians killed and scalped her mother and carried Sarah away to captivity. She was completely orphaned a few months later when her father drowned in one of the rivers while searching for her among the tribes. It is unlikely she knew this until she was redeemed from the Indians, more than ten years later. With no parents to shelter her, Sarah moved in with the Berrys. She and Nancy Hanks became close and each vowed to name her first daughter in honor of the other. Sarah Mitchell was older, but she had lived too many years among the Indians to have learned the domestic arts of a frontier wife. Nancy taught her.[3]

Thomas Lincoln's mother and brothers lived in Washington County. His father, Abraham, had been killed by Indians in Jefferson County in 1786 and his mother, Bersheba, moved her sons to the Beech Fork country. Local historians say that Thomas learned his skills as a carpenter and cabinetmaker in the blacksmith shop operated by the Berrys. Maybe it was there that he first met Nancy Hanks. He did not stay in Washington County, however. He moved to Hardin County and worked for Samuel Haycraft, Sr., and sometimes for Jacob Van Meter, Sr., with whom he also made his home. Thomas did well in Hardin County and acquired some property, but when it was time to marry, he went back to the Beech Fork for Nancy Hanks.[4]

The day before Thomas Lincoln and Nancy Hanks married, he rode into Springfield to get his marriage bond at the courthouse. Richard Berry, Jr., signed it with him. While they were there, they met Methodist preacher Jesse Head and, still needing a preacher to perform the ceremony, Thomas invited him to administer the vows. On June 12, 1806, a crowd gathered at Francis Berry's for the wedding. Sarah Mitchell was Nancy's bridesmaid; Peter Siebert, Jr., was Thomas Lincoln's best man. When the ceremony was finished, the party repaired to a feast described for future researchers by the botanist Christopher Columbus Graham. Apparently, Graham did not know either the bride or the groom. He had been out in the woods gathering plant specimens, and having heard about the wedding, just came by for some supper. Everyone was welcome; that was the kind of hospitality typical of the Kentucky frontier, especially on a happy occasion like this. Of the reception menu, Graham remembered: bear meat, venison, wild turkey and duck, mutton roasted on a spit over a slow fire, peaches and honey, maple sugar to sweeten the coffee, and whiskey.[5]

The newly wed Lincolns did not make their home in Washington County. They lived from the earliest days of their marriage in Elizabethtown where Thomas owned his land and pursued his trade. It was in Elizabethtown in 1807 that Nancy had a daughter she named Sarah. She had kept her promise to Sarah Mitchell, and Sarah Mitchell remembered her promise, too; she named her first daughter Nancy.[6]

In December 1808 the Lincolns moved out of town, to a place on the South Fork of the Nolin River called the Sinking Spring Farm. It was near Robert Hodgen's mill. There, in February 1809, Nancy had another child, a son named Abraham for Thomas' father who had been slain by the Indians.

It turned out that the title to the Sinking Spring Farm was a legal tangle, as the titles were for the claims of so many early Kentuckians. The Lincolns left the disputed homestead and moved about ten miles to Knob Creek, not far from where it empties into the Rolling Fork. The farm they rented was rich bottom land in the shadow of eight hundred foot high Muldraugh Hill. Fertile fields extended up the valley. There was the creek close by, the Louisville and Nashville Turnpike out front, and a schoolhouse only two miles away. Life would be better for the Lincolns on the Knob Creek place, Thomas was just sure.

Right away, things went wrong. Nancy Lincoln had her third baby the same year they moved, 1811, but the newborn died after only three days. It is local tradition that Thomas Lincoln was away from home when the baby died and that a neighbor named George Redmon made the tiny coffin and carried little Thomas Lincoln, Jr., to the Redmon family cemetery on top of Muldraugh Hill. The grave was marked by a fieldstone scratched with the initials "T.L." and a plain stone at the foot.[7]

It beat Nancy Hanks Lincoln down. She was only twenty-eight years old, but she never had another pregnancy, and her boy Abraham recollected his young mother's haggard appearance all the rest of his life. Once, after he was grown, he saw a woman he said reminded him of Nancy; the woman had "withered features, wrinkles, a want of teeth and, in general, a weather beaten appearance."[8]

In 1853, looking back on his boyhood, Abraham Lincoln described life in Kentucky to Leonard Swett as "stinted." Getting away from the gloomy cabin felt good to the boy. His cousin Dennis Hanks recalled, "Abe was right out in the woods, about as soon as he was weaned, fishing in the creek, setting traps for rabbits and muskrats, going on coon hunts with Tom and me and the dogs, following up bees to find bee trees, and dropping corn for his pappy. Mighty interesting life for a boy, but there was a good many chances he wouldn't live to grow up."[9]

Abraham's best chum was Austin Gollaher, but he, like many of Lincoln's acquaintances, at first discounted the new boy. In an 1894 interview, when he claimed to be the last person living who knew Lincoln on the Rolling Fork, Gollaher remembered, "At first sight I must say I didn't like Abe one bit. His appearance was not taking and I was sullen like, and had little to do with him. In a few days more me and my mother went over to see them ... we become fast friends after that."[10]

Louis Warren, who anchored his history of Lincoln's Kentucky years in the unyielding bedrock of documentary evidence, discounted most of the tales passed down by Austin Gollaher (and others) of the boy Lincoln. The one story of Gollaher's which Warren conceded might contain a seed of truth is the familiar one in which Gollaher saved Lincoln from drowning. Gollaher remembered, "It was when we were fishing one day the creek was up and we had to 'coon' it across on a log. Abe slipped and fell off, and I being the biggest got a sycamore limb and fished him out." On shore, Gollaher rolled Lincoln over and pounded him on the back until the creek water gushed out. The two boys feared punishment if their mothers learned of this misadventure, so they vowed never to tell. Gollaher kept his word to Lincoln, and did not tell the tale of the near drowning until after his friend's death in April 1865.[11]

In the winter there was Zachariah Riney's blab school to enliven things. Lincoln was a studious boy. Austin Gollaher told the 1894 interviewer, "Abe was a great learner. He ciphered on everything around and read everything he could find.... The fence corners was full of big iron weeds, and he'd gather them in the daytime by great piles to throw on the fire at night to make a big blaze so's he could see to study."[12]

There were good times, too, when Thomas was home from a job of carpentry or millwork. He brought stories from the outlying communities and new things to make life nicer on the Knob Creek place. Once he came home from an auction with a heifer and another time with a wagon that had cost him eight and a half cents. There were trips to Hodgen's Mill and to Elizabethtown where they got paid a bounty for wolf scalps. But not every memory of his father in the Knob Creek days was pleasant. Ida Tarbell related the story of how Thomas and Abraham worked all one Saturday planting corn and pumpkins in a big field of seven acres. It was the boy's job to drop two pumpkin seeds "in every other hill and every other row. The next Sunday morning there came a big rain in the hills ... the water came down the gorges and slides and washed ground, corn, pumpkins seeds, and all clear off the fields." The boy had not liked the work in the first place, now the whole field had to be replanted. It was a crushing experience for a little fellow to see his hard work all undone, and it undoubtedly contributed to Lincoln's lifelong dislike of farm life. From his early twenties on, Lincoln always lived in town—New Salem; Springfield; Washington, D. C.—and never expressed any interest in returning to live in the country until one sentimental day at the very end of his life.[13]

There was always the anticipation of company stopping by the Knob Creek cabin. It was on the main road. One visitor who came to stay a few days was the botanist Dr. Christopher Columbus Graham, the same Graham who had been at the Lincoln's wedding and remembered the banquet afterwards. At the time he stopped in to visit the Lincolns, Graham was making a study of the flora in the Rolling Fork Valley. He was an interesting man who knew Boone and Audubon, and he was a welcome visitor. The Lincolns, being naturally gracious, let him have the feather bed when he was visiting, while they slept on the cabin floor.

The grown Lincoln might recall life in Kentucky as "stinted," but Christopher Columbus Graham remembered the hospitality of the Lincoln cabin and the comfort they offered a lonely traveler on the Louisville and Nashville Turnpike.[14]

Like that of the Sinking Spring farm, the Knob Creek title proved not to be secure. George Lindsey claimed to be the owner, but in December of 1815, "a bill of ejection was filed against Thomas Lincoln and nine of his neighbors who occupied land lying within a ten-thousand acre tract claimed by some Philadelphia investors." The dispute with the Philadelphians was settled in Lindsey's favor in 1816. Thomas Lincoln stayed until September of that year, when the court ruled against him in his long-fought battle to regain the Sinking Spring Farm. It was clear to Thomas Lincoln that land ownership in Kentucky was too risky a proposition; he was ready to move to Indiana where there had been a government survey and the land office at Vincennes could guarantee a man's right to his acreage. Thomas built a flatboat with little Abraham's help; loaded it with ten barrels of whiskey and his carpenter's tools; and floated down Knob Creek to the Rolling Fork, into the Salt River, and to the Ohio. Thomas had been to New Orleans and knew how to pilot a flatboat, but once in the Ohio, something went wrong. The flatboat overturned, spilling four barrels of whiskey and many of his tools. He salvaged some of the cargo from the river's bottom and pushed on to Thompson's Ferry on the Indiana bank. He left his plunder with a Mr. Posey and went on foot to Little Pigeon Creek in Perry County, sixteen miles north of the Ohio, where he claimed a quarter section (160 acres) of land.[15] When he returned

The only known photograph of Thomas Lincoln (Library of Congress).

to Kentucky, Thomas arranged for an auction sale. Gone beneath the crier's gavel were the heifer, the wagon, the bulky furniture. What was left could fit on two packhorses. It is told that just before leaving for Indiana, Nancy Lincoln and her two surviving children climbed up through the honeysuckle and the bare winter trees of Muldraugh Hill to visit the grave of the baby who had died five years before. Finally, it was time to go. Thomas Lincoln had been made responsible by the county court for the upkeep of the Louisville and Nashville Turnpike between "the Bigg Hill and the Rolling Fork." Now he was using that same road to get out of Kentucky. Thomas and one child rode one horse, Nancy and the other child rode the other horse, and each led a packhorse.[16]

Across the Ohio River, the accommodating Mr. Posey lent the Lincolns or rented to them a wagon. They loaded the remaining whiskey and tools and the packs from the horses and moved to the half-faced camp that was their new home. It was lonely and wild compared to the Rolling Fork, and moving there meant starting over, practically from scratch.

In 1830, Zachariah Riney sold his Rolling Fork land and moved to northern Hardin County. Rineyville is named for him. He continued to teach school there. In 1857, at age ninety-four, Riney moved to the monastery at Gethsemani in Nelson County where his grandson William (known at Gethsemani as Brother Benedict) was a Trappist monk. Riney died in 1859. He barely missed seeing his former student become President of the United States.[17]

The Knob Creek schoolhouse where Riney had taught the Lincoln children was still standing as late as 1907. R. Monroe Ford stored grain in it. It is gone now and so is the Lincoln cabin. Like the school, the humble homeplace was used as a corncrib before Steve Thompson and his son Robert tore it down in 1870. The logs were burned as firewood. Thus does a country honor the memory of its heroes.[18]

Six

Steamboats and Railroads

The Rolling Fork system is an elaborate web of streams feeding into streams. Some of its tributaries are very long, long enough to be rivers in their own right. It can be confusing—where else but here would Chaplin *River* flow into Beech *Fork* and Beech Fork flow into the Rolling Fork? Think, now, in terms of smaller to larger: if the Chaplin is a tributary of a fork, should it not be busted in rank to something more modest, a branch or a run? No. It is a river.

The names of the tributaries (and of *their* tributaries) tell much of the story of the Rolling Fork, its vegetation, its wildlife, its pioneers, and even what the pioneers thought about. What plant life did the explorers observe? The tributaries answer the question. Cane, cedar, hickory, beech, white oak, and cherry. What minerals? Salt, sulphur, and slate. What animals did they see? Otter, buffalo, snake, turkey, terrapin, whippoorwill, wolf, buck, and bear. Who were these pioneer families? They included: Price, Younger, Wilson, Edlin, Murphy, Thompson, Christie, Cartwright, Hardin, Pottinger, Cloyd, Prather, Vittitow, and Moore. What did they think was good to eat? Milk and Mush Creek and Sugar Run tell us. You can almost piece together the whole history of the Rolling Fork from the names of its waters. And, if you follow Monk's Creek in Nelson County north toward its forks, you will see on your left the great tan and white stucco abbey of the Trappists and you will hear the mellow ringing of its bells and you will understand how this stream got its name.

Driven from France by the Revolution, the Trappists had first come to Kentucky in 1805. They settled on leased land near Holy Cross in Marion County, but only briefly. They returned to France after Napoleon's fall, then came back to the valley of the Rolling Fork in December 1848 and established Gethsemani. Their leader was Father Eutropius Proust. They were members of a very old order (tracing their history back to 1098) and brought ancient ways of doing things to a land that was still young. Arriving on their land—1,400 acres acquired for them by Bishop Flaget—the forty-four brothers leaped from their wagons to kiss the ground and pray that the Lord would always allow them to stay.[1]

Almost immediately, three of the brothers deserted. The ones that remained set about building a gristmill, a saw mill, and a carding mill, which would benefit the surrounding farmers as well as themselves. They cleared the land for their crops and livestock and began a Gothic abbey that would not be finished until 1866. The Trappists thought in large dimensions; the abbey was staked out to be 150 feet long and ninety feet wide.

The monks started their day with devotions at 2:00 a.m. At 6:00 a.m. there began an hour of meditation followed by an hour-long Mass. From 8:00 until 11:30 they performed manual labor and then got their one meal of the day, vegetables and milk. In the afternoon were more chores and more devotions until it was time to go to their partitioned cells. Each monk's earthly wealth consisted of a cup, pitcher, spoon, knife, fork, and napkin. The brothers worked diligently, lived simply, and spent their days quietly, for they observed a vow of silence.[2]

The monks of Gethsemani might have struck their hard-living neighbors as peculiar, but their building of a new community was not strange at all. The valley of the Rolling Fork was experiencing a boom. That was due, in no small part, to the exciting innovation of steam transportation. The first steamboat had gone down the Ohio in 1811. Before long, steamboats were coming up the Salt River to Pitts Point thence up the Rolling Fork as far as the mouth of Beech Fork. Naturally, farmers throughout the valley were anxious to make use of the river packets. Now there was a way to get their crops upstream as well as down. The number of distant markets doubled, and land values at home reflected the increase. Prices by the 1840s had jumped to $5.56 per acre in Bullitt County, $3.69 per acre in Hardin, $3.58 in LaRue, $5.93 in Marion, and an incredible $9 per acre in Nelson County.[3]

The old pioneer settlements were pulling themselves together, organizing proper governments, making civic improvements, and approving ordinances to govern the many new businesses that were moving in. One such settlement was at Pitts Point. Jacob Froman had started a settlement of the same name in 1779, but there was no formal town there until 1831 when the ferryman Abraham Froman and his wife Hannah sold 606 acres to James and John Pitts for $1,500. Froman kept his ferry out of the deal, though; it was too profitable to give up. Each ferry ride put ten cents in Froman's pocket.

Town lots at Pitts Point could be bought for $35, originally, but had increased to $250 by 1842. By 1860, the businesses included: a customs inspection office, a flouring mill, a sawmill, two hotels, two general stores, four doctors, two attorneys, two carpenters, a blacksmith, a gunsmith, a saddle and harness maker, a fish dealer, a plow maker, one banker, and one photographer.[4]

Pitts Point was thriving, but it was not the only one. Nelsonville grew up around an iron furnace begun on six hundred acres by William and Mordecai Miller and John Irwin in 1836. Howardstown on Lunar Creek was another growing town. But New Haven was the one that continued to grow. It was officially founded in 1820 and named by Samuel Pottinger, Jr., for the town of the same name, which he had admired while in Connecticut. New Haven was laid out near his father's old landing, and at least one of the warehouses was still there; the Catholics celebrated Mass in Pottinger's warehouse while they were building their church, St. Catherine, and other congregations used it, too. The town was incorporated in 1839.[5]

The arrival of new technology was transforming the valley of the Rolling Fork. The steamboats stimulated the growth of new towns and the transformation of old ones. Yet, the day of the steamboat was brief. A newer technology arrived in the late 1850s that largely shut the steamboats out and added even more town dots to the map of the Rolling Fork Valley. It was the Louisville & Nashville Railroad, a state-of-the-art line whose quality was known throughout the nation. The New York *Times* said a few years after its completion, "There is, perhaps, no line of railroad in the whole Southern country more noted for its excellent construction than that of the Louisville and Nashville Railroad. It runs ... over an excellent ballasted track, diversified with heavy grades, deep cuts, tunnels and bridges of every character—evincing in its every detail, superior engineering."[6]

Lebanon Junction was a community begun by and for the railroad. From that point on the main stem, a spur was laid to Lebanon in Marion County. The railroad built a roundhouse at Lebanon Junction, and there was a two-story hotel for weary travelers. Another town that benefited from the completion of the L&N was Boston. Boston was a sleepy Nelson County village originally located on Pine Tavern Road, so unimportant that it was not even mentioned in Collins's comprehensive 1847 history. But Boston woke up when the L&N Railroad came. The whole town picked up and moved to be near the Lebanon Branch, and commerce flourished.[7]

Those who remembered the days of ox-drawn wagons struggling through the mud of what passed for roads, and who remembered the lazy flatboat trips down the rivers with no greater speed than the current itself could provide, blinked their eyes in wonder at the changes they saw all around them. These roaring land and water monsters with their smokestacks belching black smoke into the air had transformed the valley of the Rolling Fork more than anything since the end of the last Ice Age, and it was all accomplished not by the whims of nature, but by the will of men. Progress was here for sure, and there would be no turning back.

Life in the valley had its ugly aspects, though. Slavery was one. It was not a huge presence in the Rolling Fork region, not like it was in the Bluegrass. Pitts Point, for example, had only thirteen slaves owned by six masters. This is by no means meant to dismiss the cruelty of slavery; even on a scale as small as one individual it was a terrible thing. Numbers do not matter. A soldier killed in a skirmish is just as dead as a soldier killed in a Shiloh, and the family grieves just as deeply, and the pain was the same to a slave whether he was one out of a population of thirteen or one out of thirteen thousand. The slaves ran away when they could. A typical ad in the April 4, 1835, *Kentucky Register* read, "A $20 reward for a runaway Negro from James Brown, on the 6th, named Bill, rather yellow complexion, 23 years old." Whether Bill made good his escape is not recorded.[8]

If he was not lucky, Runaway Bill might have been waylaid by thieves and sold to a distant buyer who would certainly have paid more than the measly reward of $20 that James Brown offered. Gangs of thieves lurked in remote areas of the valley. One band of outlaws operated out of LaRue County. The bandit leader was Big Bill Redmon, a "terror" who had "no more idea of mercy or kindness than the most ferocious beast." Redmon's hideout was a two-acre camp called "Robbers' Cabins." From there the bad men fanned out to ransack houses, waylay overland travelers, and ambush flatboats on the Beech Fork, Rolling Fork, and Salt River. Redmon's band sometimes got as much as $1,000 out of a single job. If they were in a humanitarian mood, they carried their victims into the deep woods and left them there to either find their way out or not. At less charitable times, the robbers executed them.[9]

That was the plan for a young Bardstown man named Forbes. He was robbed by three of Redmon's gang of $500 or so, then led through the brush to a canoe and blindfolded for the trip to Robbers' Cabins. Ten more men heavily armed with guns and knives were waiting on shore when the canoe arrived. Forbes was taken to a cabin and left alone. After a while, one of the outlaws brought him a plate of food and served it with the discouraging remark, "Captain Bill says for you to fill up, as it's probably the last you'll ever eat." Captain Bill himself later entered the cabin where the prisoner was being held and closely studied him. It came to light that the men who had captured Forbes had believed he was a deputy sheriff. Redmon knew that he was no such thing. "This man is no more a deputy sheriff than you are," Redmon told his men. A regrettable mistake had been made, but there could be no reprieve for the prisoner. Redmon turned back to Forbes and said, "It would never do to let you go inform against us. You can have from now until tomorrow to prepare for death."

Before tomorrow came, a rescue party charged into Robbers' Cabins, led by the actual deputy sheriff who had seen Forbes' abduction. A gun battle erupted. The lawmen shot four robbers dead, including Redmon, who died at the river's edge as he was trying to get to a canoe. The rest of the robbers surrendered. Forbes got his money and watch back, and his life. He later became a Mississippi lawyer.[10]

People thought that Big Bill Redmon's gang was rough, but there were rougher men coming. There was an unfortunate, uncorrectable fact about the valley of the Rolling Fork: it was centrally located and in 1861 found itself directly between the armies of two warring nations. Its attractiveness as a highway for maneuvering soldiers was enhanced by the completion of the L&N Railroad just before the war began. Hordes of men in blue and gray were coming to spill blood on the soil of the Rolling Fork country in a volume that, by comparison, made the Indian wars and the depredations of Redmon's men look like an election day scuffle. There was no way to ignore it and there was no way to escape it, even for civilians, because the marching soldiers crossing the land had to live and they were going to live off the farmers and shopkeepers in the valley of the Rolling Fork.

SEVEN

Thunder in the Valley

The spirit of John Hunt Morgan hangs over the valley of the Rolling Fork like a gray cloud filled with thunder. Other notables passed through: William Tecumseh Sherman, Simon Bolivar Buckner, Don Carlos Buell, Braxton Bragg, "Fighting Joe" Wheeler, even Nathan Bedford Forrest, but it was Morgan whose presence in the valley was most feared or most cheered and rightfully so, for the valley did often occupy his attention. Morgan was a destroyer of railroads and the L&N, always pumping supplies to the Federals in Tennessee, was his special target in 1862 and '63. But he was not the first Confederate to attack the L&N.

Late on September 17, 1861, Major Thomas Hayes, under orders from Simon Bolivar Buckner, struck at the L&N. He moved north and burned the railroad bridge that crossed the Rolling Fork between Lebanon Junction and Colesburg. When news of the arson reached Union headquarters in Louisville, department commander General Robert Anderson ordered General William T. Sherman to assemble a force of men and hurry south by train to Lebanon Junction. He found "the railroad bridge burned down and still burning," but the Rebels had retired. Sherman decided to follow. He left behind one regiment to guard the Colesburg Road and sent the rest of his command up the Clear Creek Valley toward Elizabethtown, where he later joined them. They camped on Muldraugh Hill.[1]

That was it for the Lebanon Junction campaign. Sherman assumed command of the Department of the Cumberland from General Anderson on October 8, 1861, and was so worried that he wrote on that same day to Garrett Davis in Paris, Kentucky, "I am forced into the command of this department against my will, and it would take 300,000 men to fill half the call for troops." He deployed what troops he had and begged for more, listened to the endless complaints and demands of his officers in the field, and visited his outlying defenses. The strain proved too great. Sherman had an emotional breakdown of some sort later that fall and was relieved of command. He left the department in better shape than

46

he had found it. The Union troops in the Rolling Fork Valley were concentrated at critical points such as Bardstown, where there were 996
men in November 1861, at Colesburg (822 men), and Lebanon Junction
(1,007 men). Smaller garrisons spent the autumn building stockades
at gathering points like Camp Pope at New Haven and Camp Morton,
on the Louisville and Nashville Turnpike, about four miles outside of
Bardstown.[2]

Absalom A. Harrison, a cavalryman with the 4th Kentucky Cavalry,
was posted at Camp Morton. He wrote home in that first winter of the
war.

> It was very nice in a woods pasture place when we first came here. But it is
> knee deep in mud now.... I would like to be home, but I got myself in this
> scrape and will have to stand it. But if I live to get out of this, I will never be
> caught soldiering again that is certain. We did not know what hard times
> was until we come to this place. We don't get more than half enough to eat
> and our horses are not half fed and everything goes wrong.[3]

If Harrison thought "everything goes wrong" because of some mud
and short rations, he was going to get an education, come 1862. In
that summer, General Braxton Bragg invaded Kentucky, bringing with
him twenty thousand Enfield rifles to arm the Kentuckians whom he
expected to liberate from the hateful rule of the Yankee nation.

Bragg was motivated to invade Kentucky partly because of the
optimistic report of John Hunt Morgan, who had raided into the state
the previous July. In what is called the "First Raid," Morgan introduced himself to the valley of the Rolling Fork with a strike against Lebanon and Lebanon Junction. While he directed the burning of tons of
commissary and quartermaster stores at Lebanon, he sent a detachment
toward Lebanon Junction, on the main stem of the L&N Railroad. It
was a wise move, for a troop-filled train was on its way from Louisville.
The surprise of being attacked by this small band of Morgan's Raiders
broke the confidence of the Federals, who returned to Louisville. From
Lebanon, Morgan proceeded into the Bluegrass Region, where he burned and stole and brushed Home Guard units from his path and hardly
broke a sweat. President Lincoln became aware of the confusion in his
home state and wired General Henry Halleck, "They are having a stampede in Kentucky. Please look into it." Morgan returned to Tennessee
and reported that there was a great, untapped reservoir of pro–Confederate feeling in Kentucky.[4]

Buoyed by this report, Bragg moved north. In September 1862, he
led his army through Munfordville, where he defeated the Federal garrison guarding the Green River railroad bridge, on up through Hodgenville and thence to Bardstown. There, on September 14, he addressed a

letter to his fellow Kentuckians, urging them to throw off the yoke of Northern oppression. Bragg gave the young men as much time as he could spare for them to come join him, but he had attracted few volunteers by the time his troops moved out toward Danville. As the Confederates left Bardstown, their rear guard—Colonel John Wharton's cavalry and a field battery—engaged with the vanguard of Union General Thomas L. Crittenden's column, which was approaching from the direction of Louisville. Wharton's horse soldiers counter-charged and scattered them.

Wharton's small fight did not improve General Bragg's sour mood. He brooded about the few recruits he had signed up, and he took his bitterness out on the Kentuckians in his army now and for as long as he remained in command. The fact of the matter was, Kentuckians felt no need to be liberated by the general who wooed the farm boys while at the same time his soldiers were drinking the wells dry and stealing ("requisitioning") from their old parents all the horses they could find and killing or carrying away all the chickens, hogs, and cattle. Not that Don Carlos Buell's Yankees were much better, but they were not here just now; Bragg's Rebels were.

Bragg and Buell met in Kentucky's bloodiest battle at Perryville, away up the Chaplin River, on October 8, 1862, and bludgeoned each other for an entire day. The Confederates lost about 3,100 killed and wounded; the Federals about 3,600. Bragg had won a tactical victory, but sacrificed too many men to follow up his success, especially considering that the next morning he would be facing two relatively fresh Federal corps. Bragg slipped away in the night and began his long withdrawal from Kentucky. The Enfield rifles returned to Tennessee, most of them still in their crates.[5]

Morgan played no role in the Confederate advance nor in the battle of Perryville. He had remained near Lexington with General Edmund Kirby Smith. After the battle, the retreating Bragg linked up with Smith at Harrodsburg, and together they traveled south. General Joe Wheeler, the Confederate "War Child," skillfully delayed the Yankee pursuers with obstructions in the narrow roads and ambushes. This was not the kind of action that Morgan enjoyed. After only a few miles, he asked for and received permission to double back toward the west where, he said, he could strike the L&N. He hit the railroad at Elizabethtown and inflicted some slight damage, then continued in the direction of Leitchfield. Beyond there, he turned south and west and took a leisurely route toward Tennessee.[6]

Despite the damage it had suffered during the Perryville Campaign, the L&N was still feeding and arming the enemy in Nashville and

Morgan meant to put an end to it. As fall faded into winter, he received permission to return to Kentucky. Morgan began his Christmas Raid on December 22, 1862, moving north at a furious pace, destroying railroad track by the mile, and capturing the Union garrisons at Bacon Creek, at Camp Nevin on the Nolin River, and at Elizabethtown. Then, he rode hard toward the two great railroad trestles on Muldraugh Hill, each one five hundred feet long and eighty to ninety feet high. The infantrymen guarding them were of the 71st Indiana and 78th Illinois. Their commander was Colonel Courtland Matson. The Federals had only small arms, and they were powerless to stop Morgan, who lobbed shells down on them from the hill crest. After two hours of this uneven contest the Northern boys surrendered, and Morgan burned the soldiers' shelters and the trestles and relieved the defenders of their overcoats and new Enfield rifles.

Satisfied that he had crippled the L&N for an inestimable period of time and fearing a meeting with the Yankees gathering against him, Morgan turned south. Finding the Rolling Fork swollen from the winter rains, Morgan stopped at Mrs. Hance Hamilton's fine brick home on the Hardin County side of the flooded river. Andrew Jackson had once stopped at the Hamilton House for the same reason.

On the morning of December 29, Morgan sent Colonel D.W. Chenault to burn the L&N trestle at Boston. Major Robert Bullock took two artillery pieces to demolish the bridge at Colesburg, and Colonel W.C.P. Breckinridge did not lead but sent a heavy detachment to destroy the railroad bridge at New Haven. Those officers remaining in camp at Hamilton's Ford had a court-martial to convene to consider the case of Lieutenant Colonel J.W. Huffman, who was charged with mistreating prisoners.

The court-martial was not a sham, but neither were the charges very complicated. Huffman was acquitted before noon. The officers left the Hamilton house and were preparing for the river crossing when the sound of cannon fire shook the air around them. Shells began falling from above. Federal Colonel John M. Harlan's artillery had arrived at the top of Muldraugh Hill, with 2,900 eager Yankee infantry and cavalrymen behind them. Harlan had been on Morgan's trail for three days. Now, he had Morgan trapped, outgunned, and outnumbered.

Basil Duke deployed three hundred men in a defensive line as the Federals descended the hill and approached across the valley floor. They knew Morgan, and they advanced cautiously, while four or five of their Parrott guns continued to punish the Raiders from above. The combined pressure of artillery, infantry, and cavalry was too much for Duke's valiant three hundred, and they were falling back when Bullock returned from Colesburg. He threw his five hundred men into line. They held the ground while the rest of Morgan's men continued across the Rolling Fork. Finally, it was Duke's turn to cross the river. As he and his men forded, an artillery fragment struck Duke in the head. He plunged into the river, perhaps mortally wounded. Captain Tom Quirk was on the scene, and he reached down to save Duke from drowning. The last handful of Rebels fell in behind and crossed to the Nelson County bank. The action at Rolling Fork was over. Harlan did not follow, and the Raiders made it safely to Bardstown, where Duke's wound was treated. The blow to his head was not fatal, it turned out, but it did make a temporary invalid of him, and he finished the raid riding in a mattress-filled carriage.[7]

The next morning, Morgan's men continued their ride south. At Lebanon, right in Morgan's path, the Federals had concentrated several thousand men and some artillery batteries under Colonel William A. Hoskins. It was too much. Morgan ordered Colonel Adam R. Johnson and a detachment to demonstrate in front of Lebanon and hold the Yankees in place while the rest of the Raiders made a wide circuit around unnoticed. The march to bypass Lebanon occurred after sunset on December 30, a night described as "intensely dark and bitterly cold." Duke wrote in his post-war memoirs, "It is common to hear men who served in Morgan's cavalry ... refer to the night march around Lebanon as the most trying scene of their entire experience."[8]

The Christmas Raid was over and despite the forces the Federals sent to capture them, the Confederates returned safely to Tennessee. Morgan was celebrated by old and young alike. Little boys playing war chanted, "I wish I was a cavalryman / And did with John Hunt Morgan ride / A Colt's revolver in my hand / And a saber by my side." Morgan was idolized, but the L&N Railroad was operating again within thirty days.[9]

Morgan came back through Lebanon in July 1863, on his way to Ohio, and this time he stopped to fight. The Lebanon garrison consisted of the 20th Kentucky Infantry, Colonel Charles S. Hanson, commanding. When Morgan appeared south of town and opened up with his artillery, the Federal pickets fell back to the L&N depot where their comrades had barricaded themselves. After several hours of inconclusive fighting, Morgan ordered a charge. It was successful and the Yankees began surrendering. As they did, a shot rang out that killed Thomas Morgan, only nineteen years old and the general's brother. It was an act of treachery that could not be forgiven, and General Morgan did not try to restrain his men as they plundered the town. "Morgan did not care much what the boys did," Henry C. Magruder later recalled. The courthouse, with its files of outstanding criminal indictments was one special target, for some of Morgan's men were among those named— unjustly, in the view of Ben F. Bowman, a native of Marion County. "I never stole a horse the entire time I was with Morgan," Bowman protested. "All I ever stole was ropes. It just happened that each rope had a horse on the other end of it."[10]

Blaming Hanson for Thomas' death, the surviving Morgan brothers roughed up the colonel and threatened his life, and they turned a blind eye to worse treatment than usual of the Yankee prisoners on the march to Springfield. At one time, Morgan might have laughingly paroled them, and remember, too, that back on the Rolling Fork the previous December, Morgan had court-martialed an officer for mistreating a captive. Now, he allowed his men to rob the Yankee prisoners and to abuse them, and when Sergeant Joseph Slaughter collapsed in the road, a Raider clubbed him over the head and he died.[11]

The Raiders did not linger in Springfield. They paroled their prisoners and pressed on toward Bardstown, which they reached before dawn the next morning. At Bardstown, they faced another fight. Lieutenant Thomas W. Sullivan and twenty-five men of the 4th U.S. Cavalry had ridden out from Louisville to keep an eye on Morgan's movements. Once in Nelson County, they encountered a few graycoat riders whom they chased back to Bardstown. Loyal citizens there warned Sullivan that Morgan and several hundred raiders had the town surrounded; the lieutenant had led his patrol into a trap. Sullivan wrote, "I immediately took possession of a large livery stable ... and purchased provisions for my men, to last as long as their ammunition would hold out. I then erected a small breastwork of plank and manure within the stable to command the gate." He also threw out pickets, who soon came under attack and were driven back. Hoping that this small defeat had convinced Sullivan that resistance was futile, Morgan demanded that the lieutenant surrender. Sullivan replied that he "hoped to gain the esteem of General Morgan by a gallant defense," and the fighting resumed.[12]

All through the day and night, Morgan and Sullivan skirmished. The Rebels stretched ropes across the streets to prevent the Federals from making a dash to safety, tried unsuccessfully to set fire to the stable, and kept up a continuous fire against Sullivan and his men. At daylight the next morning, Morgan again demanded surrender, and Sullivan again refused, until a scout on top of the stable called down that he could see the four pieces of Confederate artillery that had been brought up in the night. Realizing that this could only result in the massacre of his men, Sullivan surrendered. The raiders took the Yankees' hats and boots and then paroled all but two of them. In his official report of the action, Sullivan complimented the conduct of his men, and added that the "marauding chief himself (Morgan) could not help complimenting the 25 'damned Yankees,' who detained him twenty-four hours."[13]

From Bardstown, Morgan followed the railroad to its junction with the main stem. There, he captured a northbound train. He robbed the passengers, looted the express car, and then, with a touch of the old Morgan flair, allowed the train to return to Elizabethtown (going backward now) so as not to inconvenience the female passengers with a long walk back.

The Federals were hot on Morgan's trail, only a few hours behind, so he hurried on toward Brandenburg, where he crossed the Ohio River into Indiana. Raiding north of the Ohio turned out to be a costly mistake. Local militia and volunteers for the day harried and delayed Morgan across Indiana and Ohio, while hard-riding Federal cavalrymen closed in from behind. The pressure was unrelenting. Before the end of July the Raiders were all captured, save for a handful who had slipped back across the Ohio into Kentucky. The Southern prisoners were held in different places; Morgan and some of his officers found themselves confined as common thieves in the Ohio penitentiary. Morgan escaped, made his way south, and returned to service. Duty to the Confederacy kept him farther to the east after that and he was seen in the valley of the Rolling Fork no more.[14]

After the Thunderbolt, there were incidents in the valley of the Rolling Fork, but major operations were at an end. With too few resources to mount serious offensives and with so much territory irredeemably in Union hands, the Confederate effort in Kentucky was left to loosely organized, undisciplined bands of guerrillas. In the Rolling Fork country, their leaders were men like Samuel O. "One-Armed" Berry, the piratical-looking Henry C. Magruder, the boyish-faced Jerome Clark (dubbed "Sue Mundy" by the editor of the Louisville *Daily Journal*), and even the soft-eyed Missouri bushwhacker William C. Quantrill.

By the fall of 1863, the guerrillas had begun to make their presence felt in the valley. Captain Littleton Richardson seems to have been the first to attract notice. On October 9, 1863, the *Daily Journal* ran an item about one of Richardson's strikes against the Lebanon Branch of the L&N Railroad. Near New Hope, Richardson and his gang had stopped a train, robbed the passengers, and burned the cars. They tore up some track before disappearing again into the hills. "It would seem that a regular system of guerrilla warfare has been inaugurated in Kentucky," said the newspaper.[15]

Richardson's gang hit Bardstown on October 22. They "burned the depot, captured and burned a locomotive and train of cars, robbed the stores and citizens and cut the telegraph wires." The *Daily Journal* editorialized, "There is not upon the famous Newgate Calendar the name of a viler and baser robber than he and his command."[16]

Richardson had made an impressive start and might have gone on to greater infamy, but he was killed near Cave City in March 1864. It took a little while for other leaders to emerge in Richardson's place. It was not until September that the true successor to Captain Richardson appeared. In the first week of September, a band of guerrillas hit the Lebanon Branch of the L&N near New Haven. They threw the Louisville bound train from the track, looted and burned the baggage car, and robbed the passengers. The Louisville newspaper said, "We are informed by a railroad employee that the guerrillas were fifteen in number, under the command of Billy Magruder [who], as far as we can learn, is a new aspirant for guerrilla honors. We do not recollect of having ever heard of him and his band before. It is hoped that his career may be marked with disaster and speedily brought to an end."[17]

The man whom the newspaper called "Billy" was actually Henry C. Magruder, who had grown up on his grandfather's farm between Lebanon Junction and Boston. At the start of the war, he enlisted in the Confederate Army. He served with Simon Bolivar Buckner and Albert Sidney Johnston, and had finally ended up in the 2nd Kentucky Cavalry under Morgan. He had stayed with Morgan until the Great Raid of 1863, when, in Indiana, he became separated from the Thunderbolt's column. Several attempts to rejoin Morgan failed, so Magruder and others who were in a similar fix returned south and rode as irregulars, claiming the valley of the Rolling Fork as their domain, living off the plunder they took from the L&N Railroad, from village stores, and from unlucky citizens. They stole at will and killed without remorse. So persistent were their raids and so ineffectual was the Federal response that the *Daily Journal* was forced to admit in October 1861, "Guerrillas seem to do as they please in Kentucky."[18]

To stop men like Magruder and his comrades Sue Mundy and One-Armed Berry, the Federal commanders hired guerrilla hunters to range over the countryside with instructions to capture or kill the bushwhackers. One of them was Major Cyrus J. Wilson, a citizen of LaRue County. Wilson had built LaRue County's first courthouse in 1843 and had brought the first steam mill to the county in 1855. In addition, he was a Methodist preacher. When hostilities broke out in 1861, he raised a company of men and became their captain. Added to three other companies, Wilson's men were styled the 33rd Kentucky Infantry. Wilson was the new regiment's lieutenant colonel. The 33rd was at Munfordville during the battle and siege of September 1862 and were taken prisoner.

Rather than feed them, Confederate General Bragg paroled them and sent them on their way. Lieutenant Colonel Wilson went home to New Haven to await his exchange. There, he discovered his town occupied by the 3rd Georgia Cavalry, and, in an apparent violation of his parole, he decided to take action. He went to Elizabethtown where he met with the Union officers and offered to guide a party back to New Haven where they could catch the Rebels unaware. The expedition, consisting of the 1st Kentucky Cavalry and the 2nd Indiana Cavalry, set out from Elizabethtown on the night of September 28 and arrived near New Haven just before dawn the next morning. They captured the Rebel pickets without a struggle, surrounded the enemy camp, and began assembling three hundred sleepy Georgians who were astonished to find themselves staring into the barrels of Yankee carbines. Except for a handful of distant videttes, every Rebel cavalryman at New Haven was captured. Not a single shot had been fired. It was one of the most celebrated small actions of the year 1862, and Lieutenant Colonel Wilson was its author.[19]

After their exchange, the men of the 33rd reported back to Munfordville, where they remained until ordered to New Haven to help suppress guerrillas. When it became clear that the 33rd was going to remain understrength, it was combined with the 26th Kentucky Infantry. In the new organization, Lieutenant Colonel Wilson voluntarily accepted the lower rank of major. The consolidation was finalized in April 1864. Within a year's time, Wilson had left the regiment for other duties. His superiors had long taken notice of his qualities as a man and an officer, and now Major General John M. Palmer, the district commander since February 1865, offered him a position as a "secret service" agent. His job would be to chase down guerrillas. Wilson had not been in his new assignment long when Palmer ordered him to lead a strike force to Meade County where Henry Magruder and Sue Mundy were reportedly hiding out.[20]

The guerrillas had been having a high old time in the new year of 1865. In January, Magruder and Mundy made simultaneous strikes against the Lebanon Branch of the L&N and Bardstown, destroying property and murdering in cold blood five discharged soldiers of the 15th Kentucky Infantry. After these atrocities, they moved farther east and joined forces with a new player in this bloody drama, the infamous William C. Quantrill. Quantrill had lost his command to George Todd in a contest of wills in the winter of 1864–65, and he traveled east with those of his bushwhackers who remained loyal to him, men like Jim Younger and Frank James. In Kentucky, Quantrill and his band threw in with Magruder and Mundy. During the first two weeks in February, the combined gang hit Danville, Hustonville, New Market, Bradfordsville, and Simpsonville. However, by the third week of the month, Magruder and Mundy had apparently tired of Quantrill's company. They returned to the Rolling Fork. On February 23, they attacked Lebanon Junction and also Fort Jones, which overlooked the L&N bridge on the river between Lebanon Junction and Colesburg.[21]

February was a pivotal month for guerrillas in Kentucky. About the middle of the month, the CSA's Secretary of War, General John C. Breckinridge, ordered the various bands to go south and rejoin the regular army. Still believing themselves to be legitimate soldiers and subject to orders, Magruder and Mundy headed southwest to report to General Hylan B. Lyon in Paris, Tennessee. Two others, Henry Metcalf and Bill Davison, joined them en route. Near Hawesville on March 3, they ran into a company of Home Guards called the Green River Battalion. In the fight that followed, Davison was mortally wounded and Magruder was shot through the body. His comrades Mundy and Metcalf took him back toward Meade County. They found shelter in the tobacco barn of a farmer named James S. Cox. There they planned to hide until Magruder either died or grew strong enough to ride. An informer reported to General Palmer where the guerrillas were hiding, and Palmer called for Major Wilson.[22]

On Saturday evening March 10, Wilson left Louisville with a force of fifty men, most of them from Co. B, 30th Wisconsin Infantry. They traveled by paddle wheeler and disembarked at Brandenburg. From there they marched to the home of Dr. J.P. Lewis, who had been treating Magruder and could lead them to the guerrillas' lair. On Sunday morning, about dawn, the bluecoats arrived at Cox's farm. They searched his house and surrounded the tobacco barn. When they announced their presence, a firefight broke out and four soldiers were wounded. After the shooting stopped, Mundy agreed to speak to Wilson at the door. Wilson later recounted their conversation. Mundy feared that if he and Magruder and Metcalf surrendered, the soldiers would shoot them down. Wilson promised him that this would not be the case. Mundy said well, then, they would be taken to Louisville and killed there. Wilson agreed that they would certainly be executed, but that surrender would at least allow them to live a few days longer.

Rough men often respond to straight talk. Mundy asked Wilson to come inside the barn for a smoke, and there the major found Metcalf and the wounded Magruder. Magruder, exhausted and disheartened by pain, said to Wilson that "he had been a bad boy and was going to die," and he urged Mundy to surrender. So did Metcalf, and Wilson insisted again that the men give up. Finally, Mundy agreed, so long as the three would be treated as prisoners of war. To this, Wilson agreed, and the men came out of the barn. They returned to Brandenburg and proceeded from there to Louisville aboard the steamer *Morning Star*.[23]

Mundy's trial began and concluded on March 14. He was convicted and hanged the next day. Magruder's trial would be next, if he survived his wounds. But looking at him in the military prison hospital, few believed that his recovery was likely.[24]

While Magruder languished between life and death, Quantrill still rode. Trying to bring his career to an end was a guerrilla catcher who was cut from an entirely different bolt of cloth than Major Cyrus Wilson. Quantrill's adversary was Edwin Terrell, a bandy-legged little man who wore a coat that extended to the tops of his tall boots and a brace of pistols belted at his waist. His face was rodent-like and, in the one known photograph of him, he wears a sadistic leer that marks him as a killer at heart. In Terrell's case, looks were not deceiving. He killed his first man at age fourteen. When the war broke out, he first enlisted in the Confederate Army, but he was in constant trouble and ended up serving the other side. In January 1865, he was hired as a guerrilla hunter by General Stephen G. Burbridge, Palmer's predecessor, and was retained by Palmer when he assumed command. On April 1, Palmer selected Terrell for the specific purpose of tracking down Quantrill. Palmer was aware that he was in cahoots with a dangerous man; he later said, "I never let him enter my quarters without keeping a revolver at hand."[25]

Quantrill did not know it, but heading toward him was a force with a single purpose in mind: his destruction. Like those bullets found at Gettysburg that struck in midair and were welded together by the impact, Quantrill and Terrell were about to collide and their names welded together in history.

According to John McCorkle, who had been Quantrill's scout in Missouri and had followed him to Kentucky, the guerrillas spent a lot of March and April 1865 loafing around Jim Dawns' still. Someone must have carried the news to Quantrill of the capture of Clark and Magruder and also of the death of the raider Bill Marion near New Haven on April 15. Terrell and his men were in the New Haven area that day, but there were other Federals nearby, as well, and it was almost certainly not Terrell or any of his men who killed Marion. Nevertheless, Terrell took time out from hunting Quantrill to deliver Marion's body back to Louisville. He was eager to claim the credit. Besides the glory of it, General Palmer had promised him a fine horse if he took Marion down. The little newspaper war that broke out over the question of who killed Marion did not disturb Terrell at all.[26]

If Quantrill had no premonition from the thinning ranks of prominent guerrillas that the end was near, he did about a week later when his horse Old Charley was hamstrung and had to be destroyed. The Missourian understood the death of his war horse to be a foreshadowing of his own doom. "That means my work is done," Quantrill told his men.[27]

On May 10, on the James H. Wakefield farm, near the Spencer-Nelson County line, Terrell caught up with Quantrill. The raiders were inside a barn where they had gone to escape a rain storm when the Yankees attacked them. In the scramble to escape, Quantrill was shot in the back. The bullet had nicked his spine and he was paralyzed. One of Terrell's men fired a second time at Quantrill. The round hit his right hand and blasted it to pieces. A part of it that included his trigger finger flew off and landed in the mud. Terrell and his gang carried Quantrill to Wakefield's house, which they then began to loot. To satisfy them, Wakefield offered the pillagers a handful of money and a jug of whiskey. They left but promised to come back for their prisoner.

On May 12, Terrell began the slow job of transporting Quantrill to Louisville. His ambulance was a lumbering Conestoga wagon. On the second day, they arrived at Louisville. The Federal authorities who took charge of the dying prisoner assigned him to the same hospital ward where Henry Magruder lay confined to his cot by his wounds. Quantrill was delirious at the end; he and his men were about to be attacked. He was calling out encouragement to his phantom riders just before he died on June 6.[28]

Their leader was lost along with their cause, and Quantrill's men were stranded in Kentucky, far from home. John Porter assumed command of the gang and entered into talks with Cyrus Wilson about surrender and parole. They reached a tentative agreement. While they waited for General Palmer's final approval, an incident occurred that threatened to ruin everything. Two members of One-Armed Berry's group gang-raped a woman named Mary Clark on the Bardstown-New Haven Road. Not only did this outrage the Southern chivalry of Porter and his followers, but it also put their chance for parole at risk. They needed to act quickly. Frank James offered to take six men and chase the miscreants down, and Major Wilson agreed to the plan. In an ironic twist of fate, these men, who had been guilty of spreading such mayhem through the valley of the Rolling Fork, now became agents of law and order. Within a short time, James and his posse apprehended the two rapists and took them to Mrs. Clark's home. She identified them as her assailants. James's posse executed them and delivered the bodies to Wilson. A few days later, on July 26, 1865, the Missourians' paroles came through. They kept their pistols and horses and returned to the far side of the Mississippi.[29]

And Henry Magruder still lived. Since the time of his capture the people had expected to read in the newspapers of his death, but he fooled them. He lived to be put on trial; the hearings began on September 13, 1865. After two weeks of testimony, the presiding board exonerated him of eight murder charges and of a charge of rape, but found him guilty of being a guerrilla and of committing nine murders. The sentence was death by hanging. When they came to get Magruder from his cell on October 20, he commented, "It is hard, but maybe it is fair." He walked out of the prison to the sound of band music from the 125th Colored Infantry. Thirteen steps led him up to the waiting noose. While an officer read the list of charges against him, Magruder gazed from the gallows over the rooftops. A large crowd had gathered to watch him swing. Many of them commented upon how utterly calm the condemned man seemed to be. When asked if he had anything to say, Magruder replied, "Not a word." The rope was fixed, the hood was pulled over his head, and Henry C. Magruder plunged to his death. His mother claimed his body and took it back to the Bullitt County farm for burial.[30]

The war was over. The Union victory gave some new opportunities and forced others into exile out of state while still others remained and tried to make sense of a world so markedly different than the one they had known. Some could never adjust. Basil "Hermit" Haydon was one of them. Haydon was a descendant of one of the families who traveled from Maryland to Kentucky in the Catholic migration of the 1780s. At the start of the war, he was a bachelor farmer, a slave owner, and an ardent anti–Lincoln man. He came home to Nelson County from Confederate service in 1865, embittered at the changes he saw all around him. He declared that God was a harsh and unjust God to have deprived him of his slaves and he "registered a terrible oath" that from that day on he would never set foot on the earth.[31]

Haydon spent most of the next forty-five years in his room of the family's 1788 homestead. No relative was permitted to come into his sanctuary. For those times when he had to go out, he had wooden walkways built to connect the buildings of his property and when he rode to town on his horse, he called to the merchants from the street outside. Those trips to town became less and less frequent. An 1899 newspaper article said that Bardstown banker visited the hermit twice a year "and through him the recluse settles his financial matters with the outside world." Gossip said that he accumulated a sizeable fortune which he kept hidden in his home. Haydon's behavior grew stranger with every passing year. He never cut his hair or shaved after he made his oath. He kept a fire burning on even the hottest days. From his room, he managed his farm operations, sometimes to the inconvenience of his hired hands. He once had his foreman parade all the livestock past his unshuttered window for inspection.[32]

Haydon died, still clean-footed, in 1909 and was buried at St. Joseph Cemetery in Bardstown, covered by the earth he had renounced.

EIGHT

Struggling Just to Live

Hermit Haydon and a few others could not adjust, perhaps, but in those same decades that he refused to touch the earth, the rest who remained in the valley of the Rolling Fork repaired the damages of war and got on with life. The Louisville & Nashville Railroad had come out of the war more prosperous than before. The Nelsonville Furnace and the Belmont Furnace in Bullitt County had merged to better meet the demand for iron during the war, and they were thriving. The old fords and wooden bridges were being replaced by iron bridges. Lebanon rebuilt; so did New Haven and Boston. New churches were going up everywhere, and the monks at Gethsemani finally finished theirs. New railroad hotels were seen along the L&N, and new industries brought relative prosperity to the valley.

In 1867, very near the site of Zachariah Riney's schoolhouse, John McDougal Atherton built a distillery and a town for his workers. Soon, there was a stillhouse on either side of the turnpike, one to produce sour mash and the other sweet mash. Atherton built a store for the workers, a rooming house, and a three story hotel named for himself. At full production, the Atherton distilling operations used 2,220 bushels of grain daily "and produced about 6,600 gallons of whiskey," which, until shipped out via the company's spur line to the L&N at New Haven, was stored in warehouses that could hold more than 150,000 bourbon-filled barrels which were built by his own coopers. Obviously, distilling was an industry that consumed volumes of raw materials. The benefits to the local growers of grain and suppliers of hardwood can be imagined. Merchants, too, prospered by Atherton's operations, for distillery workers "typically earned $600 to $700 a year" at the turn of the century, and much of that money went into the tills of the shopkeepers in New Haven and Hodgenville. Thinking back on the good-paying jobs of that time, New Haven Mayor Bobby Johnson said, "If you had a job at the Athertonville distillery you were on top of the world."[1]

The federal government, too, began pouring money into the local

60

economy. In 1903, the War Department considered the area around West Point for a permanent military installation. In that year, thirty thousand artillerymen, infantrymen, and cavalrymen came to what was called Camp Young. It was the waning days of the horse cavalry and horse-drawn caissons. The old photos show the young soldiers looking smart in their Spanish-American War era uniforms, the brass buttons gleaming against khaki blouses, the brims of their campaign hats curled up fore and aft. The co-operation of the locals and the topography of the area impressed the government officials greatly. Here were favorable factors for the creation of a permanent fort. They did not follow up on their plans in 1903; but they would be coming back in 1918.[2]

Along the Rolling Fork, it was a good time to live, but living was chancy. Medicine was still in such a primitive state that a whole list of diseases existed against which there were no preventatives or effective treatments: consumption, pneumonia, typhoid fever, diphtheria, meningitis, le grippe, Bright's disease. They carried away hundreds of victims every year. Death stalked even the able-bodied and strong, however, and often found them in the workplace. The local newspapers published an endless litany of tragedy. Men cutting timber were killed by falling limbs or trees that fell in an unexpected direction. Farmers were crushed by farm equipment. Toddlers and young children got too close to the open fires that were necessary for hog scalding or washing laundry; the flames licked at their clothes and they ran in terror and died of their burns.

The Rolling Fork was regarded as the most dangerous river in Kentucky and many drowned in its treacherous waters, but few aspects of life were more dangerous than the railroad. Tragically familiar were accidents that killed individuals and wrecks that took the lives of carloads of passengers. An accident on the railroad bridge at Calvary in June 1900 left three people dead and fourteen injured, but the worst railroad disaster was the Shepherdsville train wreck of December 20, 1917, when a miscommunication resulted in the collision of two trains and the instant death of at least forty-six Christmas shoppers returning from Louisville.[3]

And, if the vagaries of cruel luck were not bad enough, there was the evil intent of one's neighbors. A careful survey of Carolyn Wimp's wonderful series of newspaper abstracts from Hardin, Nelson, and LaRue Counties around the turn of the century shows a tragic level of violence in the towns of the Rolling Fork. So closely was violence associated with the region that a 1911 postcard called "Night Scenes in Raywick" showed a silhouetted scene of men and women brawling in the street with clubs and umbrellas while an unconcerned policeman stands under a street lamp nearby. The implication was that riots were a common occurrence in Raywick. The region had acquired a violent, riotous image.[4]

The strangest episode of violence may have been that of Mary Thompson at Lebanon Junction in 1904. John Irvin had been in a verbal altercation with Mrs. Thompson's son, who went to tell his mother, who went to find her razor, and then went to find John Irvin. She found him. One pass with the razor was all it took to finish him; Mrs. Thompson weighed 250 pounds.

She was arrested and taken to jail, where fifty of Irvin's friends found her. The mob broke down the doors and pulled her from her cell and hanged her, but as she dangled from the stout tree limb, she snatched the knife of a man who foolishly stood too close, cut the rope that was strangling her, and fought her way out of the crowd. As she ran for it, the lynch mob drew their pistols and fired over one hundred shots in her direction. Ninety-seven shots from these sharpshooters missed her, but three found their mark and the mighty woman fell to the ground. The New York *Times* reported the hanging and shooting of Mrs. Thompson and noted that the mob "left her for dead. Later the officers removed her to a physician's office, and there she died."[5]

Judging by the poor quality of marksmanship in the Mary Thompson lynch mob, it may be surprising that there were any gun deaths at all in the Rolling Fork Valley, except accidental. In fact, the newspapers reported many. The causes of the violence were the usual and often fueled by alcohol, but not always. Sometimes it was simply a minor event that spun out of control. In August 1901, Elijah Hazel shot and killed William Hill, keeper of the Nelson County poorhouse. Hazel was a resident there and worked on the farm. Hill had given him some instructions about his work, which Hazel ignored. Later, when Mrs. Hill noticed that the orders had not been followed, she stepped in and admonished Hazel "and received some insulting replies from him." She reported Hazel's remarks to Mr. Hill, who went to Hazel's quarters for an explanation. An argument ensued and Hazel shot Hill. The wounded man turned to flee, and Hazel shot him twice more in the back. Hill died on the spot. The case seemed cut and dried, but at Hazel's trial, the jury hung. The majority favored the death penalty, but five held out for a sentence of life imprisonment. In his second trial, Hazel was sentenced to life in prison. He died in the state penitentiary in Frankfort seventeen months later.[6]

April 1904 gives us another instance of a fatal gunplay. Marshal A.F. Haley went to arrest Charles Martin on some minor charge in Lebanon Junction. John Rouzee, a longtime enemy of the officer's, took it upon himself to interfere. Things quickly became heated. Haley,

Martin, and Rouzee all pulled their guns and opened fire. A man named J.D. Gentry came running to assist Haley. The newspaper stated, "When the smoke cleared away, Rouzee and Haley were lying dead and Gentry was wounded. Martin, the cause of the disturbance, escaped uninjured, but was captured by a constable." Though he, too, had pulled his gun, Martin was later acquitted of complicity in the death of Marshall Haley. In a postscript to the tragedy, Ethel Lee Haley, the marshal's little girl, died of measles and pneumonia less than six weeks after her father was killed.[7]

Through it all, only one resident of the valley of the Rolling Fork was known to have lived long enough to see the long arc of history, from the log forts of Samuel Goodin and Benjamin Lynn, the buffalo and the Indian warrior, the shouting Baptist exhorters and the lonely priests on horseback going to celebrate Mass at some remote altar, the slave coffles, the railroads, the dusty Federal infantrymen, the brightly dressed guerrillas, and now, the iron bridges and new jails.

This ancient citizen of the Rolling Fork was a giant bullfrog who lived in the springhouse at the distiller John Ritchie's old homestead. The frog was described as having "vast proportions" and a "thunderous voice" which could be heard booming from far away. The most elderly human residents could not remember a time when the bullfrog did not live beside the cold pool of the springhouse; they felt sure that he was the original Ritchie frog of the pioneer times. In an 1897 feature in the Nelson County *Record*, Stephen Ritchie affirmed that this frog was the same one. He remembered that his grandmother had called the frog her "rain sign." The article concluded that the bullfrog, though a century or more old, was still "very active."[8]

The same could be said of the valley of the Rolling Fork.

NINE

Too Dry, Then Too Wet

The 1920s and '30s were hard years for the people who lived in the valley of the Rolling Fork. First it was too dry. Then it was too wet.

Geography and tradition had made distilling an important way of life along the Rolling Fork. The elements had always been there: plentiful hardwood forests, creeks of cold, limestone-infused water, and a soil and climate ideally suited for growing corn. In 1780, the enterprising John Ritchie had seen the parts of the puzzle as one picture, and a new way of making a living was begun. It was not an occupation for the lazy man, the stupid man, or the careless man. A distiller had to be as practical as a mechanic, as intuitive as a good cook, and blessed with the strength and endurance of a farmer. Here's how the work was traditionally done:

Shelled corn was put into a sack and doused with hot water over a period of three or four days to make it sprout. After the corn had produced "stringers" it was spread out in the sun and allowed to dry. Once it was dried, the corn was ground into a coarse meal called "chop." The chop was turned into "mash" by putting it into an oak barrel and adding hot water. The barrel was then covered. After three to five days, more hot water was added, plus some rye malt. The barrel was covered again. The mash could be heard "working," gurgling and hissing.[1]

After several days, the mash was ready to run; it was said to be "ripe." Now the distiller must hurry; he had eight hours to make his whiskey. The mash was strained through a cloth into a copper pot still. Copper was the time-tested metal of choice because copper would not corrode and poison the liquor. The cloudy, yellow liquid going into the still was called "corn beer," and this was boiled in the still over a slow, steady fire of oak or hickory. Ash was also good. As the beer started to cook, a lid was put on the still. Now the steam produced by the boiling beer had no way to escape except through the long, beak-like neck of the still and into the "worm" (a long corkscrew of copper tubing), which was submerged in a container of cold water. Ideally, this container was also set where water could flow around it—a stream bed served nicely. The alcohol steam condensed in the worm and flowed out of the end, a liquid once more, into kegs or buckets. This liquid was called the "singlings."[2]

The still had to be scrubbed out before the next run. When it was clean, the singlings were poured back into the still and the cooking process repeated. This time, when the liquid ran out the end of the worm, it was called "doublings." Fifty gallons of singlings yielded between fifteen and twenty gallons of doublings. If the distiller shook the doublings and saw bubbles the size of No. 6 shot rise to the top, then the whiskey was good, about 120 proof. He cut the doublings with five gallons of spring water. Now it was ready to store.[3]

The whiskey from the still was as clear as water—the famous "white lightning" of country songs. The golden color associated with Kentucky bourbon came not from the distilling but from being stored in charred white oak barrels. Changing temperatures over time caused a slight expansion and contraction, forcing the whiskey back and forth through the thin layer of scorched wood inside the barrel, smoothing it and coloring it. Some stored the whiskey for a longer period of time than others; it depended on the markets and the demand.[4]

That was how the early whiskey makers did it. They took pride in their work and tried to make a quality product. In the years to come, distilleries like Jim Beam, Heaven Hill, and Maker's Mark would turn John Ritchie's cottage industry into one of Kentucky's primary manufactures. The big-time distilleries were an economic boon to the area, and generations of families made a living from them directly or indirectly.

Then, the spirit of reform swept the land. In 1918, the Kentucky General Assembly outlawed liquor distribution and possession. It was the latest in a long list of individual states to do so, and the whole country went dry with the ratification of the 18th Amendment—the Volstead Act or the National Prohibition Enforcement Act—in October 1919. The distillery workers in Athertonville and Bardstown picked up their final pay envelope and went home to decide how to make a living now that the temperance movement had deprived them of their livelihood. Some went to the far, dark corner of the barn and pulled a dusty tarp off of a family heirloom—a fat-bodied, bird-looking thing made of copper, with a coiled "worm" dangling from its metal beak.[5]

For most men who went "farming in the woods," it was a matter of family finance. Men did what they had to do to provide for their wives and children. They brought out the old stills and quietly ordered new ones. A still-maker charged between $20 and $30 to make a pure copper, fifty gallon still. There had been moonshining, of course, ever since the first excise tax on whiskey was imposed in the 1790s. A moonshiner was traditionally just a tax evader, but this was something different, more widespread, now that the 18th Amendment had passed. It was more profitable, too. What had sold for $2 a gallon was now bringing $22 a gallon. It cost only ninety cents a gallon to make.[6]

The profits were great and the risks were small. A moonshiner who was caught often faced nothing more than a two-year probation for his first offense and a year plus one day in prison for his second. Enforcement of the Volstead Act fell at times to the Treasury Department and at other times to the Justice Department, but it is doubtful that such paper shuffling in Washington made much difference to the field agents; their goal remained the same: go out and stop the backwoods whiskey cookers. Men like William "Big Six" Henderson and Quinn Pearl became local legends for their ability to catch moonshiners.[7]

Riding through the hills, the revenuers watched for a smooth path through the brush with no signs of horseshoes or animal hooves or of wheel ruts. This was the "moonshine path" that might have been used by a family for years. At its end, beneath an overhanging cliff or in the mouth of a cave, was a still or a log stillhouse, half-hidden behind piles of brush. Oftentimes, a stream rather than a trail was the best clue as to where a still was hiding, since the moonshiner needed fresh water for his cooler-barrel. On breezy days, the revenuers could sometimes smell the cooking mash, but their horses were even quicker to detect the stills, for they hated the odor. Smoke sometimes gave the still location away, especially at the beginning of a run.[8]

It was a tense game of cat-and-mouse, but usually not a particularly dangerous one. There were few shootouts between federals and the moonshiners. Probation was nothing and a man could even endure a yearlong sentence, but killing a government agent meant the electric chair. So, the moonshiners hid until caught and then ran, abandoning their operation to the revenuers, who proceeded to "cut down" the still, a hard, filthy job.

Those moonshiners who successfully kept their product until time to transport it to Louisville or Fort Knox faced the possibility of being caught on the road with a cargo. Some traveled in pairs: a car in front, a truck with the goods behind. If the law got after them, the driver of the car would speed recklessly ahead and lure the policeman into giving him a ticket while the truck driver passed slowly by, a law-abiding citizen with proper respect for the speed limit. Others relied on concealment and speed. These early "trippers," screeching around the curves and punching it on the straightaways, were the start of NASCAR. If the revenuers could not be outraced, the trippers would throw out jars of

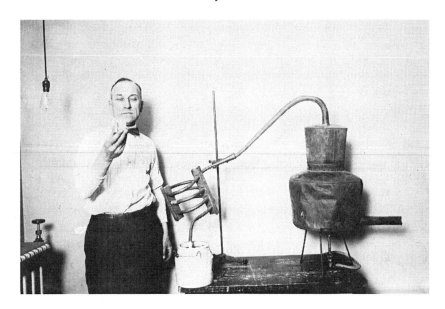

Confiscated moonshine still (Library of Congress).

whiskey to shatter on the road and flatten the tires of the dead wagons. Tacks and spikes could do the job, too. The revenuers had their tricks, as well. When an informer told them the route a tripper was going to take, they placed spiked planks end to end at the approach to a bridge, pointed side up. The best tripper alive could not get away with punctured tires.[9]

The repeal of prohibition by the 21st Amendment in December 1933 was a terrible blow to the moonshiners, but some persisted. Joe Creason, late columnist for the *Courier-Journal,* reported that in 1947, the twenty-seven Treasury agents assigned to Kentucky "were able to raid and destroy 267 stills.... A total of 376 persons were arrested and 46,325 gallons of mash seized." As late as 1952 stills were being cut down. Near Colesburg in that year, federal agents discovered and destroyed a huge electric still consisting of seventy-two fifty-gallon fermentation tanks along with three thousand gallons of mash, four thousand pounds of sugar, and over 250 gallons of whiskey.[10]

However, it was generally true that the end of prohibition was the end of the moonshiner, too. The legal distilleries went back into full production and quality brands like Maker's Mark with its hand-dipped red wax seal began to attract the world's attention to the valley of the Rolling Fork. Maker's Mark, in Loretto, is the oldest, continuous distillery in the United States operating on its original site, and it is a National Historic Landmark. It is open to tours, and in 2007 a new visitor center was built to welcome the thousands of people who stop by annually. The Jim Beam Distillery at Clermont is also a popular tourist destination. Signs along the highway boldly advertise Kentucky's "Bourbon Trail," luring families to come see what revenuers once had to creep through the underbrush to find.

The return of spirituous liquors in 1933 was followed by a chaser of icy cold water in 1937. In early January of that year, there came a powerful blizzard. A few days of warm weather followed. The accumulation of ice and snow melted, and the ground was saturated. Then came a bitter cold spell and the sodden ground froze. Finally, beginning on January 16, there came ten solid days of heavy rain. Almost twenty inches of rain fell in January, over ten inches of that between January 20 and 24. Added to this were periods of snow and sleet. The Flood of '37 was on, and the water was rising two feet an hour.[11]

There was no direction for the excess water to go but up. The farmers had to leave their low-lying farms and seek safety on higher ground. Many had to leave their livestock to perish—a necessity that some of them never stopped regretting—but a few landowners herded their animals to the top of a nearby knob. The scene from the peak was weird. The Rolling Fork was described as a "several thousand acre lake." Sallie Pope remembered her knob-top experience as like being "surrounded by an ocean, there was nothing as far as the eye could see on every side and no land visible except a few knobs, chimneys and tops of farm houses at a distance … just a surging, rippling ocean from hill to hill."[12]

Food grew scarce as the days went by. Robert L. Moser and his family tried to stay in their Bullitt County home, but finally had to be rescued. They lodged with a family named Cruise near Chapeze. Moser remembered, "After we had eaten everything the Cruise family had saved for the winter, the men went to the Distillery and got Yellow corn meal mash. We had fried mush for lunch and boiled mush for dinner."[13]

When reports of the severity of the flood reached Washington, D.C., says historian Rick Bell, "President Franklin D. Roosevelt addressed the nation and asked for support for the Red Cross. Almost immediately over $2,000,000 was given in response." Roosevelt also hired 6,500 additional Works Progress Administration personnel and dispatched them to lend a hand in Louisville. WPA administrators in regions not affected by the flood received orders to send all surpluses to the Ohio River communities. Before long, "eggs by the carload—12,000 dozen per car—canned beef, evaporated milk, Florida grapefruit, cotton and mattress ticking, overshoes, blankets, heavy underwear, shirts and galoshes were on their way." WPA workers also built skiffs to supplement the fleet of boats sent by the Coast Guard for evacuation duty. They built privies and delivered supplies, cleared debris, cooked and served meals from field kitchens, nursed the sick, and put on shows to keep the people's spirits up. In addition, the President authorized Governor A.B. "Happy" Chandler to declare martial law so that soldiers from Fort Knox could render aid in rescue and security efforts. One essential government function, mail delivery, was impossible in the flooded country, but the WHAS radio broadcasts out of Louisville reassured the isolated rural people that they were not alone and had not been forgotten. Sallie Pope said that the country people "were cut off from the world but listened to the radio both day and night."[14]

Virtually everyone in Boston had to be evacuated from their homes. Shelter was provided for them in schools and churches. The roads were all flooded. Six feet of water stood over U.S. Highway 62 at the foot of Muldraugh Hill. The Red Cross sent supplies to the water's edge at Boston, and a boat route was established to the various refugee centers and on down the valley to Lebanon Junction and Colesburg. At Colesburg, the water was ten to fifteen feet higher than had ever been recorded. The area was a natural reservoir for the rising water. Mary House, who lived there, explained why with a simplicity that would shame a geographer: "Colesburg sits right in a holler," she said.[15]

Mary House and her husband Jim found refuge in the local schoolhouse after the rising water of the Rolling Fork got in their home and carried away a pot full of beans and the table it was sitting on. A train took them to Elizabethtown where they stayed for two weeks. Almost all of Colesburg was evacuated by train on the afternoon of January 24. A second train that night rescued nine more, and a Monday morning train brought out eleven more. Finally, only two houses remained occupied in Colesburg; both belonged to Rudolph Rogers. They were on the highest ground in town. The Baptist Church, the school, and Rogers' two houses were safe, but St. Clare Catholic Church was flooded and J.H. Padgett's store held water twelve feet deep.[16]

At Elizabethtown, the Colesburg refugees were registered at the Hardin County Courthouse and fed a hot meal in the basement before being assigned to homes. Vaccinations against typhoid fever were mandatory, for the water was nasty with all manner of filth. One only had to look at the oily, rainbow-hued surface of the water and notice the rafts of floating scum to know that drowning was not the only danger carried in this swirling, stinking inland tide. It was two weeks before the flood victims were allowed to return to Colesburg. Jim and Mary House found all their belongings ruined. The Rolling Fork had reached the roofline of their home.[17]

By February 12, fewer than thirty refugees remained in Lebanon, fewer than fifty in Bardstown. The clean-up required a massive effort. The Red Cross pumped polluted water out of rural folks' wells and disposed of tons of tainted foodstuffs. Roy Troutman noted that crops laid by in the barns and corncribs were ruined by the floodwaters. As for the houses, Troutman said, "Cleaning up was an awful job because we had to get the mud out of all the homes. The smell stayed around for months." Robert L. Moser added, "Furniture fell apart, where it was glued together; wall paper fell off the walls; all the doors were swelled up until they were stuck to the floor, if open, and the door casing if shut. Nothing worked like it was supposed to. Shovel up a scoop of mud off the floor, run fingers through it for silver ware, and pitch it out the window. The floors were like a big washboard where the wood swelled up; windows all stuck in place."[18]

The loss was measured in large part in the loss of livestock. Annie Laura Jenkins of Shepherdsville wrote her parents, "The loss of stock is pathetic to me. We know one man who watched his 300 hogs drown; another lost 35 registered cows; another with 250 steers; and on and on. The stock is floating around in the water. They were able to save scarcely any. Horses and mules drowning like rats."[19]

In its final tally, given on February 18, 1937, the *Kentucky Standard* reported that flood damage in Kentucky was estimated at $61,858,000. Nelson County had suffered $20,000 in damage; $450,000 in Hardin County; and $1,711,500 in Bullitt. Shepherdsville, the county seat of Bullitt had been completely inundated for the first time in history. The courthouse held four feet of water.[20]

A government big enough and powerful enough can be a force for enormous good. The money and manpower that were poured into the effort to get the drowned communities of the '37 Flood back on their feet could not have been managed by a small, anemic government in Washington; it would have been nearly as helpless as the government in Frankfort.

For all of the expenditure of national resources in the valley of the Rolling Fork, there was still more to come. The *Kentucky Standard* announced on February 11, 1937, that Nelson County had gotten an allotment of $315,000 from FDR's Rural Electrification Administration to extend power lines to benefit an additional one thousand farm families.[21]

It was a hard country to keep down. Still is.

TEN

The Rolling Fork Today

It was expected in 1903 that the United States government, pleased with the varied terrain and the patriotic spirit of the region, would establish a permanent camp near the confluence of the Salt and Rolling Fork Rivers. West Point would be its nucleus. Neither the time nor the location was exactly right.

Fourteen years later, it was plain that the United States was going to become involved in the war in Europe and a remote camp was needed for the artillery forces then training at Camp Zachary Taylor in Louisville. So, in January 1918, the government leased ten thousand acres around Stithton and named the installation Camp Knox (in honor of General Henry Knox, General Washington's artillery commander during the Revolution and also the first Secretary of War). Many farm families and the entire population of Stithton were dislocated. The town disappeared except for St. Patrick Catholic Church, which remained to become the post chapel.[1]

In June 1918, Congress authorized the purchase of forty thousand acres in Hardin and Meade Counties at a cost of $1,600,000. The erection of facilities for 22,700 men was commenced. Quartermaster W.H. Radcliffe was in charge of construction. A new town located on the Hardin County side of Fort Knox was named after him. The armistice in November 1918, followed by army manpower reductions beginning in 1921, made Camp Knox less important. Some returning Doughboys were mustered out there, but plans were scaled back for a permanent base. The War Department did hold on to the land as a training center for the National Guard and the ROTC. One of the ROTC artillery student cadets at Camp Knox had come down from the University of Wisconsin. He was an unassuming young man, painfully shy, but before the decade was done, he had become the most famous man in the world. His name was Charles A. Lindbergh, and he came down to Kentucky to attend the Field Artillery Summer Camp in 1921, an experience he mentioned in his memoir, *The Spirit of St. Louis*.[2]

Camp Knox was also chosen for one of the nation's fifty Civilian Military Training Camps. The great American poet and novelist Robert Penn Warren was a civilian cadet at Camp Knox when he wrote his first public piece, a poem called "Prophecy," published in the Camp Knox *Mess Kit* in 1922. "Prophecy" was a little gem of a poem, but even the most perceptive admirer of verse might not have been able to see in this first effort the talent that would burst forth to lead Robert Penn Warren to the top of the literary world. The Logan County native became one of nation's most distinguished authors, winning a total of three Pulitzer Prizes, two for poetry and another for his novel *All the King's Men.* No other author has ever won Pulitzers for both poetry and fiction. Only Warren did, and he got his start as a published author at Camp Knox, Kentucky.[3]

The 1930s saw another population of young men arrive at Camp Knox. They were Civilian Conservation Corps boys, who began arriving for their six months' enlistment in the spring of 1933. By the end of the first week in June, the number of young men was fourteen thousand. The army was ordered to run the CCC camps, while the "Departments of the Interior, Forestry and Agriculture would be responsible for work projects." The boys took classes, and each one was given the chance to learn a marketable skill, and then they dispersed across the country in companies of two hundred. The trees the CCC planted, the parks they built, and the eroded land they reclaimed helped create the nation we see today, but there was another, more critical job ahead for them. Some of these same young men would return to Knox in the following decade for the training they needed to fight and defeat the Axis Powers. The installation on the Rolling Fork was about to be called back to its original intended purpose.[4]

During the 1920s, a mechanized cavalry was in development at Fort Eustis, Virginia, but the space there was limited and the terrain too uniform for the most effective training. Colonel Daniel Van Voorhis and Lieutenant Colonel Adna R. Chaffee believed Camp Knox's "larger size and varied terrain were more suited for the development of armored tactics" than Fort Eustis, and they were authorized to relocate the program in November 1931. Van Voorhis and Chaffee were really the fathers of Fort Knox and, one might insist, the architects of American victory in Europe during World War II, since the winning tactics used by tank commanders like General George Patton were largely refined at the newly named Fort Knox. The Armored Force School was established at Fort Knox in October 1940. Its job was to teach ways to counter the Nazi Panzers. The 864 buildings on post were inadequate to house and train the nearly two thousand officers and men of the Armored Force

School, so a building expansion was approved. The officers and trainees soon numbered more than 4,200, and "by 1943 Fort Knox had expanded to more than 106,861 acres and had 3,820 buildings."[5]

Another building project had been completed by this time. The Treasury Department decided in the thirties to build the U.S. Bullion Depository, popularly called the Gold Vault, at Fort Knox. The fort was located in the nation's interior and was easily accessed by highways and railroads. The depository cost $560,000 to build. Its outer walls were granite lined with concrete; the vault itself created a building inside a building. The doors of the vault weighed thirty tons and could only be opened by a combination of numerical sequences. Several staff members were involved in every opening of the doors, but each one knew only his part of the total sequence. Guard boxes at each corner and a guarded entry gate added extra layers of security to the grounds of the gold vault.

The first gold shipments arrived in 1937, a busy year for the men at Fort Knox since many of them were helping rescue and evacuate victims of the great flood. The gold came by rail from New York and Philadelphia. Each gold ingot carried from the train and stacked inside the depository measured slightly smaller than a regular brick but weighed 27.5 pounds. The value of the gold was estimated at nearly $23 million. (As of 2019, the gold housed at the vault was valued at over $6 billion.)[6]

U.S. Bullion Depository at Fort Knox (Library of Congress).

On December 27, 1941, treasures of another sort were shipped to the gold vault. The widening world war made essential the safety of treasures rarer than gold: the Magna Carta; a Gutenberg Bible; the Declaration of Independence; the Articles of Confederation; the original, signed Constitution; an original, signed copy of the Gettysburg Address; and the original, signed manuscript of Lincoln's 2nd Inaugural Address. They were stored inside the vault. One wonders what would have become of these samples of man's greatest efforts to be better than he was if our enemies had won.[7]

The personnel at Fort Knox were determined that our enemies would not win. By 1943, two daily shifts at the Armored Force School were required to train the soldiers headed off to Europe or the Pacific. By the end of the war, there were sixteen armored divisions at Fort Knox, as well as more than one hundred tank battalions and mechanized cavalry squadrons. War had always been a part of the valley of the Rolling Fork, but this was war supersized for a nation forced into a gluttonous, and soon habitual, appetite for military spending.[8]

Since 1945, Fort Knox has scarcely looked back. The brigades and military training schools there have rotated and changed through the years, but the overall mission has always remained the same, to train officers and men to defend the United States and to protect a sizeable portion of its gold reserves.

As important as it is and in spite of its location on the map, Fort Knox is not culturally a part of the Rolling Fork. Not really. It is all numbers, and straight lines, and hard edged, humorless men who are devoted to the essential task of national security. Fort Knox has brought to the Rolling Fork region worldwide attention, but it stands apart, and what goes on behind its guarded approaches is a mystery to the surrounding civilian population, unless they work there. It is easier to admire Fort Knox than it is to love it. Fort Knox is the smell of gasoline and tire rubber instead of horses and harness leather. It is the throbbing sound of heavy guns rather than the flat crack of a flintlock rifle and it is razor wire and security checkpoints instead of the rail fence and welcoming cabin.

Nature itself has been required to bend to serve the military needs of modern times. The Rolling Fork River is 107.9 miles long, all of it open to the rafter and the canoeist, except for its lower stretch, which is within Fort Knox's boundaries. There, river travel is forbidden. Apache helicopters patrol the river to prevent trespassers in this domestic no man's land. Even if the Apaches did not catch them, trespassers might be in danger. There has been so much gunnery practice around the river and so much unexploded ordnance lies in its channel that the Rolling Fork is likened to an aquatic minefield. The river that Benjamin Lynn and John Ritchie knew so well is probably gone forever.[9]

More in keeping with the heritage of the Rolling Fork than Fort Knox is Bernheim Forest, one of the great nature preserves in the East. Isaac W. Bernheim was a nineteen-year-old native of Bavaria when he migrated to New York in 1867. He had $4 in his pocket and only a rudimentary grasp of the English language. He borrowed $200 for a supply of peddler's goods—needles, thread, socks, suspenders, stockings, and such—and took to the highways and byways. He prospered until the fall of 1867, when a series of setbacks, including the death of his horse, sent him looking for a fresh start in the West.

Bernheim made his way to Paducah, arriving in May 1868. There, in partnership with his brother, he established a distillery in 1872. In 1888, the Bernheim brothers moved their firm to Louisville, a regional center for liquor distribution. In Louisville, the Bernheim brothers continued to expand. They became distillers as well as distributors, and their fortunes soared. Isaac Bernheim used part of his for a generous but shy sort of philanthropy. He was a silent contributor to Louisville's renowned Jewish Hospital, for instance. He made a gift to his community of the 1899 Thomas Jefferson statue in front of the Jefferson County Courthouse and of the 1922 statue of Abraham Lincoln in front of the Louisville Free Public Library. He also donated money for the statues of Henry Clay and Dr. Ephraim McDowell in Statuary Hall in the U.S. Capitol Building.[10]

The towering things of nature appealed to him, too, and in the tall knobs of Bullitt County and Nelson County, in country that was carved by the tributaries of the Rolling Fork, Bernheim found the inspiration for his greatest legacy. In 1928, he bought fourteen thousand acres as a nature preserve for the enjoyment of the public. He set up a nonprofit organization, the Isaac W. Bernheim Foundation, to hold title to the land and set up the Bernheim Trust to manage the endowment he left to the foundation, and he was specific about what he wanted to come from his generosity. Among them: "A sanctuary for birds that fly, and fowl that find their home on water, Foot paths and motor roads, Trees labeled carefully and protected, A natural park with a profusion of things that gladden the soul and please the sight." And he also shared his thoughts about what he did not want: "No pistols, rifles, or shotguns; No trading or trafficking [sic]; No discussion of religion or politics; No distinction to be made between rich and poor, white and colored." These were the benefactor's principles. Bernheim Forest was opened to visitors in 1950. Isaac Bernheim was not present to appreciate the splendor of his gift. He retired in 1922 to Denver, Colorado, and died while on vacation in Santa Monica, California, in April 1945.[11]

Ten thousand acres of Bernheim Forest are now open to the public between March 15 and November 15 each year. The reserve contains more than sixteen thousand acres. More than a half million people go there annually to take advantage of the opportunity to see an expanse of land as near to unspoiled as one can find anywhere in Kentucky. The improvements are made with the idea of perpetuating that philosophy of low impact. A $3.5 million visitor center at the park, erected in 2005, was "designed to be environmentally friendly.... Its windows are angled to maximize light and heat, the building was constructed from recycled materials, including beams made from old Heinz pickle vats and a ceiling of wood from former Jim Beam bourbon rack houses." It features geothermal heating and a peat system to filter sewage. Visiting Bernheim Forest is a wonderful experience for those who are interested in sustainability, modern botanical science, and in what the valley of the Rolling Fork once was.[12]

The monastery at Gethsemani is another reminder of earlier days, but even it has not been impervious to change. Not that the foundations of the monks' life changed. They still lived a life that was simple and ordered and tempered by a discipline that even Fort Knox might envy, but which was based on some very different principles: prayer, work, study, community, silence, hospitality and love. If one could balance these elements in his life, and cleave unto them, he was fit to be a contemplative at the quiet enclave of Gethsemani.

But, in the 1940s, Gethsemani began to attract a degree of attention that made the observance of the traditional way of life more of a challenge than it had ever been. It was partly the monks' own fault. A mail-order food business in bourbon fudge, fruitcake, and white Port du Salut cheese began replacing agriculture as the most important source of income at Gethsemani. An income was essential, for the Catholic Church does not support Gethsemani. The monks abide by the Rule of St. Benedict which requires them to "live by the labor of their own hands."[13]

The cheese became particularly well known, and it is still the main product that many people associate with the monastery. One taste and one whiff will help explain what makes it so unforgettable. Gethsemani cheese is not for the fainthearted. Brother Raphael describes it as "cheese with character." Now, there is a gift shop at Gethsemani where visitors (upwards of 100,000 annually), along with mail-order and internet customers, spend over $3 million a year on the cheese, fudge, and cake, as well as recorded music, handcrafted crèches, and religious texts. Among the texts on sale are the writings of Thomas Merton, who lived at the monastery beginning in the 1940s and wrote, while living there, his best-selling autobiography, *The Seven Storey Mountain*.[14]

Born in France in 1915, Merton displayed a brilliant mind for literature and attended Cambridge University in England. He had strong worldly appetites and fathered an out-of-wedlock child who, along with its mother, was later killed in the Nazi bombing of London. Merton enrolled at Columbia University in New York in 1935. He was an accomplished, talented young man, but he was dissatisfied. He hoped to fill the emptiness inside him by a life in the Franciscan priesthood. However, when the excesses of his past life became known, this was not permitted. His youthful indulgences had robbed him of the one great desire of his mature years. Bitterly hurt, he accepted a teaching position at St. Bonaventure University in Olean, New York.

Still, he searched. At Easter, 1941, Merton scheduled a personal retreat at Gethsemani. Studying the *Catholic Encyclopedia* to learn more about the Trappist monks with whom he was about to spend his vacation, Merton experienced an epiphany. He later wrote that it "pierced me to the heart like a knife." He said, "What wonderful happiness there was, then, in the world! There were still men on this miserable, noisy, cruel earth, who tasted the marvelous joy of silence and solitude, who dwelt in forgotten mountain cells, in secluded monasteries, where the news and desires and appetites and conflicts of the world no longer reached them."[15]

Merton's Easter retreat turned into a lifetime of service. "Father Louis," as he was known at the monastery, wrote of his spiritual journey, and his life at Gethsemani, in *The Seven Storey Mountain*. The book's initial printing was for twenty thousand copies to meet the demands of three book clubs. In the first month, it sold over 12,900 copies; by the end of the second month, sales were over 31,000; and by the end of the first year, over 600,000. Since then, Robert Giroux calculates the sales number to be in the "multiple millions."[16]

Merton continued to write and his ongoing discussion of the Christian's duty in a world of racism, poverty, and war are, to many readers, the richest and most thought-provoking of texts for those who are searching for their way in a sad and maddening world. More than sixty of his writings are still in print. Merton's life ended in 1968. His interest in the monastic life and in Eastern religions led him finally to Bangkok, Thailand. He died there by accidental electrocution on December 10, 1968. He was fifty-three years old. Friends and fans mourned him, but he had left the world a genuine masterpiece, *The Seven Storey Mountain*, written among the monks in the valley of the Rolling Fork.[17]

The quality of his work notwithstanding, Merton was not a native son, and he lived in virtual isolation from the secular world outside the monastery, and so it is perhaps understandable that the locals were slow in appreciating him. More puzzling is their tardy interest in Abraham Lincoln. One explanation is undoubtedly a nascent resentment dating back to the Civil War, when Lincoln's troops occupied the valley and his policies freed the slaves. It took a full quarter-century after the rest of the nation had memorialized the boy from Knob Creek for the people of his native home to decide that, in the end, maybe he *had* amounted to something.

On Decoration Day 1933, a team of government relief workers was cleaning a graveyard on Muldraugh Hill between Hodgenville and New Haven. Jim Taylor was their foreman. Near a walnut tree at the center of the graveyard, Taylor's grubbing hoe hit a tombstone that had toppled over. Taylor remembered, "I couldn't make out the letters very well so I went down in my pocket and got out a nail and scratched out the letters. That made it plainer to see. Then I set the stone back practically where I found it and they mounded up the grave."[18]

The letters Taylor scratched out with the nail were: T.L. Jim Taylor went on, "We'd all heard that a Lincoln was buried there. My father had said his parents had said that." One of Taylor's great-grandfathers was George Redmon, who had buried the baby Thomas Lincoln, Jr., in 1811. The discovery of Thomas Lincoln, Jr.'s, gravesite was of national interest. *National Republic* magazine ran an illustrated article telling the whole story. One of the photographs in the story showed a new log building, with two large bays, some dormers, and a long front porch. Inside were a restaurant and gift shop, but what was the attraction that was going to draw those hungry souvenir buyers? It stood next door—a one-room cabin that had been assembled near the site of Thomas Lincoln's old place on the Louisville and Nashville Turnpike, now called U.S. 31-E.[19]

Robert Thompson, who had helped his father tear down the original Lincoln cabin for firewood in 1870, came back in 1932 to direct the assembly of a duplicate cabin using logs from the Gollaher place, the very home where young Abe had visited with his chum Austin. Mr. Thompson was ninety years old and the Lincoln cabin was replicated from his memory. Chester and Hattie Howard now owned the property, and they operated it as a tourist attraction. The Howard family owned the Knob Creek place for decades, but in 1986 it was for sale again. An auction sale was announced. Paul Harvey covered the story on his radio broadcast. ABC and CBS reported on it, too. The day of the sale, when auctioneer Cordell Tabb dropped the gavel, the property still belonged to the Howards, or at least to their descendants. Twelve members of the family formed a consortium that bought the gift shop/restaurant and 228 acres for $120,500. Tabb had hoped it would go for a little more, and the Howard descendants knew that they had gotten a bargain. One said, "We got it for a real good price." It was an *especially* good price if their hope came true that the federal government would buy the place as a companion property to Lincoln's Birthplace ten miles away. The new owners planned to ask $1 million for the farm. In the meantime, while waiting for the government to pony up, the Howard descendants were hosting 35,000 visitors annually to their private park, April through October, at $1 for adults and fifty cents for children. Some came from as far away as the Ukraine to honor Lincoln on the land of his first memories.[20]

Kentucky's U.S. Congressional delegation, Democrats and Republicans alike, sponsored legislation to allow the park service to acquire the Knob Creek Farm. President Bill Clinton signed it into law on November 6, 1998. It was not a done deal, even then, for the Gramm-Rudman Act made it impossible for the park service to buy the land outright. The purchase price had to be privately raised; only then would the government assume control. A group called Preservation of Lincoln's Kentucky Heritage was organized, and local citizens, as Jim Taylor would have said, "went down in their pocket." So did nearby businesses and the Kentucky General Assembly. The Kentucky Heritage Land Conservation Fund made a grant of nearly a half million dollars. It was a noble effort. Director Fran Mainella of the National Park Service said she would tell the story nationally of how those in LaRue County had pulled together to finance the preservation of Lincoln's boyhood home.[21]

The necessary money raised, the park service took charge of the Knob Creek property in November 2001. A geological and archaeological survey was arranged with hopes that government archaeologists could discover the footprint of the cabin where young Abraham Lincoln had lived. They descended on the site with their magnometers and shovels. For nearly a week, the archaeologists went about their work, but in the end, the location of the cabin remained a mystery. Probably, the development of the little park and the work along 31-E had long since obliterated all traces of the exact spot where the cabin sat.

The vanished cabin is a symbol in itself. Like the Indian villages, the frontier forts, Goodin's grave, and Riney's schoolhouse, it was gone forever. So much of the history of man has vanished in the valley of the Rolling Fork. But the land endures and the river still flows, a reminder of what once was to the people who live along its storied banks.

Part Two

The Nolin River

The Nolin River Valley

Elizabethtown
Glendale
Hodgenville
Nolin
White Mills
Buffalo
Bonnieville
Millerstown
Wax
Bee Spring
Sweeden
Mammoth Cave
Brownsville

Valley Creek
Middle Creek
North Fork of Nolin
McDougal Creek
South Fork of Nolin
Nolin River
Bacon Creek
Nolin River Lake
Green River

Map by Sasha Jovanovic.

Introduction

The Nolin River is not an angry, violent river like the Snake. It drops only 2.13 feet in every mile and has no rapids to speak of. There is some unruly water where Valley Creek enters the Nolin, and there is some accidental whitewater at Star Mills where rubble from the partly collapsed mill dam creates a turbulence, but those are the exceptions. For most of its length, the Nolin is a slow, peaceful river.

The Nolin is not a long river like the Missouri. A report of the United States Geological Survey in the spring of 1932 stated that it *is* the crookedest river in the U.S., with twenty river miles to six straight-line miles, but even if you straighten out its 114 bends, the Nolin still measures only 122 miles. Almost any river whose name you know is longer and drains a larger basin. The Nolin catchment area is just 728 square miles.

The Mississippi River inspired Mark Twain's classics, and the Hudson gave the world Robert Fulton's steamboat. Even little Antietam Creek in Maryland is renowned as the red-stained scene of America's bloodiest day in September 1862. The Nolin cannot claim anything to compare with these. No fine books, no great battles, no advances in technology came from the valley of the Nolin.

But there are two other things that will bring a river fame: geological wonders and famous citizens, and the Nolin is uniquely rich in both of these. The Nolin River begins its winding journey in LaRue County, Kentucky, and on its south fork in February 1809 Abraham Lincoln drew the first breath of an indispensable life. The Nolin ends in Edmonson County within the boundaries of Mammoth Cave National Park, where earth's longest cave system, with 420 miles of mapped passage (and who knows how many more unmapped) is preserved for the wonderment of all the world. Lincoln's birthplace and Mammoth Cave—not bad bookends for a small, slow, crooked river in the rolling country of west central Kentucky.

Between these bookends, the birth cabin and the big cave, are the unrecorded lives of the people who called the land home. They deserve some notice, too. They sweated and strained to develop the valley of the Nolin. They dammed the river and made it work for them, and sometimes the river hit back, washing their houses and stores away. They hated the land and cursed it and they loved the land and fought to defend it. When they died, they were laid to rest in it, and often, after a few generations, no one even remembered their names or where they were buried. Thousands of lives and each one a page in the history of the Nolin River.

ELEVEN

The First People

The date of the arrival of the first Kentuckians, the Paleo Indians, is not agreed upon by all. Harrison and Klotter say that they wandered into Kentucky about 10,500 BCE, but they add that "the dates may well be pushed back into the past as more is learned." Indeed, other scholars already consider the above date to be too late by more than two millennia. Philip DiBlasi and other historians, including some of the conservative National Park Service, believe that the Paleo Kentuckians arrived about 13,000 BCE. All agree that they were migratory hunters. The flint projectiles that tipped their spears, most notably the lovely and deadly Clovis points, have been discovered all through the basin of the Nolin. Sometimes in their travels they happened upon an outcropping of high quality flint. Then they stopped awhile to make blades, but any stop was necessarily brief. To survive, they must keep moving, following the mammoth herds. Luckily, these first inhabitants of the Nolin River Valley did not have to endure the worst of the Ice Age. The climate turned progressively warmer and the glaciers began to move north. If they looked toward the Ohio River, the Indians near the Nolin could see the jagged, two-mile high southern faces of the retreating glaciers.[1]

Over time, the big game grew scarce. Only the small game remained, deer, elk, and buffalo, primarily. The people needed to migrate but very little to hunt these, and because the animals were smaller, so were the projectile points. The Indians ate mussels from the waterways and piled the shells into tall mounds. They gathered nuts and berries from the maturing forests. Their lodges were more substantial than the skin tents of their migratory ancestors. Burials became more elaborate. This second culture of Indians in Kentucky is called the Archaic culture, and they were really the first to admire and use the Nolin Valley. The Paleo Indians were there but they might have been anywhere; they were simply following the big game, wherever it led. The Archaic Indians were there, and they liked it well enough to stay.

The benefits of this more stable lifestyle in a friendlier climate can be imagined. A more-or-less permanent village site meant the opportunity to grow food. The Indians could plant their crop of sunflowers, squash, and goosefoot in the spring and be there in the fall to gather it. The improved diet meant a longer, healthier life. A tribal hierarchy began to form, a simple political system of chiefs who led the village in the physical world and a priesthood who saw into the world of the spirits. There was division of labor. Some knapped flint and some cured hides. Weavers made moccasins, fishing nets, and pouches from local plant fibers. Some hunted while others farmed, and a few eventually carried torches deep into Mammoth Cave where they mined gypsum and mirabilite, minerals that were useful as medicine and valuable in trade. Some Indians lived in the cave, and some died and were buried there.[2]

There was always some wandering, of course. When they traveled, the Archaic Indians often stayed in rock shelters or shallow caves, and it was here that they left some of the most intriguing clues about their way of life. Under the protective overhangs they left petroglyphs (designs pecked or abraded into the rock surface) and pictographs (designs painted on rock). In a small cave in Edmondson County, near Bee Spring, Fred E. Coy and Thomas C. Fuller documented a petroglyph consisting of two spirals and some bird tracks. The larger spiral is at the twelve o'clock position, the smaller one at about four o'clock, and extending below and to the left of the small swirl are four incised tracks obviously meant to represent turkey tracks. At other locations in the region there have been found the pecked or rubbed representations of raccoon, deer, and rabbit tracks, and in one surprising instance near Grayson Springs in Grayson County, tracks of human feet. Nineteenth-century historian Lewis Collins said that they were perfect, "the toes, heel, length, and breadth of the feet are imprinted with wonderful exactness."[3]

Near Brownsville, not far from where the Nolin enters the Green, there is a rock shelter containing pictographs executed by some ancient hand in a dull red pigment. One figure is humanlike and has his arms outstretched and flexed at the elbow in what looks to a modern observer to be the gesture of surrender. The figure is either wearing a cat-costume or has a painted face and body. Near the cat-man is "a large circle, 41 cm (1.4 ft.) in diameter, with several geometric figures within the circumference. Some of the geometric elements appear to be placed inside zones delimited by curvilinear lines. Beneath the circle is an hourglass shaped figure ... lines enclose the circle and the hour-glass shaped figure on each side, but do not close at the top or bottom." Two smaller designs, one of a human head and the other resembling a bird, are seen between the cat-man and the circle/hourglass. Coy and Fuller say that this site "is outstanding because it is one of only two well documented pictograph localities that still survive in the state."[4]

These images were presumably etched or painted in rock shelter walls when the people were out hunting or on a trading expedition. Trade came to be of growing importance during this period. Kentucky's Natives traded basketsful of minerals quarried from the caves for such luxuries as obsidian and bear claws, copper, sea shells and shark skins. Contact with Indians from the outside undoubtedly enriched the lives of the late Archaic Indians with new ideas as well as with exotic goods.

As these Archaic Indians became more dependent on trade and fascinated by death (especially the rituals surrounding burials), their way of life evolved into a third culture, the Woodland. The Woodland Indians occupied the valley for the next two thousand years and impressively so. When Jesus of Nazareth was struggling up the rugged path of Golgotha, the Woodland Indians were trading along an elaborate web of foot trails that connected their villages with the Rockies, the Great Lakes, the Chesapeake Bay, and the Gulf of Mexico. They were building their burial mounds when the Great Wall of China was rising stone by stone and the Dome of the Rock was under construction in Jerusalem. Like the people of the Old World, Kentucky's Indians were experiencing a time of grand cultural expansion. The Woodland culture represented the golden age of Kentucky's pre–Columbian people.[5]

The Woodland Culture was widespread. Mounds containing layers of burials are found throughout the eastern half of the United States, including along the Nolin River and its tributaries. Even away from these mound sites, there is abundant evidence of the Woodland Indians. Their projectile points are commonly discovered in the Nolin River Valley.[6]

This period of pre–Columbian Indian life was certainly the most affluent, but evidence shows that it devolved into war. There had been small-scale conflict well before this. At the Ward Site, a late Archaic village in McLean County (which is not in the Nolin River Valley, but which was home to the same culture), archaeologists excavated the skeletons of four adult males, all of them with "cut marks indicative of scalping." One of them was buried with three females, none of whom showed signs of skeletal trauma, but the male skull displayed "scalping cut marks on the mid- and right portions of the frontal bone." He was missing the lower portions of his right and left legs, and his ribs showed evidence of many stab wounds. Curiously, this victim was buried with a "drilled and incised Gulf Coast shell placed over his face." The second individual had several cut marks on his skull and, like the first man, was missing his lower legs. The third victim was found in a burial trench and also had unhealed cut marks around his skull. The fourth, an adult male buried in a single grave, had been scalped, and was buried with a trophy—a right arm that was missing its wrist and hand. The point is that violence was not unknown, but it was rare.[7]

However, about 1000 CE, as the Woodland period transitioned into what is sometimes called the Late Prehistoric (or, as DiBlasi says, the Mississippian-Fort Ancient Period), the number of violent deaths increased significantly. This period of one thousand years ago is dimly understood and the causes for the unmistakable increase in intertribal or interregional conflict are unknown. Probably they were not different from the causes of war throughout history. Maybe the accumulation of wealth from trade-inspired raids from poorer groups, or maybe the groups whose territory was crossed by the trails demanded tribute from the travelers who passed. Maybe there was a simple disagreement over the terms of a trade, and it got out of hand. Maybe there was competition for resources as the population increased. Maybe war erupted because of an intensified interest in crop cultivation and in mound building. This last one requires some explanation.

The predominant Late Prehistoric group in the valley of the Nolin and areas west is known as the Mississippians. This powerful native culture kept the burial mound tradition of their ancestors and continued to grow crops, but both agriculture and mound building became more pronounced. Corn, beans, and squash were intensively grown, and, in addition to the burial mounds, the Indians now began to construct flat-topped platform mounds on top of which were the dwellings of their leaders. The Mississippian leaders are thought to have held hereditary power, and they carried symbols of their authority, as evidenced by the elaborate stone mace discovered in Edmonson County.[8]

The platform mounds could be of impressive size. One in Butler County, Kentucky, measured approximately ninety-nine feet long, eighty-two feet wide, and thirteen feet high. They wanted them tall for effect. Charles Stout and R. Barry Lewis observe, "Platform mounds are the most physical evidence of most Mississippian towns. Their visibility is the key to their existence. Mississippian peoples, like societies around the world, were well aware of the powerful psychological and visual impacts of height relative to the observer, whether in the form of a towering headdress, a platform mound, or a temple roof line."[9]

How did a greater emphasis on mound building and farming lead to war? Some believe that the Indians began raiding their neighbors to obtain slaves, whose labor was needed in the larger-than-ever fields and also in the towns where the platform mounds were rising. Raids begat more raids. Periodically, the people retreated behind defensive palisades. Archaeological evidence shows that during peaceful intervals the palisades were allowed to decay and go to ruin, but in times of war new ones were built. The walls were defended by men armed not only with the long-reliable spear but with an innovation in weaponry, the bow and arrow. The arrowheads of the Mississippians are found throughout the Nolin Valley: unadorned triangles of flint with no particular artistry. A basic killing tool, grim in its simplicity, this projectile point is known to collectors as the war point.

When war came to the Nolin River Valley, the Indians were serious about its defense. In Edmonson County, near where the Nolin enters the Green River, is Indian Hill. Collins described it as "circular at its base, and one mile in circumference—its altitude eighty-four feet, and, except on one side, which is easy of ascent on foot, perpendicular. The remains of a fortification are seen around the brow, and a number of mounds and burial places are scattered over the area. A spring of fine water issues from the rock near the surface." There is another pre–Columbian fort in southern Hardin County.[10]

There is little doubt that warfare had become a factor in the pre–Columbians' lives. Scholar John H. Blitz writes, "Archaeological evidence for increased intergroup conflict indicated by small projectile points lodged in human bone, groups burials of such individuals, and the appearance of fortified communities, or placement of sites into defensive positions, closely correlates with or follows soon after bow introduction into many areas of North America." These areas include Kentucky and the Nolin River Valley.[11]

Bennett Young, in his classic *The Prehistoric Men of Kentucky*, observed, "The care, skill, and labor expended in these stone fortifications show that in those prehistoric days the wars were real, that the conflict between the parties who built the fort and those on the outside must have been long and fierce. How these struggles ended we cannot tell." It was an ugly end to a long epoch of Indian life in Kentucky.[12]

The "long and fierce" wars may have been one factor that contributed to the Indian abandonment of Kentucky about 1600 CE. After that, Kentucky was as empty of residents as it had been before the Paleo Indians followed the first mammoth through the snow. Except for an occasional hunter or war party, no human would lay eyes upon the Nolin River for the next 180 years.

TWELVE

The River Gets a New Name

In 1780, a party of white hunters came into the valley of a slow-moving, wildly crooked river that earlier people had called the Elk Garden. At least, that is how it translated into English. Anyone who saw these hunters would have mistaken them for Indians. Their hair was long. They dressed in moccasins and fringed hunting shirts. Tomahawks and skinning knives gleamed in their belts, and they carried long barreled rifles. Their light-footed walk showed that they were at home in the forest, and their alert response to every sound and sign showed they were accustomed to its dangers.[1]

They scattered during the day, each man making his own hunt, gathering each evening back at the main camp where the camp keepers had stayed to flesh the hides and stretch them to dry and to roast the best cuts of meat over small fires, small enough that their smoke would not attract the attention of Indians. The threat of Indians was never far from their minds. The British armed the warriors of the Northern tribes with muskets and scalping knives and sent them swarming across the Ohio. They earned a bounty for each Kentucky scalp they brought back to the Redcoat forts north of the river. It had been a bad four years in the settlements off to the east; Boonesborough, Logan's Fort, and Harrodsburg had all suffered their share of scalp raids. These hunters knew it paid to watch the shadows.

One hunter was a thirty-year-old lieutenant in the Kentucky County Militia named Benjamin Lynn, and he knew the Natives well. He had left his Pennsylvania home while still a teenager to go live among them. He was fluent in the languages of the Delaware, Shawnee, and other tribes; he had hunted with them as far west as the Mississippi River and as far south as present-day Natchez. Lynn had moved to Kentucky in 1776 and had wandered over its prairies and explored its interior rivers. He had once traveled the length of this same crooked stream where the hunters now camped. He had liked the looks of it, and he later appeared before a panel of land commissioners at Harrodsburg to claim one thousand acres near its headwaters. He told the commissioners that he had made improvements—possibly nothing more than tomahawking some boundary trees—before January 1, 1778.[2]

Lynn lived first at Harrod's Fort. Living there at the same time was George Rogers Clark, himself a recent emigrant from Virginia, only twenty-three years old but already a leader in the defense of Kentucky's scattered forts. Lynn became Clark's right hand. In January 1777, when Clark returned from Williamsburg with five hundred pounds of gunpowder he had obtained from the Virginia Council, Lynn helped retrieve the cache from its hiding place near Maysville and distribute it among the settlements. Three months later, in April 1777, when Clark decided that the key to Kentucky's defense was to carry the war to the enemy north of the Ohio River, it was Lynn he chose, along with Samuel Moore, to go spy out conditions in the British-held Northwest Territory.[3]

Tradition says that, from Harrodsburg, Lynn and Moore followed the Rolling Fork west and crossed the divide into the valley of the Elk Garden. The two spies followed the Elk Garden to where it emptied into the Green River. They then followed the Green to where it enters the Ohio and continued west from there. Lynn and Moore made their way to St. Louis and listened for information. Then they crossed back into the Illinois Country, presenting themselves as simple hunters with no stake in a distant war in the East. Their act was so convincing that Lieutenant-Governor Phillip Rocheblave himself, commander of the British fort at Kaskaskia, hired them to bring in meat for his troops. Lynn and Moore counted Redcoats and Indians at the same time they fed them. When they learned that the Indians had become suspicious of them, Lynn and Moore fled by the light of a full moon. They reached Harrodsburg on June 22 with the information Major Clark wanted. The enemy numbers were few and their confidence too high. An attack would be an utter surprise. Clark was so pleased with the success of the mission that he rewarded Lynn with the rank of lieutenant in the Kentucky Militia.[4]

Lieutenant Lynn agreed to go with Clark to Williamsburg to argue the need for a campaign against the British forts in the Northwest, but he had personal business to attend to first. Besides George Rogers Clark, someone else had been watching for Benjamin Lynn's return. Hannah Severns was a young Pennsylvania woman with a story of her own to tell. She had endured six years of Indian captivity before emigrating to Kentucky. She and Benjamin Lynn were married on July 9, 1777, only two weeks after his return from the Illinois Country. Squire Boone, Daniel's younger brother and a Baptist preacher, performed the ceremony. It was an occasion of "great merriment," Major Clark remembered. During the festivities, a buffalo bull wandered right up to the walls of the fort along with the cattle and quickly became part of the wedding feast.[5]

Lynn's and Clark's journey to meet with Governor Patrick Henry in Williamsburg occurred three months later, in October 1777. The Kentuckians traveled six hundred miles in thirty days and got the authority they sought. Secret orders allowed them to raise an army of up to 350 men for a western campaign against the Redcoats and the Indians in *their* homes north of the Ohio River. Clark, now a lieutenant colonel, appointed Lynn to circulate among the settlers of the Ten Mile Country of southwestern Pennsylvania and recruit men for the next summer's expedition.[6]

It was not until May 1778, that Clark and his 150 men returned to Kentucky. Recruiting had proved hard, and Clark's little army was two hundred men short of what Virginia had permitted. Still, Clark was determined to proceed with his plan. Traveling by rafts down the Ohio River, they stopped at Corn Island, a sliver of land in mid-stream at the future site of Louisville. It was here that Clark trained his men before they struck out for the Northwest. It was here, too, that Clark detached Lynn from the Illinois Regiment. He was put in charge of a company of seventeen men and ordered to return to Harrodsburg to protect the women and children there.

The Illinois Regiment shot the Falls of the Ohio in the dim light of a solar eclipse on June 24, 1778, and by July 4 Clark and his men were crouching in the tall grass just outside Kaskaskia. The history books tell how George Rogers Clark and his band of "Long Knives" conquered three British forts in the Northwest before the end of 1778, employing the element of surprise so well that they never fired a shot in anger nor lost a man; how Clark spent the winter negotiating peace with the Indian tribes; and how, in February 1779, they had to re-capture the fort at Vincennes after a brutal wintertime march across the flooded prairie. The region now secure, Clark hoped to gather enough volunteers that he could march on to Detroit. The conquest of Detroit would deprive the Indians of their British benefactors, and Kentucky would be safe. He expected five hundred volunteers to come join him. A few did come, including Lynn and fifteen men from Harrodsburg, but never enough to take the offensive. Spring and summer passed while Clark waited. Meanwhile, Detroit was growing stronger. In August, a disappointed Clark sensed that the opportunity had passed. He placed small garrisons to hold what he had won in the Northwest and returned with the rest to the Falls of the Ohio.[7]

It was the following year that Benjamin Lynn and his party of pelt hunters entered the valley of the Elk Garden. One day, while hunting alone, Lynn found an Indian trail that interested him and followed it so far that he could not get back to the camp that night. His fellow hunters did not begin to worry until the second night when Lynn still had not returned. Maybe the Indians had gotten him. Maybe their friend had drowned; almost none of the old frontiersmen could swim. Whatever had happened to Lynn, they could not go back without knowing what had become of him. They interrupted their hunt to search the river-banks for some sign of Lynn, returning each evening to the main camp, unsuccessful. As the men came in one by one, the others looked up to see the disappointment in their faces. A two-word report summed up their failure: "No Lynn," they said.

It was "No Lynn" for several days before the missing hunter was discovered camping further south, in present day Hart County, along the tributary of Green River which they named Lynn Camp Creek. He had never been lost; he had just been looking. The river where his friends had *presumed* he was lost carried a new name from that time on—the Elk Garden River had become the Nolynn, or as it is rendered today, Nolin.[8]

In time to come, more hunters came and made claims for the fer-tile land along the Nolin. Others, hearing their tales of rich land to the west, came after them. Some hired agents to spy out and mark their claims. Squire Boone, brother of Daniel, explored the Nolin River Val-ley as early as 1778, working as a freelance locator of prime land for oth-ers who were interested in settling in the valley. In one case, Boone gave a deposition before a panel of Kentucky land commissioners and testi-fied that he had located eight thousand acres on the Nolin and entered a claim for James LaRue. Elisha Freeman claimed eight hundred acres on the river in December 1782. Joseph Carmen made his claim for one thousand acres in February 1783. Jacob Van Meter, Sr., claimed three thousand acres in April 1784, and his nephew whose name was also Jacob Van Meter (and who was called "Bacon Creek Jake" for his explo-rations along that tributary and also to distinguish him from his uncle) claimed 4,508 acres in the area.[9]

Some of the land was forested with old growth timber, but much of it was what settlers called "barrens," areas that the Indians had kept burned off to make hunting easier. It was an ancient practice. When James Knox and the Long Hunters were in the Barrens in 1770, they did not find so much as a stump or a rotting log. The land was open prai-rie, a vast luxuriance of grass. Local historian Bessie Miller Elliott said that, according to an old tradition, "one could ride from the station on Nolynn to the Severns Valley Station without being able to find a riding switch."[10]

The pioneers preferred the wooded land. Land that would not grow trees would not grow crops, they believed. Besides, they needed the trees for forts and cabins, for firewood and fences and barns. The forts, sometimes called "stations," were begun as soon as the settlers arrived. Their memories of Indian raids were still sharp, so they built their stockades and blockhouses and were watchful. The fear of Indians haunted them for years to come.

Andrew Hynes built his fort on a tributary of the Nolin in 1779. Thomas Helm, Samuel Haycraft, and Jacob Van Meter built theirs in 1780. Van Meter had led one hundred people on twenty-seven flatboats down the Ohio River in the fall of 1779. It was one of the largest parties of pioneers to come into Kentucky in this early day, much larger than the groups led by Boone or Harrod. The Van Meter colony floated from Fort Pitt to George Rogers Clark's fort at the Falls where they spent the winter of 1779–80. In the spring, some of Van Meter's one hundred crossed overland to Valley Creek, a tributary of the Nolin. There, Jacob Van Meter built his fort. Another fort was Phillip Phillips's, built on the North Fork of the Nolin in 1781.[11]

Soon the settlers moved outside the forts to clear the land for their little cabins and the crops, which they planted among the stumps. The Indian raids they continued to fear never materialized in the valley of the Nolin; there was an occasional incident, but never any sweeping attacks like they had experienced further east during the Revolution. The main reminder of the Indians now was the arrowheads the farmers found in the dirt behind the plow. With the land safe and cleared and cultivated, some began to leave the tilling of the soil to others.

Robert Hodgen, an Englishman by birth, moved out of Phillips's Fort to start a store and a tavern on the North Fork of the Nolin. He also had a saw mill and a gristmill, was a justice of the peace, and later represented Hardin County in the General Assembly. Small wonder that the surrounding community was later named for this enterprising man. Pennsylvanian George Close was a miller and so was his son-in-law George Highbaugh. Highbaugh's story was one of almost unending adventure. He was a German whose ambition was to reach America. His chance came when King George III contracted with several German states to provide mercenaries to help crush the rebellion in the colonies. Highbaugh enlisted and made the long voyage to America. Then one night, off the coast of Georgia, he slipped over the ship's side. On shore, he began walking north toward the American lines. At Fort Sunbury southeast of Savannah, he surrendered and was so passionate in his statement to the fort's commander that he was allowed to take the oath and enlist in the American army. When the British arrived to besiege the fort, Highbaugh was one of the few who escaped. He and a small band of others made their way to where other Colonial forces were gathering under Lieutenant Colonel Samuel Ebert. In a skirmish shortly after, Ebert's small command was attacked and captured by the British. After three months, Highbaugh escaped. Once again, he made his way to American lines. He continued with the Continentals until September 1782, when he was discharged near Savannah. He traveled to Philadelphia where there was work in the shipyards, but after a year he moved west to Pittsburgh. At a fort south of the settlement, he met the Close family and was caught up in their dream of moving to Kentucky. He built them a river-worthy raft and traveled with them to the Falls of the Ohio, landing in May 1785. For the next four years the Close party remained in the settlements near the Falls. In 1789, they moved southwest to the Nolin River Valley in what would become Hardin County. That same spring, George Highbaugh and the fourteen-year-old Catherine Close married. The new husband bought one hundred acres of land, built a cabin and went to farming. His adventures were not over, though. He joined the 1791 expedition of General Arthur St. Clair against the Northwest Indian confederacy led by Little Turtle, Blue Jacket, and Buckongahelas. The expedition was a disaster. St. Clair marched into an ambush that cost him 832 casualties out of a column of about one thousand officers, men, and camp followers. Highbaugh was one of the survivors. His close call seems to have dulled his appetite for soldiering, for he never served in the military again. After his return to Hardin County, he and Catherine set about building a family and a fortune. In 1798, they moved to a new place on Bacon Creek, and there they prospered. Highbaugh owned no fewer than four thousand acres of rich farmland and a gristmill when he died in 1840, at age eighty-five. Catherine died in 1858, the widow of one of the wealthiest men in the Nolin Valley.[12]

Conrad Walters had a tannery on the South Fork of the Nolin. Jacob Miller built a gristmill next to his cabin further down the river near where the future counties of Hardin, Hart, and Grayson came together. Jacob Van Meter, Sr., built a gristmill over on Valley Creek; his namesake nephew, "Bacon Creek Jake," also had a gristmill on Valley Creek, but further down, nearer to where it enters the Nolin. Bacon Creek Jake set up a whiskey still, too. Some of the pioneers entered politics; county judges and jailers began taking office. Public buildings were erected and county-ordered roads began to stitch the settlements together.[13]

Benjamin Lynn went in a different direction. He became a traveling preacher, chasing the Devil across the frontier. The countryside today is dotted with churches planted by Benjamin Lynn.[14]

The recorded history of the Nolin River had begun.

Thirteen

Devil on the Loose

Louis-Philippe, royal fugitive from the Reign of Terror in his native land, was not the first Frenchman they had seen at Robert Hodgen's tavern. He was the second one in four years.

The first was André Michaux, back in 1793. He was a botanist, and his bona fides were impressive. He traveled with letters of introduction from Secretary of State Thomas Jefferson, U.S. Senator John Brown, and Kentucky Governor Isaac Shelby. Michaux had been wandering around the country since 1785 when King Louis XVI had sent him to America to seek useful plants that might be transplanted and successfully cultivated in France. In America, he took his instructions from Edmund Genet, French envoy to the United States. Michaux toured the East first, then, as ordered, he crossed the mountains to Kentucky where he met with General George Rogers Clark before continuing his plant collecting. His rambles brought him into the valley of the Nolin.[1]

It soon became evident to all that André Michaux was attempting to collect something more on his travels. Michaux was pursuing a secret agenda for his king, attempting to recruit an army of westerners to advance on New Orleans and take it from the Spanish. Michaux offered Clark the rank of major general in France's American forces if he would raise and lead the volunteers. Clark, impoverished and bitter about his treatment by the U.S. at the end of the Revolution, accepted the rank, agreed to lead, and set about gathering ammunition and rations. The scheme might have succeeded; Kentuckians remembered kindly the help France had given America in the War for Independence and many had a grudge against Spain. Kentuckians loaded their furs, tobacco, and whiskey onto flatboats in the early winter, floated down to the Ohio and then on down the Mississippi to the markets at New Orleans where they sold both their cargoes and flatboats before walking back home with goods in their baggage and money in their pockets. It was a workable system. The trouble was Spanish fickleness. Sometimes a man got halfway down the Mississippi only to learn that the Spanish, without fair

96

warning, had closed the river to traffic from the North, leaving the Kentuckian stuck, with no way to go ahead, no way to go back, no choice at all but to leave the flatboat and the goods on board in the middle of nowhere; a year's worth of work gone for nothing. If France controlled the river, these outrages would stop. Already there had been anti–Spain protests around the state, but protests alone were no solution. Action was needed. The men in Hodgen's Tavern thought about their long rifles hanging on the cabin wall and about the chance to shake off the dust of ignominious peace and campaign with Clark again. These men were ready for an adventure.[2]

But President Washington was trying to keep the young United States out of conflicts between the European superpowers. He learned what Michaux was up to because of a miscalculation by General Clark. Clark felt so assured of popular support for the cause that he "openly proclaimed his purpose and solicited volunteers." Washington ordered Governor Shelby to put an end to any talk of an army of Kentucky soldiers marching under a French flag to take control of Spanish New Orleans, and he ordered General Anthony Wayne to prepare to mobilize U.S. troops on the Mississippi. When Genet was summoned back to France, the scheme lost its motivating force. Michaux returned east and the men at Hodgen's went back to whittling and forgot about following General Clark again.[3]

Now, here was this Louis-Philippe, a twenty-four-year-old coxcomb traveling with his two brothers and a servant. Kentuckians suspected that Louis-Philippe was up to something, like Michaux had been, but Louis-Philippe was genuine. He was running for his life, trying to stay ahead of the French revolutionaries who had guillotined the royal family and were now after him.

Louis-Philippe liked what he saw at Hodgen's. In his journal he wrote, "We rode down off the plateau of the Barrens and at Mr. Hodgen's place ... found a fine farm, much better than any we had seen for a long time. The orchard is mature, and the trees at least seven or eight years old." He apparently found the company at Hodgen's tolerable, for he did not complain of their manners. The night before he called the wife of his host an "intolerable chatterbox."[4]

Louis-Philippe found Americans to be generally surprising and frequently annoying. Three nights before he reached Hodgen's, he had had an uncomfortable experience with a frontier family, an episode that shocked even a Frenchman. As he told it:

> I should not want to omit here a frank report of what we all witnessed at Captain Chapman's. There were only two beds in the one room that was the house's entire living area and we were granted only what they call here

house-room, that is, permission to spread our blankets on the rough planks of the floor ... between the two beds. Captain Chapman got into one bed with his wife, which seemed perfectly straightforward to us. A rather pretty girl who we knew was unmarried got into the other, and that too seemed straightforward. A strapping young man of about 20 or 22 arrived shortly afterward ... he undressed and plunked himself into the girl's bed [and] it occasioned a certain surprise on our part. It had no such effect on the captain.... Nor was he distressed by the young man's intimate manner with his daughter. His other daughter blew out the candle and slipped into the young people's bed, so that the young man was in the middle. That seemed to us even more extraordinary. We four paid close attention to these goings-on, and saw to our left, by the gleam of the fire, the young man and the first daughter get up and settle again at the foot of the bed; in a word, we saw all that one can see.[5]

All the while, Captain Chapman and his wife whispered to each other what "odd fellows" their French visitors were.[6]

Frenchmen and fornicators. The Devil was on the loose, for certain, but he would not win Kentucky without a battle. One who was ready to fight him for frontier souls was the same Benjamin Lynn, that man of many rivers, whose temporary disappearance from his hunting companions gave the Nolin River its name. Lynn's wife Hannah taught him to read and write. He felt the call to preach, and once he was armed with a newfound, literate knowledge of the Bible, he began to combat sin with all the same zeal he had once fought British regulars and Shawnee braves. He preached the first sermons in Phillips's Fort. With James Skaggs, he organized South Fork Baptist Church in 1782, and he performed the first baptisms in Kentucky; seven sinners' transgressions were washed away in the South Fork of the Nolin while armed guards stood nearby to protect them from Indians. He preached at Severns Valley, Level Woods, Pottinger's Creek, and Cedar Creek. In 1792 he moved to the Green River region to preach. Benjamin Lynn delivered the first message at Brush Creek Baptist Church in the Green River country, and he pastored that congregation through the early years until membership grew to one hundred. It was a straight and narrow road these early Baptists trod. The deerskin-bound minute book of Brush Creek listed the rules: no lingering around a place where drunkenness occurred, no betting on horse races, no carrying a pistol or dirk, no laughing or whispering during church, and no skipping services. An explanation was expected from any member of the congregation who missed two meetings.[7]

Lynn ranged far in his war with Satan. He went preaching to Ohio and Illinois, even to Arkansas. Then, a stumbling block was thrown in Lynn's way. He attended the 1801 "Great Revival" at Cane Ridge and, though he did not preach there, he was transformed by what he saw and heard. When he returned, his old churches "received him coldly." They were not patient with a preacher whose vision of the Good News suddenly changed after twenty years, and reports of the barking, twitching, and rolling-on-the-ground behavior of those who attended Cane Ridge offended them. The Brush Creek congregation dismissed him as its minister. The Green River Association of Baptists issued a warning to its brethren not to let Lynn preach to its congregations henceforth.[8]

Before the sting of that disappointment was over, more trouble came to Lynn. It was the same trouble that eventually drove the Boone brothers, Simon Kenton, and many of the earliest pioneers out of Kentucky: shingled claims. Because there had never been any official government survey of Kentucky, the settlers just used natural features of the land—trees, stones, sink holes, and so on—to mark the corners of their land. Later settlers came along and, not recognizing any signs that the land had been claimed, would claim a tract of their own using other trees and stones and sink holes for their corners. As a consequence, the land claims overlapped like the shingles on the roof of a house; ownership was hopelessly confused. Kentucky became a paradise for lawyers. Often times, the earliest claimants lost out and this is what happened to Lynn. It was a double disappointment to the most colorful character of the early days on the Nolin; first his church and then his land were taken from him. An old black woman who had known Lynn later recalled, "folks did not treat Massa Lynn right—and he left the neighborhood on that account." Benjamin Lynn moved to Tennessee, away from the land of bad titles and disapproving Baptists, and there he continued to preach. About 1809, Lynn moved to Madison County, Alabama, to live with his daughter and her family. The old explorer died there at age sixty-four on December 23, 1814.[9]

Other veterans of the Revolution came to the Nolin River Valley to wage war on the Devil during the early years. Alexander McDougal owned four hundred acres on a LaRue County branch of the Nolin that now bears his name. He was an Irishman by birth, born in Dublin in May 1738. About 1759, he came to America. He settled briefly in North Carolina, before moving to Union District, South Carolina, where he made his home. McDougal had been raised as a Presbyterian, but he joined the Baptists in South Carolina in 1770 and began to preach about 1775. Three years later, the Revolution found him. He served under several different officers between 1778 and 1782, but never as a regular. He seems to have been one of those guerrilla fighters in the style of Francis Marion, and his main enemy was not Redcoats, but Tories. When the war was over, McDougal moved to Kentucky, took up his land on the

Nolin, cleared it with the help of his slaves, and preached the Gospel. He was the minister at Severns Valley Baptist Church between 1803 and 1820, was a charter member of Gilead Baptist Church in 1824, and preached at Nolin Baptist Church in LaRue County until he gave up the pulpit at last, when he was ninety-five years old. McDougal died, aged 102 years, in March 1841. He is buried in the beautiful old graveyard beside the church.[10]

Warren Cash was the preacher at Star Mills and also at Otter Creek Baptist Church (in Meade County), but his name is more closely associated with Gilead Baptist Church on the Nolin near Glendale. Cash was only sixteen years old in 1776 when he enlisted as a Patriot soldier in Albemarle County, Virginia. Thomas Jefferson, another citizen of Albemarle County, wrote the Declaration of Independence that same year. Cash fought to make Jefferson's words a reality at Brandywine and Monmouth Courthouse; he endured the Valley Forge winter with Washington's army and soldiered on until his discharge in 1784. He was rough, illiterate, and a "bold sinner," but a wife and infant son soon began to reform his bad habits. A new land was needed for a new life, so with his rifle "Old Walnut Rail" in hand, Cash led his little family through Cumberland Gap in 1785 and settled in Woodford County, Kentucky. There, Cash was baptized. Shelby County was his next Kentucky home. He was ordained there in 1799. From Shelby County it was on to Nelson County and finally to Hardin County, where he arrived in March 1806.[11]

In March 1824, Cash organized Gilead Baptist Church with nineteen members, including other veterans of the war and their slaves. The congregation moved into a meeting house built by Thomas Dorsey on an acre of Nolin riverbank in 1807 and only three years later erected a brick building. For sixteen years Warren Cash was shepherd to the Gilead flock, a preacher of only middling ability but one who, at his death in 1850, was remembered for his piety and his determination to do good in the name of the Lord.[12]

Determination was a quality these early preachers needed in abundance. It was bad enough that Sheriff Isaac Hodgen got drunk and demolished a store in Bardstown. It was tragic that a man had murdered his wife only eight miles from Hodgenville and had left her body lying across the threshold of their cabin until the hysterical cries of the children, two small girls, drew a crowd (that included, it is said, Thomas Lincoln and his little boy who were returning from a trip to Elizabethtown). The crowd attended to the body and hauled the murderer away. It was humiliating that revelers met to throw their money away and tempt the Devil at racetracks, one as close as Middle Creek, halfway between

Hodgenville and Elizabethtown. These were a tribulation to the early preachers, but sometimes their own parishioners backslid into behavior that brought shame to the church.[13]

Take Jacob Van Meter, for example. "Bacon Creek Jake" was an accomplished man. He was a pensioned veteran of Clark's Northwest Campaign, 1778–1779, and of the 1782 Shawnee Campaign. He was the father of a large family of children and the owner of more than four thousand acres of rich Nolin Valley farmland. He lived in an unusually fine two-story log cabin with glass windows and a brick chimney seventeen and one-half feet wide. Bacon Creek Jake was a community leader and a founding member of Gilead Baptist Church, yet he had to be "excluded" from the congregation on the second Saturday in May 1828 for having "drank [sic] too much spirituous liquor." Another member was admonished that day for swearing, and another for not attending church.[14]

There was an evil on the land worse than drinking and swearing, though, and the congregations struggled with it, even split over it, all through these early years. Slavery was the question. As far back as Benjamin Lynn's day, the question was a divisive one. The 1790 Kentucky census showed that twenty percent of the population was black, so slavery was no small issue. Many settlers on the Nolin frontier came from slaveholding Virginia and the Carolinas, but many others emigrated from Pennsylvania, where the Quakers had been condemning slavery for one hundred years. Lynn's Brush Creek congregation added their names to a petition asking the 1792 Kentucky Constitutional Convention to outlaw slavery. And at the Great Crossings convention of Kentucky Baptist associations, the delegates drafted a resolution that began, "Slavery is a violent deprivation of the rights of nature and inconsistent with a republican form of government." All across the region, church congregations were coming to the same conclusion: slavery should end. Other churches were deciding the opposite. And in many cases, a congregation meeting under the same steeple and asking the same God for guidance reached both conclusions at once, leaving no alternative but to divide. In 1808, fifteen members left South Fork Baptist Church in a dispute over slavery. The Lincolns were among those who split with South Fork, although "existing records do not document whether Thomas Lincoln presided over the split." The Lincolns began attending services at the anti-slavery Little Mount Baptist Church, one of the "emancipation Baptist" congregations.[15]

The log cabin frontier was a great leveler: master and slave worked side by side to clear the land, to set out the crop and to bring it in, and all for the same pay—namely, subsistence-level food and shelter. The charter members of Gilead and Severns Valley included slaves; their names appear alongside those of their masters in the early records. It is also true that masters granted slaves their freedom with surprising frequency. One example is that of Jacob Van Meter, Sr. In his 1792 will, Van Meter not only freed his slaves when they reached age thirty, but also gave "three hundred acres of land on Nolin at Rock Dismal [Edmonson County] ... to my faithful Negro man Bambo, to him, his heirs and assigns forever."[16]

Other aspects of slavery were troubling, however, and would give no rest to people of conscience. They asked: how can a nation that fought for freedom from the British continue to deny freedom to black people? Another uncomfortable question had more to do with the future than the present. Now, in the early days of settlement, the work might be the same for all, but in the end, the master was going to profit from his own labor and that of his slaves. The master would move up in the world, but the slave never would. Did not blacks have the moral right to benefit from their work just as whites did?

Underlying all the economic questions were the most unsavory elements of slavery: the cruel mistreatment of slaves and the dividing of slave families. Unable to reconcile slave-holding with a Christian life, more and more Kentuckians were deciding that slavery was a sin, while others insisted that slavery was not only necessary, but also proper, and permitted by the Bible itself. This vexing issue that was disturbing the prayers of Kentucky's churchgoers would soon become the rock upon which the back of the nation was broken.

FOURTEEN

Two Presidents, Two Fathers

Thomas Lincoln was an anti-slavery Baptist. All his life he had seen the relatively mild version of slavery in Kentucky and Virginia, and in 1806 he had seen the harsher brand of Deep South slavery when he was on a flatboat trip to New Orleans with his friend Isaac Bush. Slavery was an ugly thing, and Thomas Lincoln was against it. But there was more to it than just right-and-wrong. Lincoln was a cabinetmaker and a carpenter, and it was hard to find people who would hire a man to do a job when a slave who had the skills could be made to do the work for nothing.

Thomas Lincoln got some work, of course. People admired his set of tools, and most everyone agreed that he knew how to use them. Still, he had to scratch to find enough work around Elizabethtown to support his pregnant wife and his young daughter, Sarah. He had had to struggle for as long as he could remember. His father, Abraham, had left Rockingham County, Virginia, for Kentucky in 1782, when Thomas was six. They settled in Jefferson County and might have done well there, but in 1786, while Abraham worked a crop near his cabin, an Indian shot him from ambush. Thomas was beside his father when he fell. The brave dashed out of the woods to scalp Abraham and was about to kill or kidnap the little boy when a rifle cracked from the cabin and the Indian fell dead, blood spurting from a hole in his chest. Tom's older brother Mordecai had shot the man, drawing a bead on a shiny pendant he wore on a string around his neck, and by his calm marksmanship he saved his little brother's life.[1]

The widow Bersheba Lincoln moved her brood to Washington County after Abraham's murder. By 1796, at least, and perhaps earlier, Thomas had left his mother's house and was in Elizabethtown, helping Samuel Haycraft, Sr., build his mill on Valley Creek and also working for Jacob Van Meter, Sr., with whom he lived. In *Lincoln and the Lincolns*, Harvey H. Smith quotes from an interview that Dr. William Smith (a boyhood friend of Thomas Lincoln) conducted in later years with Bersheba Lincoln. She said, "Thomas did not live with us long in Washington County. He came down to Hardin County with Josiah [his brother] and he worked for Jacob Van Meter before he was grown, living with him, and at times he worked for others." Another witness is quoted as saying that young Thomas Lincoln "lived with Jacob Van Meter a good deal."[2]

Van Meter and Haycraft seem to have had a powerful influence on the fatherless young man. Smith concludes that Samuel Haycraft, Sr., and Jacob Van Meter, Sr., "had more to do with the life of [President] Abraham Lincoln's father that all the balance of his associates."[3]

Thomas Lincoln weighed a solid 185 pounds and stood about five feet, nine inches tall. His eyes were never bloodshot from too much drinking, but he bought tobacco by the pound. He could write his name. He played the fiddle. He was a casual, slow-moving man who liked a story or a joke. Thomas Lincoln was a man with a temper, though, and he was known to fight when it was necessary. One time, thinking a woman had been insulted by the comments of another man, Lincoln fought him and gnawed off a piece of the man's nose.[4]

Thomas Lincoln was a reliable citizen. He was appointed by the county court to help maintain the road between Hodgen's Mill and New Haven, and he was occasionally a slave patroller—an assignment which may have galled him, considering his anti-slavery views. The community trusted him. He signed his name to a promissory note of Jacob Van Meter, Jr., (the son of his old mentor) to Samuel Haycraft, Sr., for the considerable amount of £26:17:3. He was a juryman when called, and when he was not in the jury box, he was sometimes found in the witness box. He once won a lawsuit against a man who had slandered his work as a carpenter. And, as his reputation increased, so did his good fortune. Thomas Lincoln did a little farming, in addition to his carpentry, and he owned quite a few head of livestock. On February 18, 1806, he sold to the Elizabethtown merchants Bleakley and Montgomery 2,400 pounds of pork and 494 pounds of beef which gave him a credit of £21:14:1½ at their store. He used some of that credit for his wedding clothes.[5]

In 1806, Thomas Lincoln married Nancy Hanks of Springfield. On his wedding day, he wanted to make the best impression on his bride and her neighbors. He showed up at the Berry cabin wearing new calf-skin boots and a new suit that someone had tailored for him in Elizabethtown. He had on a new hat and a pair of new suspenders. He had even adorned his horse with a decorated bridle. After the ceremony and the wedding feast, the couple returned to Elizabethtown, where they made their home. It was there, in 1807, that Nancy Hanks Lincoln gave birth to a daughter whom she named Sarah.[6]

In December 1808 the Lincolns moved to a three hundred-acre farm on the South Fork of the Nolin. Their new home was a snug little cabin eighteen by sixteen feet, already built. Thomas paid $200 for the house and land. Of that South Fork farm, Thomas and Nancy's boy Abraham (named for the grandfather the Indian had killed) would later write, "I was born February 12, 1809 in the then Hardin County, Kentucky, at a point within the now recently formed county of Larue, a mile, or a mile and a half from where Hodgin'sville now is. My parents being dead and my own memory not serving, I know no means of identifying the precise locality. It was on Nolin Creek."[7]

Thomas Lincoln made the rounds to tell the kinfolks and neighbors about Nancy's new baby boy, and they came to find the mother and the child under a bearskin cover, the red-faced baby in a little yellow gown. Surely, all Thomas Lincoln could see that Sunday when Abraham was born were the possibilities ahead. Maybe he imagined teaching, by and by, this child just born the names and uses of those good carpentry tools; maybe he imagined the boy following him in the field, dropping corn and pumpkin seeds in the rows and, as he grew taller and stronger, the boy himself guiding the plow through the soil of Sinking Spring Farm. Maybe the new father remembered the day he was in the field with his own father Abraham and a gunshot rang out. It is a poignant moment to consider because, although Thomas Lincoln in this hour of joy and imaging could not know it, his troubles had just begun—he had paid $200 for them sixty days ago. The road he was now on would lead him and his family to ruin.

In the woods around them, the pioneers found cures for almost everything. If arthritis troubles you, said the folk doctors, eat a pokeberry a day for nine days. The juice of the jewelweed is good for burns, and if your heart is acting up, why, just drink some milkweed tea. Cancer is cured by tea brewed from red clover blossoms. A tea made from the inner bark of the white walnut tree will bring your constipation to an end, and if you go too far the other way, blackberry syrup will cure your diarrhea. They will tell you with a wink that whiskey will do the trick for a whole list of ailments. But there was no known preventative for misfortune, and Lincoln was in the early stages of an incurable case of it.[8]

Once again, as was the case with so many others, the trouble was a disputed land title—not the result of shingled claims this time, but of carelessness. The Sinking Spring Farm was originally part of the fifteen thousand acres of Richard Mather, who had come to the Nolin Valley from Philadelphia in 1801. Mather had sold the Sinking Spring land to David Vance, who bought the farm, not outright, but with an agreement to make payments. Vance had sold the farm to Isaac Bush and Bush to Lincoln. The problem was that Vance had never completed his payments to Mather, so it was not his to sell. Nobody since Mather had ever held clear title to the land. Thomas Lincoln was forced to move, but he was determined to get legal possession of the farm. Five years of litigation followed. In the meantime, he took his family to live on a rented farm on Knob Creek. He had suffered a setback, but he was not yet a failure. The Hardin County tax list for 1814 showed that Thomas Lincoln was still in the top one-fifth of property owners; "only fifteen persons out of ninety-eight listed had a greater property value" than Lincoln's.[9]

But bad luck was not done with Thomas Lincoln. He barely missed being evicted from the Knob Creek farm when the presumptive owner, George Lindsey, was sued by some Pennsylvanians who claimed to own a vast tract of land that included Thomas Lincoln's farm and nine others, as well. The lawsuit was settled in Lindsey's favor in 1816, but later that same year the court ruled against Lincoln in his effort to keep the Sinking Spring Farm. Thomas Lincoln had had enough. He decided to take his family to Indiana, where he could get a guaranteed title to his land from the government. And there was another reason to move north. Slavery was illegal in Indiana, meaning that people had to *hire* work done unless they wanted to do it themselves. Valid titles and no slavery. Life would be better for the little family in Indiana. They moved north that winter.[10]

Something essential had gone out of Thomas Lincoln, though. He never could seem to get the same traction in Indiana that he had in his early days in Kentucky. Some wound to his spirit robbed him of his vigor and caused him to stall. The first winter and for some time after they lived in a half-faced camp, basically a roof propped up on stilts at one end with the whole front open to the wind and snow. Later, Tom Lincoln, the master carpenter and joiner, did stir himself enough to build a crude cabin, but he could barely find the energy to chink the walls, and they leaked when it rained. He did not put in a floor at all. The door opening was covered by a flap of animal hide.[11]

After two years in Indiana, Nancy died of the milk sickness. Tom Lincoln returned to Elizabethtown for a wife. He found the widow Sarah Bush Johnston washing clothes in the front yard of her cabin on Valley Creek and, with no flourishes or flowery speech, asked her to marry him. They had known each other since both were young; Sarah remembered fondly the cabinetmaker who had courted her back then, and she agreed to his proposal. A Methodist preacher married them and they headed north in a wagon loaded down with her three children and her household plunder. Under her attentive care, her children and Tom's were knitted into one family and Abe, especially, thrived. "She proved a good and kind mother to me," the grown Abraham recalled.[12]

Tom grew more and more frustrated. He argued with Abe over the boy's inclination to waste time reading instead of working, and a Hanks cousin remembered that Tom would "sometimes knock him over." Sarah interceded on behalf of the boy. She tried to buy her stepson time to study, making Tom leave him alone. She saw something in the boy, even if Tom could not.[13]

The damage was done, though, between father and son. They were never again close. Abe helped the family move to Illinois in 1830 and then, legally able, he left the family. After that, he rarely ever saw his father again, and once he was established as a successful lawyer, he may not have seen him at all. He did rescue his father financially through the years; sometimes even $20 was more than the old man could scrape together, but Tom was never invited to Abraham's Springfield home, never met Mary Todd, never saw his four grandsons. Tom Lincoln died in 1851. Abraham, though summoned by his stepbrother, did not go to his father's deathbed.[14]

So much in Thomas Lincoln's life had gone wrong, beginning with his loss of the Sinking Spring Farm. One might be tempted to say that he and the other old "buckskins" were too ignorant to make their land titles secure, but the fact is that Easterner speculators in Kentucky land had their problems with murky titles, too.

In March 1796, James Dickey, Robert Johnson, and James Buchanan, Sr.—a trio of Pennsylvania investors—bought almost six thousand acres of land lying on both sides of the Nolin River in Hardin County. It had been part of the estate of John LaRue who had died in 1792. The executors, Isaac LaRue, Robert Hodgen, and Phillip Phillips had sold the land to men who had, in turn, sold it to Dickey, Johnson, and Buchanan. The trouble started when the heirs of John LaRue brought suit, claiming that the land should never have been sold at all. The Pennsylvanians found themselves stuck in a classic Kentucky land dispute quagmire.[15]

James Buchanan, Sr.'s, son and namesake was a lawyer of one year's experience. In 1813 the old man dispatched the young man to Hardin County to defend his rights to the land. Buchanan came down the Ohio River on a flatboat from Pittsburgh with a cargo of merchandise bound for the store and tavern of Major James Crutcher. Buchanan probably lived with the Crutchers in Elizabethtown.[16]

Elizabethtown was the home of several gifted attorneys at the time. If James Buchanan thought that he was going to come down and teach the yokels how to practice law, men like John Rowan, Felix Grundy, and

Ninian Edwards soon cured him of that notion. Ben Hardin was another with whom Buchanan bumped heads in court. Buchanan at first discounted Hardin because of his rustic appearance, but it was not long before he realized that he was outmatched. For his part, Hardin was not intimidated by young Buchanan's store-bought clothes and neither was he impressed by the Easterner's legal talents, which he judged as little more than adequate. Hardin said that, after a few encounters with members of the local bar, Buchanan "began to look unhappy."[17]

James Buchanan did not stay in Hardin County long. He could not untangle his father's legal problems, so in 1814, he went home to Pennsylvania. He is said to have remarked as he was leaving, that "every horse-thief and jail-bird in the West knew more about land law than he did." Buchanan resumed his law practice in Lancaster amidst a more affable clientele, and he began to dabble some in politics.[18]

The lawsuit was finally resolved in 1821, by which time Robert Johnson had died. It was something of a split decision. The heirs of John LaRue received the money from the improper land sale; Buchanan Sr. and his one surviving partner were awarded the land. It had taken twenty-five years, but they had clear title to the Nolin River land, at last, and they began selling it off. White Mills was started on some of it, and so it was profitable, after all.[19]

It does not mean much, really, but it is an interesting historical curiosity that the fathers of the 15th and 16th presidents owned land along the Nolin River at the same time, that their sons lived in Hardin County at the same time, and that the two sons would attain the White House at the crucial moment of American history. James Buchanan would preside over the dissolution of the Union, and Abraham Lincoln would put it back together again—this time free from the stain of slavery.

FIFTEEN

The Remarkable Stephen

By the 1840s, slaves in the Nolin River Valley had pretty much the same lot in life as slaves elsewhere in the upper South. It was a lifetime of work with slim chance of manumission. A few were artisans, a few more were house servants, the majority were farmhands working in the tobacco, hemp, and corn.

Counted among the slaves, however, was a small population in the region of the lower Nolin where it enters the Green whose work was unique. They pocketed money from their work and were the respected leaders of the whites whose lives were temporarily in their care. They were the first guides at Mammoth Cave. Stephen Bishop, "The Remarkable Stephen," was their patron saint.

The legend that an Edmonson County hunter named Houchin chased a bear into a hole in the ground and became the white discoverer of Mammoth Cave may or may not be true. The year that white men first visited Mammoth Cave is not even certain. What is accepted as fact is that in 1798, a man named Valentine Simons claimed two hundred acres surrounding the cave and began to commercially mine saltpeter. Saltpeter, a nitrate, was the primary ingredient in the production of gunpowder, and Mammoth Cave saltpeter was of the finest quality. It was refined by a process of boiling and drying similar to the way salt was made. Ownership of the cave passed through several hands—John Flatt, the brothers George and John McLean, and finally Fleming Gatewood and Charles Wilkins, who bought it from the McLeans for $3,000 cash in August 1812. The Gatewood and Wilkins partnership seemed well timed, for the United States had gone to war with Great Britain in June 1812, and the demand for gunpowder was high. Saltpeter prices jumped from seventeen cents a pound to one dollar a pound, and, with a work crew of seventy slaves, production at Mammoth Cave was projected to reach five hundred pounds of nitrate per day. The estimate proved overly optimistic. Saltpeter extraction in Mammoth Cave was hampered by the effects of the New Madrid earthquake that had occurred in December 1811. No lives were lost at Mammoth Cave when the earthquake hit, but the mining equipment was badly damaged. Necessary repairs took time, and continuing aftershocks kept the totals below expectations. Perhaps this is what convinced Fleming Gatewood to get out. Before the end of 1812, he sold his half interest to Hyman Gratz, and the mining went on. The DuPont Company bought all the nitrate that Gratz's slave gangs could take from the cave.[1]

Nitrate was not all that the miners found in Mammoth Cave. They uncovered ancient relics, and one work crew in 1812 found the mummified body of a pre–Columbian woman in a shallow grave under a slab of stone. When journalist and poet Nathaniel Parker Willis visited the cave in the 1850s, he was beguiled by the story of the discovery of the ancient woman's body. In his book *Health Trip to the Tropics*, he quoted at length an 1813 account by a man who had seen it: "The body was in a state of perfect preservation, and sitting erect. The arms were folded up, and the wrists were laid across the bosom; around the two wrists was wound a small cord, designed, probably, to keep them in the posture in which they were first placed." The woman was wrapped in deerskin and outside of this was a fabric woven from the inner bark of a tree. As for the body: "The hair on the head was cut off within an eighth of an inch of the skin, except near the neck, where it was an inch long. The color of the hair was dark red; the teeth were white and perfect." And then, the witness made an intriguing revelation. "I discovered no blemish upon the body, except a wound between two ribs, near the back bone; and one of the eyes had also been injured." Beside the woman in her grave were a pair of moccasins and a light robe, both made of woven bark, and a knapsack. In the knapsack were a woven bark cap, seven bird-quill headdresses, strings of beads, a fawn-hoof necklace, another necklace with an eagle-claw pendant and yet another with a bear-jaw pendant, two rattlesnake skins, some deer sinews, seven needles, two whistles made of cane, and a packet of vegetable dye pigments. It was a discovery that abounded with mysteries, and Willis' fascination was complete. He called the woman "Kentucky's posthumous belle."[2]

Cave owner Hyman Gratz was an artifact collector, and he sent some of the pieces found inside Mammoth Cave to a doctor named Samuel Mitchell in New York. In one letter that accompanied a package of Indian items, Gratz wrote:

> There will be found in this bundle two moccasins in the same state they were in when taken out of the Mammoth Cave about two hundred yards from its mouth   it will be perceived that they are fabricated out of different materials. One is supposed to be made of a specimen of flag or lily which grows it the southern part of Kentucky; the other of the bark of some tree,

probably the papaw [sic]. There is also in this package a part of what is supposed to be a kinniconeche pouch, two meshes of a fishing net, and a piece of what we suppose to be the raw material out of which the fishing net, the pouch, and one of the moccasins were made.[3]

During the war years, government and business officials who inspected the mining operation came out of the cave amazed at its size. They spread the word about this phenomenon in the Kentucky backwoods, and after the war ended in 1815, as the saltpeter business declined, another came to take its place, tourism. So many travelers came to see Mammoth Cave that, after Charles Wilkins' death in 1827, Gratz bought out his partner's half-interest from his estate, added fourteen hundred acres to the property and built a log inn. Slave cooks and chambermaids attended to the comforts of the sightseers, but the real star of the black community of Mammoth Cave was about to appear.[4]

In 1838, Franklin Gorin, a Kentuckian, bought the cave and surrounding forest for $5,000. He brought in new guides: his own seventeen-year-old slave, Stephen Bishop, and two slaves whom he leased, Nick Bransford and Mat Bransford. The two Bransfords were not brothers, but they belonged to the same master, Thomas Bransford of Glasgow, and they used his surname as their own. Earlier guides taught the novices the routes of the short tours they conducted, and the young men were on their way. It was Bishop, however, who came to be referred to as the "high priest" and "prince of guides" at Mammoth Cave.[5]

Stephen Bishop was a wiry five-feet, four-inches tall. N.P. Willis thought that he resembled a Spaniard and spoke of his "broad chest and shoulders, narrow hips, and legs slightly bowed," and added, "His intelligent face is assured and tranquil, and his manners particularly quiet—and he talks to charming ladies with the air of a man who is accustomed to their good will and attentive listening." One of those "charming ladies," the Englishwoman Marianne Finch, was fairly smitten with the guide. She wrote that Bishop "looks so handsome—with his white teeth and flashing dark eyes." She could hardly believe that he was a slave.[6]

Bishop had an unnaturally keen memory for the dark passages of the underground maze that became his profession and his playground. He confidently explored regions that no man had seen before. He crossed the one hundred foot–deep "Bottomless Pit" that had thwarted every other explorer, and he discovered the cave's eyeless fish, even while he perfected his patter for the tourists. Gorin said of Stephen, "He had a fine genius, a great fund of wit and humor, some little knowledge of Latin and Greek, and much knowledge of geology, but his great talent was a knowledge of man."[7]

The cave tours began after breakfast when the visitors walked down from the hotel to the mouth of the cavern to meet their guide. They may have thought that Bishop's outfit of green jacket, striped trousers and brown slouch hat was eccentric, but he looked no stranger than they did in their padded skull caps and mustard-colored cave costumes, which they rented for one dollar at the inn. Each tourist carried a lantern, as did Bishop, but he was also burdened with a canteen of lamp oil, some Bengal torches, and a large picnic basket loaded with "fried chicken, apples, [and] biscuits"—lunch for the whites.[8]

The tour was not for weaklings. It covered eighteen subterranean miles, nine miles in and nine miles out. Willis described it as "eighteen miles of pathway over broken rocks to be traversed lamp in hand—ladders to be ascended and descended, precipices to be climbed, half-mile holes to be crept through, tight places to be squeezed in and out of, crags to be scaled, hanging rocks to be crawled under, and chasms to be scrambled over." To keep the visitors' minds off of the physical challenge of the tour, Bishop entertained them with an amusing and informative monologue. Journalist Bayard Taylor said that Bishop had "a smattering of Greek mythology, a good idea of geography, history, and a limited range of literature, and a familiarity with geological technology which astonished me." To further impress the visitors with the cave experience, Bishop would light the Bengal torches and raise them high to illuminate a dome or drop them down a chasm to demonstrate the depth. At other points, he would extinguish all lights and allow the visitors to undergo the most perfect darkness on earth. It was a test that proved to be overly frightening for many visitors, and it was given an ominous name, "trying the dark."[9]

Stephen Bishop (Library of Congress).

Bishop's witty presentation on the torchlight tours and his learned explanation of the creation and formations of the cave made him the favorite guide of the celebrities who visited the cave. They demanded Stephen. Ralph Waldo Emerson came to Mammoth Cave. So did Charles Dickens. The "Swedish Nightingale" Jenny Lind visited, as did Edwin Booth and Olé Bull, and George D. Prentice, the editor of the Louisville *Daily Journal*. More than once Bishop had to carry out on his back the white tourists who became too exhausted or too frightened to continue—he had to carry one six miles—and always he had to be cheerful.[10]

Bishop understood that his life was being played out in a moral and social labyrinth; he was leading whites and sometimes giving them orders, but at the same time, he remained a slave. Below the surface, he could get by with behaviors that would have been unthinkable above. It was a precarious situation and required exquisite balance on his part. He was careful not to step over the social boundaries when he was leading a party. For example, in addition to guiding whites through the darkness, his duties included spreading a luncheon for them. After five hours, when it came time to eat, he prepared their meal and then took his own over to another spot. He ate apart from his party of tourists unless they insisted that he join them, which did occasionally happen.[11]

After a lunch in Washington Hall, the cave parties pushed on past Rocky Mountains and Dismal Hollow to mile nine, the farthest end of the tour. Here they found the names of previous visitors who had smoked their names on the crystalline ceiling with lit candles. It was a disfiguration that offended some of the visitors and Stephen Bishop as well. He could not very well prevent it, however. As Willis observed, "a slave's remonstrance would not be much, with the kind of white man that would thus immortalize his own bad taste." He did try to prevent them from breaking off and taking stalactites and stalagmites as souvenirs.[12]

The return trip to the mouth of the cave took another six hours. Emerging, the visitors were startled by the heightened aromas of cedar, soil, and rain. They returned to their rooms and reflected on what they had seen. Many put it into writing. In his book *At Home and Abroad*, Bayard Taylor said, "What are the galleries of the Vatican, the Louvre, Versailles, and the crystal palaces of London and Paris to this gigantic vault hewn in the living rock?" Nathaniel Parker Willis made a little joke about the size of the cave. He said, "The Mammoth Cave is as large as a county, but having another county on top of it, it is not represented, I believe, in the Kentucky legislature." Then, growing serious, he said, "The Mammoth Cave is certainly a wonder of indescribable variety and beauty. It will increase in attraction as the world knows more of it, and, Kentucky, rich in so many specialties will be rich in a viaduct of cosmopolitism—having that which the intelligent of all nations must needs come and see." That their tours had been a success was largely due to the temperament, the knowledge, and the showmanship of Stephen Bishop.[13]

In 1839, Franklin Gorin sold Mammoth Cave to Dr. John Croghan, a nephew of General George Rogers Clark, for $10,000. Bishop was part of the deal. He traveled up the Louisville and Nashville Turnpike to Locust Grove, Croghan's Louisville home, where he drew from memory the first detailed map ever made of the cave. It was published and attributed to him in a book called *Rambles in the Mammoth Cave During the Year 1844*. At Locust Grove, Bishop also met the slave woman Charlotte. She was evidently dazzled by the literate visitor from Edmonson County whose conversation was both witty and learned. Shortly thereafter, Charlotte became Mrs. Bishop.[14]

The birth of Stephen's and Charlotte's son Thomas in 1843 inspired one of his most far reaching explorations. In an excellent article about Bishop in the *Courier-Journal*, Laurence Muhammed described how, far back in the cave, in an area tourists almost never see, the modern spelunker is surprised to come upon a heart drawn on the rock wall and inscribed with the words: Stephen L. Bishop, Guide, M. Cave, Mrs. Charlotte Bishop, 1843. Outside the heart, Stephen wrote more: Mrs. Charlotte Bishop, Flower of the Mammoth Cave. Bishop's passion for Charlotte caused him to give into an urge he disapproved of in others, to leave his own mark on the underworld kingdom of which he was the master.[15]

Bishop, carrying his ladder and his lanterns, loved exploring deep in the cave alone, free from the need to perform. There was so much left to see. Like all professionals, he undoubtedly grew to hate the outside demands on his time. More and more visitors were coming on the Louisville and Nashville stagecoach to see Mammoth Cave. Dr. Croghan had estimated that one thousand tourists came to the cave in 1840 and wrote a friend that he expected three thousand in 1841. By the mid–40s the number had increased even more.[16]

The enterprise was successful, but Dr. Croghan's head was bursting with new ideas for Mammoth Cave. He built good roads to the cave property, and he greatly expanded accommodations for visitors from Gorin's one small guest lodge to two two-story cabins of four rooms, more than a dozen one-story cabins, and a grand two-story hall 30 × 90 feet where guests dined and danced. He corresponded with Victor Audubon, hoping to obtain his artistic talents for commercial purposes.

Perhaps it was an attempt at persuasive flattery when Croghan gave one section of the subterranean trail the name "Audubon Avenue." If so, the flattery failed, and when the young Audubon declined Croghan's offer he engaged two other artists who did produce paintings from which engravings were made for use in Croghan's guide book.[17]

Another of Dr. Croghan's ideas was medical in nature. He built cottages inside the cave, a quarter mile from the mouth, as a tuberculosis sanatorium. He wrote, "Owing to the uniformity of temperature throughout the year 60 Faht. the dryness of the atmosphere and the continual purification thereof by the constant formations of salt Petre, I have no doubt there is nowhere to be found a spot so desirable for persons laboring under pulmonary affections." It was utter nonsense, of course. The sodden, still air of the cave was disastrous to the TB patients. Smoke from the cooking and heating fires hovered in the cave and aggravated further the invalids' respiratory ailments. The slave Alfred looked after the consumptives, and he told Bayard Taylor, "I was one of the waiters who attended upon them. I used to stand on that rock and blow the horn to call them to dinner. There were fifteen of them, and they looked like a company of skeletons more than anything else." By 1843 the experiment had ended. Four of Croghan's patients died, the others failed to improve, and the unusual experiment was brought to an end, a sad failure.[18]

When the unmarried Dr. Croghan died of tuberculosis in 1849, his nieces and nephews inherited the cave and surrounding acres. The appraisal of his estate listed his twenty-nine slaves and gave their value. Stephen, age 28, was valued at $600, which seems low, but it was higher than any other slave except Alfred, who was also appraised at $600. Charlotte Bishop, age 26 was valued at $450, and little Thomas Bishop, age 6, was listed at $100. The doctor's will instructed his heirs to set the slaves free in seven years. The heirs kept their part of the bargain. They emancipated Bishop and the others on February 4, 1856. The date of his freedom is the last definite fact known about the life of Stephen Bishop. Beyond here, his trail becomes confusing to follow. Some report that he was enthusiastic about a future move to Liberia, but there is evidence that this was another example of his knowledge of man. John A. Alexander points out that the relocation of blacks to Africa was a popular idea in the 1840s and Bishop may have told his tour groups that moving to Liberia was his dream simply as a ploy to collect greater tips. He had a particular use in mind for those tips, one which seems to contradict his supposed Liberia plan. In 1856 or 1857 Bishop made a down payment of $400—money from his gratuities—on land adjoining the cave. Then, another mystery. Within weeks of his purchase, he sold the land he had bought. Perhaps he had decided on a career change and needed the money to tide him over. It is said that he expressed a desire to become a lawyer. Whatever his future plans were, they ended when he died in 1857. He was buried on the cave property.[19]

After Bishop came a succession of African American guides at Mammoth Cave and a black community grew up nearby. There were a school and a church and a twenty-room inn run by entrepreneur Henry Bransford for the black visitors to Mammoth Cave in those segregated days. These generations of successful black citizens at Mammoth Cave were the best memorial to the life of "The Remarkable Stephen."[20]

The decades when Stephen Bishop earned his fame, the 1840s and 1850s, were a breathing spell for the Nolin Valley. The hard labor of clearing the forest for pastures and cropland was largely accomplished. The fear of Indian attack had passed long ago. It was something Grandfather talked about. The new generation was dressing up the old cabins with weatherboard and paint. Good roads crossed the region; the major ones were the western and eastern branches of the Louisville and Nashville Turnpike. Andrew Jackson, in his many trips to Washington, D.C., and back home again to the Hermitage, had used them both. From Louisville, steamboats carried travelers up the Ohio River to the great cities of Cincinnati or Pittsburgh. A railroad was soon coming to parallel the western branch of the Louisville and Nashville Turnpike, whose name it would share. It would cross the river at the village of Nolin in Hardin County. Land prices were fair. An acre of LaRue County land cost $3.58; in Hardin County, $3.69; in Hart County, $3.15. Only in Grayson County ($1.33) and Edmonson County ($1.97) were the land prices very low.[21]

New communities had sprung up and were still springing up all along the Nolin River: White Mills, once part of the disputed James Buchanan land, was one. Asa King had hired Aaron Hart to build him a gristmill there in 1834, and later he added a saw mill to it. The gristmill washed away in the great flood of 1854, but the site was profitable enough that Dan Wortham rebuilt it right away, this time with an improved dam of dressed stone. There was also a mill at Harcourt and another at Spurrier, down on the Hardin-Grayson County line. The village of Nolin was populous enough to get a post office in 1836. Buffalo, on the South Fork, was settled by the Creal family in 1848 and became an important stagecoach stop.[22]

The most active antebellum community on the Nolin River may have been Millerstown, the first town in Grayson County, a town with surveyed streets. Jacob Miller settled there in 1790. He built a gristmill near his home, a poplar log cabin with a cedar roof. The town was incorporated in 1825. A blacksmith shop, a well-stocked store, a post office, a school, and a jail kept the village hopping, and several congregations met to worship there, sharing the one church house on alternate Sundays.[23]

The people of the Nolin Valley were hardworking and good-natured and seemed, sometimes, to mock the pretentious customs of their more aristocratic citizens further south. A famous duel, for example, was fought in Millerstown in the 1840s between the Presbyterian minister, William Bowman, and the resident blacksmith whose name is lost to history. The blacksmith felt he had been singled out for criticism in one of Pastor Bowman's sermons. He challenged Bowman to an appointment on the field of honor. As the challenged party, Bowman had his choice of weapons; he selected potatoes at forty-five feet.

The weapons were unorthodox, but the *code duello* was clear on the point and the blacksmith who had insisted on this solution had no choice now but to abide by the rules and see it through, even as the laughter began to build. A crowd gathered to watch on the appointed hour at the appointed place where the duelists met. At the signal, the blacksmith began a hot but inaccurate barrage with his arsenal of spuds while Pastor Bowman ducked. When the blacksmith bent over for more ammunition, the preacher pelted him with all the accuracy of little David against the giant Philistine—but on the other end. After a half-dozen or so direct hits on a delicate part of his anatomy, the young blacksmith's appetite for individual combat was satisfied and he conceded. The great potato duel was declared a victory for the challenged party, a doctor was summoned, and the bruised blacksmith was put to bed for his recovery.[24]

The duel was comical, but there was a more serious fight coming. This time the ammunition would not be tubers but iron and lead and the cost would not be measured in bruised egos but in blood.

Armies in blue and gray were coming to the valley of the Nolin River.

SIXTEEN

Blue and Gray on the Nolin

The election of 1860 saw Abraham Lincoln, native son of the South Fork of the Nolin, defeat three other candidates for the Presidency. The result was unacceptable to the Deep South, and states began withdrawing from the Union to create a nation of their own, the Confederate States of America. In April, Confederate shore batteries fired on Federal troops at Fort Sumter, South Carolina, and President Lincoln called for volunteers to put down the rebellion. More states left the Union to join the newborn Confederacy. The situation was tense in Kentucky. Governor Beriah Magoffin was receiving emissaries from the South, urging him to lead his state into the CSA. Whether Kentucky remained with the north or allied itself with the south, the state was likely to become a battleground. Finally, the legislature decided that the only safe course was to declare Kentucky to be in a state of armed neutrality.

Neutrality might be the state's *official* stance, but it did not reflect the passions of the individual citizens. In their hearts and minds, the people had chosen sides, and the young men were eager to take up the rifle. However, because of the state's neutrality, those who wanted to enlist had to go outside of Kentucky. Boys who wanted to fight for the South went to Camp Boone, Tennessee. Those who wanted to fight for the North went to Camp Joe Holt, in Jeffersonville, Indiana. The trip was not always easy.

Hiram Wheeler was for the Union. He lived in his family's mansion at Wheeler's Mill on the Nolin, a short distance below Millerstown. In July 1861 he decided the time had come to make his way to Camp Joe Holt. He had barely started when he and his friends were accosted. Some Rebel boys at Millerstown tried to stop them. Wheeler wrote his parents, "More than once I had a revolver pointed at my breast while endeavoring to keep a friend out of the fray. Nevertheless, we came out all right and started."[1]

Wheeler and his friends walked from Millerstown to Sonora, and from there took the train to Louisville, where they ate a welcome meal of "baker's bread, bacon, coffee and sugar." They crossed the Ohio River and joined the forces gathering at Camp Joe Holt under the command of Colonel Lovell Harrison Rousseau.[2]

By late summer of 1861, Kentucky's brief experiment with neutrality was at an end. In June, in the first of two special elections, Kentucky had filled its congressional delegation with Unionists, excepting only the representative from the Jackson Purchase. In August there was a special election for members of the state legislature. When the votes were tallied, Unionists had won enough seats to dominate the legislature by a margin of three to one. Kentucky had made her choice: Union. Kentucky's loyalties having been made obvious, the Federals began establishing recruiting and training camps inside the state. Governor Magoffin protested, but President Lincoln ignored him. The Confederates used this as their excuse to move into Kentucky. Rebel forces commanded by General Leonidas Polk occupied Columbus on September 4. Felix Zollicoffer's Confederates eased into Kentucky through Cumberland Gap, and on September 17, General Simon Bolivar Buckner's troops occupied Bowling Green. Buckner threw detachments forward to Cave City, Munfordville, and a detail to the tiny village of Bacon Creek (modern day Bonnieville). Buckner had to defend the railroad that would serve his interior lines and, at the same time, to prevent it from becoming an avenue of invasion by the Federals. That meant giving part of it up. He ordered the railroad bridge over the Rolling Fork at Lebanon Junction to be burned and also the L&N bridge over the Nolin River at the village of Nolin. Captain Phillip Lee of the 2nd Kentucky Infantry, CSA, burned the Nolin bridge.[3]

The invasion of Kentucky was only two weeks old, and already the valley of the Nolin found itself at war. To protect the L&N against further Confederate outrages, department commander General William T. Sherman dispatched Lovell Harrison Rousseau (now a brigadier general) to establish a camp and to rebuild and guard the L&N bridge. On October 9, 1861, Rousseau selected a site near Nolin on the 430 acre farm of secessionist David Nevin, and in sardonic appreciation of the landowner's grudging hospitality, he named the camp Camp Nevin.[4]

Rousseau was a Louisville lawyer, a veteran of the Mexican War, and a natural-born soldier. An observer who saw him a few months later said, "Today I saw a perfect impersonation of war, as Gen. Lovell H. Rousseau, on an immense black charger, with his full staff—all in full uniform wearing soft felt hats with black plumes—galloped by— at full speed. Gen Rousseau is six feet, four inches tall, large but not fat and carried himself superbly. He might well make Mars envious." Rousseau went on to perform with valor at Shiloh, Perryville, and Stones

River, and he led one of the great cavalry raids of the war in Alabama in 1864.[5]

That was in the future. For now, Nolin was the focal point of Rousseau's attention. From his headquarters at pioneer Adam Monin's 1793 cabin, he ordered one group of Camp Nevin soldiers to begin rebuilding the L&N bridge and another to start building a fort with guardhouses at the corners. In mid–October, General Rousseau turned over command to General Alexander McDowell McCook, and assumed command of the First Brigade. By the end of the month, there were four brigades of infantry on duty at Camp Nevin, plus three batteries of artillery and one regiment of cavalry. They were styled the Second Division, Army of the Cumberland. General William T. Sherman estimated the camp population to be 13,995 men. At Camp Nevin's height, there would be many more. Men were pouring in. Alpheus Bloomfield, a gunner in Captain C.S. Cotter's Ohio Battery, wrote his parents in late October that there were "about 35,000 in this camp." Camp Nevin grew to encompass several farms. It spread six miles from end to end, over both sides of the Louisville and Nashville Turnpike and eventually across the Nolin to the south bank. This camp beside the river was the center of the Union line in Kentucky, the protector of its most vital railroad and the defender of Louisville. Sherman wrote McCook, "The safety of our nation depends on you holding that ground for the present." McCook, a West Pointer from the Buckeye State, understood his responsibility and foresaw great things for his division. He crowed to Ohio Governor William Dennison on November 15, 1861, "I am now in command of the most important army in the field.... I can break the Back of this rebellion in three moves, and thank God I have the confidence in myself to do it." It was a lot of brag for a short letter.[6]

Never mind breaking the back of the rebellion; simply commanding the camp strained the talents of the vain but limited McCook. There was the problem of contrabands, for example. The proximity of the large Federal force at Camp Nevin attracted runaway slaves from all over the region. Their presence burdened and baffled General McCook, who wrote to General Sherman, "Ten have come into my camp in as many hours and from what they say there will be a general stampede of slaves from the other side of Green River." McCook wanted instructions about what to do with the runaways. In the meantime, he said that he had "put the Negroes to work. They will be handy with teams and generally useful."[7]

Sherman replied, "I have no instructions from the Government on the subject of Negroes. My opinion is that the laws of the State of Kentucky are in full force, and that Negroes must be surrendered on application of their masters or agents or delivered over to the sheriff of the county." In other words, get them out of camp.[8]

McCook did not follow Sherman's instructions to the letter. At least some of the runaways remained in camp to do menial chores such as cutting wood, cooking meals, and doing laundry. In addition, they served as guides in military expeditions to hostile territory south. One of them is known only by his given name, John. A soldier in the 49th Ohio mentioned John admiringly in a letter to his hometown newspaper, the Fremont *Journal*. Using the pseudonym "Redstick," this soldier said, "Captain James Patterson and John, the scout, are now out scouting.... John is a negro and makes a valuable man in the scouting service."[9]

Both cavalry and infantry went out on frequent scouts, but the camp itself was the most effective bulwark against Rebel outrages north of the Nolin. An article in the New York *Times* emphasized that Confederate activity was all *south* of the camp, nothing to the north. It said, "The enemy's horse [cavalry] are scouring the country below our pickets, plundering, robbing, and destroying everything they can lay their hands on."[10]

The Federals tried with mixed results to prevent Rebel depredations. In one particularly successful expedition, McCook ordered a squad of infantrymen from Camp Nevin south toward Bacon Creek to seek out a band of Confederate raiders. A soldier of the 39th Indiana remembered, "It was near this camp [Camp Nevin] that the first blood of the Rebellion, which fell upon Kentucky soil, was shed. Forty picked scouts ... were sent under Lieutenant-Colonel Jones against a marauding body of two hundred Rebels, near Bacon Creek. Taking a position in a log house—the residence of the notorious villain John A. Murrell—this squad, without receiving any injury, repulsed the Rebels, wounding several." Later reports said that five Rebels were killed and three wounded. It was a small action, but a successful one, and one imagines that the men of the 39th Indiana returned to camp the envy of those who had not yet received their baptism by blood.[11]

The soldiers stationed at Camp Nevin complained about the endless delays in a general advance south to challenge the Rebels, but they wrote thousands of letters home in which they praised the beauty of the land and the Nolin River, and they liked their camp even better after they had had the chance to improve their quarters. In a letter to the Belmont *Chronicle* dated November 28, 1861, a soldier of the 15th Ohio wrote, "We have been over a month in Camp Nevin, and our quarters are quite cozy and home-like. We have erected ovens for baking purposes, put up stoves in some of our tents, and, in some, have made flues under ground to aid us in keeping dry and warm." Alexis Cope of the 15th Ohio Infantry wrote less about beauty and comfort and more about the camp in terms of its suitability as a staging area for the Army of the Cumberland. In his regimental history, he said, "Camp Nevin was well selected with a view to the health and comfort of the men and as a point for the massing of a large force to operate directly against the enemy. It was on the Louisville and Nashville Railroad over which it could draw its supplies and not far from Nolin's creek which furnished an abundant supply of good water. The region was well timbered and there was plenty of wood for fuel. The country was an undulating plain and offered good opportunities for drainage." Let other men admire the sylvan beauty of a timbered slope in the slanted autumn light; Cope liked it for more practical reasons, water, fuel, and drainage.[12]

Relations between the soldiers at Camp Nevin and the surrounding civilians were comfortable at times, strained at others. Certainly, the nearness of thousands of uniformed men changed the regular rhythms of life. From August 24 to December 21, 1861, Gilead Baptist Church had no services, because of "the large army encamped in our neighborhood." The soldiers often went among the populace to see what good home-cooked things they could buy and then complained about the prices the farmers charged. Believing that they were being gouged, the soldiers felt free to raid the farmers' truck patches for sweet potatoes, their barns for tobacco, and to strip whole fields of corn. "Redstick" slyly admitted as much in a letter to the Fremont *Journal*. He said, "Our camp does not abound with luxuries. It is hard bread, bacon, rice, beef, potatoes, coffee, etc.; the etc. being what is *accidentally* picked up by the men."[13]

Another excuse for such larcenous behavior was the opinion of many of the soldiers that their camp was in the midst of a disloyal population. Soldiers believed the locals guilty of carrying intelligence to the Confederates a few miles south. Those who were suspected of secessionist leanings were liable to lose their teams, which were then used to haul timbers for the rebuilding of the Nolin railroad bridge. Local merchant R.L. Rains suffered even worse treatment. He was thought to be a saboteur, a bridge burner. On or about November 12, men of the 6th Indiana, while on picket duty, attacked Rains' store and home. Rains was "thoroughly cleaned out" by the soldiers, who also ripped all the siding from his buildings. But it was not over for Rains. Eight days later, it was the turn of the 49th Ohio, who finished the destruction of Rains' property by "burning it up." In another case, a soldier correspondent wrote of seeing "a brick dwelling house of very good appearance, but one wall had been entirely removed. I asked some soldiers standing near, why so good a building had been pulled down, and the reply was, 'Oh, we wanted some brick to build our ovens.'"[14]

Hosting visits of visiting dignitaries was a frequent occurrence that added interest to the days in camp, and, as sickness spread with the onset of rainy autumn weather, there was the more somber duty of attending regimental funerals. Lyman S. Widney wrote in his journal on October 30, 1861, "The saddest sight of our camp life is a soldier's funeral. One passed today from the hospital to the hillside beyond, where a newly dug grave awaited an occupant. The procession was headed by two fifes and two drummers, with muffled drums, playing the funeral dirge, then the body upon a stretcher, carried on the soldiers of 4 comrades. The co. followed slowly, with reversed arms. At the grave, the funeral service was read by the Chaplain, the body was lowered and the grave filled, then the co., drawn up in line, fired a volley and paraded by to camp with shouldered arms and the liveliest music."[15]

Death was a real presence in the camp: death by disease, by accident, or by encounters with the enemy. Buckner's Confederate pickets were only about ten miles south, but worse were the prowling men of John Hunt Morgan. Morgan and small groups of selected men made frequent nighttime excursions to the Union lines at Camp Nevin, where they counted regiments, listened for news of a Federal advance, and shot down unwary pickets with shotguns. Morgan's killings threw a terrible scare into the untested boys who had to stand their turn at picket duty. Little wonder that the skittish Union pickets sometimes shot and killed their own comrades in the dark.[16]

Terrible as they were, Morgan's skulking attacks on Union pickets were militarily insignificant and had no effect on the overall strategy of either side. Then, on December 5, 1861, he committed an act that shocked the Union high command into action. He burned the nearly rebuilt bridge over Bacon Creek just one day before it was to reopen. The response was immediate. General Don Carlos Buell (General Sherman's successor) ordered McCook to move his division to Bacon Creek. A correspondent of the 49th Ohio described to the Hancock *Courier* how excited the men were to be advancing at last. "I rather think it would have made you suppose a President had been elected, to have looked over that camp in about five minutes—barrels piled ten high and everything in a blaze." Between December 9 and December 17, McCook shuffled his men forward to Bacon Creek, as ordered. He left behind at Camp Nevin only the sick and three officers and a handful of guards to watch over the railroad.[17]

The Bacon Creek camp was called Camp Jefferson. The bad weather that had begun at Camp Nevin in December did not moderate. Robert

Caldwell, 21st Ohio Infantry, wrote to his father, "The most staple article now in camp is, mud, mud, mud, the wagons are covered, the horses are covered, the drivers are covered, and in fact everything about camp is deluged with the same sticky substance. It is almost impossible for those with shoes to get about."[18]

The soldiers were hard put to keep dry. Caldwell wrote his father, "I have found it necessary, on account of the wet weather and bad roads to buy a pair of boots for which I am to pay when we receive our next Pay. They are a good pair and come almost up to my knees. I am to pay $5.00 for them." That was more than a third of a month's pay. Even so, Caldwell thought he had found a bargain. He wrote, "The sutler charges $7.00."[19]

The continual rain was more than just an inconvenience; it became a security issue. The roads became impassable. The men could not move and supplies could not be delivered. However, General Ormsby S. Mitchel, the camp commander, had been a soldier for more than thirty years, and he knew the answer to almost any military contingency, including this one. He described his difficulties to his superiors in a letter dated January 16, 1862, and he added, "I will make a wooden road tomorrow." The general detailed eight hundred men to build it, and it was done without delay.[20]

The Camp Jefferson garrison received its marching orders on February 9, 1862. The boys began moving out at seven o'clock the next morning, and reached Munfordville about noon of the same day. With this, the war passed out of the valley of the Nolin, at least for a little while.[21]

In late summer of 1862, General Braxton Bragg invaded Kentucky. Louisville was his expected destination. Bragg's men kept a sizable lead between themselves and Buell, who was pursuing. Buell was still miles behind when the Confederates launched an attack on the Union garrison at Munfordville. At the end of the three-day fight the Federals surrendered. The victorious Rebels occupied Munfordville and pretty well emptied the town of foodstuffs before they moved out again. As they marched north, they skirmished with Buell's cavalry and lived off the local farmers. A Confederate captain—probably an officer in Wharton's Cavalry—became a miller for a week and kept the buhrs at Eagle Mills and Red Mill turning, grinding out cornmeal to feed his men. Another, Captain J.M. Wampler, an engineer in General Leonidas Polk's wing of the Army of the Mississippi, discovered two hundred bushels of wheat at Sonora. They had been bound for the markets in Louisville, but the Rebels took them.[22]

While the Rebels fed off the land, General Buell kept pushing.

North of Camp Nevin, the men of Buell and Bragg clashed. Bragg's column had unexpectedly turned off the main road and headed east toward Hodgenville. "Fighting Joe" Wheeler's Rebel cavalry stayed behind, lying in ambush, and on September 22, when Buell's men appeared, Wheeler hit them. The fight occurred at Dorsey's Branch, near Sonora in Hardin County. Wheeler reported,

> The enemy's advance reaching me about noon, my brigade was moved rapidly to a favorable position to receive him. The artillery and most of my cavalry were secreted until the head of a column of not less than 1,500 cavalry had arrived within about 350 yards of our position, when we opened upon them with canister and shell, killing and wounding many men and horses. The enemy deployed as skirmishers and brought up their artillery, engaging us warmly until dark, when they went into camp.[23]

Despite Wheeler's claim of "killing and wounding many men and horses," casualties on both sides in the fight at Dorsey's Branch were light. Wheeler rejoined Bragg's column as it passed through Hodgenville and continued to Bardstown. Buell, in uncontested possession of the turnpike now, pressed on through Elizabethtown and West Point to the City at the Falls.

General Bragg's Kentucky campaign was ill-fated. Kentuckians had made their choice and they were sticking to it. They did not rush to join the Rebels, and Bragg's instillation of a Confederate government in Frankfort was farcical. He fled before the ceremonies were concluded when a Federal force approached. The culmination of the campaign was on October 8 at Perryville, where Bragg and Buell battered each other for an entire day before the Confederate general, who had won the battle on this one day but faced much stiffer odds the next, began a long withdrawal into Tennessee. Kentucky was saved for the Union.[24]

John Hunt Morgan was dissatisfied with the results of Bragg's campaign. The L&N Railroad was still sending supplies from Louisville south to the Federal army occupying Tennessee. During Bragg's retreat, Morgan received permission to swing back toward the west and sever the railroad if he could. On October 20, Morgan's Raiders appeared in Elizabethtown, where they burned an L&N Railroad bridge. They camped just outside of town, under the great hemlock trees at Jacob Van Meter, Sr.'s, old place on Valley Creek, but it was a short night's sleep. Early in the morning a troop train from Louisville approached town and Morgan's men fought a skirmish with the bluecoats before galloping off toward Leitchfield in Grayson County.[25]

Morgan behaved as a brigadier general, but he was really just a colonel until December 1862, when he officially received his general's star. To celebrate, he planned a new raid against the L&N Railroad in

Kentucky. They called him the "Thunderbolt of the Confederacy," and now the Thunderbolt was coming north with thirty-five hundred men to destroy the L&N. On Christmas Day, 1862, a detachment of Morgan's Raiders led by Lieutenant Colonel John Hutchinson appeared at the Bacon Creek camp in Hart County and attacked the Union soldiers guarding the railroad bridge. They were a detachment of the 91st Illinois Infantry, and though outnumbered, they proved to be surprisingly stubborn. The fight went for hours until, having acquitted themselves honorably, the defenders of Bacon Creek surrendered, not so much because the Rebels had outfought them as because of the appearance of him whose name was worth a field battery—the Thunderbolt himself. He had been in Upton with another contingent of his men, waiting impatiently for Hutchinson to come up. When he did not, Morgan rode down to investigate. Once he identified himself, the Yankees knew they were, in the vernacular of the time, "up the spout." They conceded the contest. The victorious Confederates burned the stockade and the L&N bridge and paroled the sixty-four Union defenders.[26]

Simultaneous with the fight at Bacon Creek, Colonel Basil Duke was moving against the Camp Nevin garrison. The fort there had never been finished, and the garrison consisted of only seventy-six men and officers, another contingent from the 91st Illinois. Seeing Duke's men come near and begin placing their artillery, the prairie boys quickly decided to surrender. They watched as flames consumed the bridge and the unfinished fort they had bravely guarded—until the enemy showed up.[27]

Arriving at Nolin later with the rest of his command, Morgan helped himself to some supplies from the Monin farm (recently General Rousseau's headquarters) before moving against Elizabethtown on the morning of December 27. A twenty-minute artillery barrage of 107 rounds and the death of twenty or so Union soldiers convinced the Illinois garrison in Elizabethtown to surrender. The Raiders stripped their Union prisoners of their boots and overcoats and confiscated their weapons. The L&N depot was destroyed and the railroad bridge burned. Morgan and his men enjoyed their day-long visit to Elizabethtown. They shopped for new clothes in the stores around the square and paid the unhappy merchants with worthless Confederate currency.[28]

That night, Morgan and his officers slept in featherbeds, but the next morning they rode out again and headed for their grand prize, the two L&N trestles at Muldraugh Hill. Illinois and Indiana men defended the trestles, but not too well. Morgan defeated them, burned their camps and the trestles, and began a hurried return to Tennessee. There were skirmishes during Morgan's retreat (including the action at the

Rolling Fork where Colonel Basil Duke was wounded) but the Christmas Raid of 1862 was over.[29]

There was some guerrilla activity in the valley of the Nolin for the next two years. In September 1863 Confederate captain Littleton Richardson and his company of raiders swooped down on Nolin and burned the railroad bridge, and tradition says that they retreated by way of White Mills where they captured and paroled a detail of Federals after a brief fight. Henry Magruder was another bushwhacker who paid White Mills a call. In his confession, Magruder told about leading an attack in July 1864 upon a group of Union soldiers who were guarding the ford across the Nolin River there. Magruder remembered that he and his men

> came upon fifteen Federal soldiers. We saw them on a hill, with their horses hitched, and they were playing. We saw that their guns were stacked, and saw how many there were. We went down the hill and charged them, and they took to the houses and began firing. The boys ran into the houses and captured fourteen and wounded one, and got their arms, etc. We took them out of town and paroled some of them.[30]

It is a bit sinister that Magruder said that he paroled "some of them." One wonders what became of the others.

There was guerrilla activity from one end of the Nolin Valley to the other. Bushwhackers hit Brownsville on August 21, 1864. The Louisville *Daily Journal* described how Captain Jake Bennett rode into town at the head of a gang. They fired their pistols at any blacks they saw on the street and then rounded up the white citizens. They herded them into the courthouse "where a guard was stationed over them. Each prisoner underwent a search, and was relieved of what articles of value found on his person.... The stores were broken open and plundered. Some trouble was experienced in forcing the locks of Hancock & Weir's establishment, but the robbers persevered, and met with success." The irregulars fled when a mounted detachment of the 26th Kentucky Infantry approached.[31]

Such Confederate attacks continued long after there was any possibility of them affecting the outcome of the war. In December 1864 Confederate General Hylan B. Lyon appeared in the valley of the Nolin. He had left his base at Paris, Tennessee, and made his way north and east toward central Kentucky and the L&N Railroad: Hopkinsville, Madisonville, Hartford, Leitchfield; there was little doubt as to his destination. On December 23, he came roaring out of Grayson County. Approaching Elizabethtown, Lyon dispersed his men to hit the L&N in several places at once. One detachment overpowered the Elizabethtown garrison (13th Kentucky Infantry), destroyed the railroad depot and the half million dollars' worth of army stores inside, and burned the military stockade. They forced the townspeople to carry fence rails and other flammables to the railroad trestles, which they also burned.[32]

While these men demolished railroad property in Elizabethtown, Lyon and the rest of his raiders continued toward the Federal encampment at Nolin. A few men broke off to torch the L&N depot at Glendale. The others went on to Camp Nevin where Lyon had little trouble in persuading the defenders, another handful of men from the 13th Kentucky Infantry, to surrender. As the Rebels demolished track and prepared to burn the railroad bridge and the stockade, they got a bonus. A northbound troop train pulled in. They captured and paroled the men on board, then burned the cars.[33]

It was a splendid evening, a night to celebrate, until Lyon heard the "demoralizing" news that made all of his raiders' successes meaningless. Hood's Army of Tennessee had been defeated at Nashville. The three corps that Lyon had expected were not coming, not a brigade, not a regiment; just the opposite, the whole army was retreating south. Every passing hour put Lyon farther and farther away from Confederate lines. There was no time to lose. The raiders left Kentucky via Hodgenville, Campbellsville (where they burned the courthouse), Columbia, and Burkesville (where they burned the courthouse and the bridge over Cumberland River). They passed out of Kentucky and continued through Tennessee toward Confederate lines in Alabama. Lyon's Raid was over, and it had all been pointless.[34]

There were only a few weeks of war left. Robert E. Lee surrendered at Appomattox Courthouse in April 1865, and the South's bid to become an independent nation came to an end. Tattered soldiers began returning home to rebuild their lives and fortunes from the ruins of war.

Ruin is the word. The people of the Nolin Valley had paid a heavy toll to the troops moving constantly along its length. Statistics show that in the years 1861 to 1865, Hardin County farmers lost one thousand horses; three thousand cattle; 2,500 slaves; and uncounted tons of grain, hay, cord wood, and personal property confiscated by the bummers of both armies. Similar figures would hold true for each county in the region, and much of what was lost came from the agricultural Nolin River Valley.[35]

Unlikely as it seems, the Nolin was about to experience its greatest period of prosperity.

SEVENTEEN

The Prosperous Years

In 1867, a thin man with cheerful eyes and a head of heavy dark hair came walking down the Louisville and Nashville Turnpike. He stopped often to watch a hummingbird robbing the cardinal flower or to study the rattlesnake root and big bluestem that bordered the road. He stroked his beard as he looked, and sometimes he took a notebook out of his backpack and wrote something down. He was an oddity, for sure.

His name was John Muir. He was a limber-legged young man of twenty-nine years, but unlike others of his generation he had not been in the war. He was a student at Wisconsin State University during the early years of the Rebellion. He laid low until March 1864, when he went to Canada, where his brother Daniel had already gone to avoid military service. He waited out the unpleasantness, working in a saw mill for his pay and botanizing for his pleasure. He returned to the states in 1866 and found a job in an Indianapolis wagon wheel factory, but botany remained his passion. After an accident to one of his eyes in March 1867, Muir was confined for six weeks, time he used to consider the direction his life was taking. He decided that laboring in the dusty indoors for a few dollars a week was not how he wanted to spend the years remaining to him. Henceforth, he would devote his life to the study of plants.[1]

Muir began his new life just as soon as his vision returned, and he chose Kentucky as his first field of study. On September 1, 1867, he trained down from Indianapolis to Jeffersonville, Indiana, crossed the river at Louisville, and from there began his long saunter to the Gulf of Mexico. His walk had only just started, but he already loved what he saw. In his notes, later published as *A Thousand-Mile Walk to the Gulf,* Muir enthused about Kentucky's botanical treasures, especially the oaks. He wrote, "The oaks of Kentucky excel in grandeur all I had ever before beheld." He came to the Rolling Fork on September 3. A concerned black woman on the far bank saw him preparing to ford on foot. She called out for him to stop, the water was deeper than he supposed

and too swift; he would surely drown in that dangerous river if he tried
to wade across. She sent for a horse and in a few minutes Muir crossed
the Rolling Fork on the back of a tall white horse steered by a "little sable
negro boy." He emerged from the river on the Hardin County bank.[2]

He walked south up Muldraugh Hill to the plateau on top, passed
through Elizabethtown, and bedded down for the night in the country beyond. Muir's journal entry for September 4 read, "I was awakened
by the alarm notes of birds whose dwelling in a hazel thicket I had disturbed. They flitted excitedly close to my head, as if scolding or asking
angry questions, while several beautiful plants, strangers to me, were
looking me full in the face." He lingered about this "most beautiful" of
camp grounds, "enjoying its trees and soft lights and music."[3]

Muir crossed the Nolin River later that morning, and that afternoon he came to "a sandy stretch of black oak called 'Barrens,' many of
which were sixty or seventy feet in height, and are said to have grown
since the fires are kept off, forty years ago. The farmers hereabouts are
tall, stout, happy fellows, fond of guns and horses. Enjoyed friendly
chats with them."[4]

Sticking to the turnpike as he did, Muir bypassed most of the towns
which were over on the railroad. Had he seen the villages, Muir might
also have been impressed with the flowering of man's good works in the
Nolin Valley. If he had hiked over to Glendale, for example, he would
have appreciated the enlightened citizenry. Glendale only dated back to
the building of the railroad. It was a new town compared to some, but
it was progressive. A woman's suffrage association, the first one in Kentucky, was organized there with fifty members the year that the botanist strolled by. Muir might have noticed a newly built two-story brick
building flanked by two large frame dormitories. This was Lynnland
College. It had cost $32,000 to construct. The college was chartered by
the Kentucky General Assembly on February 11, 1867, and was guided
in this first year by the Reverend G.A. Coulson, the minister at Warren Cash's old church, Gilead. The college boasted a curriculum that
included German, French, instrumental music in piano or guitar, drawing, and oil painting. One instructor who would shortly arrive was John
Payton Hobson. He carried a letter of recommendation from General
Robert E. Lee, now president of Washington College in Lexington, Virginia. Hobson had recently graduated under President Lee there.[5]

If Muir had drifted over to Nolin, he would have found a village
recovering nicely from the war. Beaufort G. Beavers, a veteran of the
Union 6th Kentucky Volunteer Infantry, had opened a dry goods store.
Taylor Watkins and Jerome Albert operated the Nolin Milling Company
and Nolin Mercantile Company. The milling company was especially

profitable. It was buying local wheat and corn by the ton and shipping flour by the carload. The company would soon build for Albert one of the finest houses in town, a two-story affair with dormers on either side of a central gable, milled porch posts, and delicately carved bric-a-brac. L&N trains stopped every day at the Nolin depot. There was a hotel and before too many years passed, a two-story brick bank building with Romanesque style arches out front and a pressed metal ceiling inside. If Muir fell ill, Dr. W.F. Combs might have treated him in his Nolin office.[6]

At nearby Red Mill, Muir would have found a village of five or six residences clustered about the mill. Of course, there were mills all up and down the river valley. Eagle Mills, near where Muir crossed the Nolin, was three stories high. There was a post office on the bottom floor. The surrounding village also boasted a general store and two blacksmith shops. At Harcourt was Buckles' Mill. John Cofer, D.C. Swan, and John Buckles were its first owners, ambitious men who had an early understanding of the importance of publicity. Their maiden advertisement appeared September 12, 1835, in the *Kentucky Register* and promised that customers would always find quantities of cornmeal, flour, and even salt on hand. "We would say to the public in the spirit of candor and truth, that we are determined to use every exertion to merit patronage. For proof of this assertion, call and examine the article we manufacture."[7]

Dan Wortham's mill at White Mills produced forty barrels of "White Frost" flour a day. The village would have a metal truss bridge crossing the river near the mill before the turn of the century; until then, wagons and horseback riders had to use the ford just downstream from the dam. A wooden footbridge joined the people on one bank of the river to their fellow citizens on the other. Perhaps, if he had visited White Mills, the people would have recounted to Muir the mysterious, recent death of Uncle Wes, the freed slave of William P. Carroll. Uncle Wes was emancipated at the end of the war and had been given a gift of land adjoining the river. Uncle Wes was in the habit of having a midnight snack of cornbread and buttermilk. One night his wife Aunt Betsey awoke to see him eating, but there was no trace of him in the cabin next morning. Searchers discovered tracks in the light snow that had fallen in the night; the footprints led to a cliff overlooking the Nolin. Below, they saw Uncle Wes' dead body wedged between a tree and the cliff just above a cave at the river's edge. Signs of his struggle to free himself showed that Uncle Wes had not died in the fall itself but from his injuries and from exposure. The cave was called Dead Man's Cave after that, and canoeists began telling stories of seeing a strange sight at certain times in certain lights, a man standing inside the mouth of the cave, just watching them float by. Everyone knew it was the spirit of Uncle Wes Carroll.[8]

That was White Mills, only one of many. Hodgen's Mill, Kirkpatrick's Mill, Eagle Mills, Buckles' Mill, Webb Mill, Wheeler's Mill, Dickey's Mill—there were mills every few miles along the river. The valley fairly hummed with the turning of their grindstones.

Though he bypassed most of the villages and had nothing to say about them, Muir liked the people and he loved what he saw. He wrote, "Another day in the most favored province of bird and flower. Kentucky is the greenest, leafiest State I have yet seen ... the grandest of all Kentucky plants are her noble oaks.... Here is Eden, the paradise of oaks."[9]

Muir continued south to Edmonson County where he did make a side trip to visit Mammoth Cave. Tourism had scarcely slackened during the war. Soldiers marching south from Camp Nevin and Bacon Creek to drive the Rebels from the state had stopped by to see the cave. In a letter dated February 22, 1862, an unnamed soldier of the 1st Ohio Light Artillery wrote to his hometown newspaper:

> Yesterday a party of about twenty visited Mammoth Cave. The spacious hotel near the Cave has been nearly ruined by the rebels, who had possession of it up to last Sunday. The proprietor, Mr. [Edward King] Owsley, is as good a Union man as lives in the State, and for this crime he was made to suffer a heavy loss. He was driven from the house about three months since, and did not venture to return until last Wednesday. The windows and window sash, doors, and a large iron safe were all broken or burned up. The bedding was carried away, and all the furniture destroyed. All he saved was a box of silver, which was hid in the cave. The box was shown to us by the proprietor, who accompanied our party through the cave. We were fortunate enough to obtain the services of "Mat," the oldest guide on the premises. The proprietor, who thinks the rebellion is about crushed, informed me that he would immediately proceed to repair and refurnish the house and would be ready to receive guests in the course of two months.[10]

Muir arrived at the cave on September 6, 1867. He was not entirely prepared for what he saw. He wrote, "Arrived at the great Mammoth Cave. I was surprised to find it in so complete naturalness. A large hotel with fine walks and garden is near it. But fortunately the cave has been unimproved and were it not for the narrow trail that leads down the glen to its door, one would not know that it had been visited. There are house-rooms and halls whose entrances give but slightest hint of their grandeur. And so also this magnificent hall in the mineral kingdom of Kentucky has a door comparatively small and uncompromising. One might pass within a few yards of it without noticing it."[11]

Muir continued, "I never before saw Nature's grandeur in so abrupt contrast with paltry artificial gardens. The fashionable hotel grounds are in exact parlor taste ... the whole pretty affair a laborious failure side by side with Divine beauty."[12]

Muir did not name his cave guide. It was his loss if it was not the celebrated Mat Bransford. He was still conducting tours at the time of Muir's visit. Another visitor of that time, A.D. Binkerd, wrote of him, "Mat is a fair average specimen of the Anglo African race, improved by a considerable degree of culture, acquired by contact with scholars, professors of every science, and especially of geology and mineralogy ... he has collected a vocabulary of scientific terms that would do credit to a man of letters." If Mat Bransford did not have the easy humor of Stephen Bishop, it was understandable, for he had suffered one of the all-too-common tragedies of slave life. Bransford and his wife had seen three of their four children sold away during the days before emancipation.[13]

John Muir continued his long walk all the way to the Gulf. Later he became the most eloquent champion for the preservation of Yosemite Park in California. He never returned to hike in Kentucky. If he had come back, say, thirty years later, he might have been impressed—or perhaps dismayed—by the unregulated growth of the communities in the Nolin Valley. They would have been harder for him to miss, this time.

No community did better than Buffalo, on the South Fork of the Nolin. The town was originally settled in 1848 and was called Buffalo Wallow after a bison bone was found on the riverbank. A legend says that it was a buffalo jump, where Indians killed bison by stampeding them over the edge of a bluff. In the early days, Buffalo was a stagecoach stop on the eastern branch of the Louisville and Nashville Turnpike. Now, with the turn of the century in sight, Buffalo had "two general merchandise stores, two grocery stores, two millinery stores, four dressmakers, two livery stables, two blacksmith shops, two churches, four preachers, a grade school, a drugstore, an implement and hardware store, a furniture store, a lumber mill, a printing shop, a telephone exchange, a piano dealer, a photographer, a barbershop, a bank, a tobacco warehouse, a dentist, three doctors, five carpenters," and a two-year school called East Lynn College. It was the perfect picture of a cultured, energetic town. All that held Buffalo back was the lack of a railroad connection. Hodgenville got the spur line instead and it became the county seat. But Buffalo was *the* town in LaRue County.[14]

Its leading citizen was Edward Stanton Ferrill. In 1883, Ferrill paid $450 for the drugstore in Buffalo and was soon doing a remarkable $30 worth of business every single day. Ferrill's profits jumped even more when, as a sideline, he began to sell salt as both as a retailer and a wholesaler. Next came farm implements and fertilizer. After that Ferrill added lumber, hardware, stock feed, nails, and even Florida oranges. Ferrill's agents spread out through the thirty surrounding counties. In 1901, Ferrill became the president of the town bank, but he never left the business that gave him his start. He kept his desk in the drugstore between his bank on one side and his hardware store on the other. He had the Carnegie touch and his profits increased every year.[15]

Ferrill may have been the most celebrated of all who pursued their dreams in the Nolin Valley, but the history of the region was shaped by the work of many men and women. And they represented many nationalities. The nameless Native Americans who came first, followed by the two Jacob Van Meters whose ancestry was Dutch, the Irishman Alexander McDougal, the Englishman Robert Hodgen, Adam Monin of Switzerland, the Germans George Highbaugh and Hyman Gratz, the African Americans Bishop and the two Bransfords—it was a colorful patchwork of settlers who had pieced together an attractive way of life along the river.

Another square was added to the quilt in 1883 when a party of Swedes settled near Bee Spring. They called their colony the "Scandinavian Temperance Colony" and they squandered no time after they arrived. First, they built a school and then a church, Sweeden Missionary Baptist. Soon after there was a gristmill, a saw mill, and a planing mill. The talented Norene family, who had journeyed from Sweden, began a small orchestra for the community. Their children performed on the accordion, flute, organ, violin, and guitar.

One of the founders of "Sweeden" reported, "Our colony is doing better by the week. We have recently got some settlers from Illinois, first class farmers—they have already their houses built." There were soon one hundred persons in the colony and another hundred scattered nearby along the Nolin, families with strong Scandinavian names like Olsen, Thunstrom, Seaburg, Bloyquist, and Bjorkman. Despite its good start, the colony was short lived. By the turn of the century the experiment was ended; even the Norenes had moved to Brownsville in 1896. But the little community named Sweeden remained, a reminder of the Scandinavian presence in the lower Nolin, and many still today trace their family history back to these industrious pioneers from the north country.[16]

And then there was the Scotsman Muir. There is a famous 1903 photograph showing John Muir, his long russet beard now turned gray, standing beside President Theodore Roosevelt atop a mountain in Yosemite. Muir was trying to persuade Roosevelt—successfully, in the end—to allocate more money for the administration of the park. Muir and Roosevelt shared a deep appreciation for the redwoods and mountain waterfalls of Yosemite, and, though neither man probably ever spoke of it, they also shared an interest in a far distant and far different locale, the Nolin River Valley. In Muir's case, the interest was botanical; in Roosevelt's it was historical. The specific object of Roosevelt's interest was the preservation of Abraham Lincoln's birthplace.

The cabin that Thomas Lincoln had found on the Sinking Spring Farm when he bought it in 1808 had led a troubled existence. Much of its history is given in affidavits collected by the Hodgenville law firm of Williams and Handley on behalf of the Lincoln Farm Association in 1906. In one of these affidavits, Lafayette Wilson stated that, in the spring of 1860, he had moved the cabin from its original site to the nearby farm of George Rodman and reassembled it, replacing a few rotten logs in the process. Rodman used the cabin as a tenant house. In another affidavit, Zerelda Jane Goff supported what Lafayette Wilson said and added details of her own. Mrs. Goff stated that she had known the Lincoln cabin since 1831 when she and her family moved to a farm adjoining the Sinking Spring farm. "I have spent many days when a mere child playing about the Spring and the Lincoln Cabin," she said. "I recollect the time these logs were taken away from the place—I mean the logs making up the original Lincoln Cabin ... these logs were taken up to the George Rodman place and were used by him in building a tenant house. This Rodman property is now the property of Mr. John Davenport." She continued that she "saw the cabin on the Rodman place which was built out of these logs from the Lincoln Cabin and recognized them from the manner in which they were hewn."[17]

In 1894, promoter Alfred Dennett bought the Sinking Spring Farm, and in 1895 he bought the birth cabin from John A. Davenport. His agent in the purchase of the cabin was James W. Bigham, a Methodist minister. Dennett had told him "to find and reconstruct the original Lincoln birth cabin." Bigham and his son moved the cabin back to the knoll above the Sinking Spring in November 1895 and took a series of photographs.[18]

In 1897, Dennett had the cabin taken down. It was shipped to Nashville. There, at the Tennessee Centennial Exposition, it was displayed with the poorly documented Jefferson Davis birth cabin. In 1901, the two cabins were again put on display, this time at the Pan-American Exposition in Buffalo, New York. After years of trying without much success to make a profit out of displaying the Lincoln and Davis cabins to the paying public, Dennett found himself to be in some financial trouble. The exhibitions came to an end, and then Dennett made

Lincoln's traditional birth cabin (Library of Congress).

a mistake that has confused the matter of authenticity ever since. He stored the logs of the two cabins—142 pieces in all—in the basement of the Poppenhusen Mansion in College Point, Long Island. There the logs rested, safe from the weather, but pitiful and ignored and apparently intermingled.[19]

In 1905, Richard Lloyd Jones, editor of *Collier's Weekly*, was able to interest the magazine's owner, Robert Collier, in a proposal to buy the farm in LaRue County and return the cabin to it. The deal was concluded the next year. They bought the farm and bought the logs that were stored in Long Island. They also organized the Lincoln Farm Association for the purpose of raising funds to erect a classical memorial to Lincoln on the land of his birth. The L.F.A. moved the logs to Louisville in time to reconstruct the cabin for viewing at Kentucky Homecoming Week. In their haste or in their ignorance, the builders mixed up the Lincoln/Davis logs and ended up with a monstrous hybrid of a cabin with all of the windows and doors in the back wall. After a week, the cabin was dismantled and the logs were stacked in a Louisville warehouse. For the next three years they rested there while the L.F.A. perfected a plan to have the site in LaRue County ready to receive visitors on the centennial of Lincoln's birth, February 12, 1909.[20]

On February 10 of that year the logs were loaded in an Illinois Central baggage car and sent to Hodgenville where they were reassembled on or near where the wandering birth cabin of Lincoln had originally stood. This time, there was no mixing of the logs; the reassembled cabin was identical to the one shown in Dennett's and Bigham's 1895 photographs. February 12 was a gray, wet day. The eight thousand people who came early saw that a tent was pitched on a platform draped in patriotic bunting and the whole stood on the hill above the spring. Architect John Russell Pope's granite and marble temple which would eventually shelter the cabin was not yet begun. The cornerstone, suspended from a crane above, was to be laid this day.[21]

After a while, there was a stir among the crowd and through the middle came President Theodore Roosevelt. With less than a month left in his term of office this was one of his last public acts. Roosevelt climbed atop a chair to deliver his appraisal of Lincoln's influence on the Presidency and on the country he saved. Roosevelt praised Lincoln's patient, methodical leadership during the Civil War and the effort to end slavery. He spoke of Lincoln's sound common sense. When Roosevelt was done, a signal was given and the cornerstone was lowered. Roosevelt placed inside, among other documents, a copy of the United States Constitution. A copy of the Emancipation Proclamation was also put inside, but not by the hand of the President. I.T. Montgomery, a former slave, once the property of Jefferson Davis, laid the Emancipation in the cornerstone and spoke of the gratitude felt by those he represented on this day, "ten million Negro citizens." Theodore Roosevelt applied the first trowel of mortar and the ceremony was concluded.[22]

Two years later President William Howard Taft came to dedicate the memorial building and five years after that, his successor President Woodrow Wilson, traveled to LaRue County to accept, on behalf of the American people, the farm and an endowment fund of $50,000.[23]

Nowadays, skeptics consider the cabin a piece of fraudulent bunk. They point to an affidavit from a local deponent in 1906 saying that the cabin memorialized in Hodgenville was not Lincoln's birthplace, without mentioning the other affidavits from the same period that affirm the cabin's authenticity. They say that the cabin was not built of old growth timber, asserting that this proves its relative youth, forgetting that there *was* no old growth timber in the "Barrens," a region of so few trees that even a riding switch was a rare find. They say that visitors to the old farm in the last years of the nineteenth century found no cabin, without telling what the locals all knew, that the little cabin on the Sinking Spring Farm had been moved the short distance to a neighboring farm in 1860.

They point out with satisfaction that a dendrochronology test performed on the cabin in 2003 showed the cabin dated no earlier than

1848, without mentioning (as was told to the author by one who was in a position to know) that only the newest logs were tested because the older logs were too fragile to risk. The National Park Service itself decided in the 1940s that the cabin should be called "symbolic," but in an earlier, less cynical time, Mark Twain, Ida Tarbell, William Jennings Bryan, Theodore Roosevelt, William Howard Taft, Woodrow Wilson, Chief Justice Charles Evans Hughes, and others believed there was no doubt that they were contributing their money and prestige to the preservation of the authentic cabin where Lincoln was born. The respected Lincoln scholar Louis A. Warren wrote in 1926, "There is no question in the mind of the writer that the logs now comprising the Lincoln cabin, with the possible exception of a few used for repairs, are the same as those purchased by Dr. George Rodman and removed from the Lincoln Farm about 1861." Some scholars closer to the present time agree that there is a certain degree of authenticity to the cabin. Lowell Harrison says in his 2010 book *Lincoln of Kentucky*, "It is believed that at least some of the logs had been in the original structure."[24]

Abraham Lincoln received only three votes from LaRue County in the 1860 election and only six in Hardin County. His armies had marched across the Nolin River Valley, had spilled blood there, and finally had freed the slaves. His assassination had been cheerfully greeted in Elizabethtown. Over the years, attitudes changed, and on February 12, 1909, Abraham Lincoln, a son of the South Fork, found honor, at last, in his own land.[25]

Eighteen

Progress

Imagine White Mills in 1914. The houses are all white and splashes of sunlight dapple the lawns that slope down to the river road. Vacationers are arriving by surrey from the Illinois Central Railroad depot at East View. They may have to board with the townspeople; the Hatfield Hotel (twenty-two rooms with a one-hundred-guest dining room) and the larger Richardson Hotel (fifty rooms and a dining room with seating for two hundred guests) are full. The Richardson Hotel, the largest frame house in Hardin County, is particularly popular. For $4 a week, a guest gets a room and three meals a day for seven days. "The table will be supplied with the very best and be served in the country style," one advertising pamphlet promises. "We grow our own vegetables, and they come fresh from our garden each day to the table. We serve you fried chicken and country ham." The guests appreciate the efforts of the kitchen staff and find that the clean country air has a salubrious effect on their appetite. Some groan in letters home that they ate an entire chicken and all the fixings. On Sundays there are often three sittings in the Richardson Hotel's dining room. A postcard from Katherine and Dora to Miss Katherine Michael of West Market Street, Louisville, says, "This is our fourth day here and we like the place fine."[1]

More than the food, though, the Richardson Hotel has a nightly display that dazzles even city people: a galaxy of electric lights, hundreds of them, given power by a generator turned by the water falling over the mill dam. They shine like the Milky Way in the otherwise dark village. "What a wonderful sight it was to see," Josie Richardson later remembered.[2]

After the meal, there are comfortable chairs beckoning in the shade of the maple and locust trees. For those who would rather, there are motorboat excursions up to Dead Man's Cave or Pearl Island. The Richardson Hotel has a fleet of twelve rowboats, twelve canoes, and one powerboat for the use of the guests. The water calls, but not until the specified thirty minutes for digestion has passed. Killing time until then, half-clad bathing beauties parade down the road, a pleasure to some and a torment to others. So scandalized is Charles Nelson of White Mills that, in a few years, after he becomes a representative in the General Assembly, he will introduce a bill to end the daily beauty pageant. "It's perfectly disgraceful," Nelson will say, "the way they walk around right into the post office and department stores and everywhere. They never think of dressing any other way until it's time to dress for the ball." Oh, the ball! There is a nightly dance at the dance hall between the hotel and Dan Wortham's 1855 gristmill. Bands come from as far away as Bardstown to play. Comfortable lodging, excellent food, swimming, boating, bathing beauties on parade, and nightly dancing—with all of these attractions, it is not hard to understand why White Mills was chosen for the 1911 convention of the Kentucky Pharmaceutical Association.[3]

Those tourists who cannot put their business entirely out of mind can call the office from the telephone in Spurrier's store, and those who are not interested in river scenery pass their vacation in the wood paneled hotel lobbies just chatting with the other boarders or reading magazines. The Hatfield Hotel subscribes to half a dozen or more, *Ladies Home Journal*, *Country Gentleman*, and others. More serious readers may get a book at the village library, operated by the White Mills Glee Club.

And, of course, there is church on Sunday. The 1839 Union Church has amicably divided. The Baptists built a church in 1901 on the other side of the gravel road from where the Union Church once stood, directly across from Dr. Clyde Carroll's office. The Christians remained within a few yards of the old church site and on the same side of the road when they built a new sanctuary in 1907. On warm Sunday mornings when the windows are open, the beautiful hymns coming from the Christian Church echo along the river like heaven is descending. Catholics can travel a mile or two out of town to St. Ignatius at Harcourt. A small Catholic colony of five families settled near Harcourt in the early days and worshipped in the home of Sylvester Boarman. His leadership "led to the 1842 construction of the first St. Ignatius Church," but there's a new church now on the main road between White Mills and Sonora. Catholics spending a week or two on the Nolin can attend Mass there. Methodists and Presbyterians vacationing in White Mills have to improvise.[4]

Whatever a vacationer does in White Mills in 1914 is accompanied by the hypnotic background music of water going over the milldam. It is no mystery why the city people return year after year to this little village for their summer vacation. White Mills combines the best of scenic beauty, a tranquil pace of life, and modern conveniences enough to satisfy any ordinary needs. But for the people who *live* there, White Mills is just as appealing. The gristmill has been joined now by a flax mill and two carding mills. The town also boasts a saw mill, a planing mill, three stores, and two blacksmith shops. For a small village of its size, there is an impressive professional population of two dentists, three doctors, three preachers, two music teachers, and nine school teachers. The Elizabethtown *News* gets it right when it later describes White Mills as "A splendid and hustling little village."[5]

The whole valley was this way, prosperous and happy. Since the turn of the century, new banks were started at Buffalo and Nolin. Farm prices were good and small industry was thriving. All along the river one still found the various types of water-powered mills. There were sumac factories, and some mineral production. Down in Edmondson County there was a booming business in the production of rock asphalt, dug from the ground and exported to wherever paving material was needed.[6]

The nearness of rock asphalt deposits made it ironic that the valley's own roads were still gravel and dirt. They could have been better, it is true, but two good railroads served the region, and when travel was impossible there were telephones, not only in White Mills, as mentioned, but also in Millerstown, Sonora, and the other small towns. One was never completely cut off from the news and gossip. There were abundant amusements to be found, sponsored by different civic groups in the valley: community glee clubs and libraries and baseball teams, in addition to the political speeches in campaign season, the visiting lecturers, and the traveling carnivals. Millerstown, especially, was known "as a good show town." The visit of one traveling circus was memorable for the elephant that broke free and plunged into the nearby mill pond. A crowd gathered on shore to watch as the elephant "proceeded to stroll along the Nolin River bottom with only the tip of its long truck showing." This was undoubtedly the first pachyderm that had bathed in the Nolin River since the Ice Age. The trainer frantically walked up and down the bank, following his submerged elephant by watching the tip of his truck above the surface and trying to find a way to lure him back to dry land. Nothing worked until the elephant himself "finally tired of the sport and emerged."[7]

The twentieth century was in full swing. The valley of the Nolin was enjoying many modern amenities without having to surrender much of its traditional charm and habitual tranquility. Back in the early seventies, Colonel George Armstrong Custer and a detachment of his 7th Cavalry were posted in Elizabethtown to suppress

moonshining and Ku Klux Klan activity. He found so few lawbreak-
ers in the area that he was bored. He visited Mammoth Cave. He
attended the races and horse sales in Louisville, hunted foxes with his
pack of hounds down the Nolin Valley, and wrote the articles for *Galaxy* magazine that were later collected into the book *My Life on the
Plains*. The harmony that Custer had found forty years earlier still
prevailed. While blood feuds and night riders kept other sections of
the state in an uproar, the valley of the Nolin was peaceable. The state
militia never had to be called in to quell disturbances there. Crime
was uncommon along the Nolin River.[8]

Still, it was not completely unheard of. One notorious case was
that of Silas Esters, who was accused of forcing a fifteen year-old boy "to
commit a crime." Esters was jailed in Hodgenville. At two in the morning on October 31, 1901, a mob of LaRue Countians went quietly to the
jail, demanded the keys to Esters' cell, and dragged him outside with a
noose around his neck. Esters slipped the noose and made a run for it,
when the white men, "crazed with anger, made after the negro, howling and firing at him with guns and pistols." Esters fell, and the mob
dragged him back to the jail where they hanged him. A photographer
captured the ghoulish scene, and then, the newspapers said, "the members of the mob quietly dispersed and went to their homes."[9]

Another lynching resulted from the murder of Deputy Robert L.
Reid on July 10, 1902. A party of black Hardin Countians were having
a picnic on Utopia Island in the river near Nolin. Deputy Reid was dispatched to the picnic, just as a precaution. A man named Harlan Buckles came down on the train from Glendale to attend the picnic, and
he was heard to threaten the deputy. No reason was given for Buckles'
grudge against Reid, but he was drunk and continued to make trouble
through the afternoon. Upon Buckles' third disturbance of the day, Reid
attempted to arrest him and was shot to death. Buckles stood trial for
the murder, was convicted and was sentenced to hang, but on appeal
the sentence was reduced to a life sentence. The law-and-order citizenry
was outraged and some of them decided to apply their own remedy to
what they believed was a miscarriage of justice. On November 16, 1902,
mob of fifty men approached the Hardin County Jail where Buckles was
waiting to be transported to the state penitentiary. Jailer D.B. Patterson was four blocks away, helping his brother load some livestock onto
a car down at the railroad depot. His son Leslie Patterson was on duty,
and when the mob presented their rifles and shotguns, he let them have
Buckles. They dragged the prisoner down to the Elizabethtown public
square and lynched him. The body dangled on display overnight and
was cut down by lawmen the next morning.[10]

There were other murders scattered across the years. Special Deputy James Wood and Hardin County Sheriff Robert McMurtry were killed in the line of duty in December 1914. It was understood that they were in a dangerous line of work and dealt with hard-bitten characters, but their murders were nevertheless shocking to a generally peaceful people. However, no crime outraged the community more or lived longer in its memory than the murder of Tom Tillery. It was particularly frightening because of its senseless, random fury, committed inside the victim's home by strangers who simply appeared in the middle of the night and began killing. On April 7, 1931, three black men drove down 31-W into Elizabethtown. They were Charles Rogers, Walter Holmes (who went by the alias Jack Strong), and Walter Dewberry, and they were on a crime spree. They had stolen a car in Chicago and burglarized homes all along their route south. They committed several home invasions in Elizabethtown before officers got on their track. Trying to escape, they ended up on a one-way street, and when they saw another car coming up behind, they left their own car and ran. They crossed farm fences and fields until they came to a railroad and followed it. About 1:30 the next morning they reached the Middle Creek neighborhood on the Hardin/LaRue County line.

Living near the tracks were Tom Tillery, a farmer, and his wife. The fugitives decided to rob them and take their car. They knocked on the farmhouse door. Mr. Tillery awoke and answered them from a window. They asked, as a deception, to borrow an automobile tire pump. He refused. They broke into the house and began firing their pistols. Tillery was hit in the abdomen. Mrs. Tillery crawled underneath the bed while they dragged her wounded husband out to the spiked cattle guard on the railroad tracks and began beating him. She could hear him crying for help. In another part of the house were her daughter and son-in-law, who, strangely, had slept through the commotion. Mrs. Tillery woke up her son-in-law. He heard Tillery say, "They're killing me," before he fired his shotgun in the direction of the assailants and they scattered.[11]

Mr. Tillery died at a Louisville hospital the next day. By that time Sheriff W.S. Long had deputized store-keepers and farmers and mechanics and they were combing the countryside in search of the killers. Dewberry was soon caught. Some in the posse were in a lynching mood and called for a rope, but the others put an end to such talk and returned to Elizabethtown with their prisoner. The newspaper said, "Vigilance of the officers, and the law abiding spirit of the people combined to defeat mob violence, though the circumstances were most provocative." Rogers and Holmes had hopped a train south, but they were arrested before the end of the second day, Rogers in Munfordville and Holmes in Bowling Green. They and Dewberry were taken to Louisville to wait in protective custody for their arraignment and trial.[12]

On trial day, April 28, the curious crowded the streets of Elizabethtown. Thirty extra deputies were on duty to maintain order and twenty state militiamen guarded the jail. The attorney for the defendants was jostled a bit on the street and had to be rescued. Aside from that, justice unfolded in an orderly and respectful way. Deputies searched people entering Judge George Hobart's courtroom for weapons, the doors were locked, and the trial began. The evidence against the accused was solid, two eyewitnesses testified to what had happened on the night of the murder and identified the attackers, and other victims of their crimes before the attack on Tillery testified as well. The jury convicted all three and sentenced them to die in the Eddyville electric chair.

Appeals delayed the executions for a year, but early on the morning of April 29, 1932, Rogers went to the chair. That morning, Holmes attacked a prison guard "with a crude weapon made from a water bucket handle" and inflicted a minor wound. When they came to get him for his execution, he threw a pail of hot water on two of them and brandished an iron pipe he had ripped from the plumbing. It took tear gas to subdue him. A priest escorted Holmes to the chamber, and he died. Dewberry lost his final appeal and was executed on November 10, 1933.[13]

Capital crime was not a frequent occurrence in the Nolin River Valley, but it did happen, and when it did, retribution was meted out. It was a sign of progress, however, that the citizens were beginning to rely on the justice of the courts rather than that of the mob.

NINETEEN

Hard Times

By the time of Tom Tillery's murder, hard times had come to the Nolin valley. The first signs of trouble came in the 1920s. World War I had touched the region heavily. The bond rallies were fun, but then the young men went off in uniform. When the war was won, many of the young men who had seen the world had little interest in returning to the Nolin. The population began to decline. The agricultural economy began to falter, always a foreshadowing of worse times to come. Some people got desperate. The manager (some say it was a cashier) at the Glendale Banking Company embezzled $19,000 in 1923 and the bank had to close the next year. The town, which had suffered a devastating fire in 1916, almost did not survive this latest disaster. The L&N Depot closed and the doctor left town.[1]

Some towns fought back. Millerstown historian Paul McClure says that his hometown was one. "On October 2, 1936, the people joined ranks to put on a School Fair, that was said by many to be the greatest day in the History of the Town. Numerous school children from the surrounding countryside (some of them dressed in costume) came and paraded with the Millerstown scholars through the town, and competed in many contests (for prizes) in the classrooms. There was a four-school, Invitational High-School Basketball Tournament [which Upton won] … An immense crowd of people came into town for the event, and the refreshment stands took in a whooping $150." It was a red-letter day, everyone had fun, but McClure had to admit that "it did no lasting good—and things soon returned to normal."[2]

The problems of the towns were just a magnification of the problems faced by individuals. Some men were skilled trappers and supplemented their income by selling mink and muskrat pelts, and some did a little moonshining, but those who relied strictly on farm wages were hurting. Farmhands earned only a few cents a day. The landowners themselves could not make any money. Tobacco growers sometimes received as little as $10 for their year's work and occasionally it was worse than that. L.H. Oldham's family remembers that he earned only thirty-eight cents for his 1932 tobacco crop. Still worse, farmers sometimes ended up in debt to the warehouse for selling charges. Paul McClure tells of a lady who, when presented with a bill instead of a check after selling her tobacco crop, said to the warehouse manager, "I'll pay you in the Sweet Bye-and-Bye. If I go to Heaven I'll send it to you; and if I go to Hell, I'll hand it to you."[3]

When a farmer could not earn the money to pay his bills, then more stores had to close, and the hard times spread and got harder. Even nature seemed to turn against the people and the gentle Nolin went on a tear. Once before, in 1854, it had gone mad and washed away the mill at White Mills; 1880 was another flood year. In 1937, the river decided to flex its muscles again. Early that year a blizzard struck, then a cold snap froze the ground, and after that came ten days of heavy rain. With the river full and the ground so hard that the rain could not sink in, the water inexorably rose. It rose with surprising speed. Ern Joyce, the storekeeper at Spurrier, loaded his inventory into two boats and stored it in a nearby barn. The water was ankle deep when Joyce began emptying his shelves; it was waist deep by the time he finished.[4]

At White Mills the river rose five feet over the floor of the 1899 bridge. There was woven wire on the sides of the bridge, and the wire caught all the debris coming down the river. Trees, furniture, outhouses, and all kind of trash piled up until the bridge began to bow in the middle; it was feared it would collapse. The dance hall washed away. The river spilled into the two hotels, and the school closed. The post office floated away. People were stranded. They ate what they had, and then they ate what was left, sometimes only lard and flour.[5]

Though they were themselves suffering from the effects of the flood, the people of the Nolin Valley who could aided refugees from hard-hit Louisville. Glendale sat back from the river and was safe. It provided shelter for several Jefferson County families in the high school gym, and local people brought them food, bedding, and linens. Warm food and dry shelter were precious, for the weather had remained cold; sleet fell from the clouds and there was skim ice in those places where the water was still. After a few weeks the river began to behave again. The refugees went home and the people of the Nolin, poor from the Depression and made poorer by the flood, struggled to repair their houses and prepare for the planting season to come. In the trees hung the bloated carcasses of drowned animals.

The great 1937 flood was just another blow to a country already reeling under crushing economic strain, but the strain was not distributed evenly. Take, for example, E.S. Ferrill over at Buffalo. In 1932, by which time the economy in most of the small town in the Nolin Valley had collapsed, Ferrill had $250,000 in sales. The Depression did not noticeably hinder him. By 1940, sales had grown to $1.25 million per year. The *Saturday Evening Post* featured Ferrill in an article that spelled out the secret of his success: no debt. He never added a new line until he could pay for it in cash. The business itself was made to pay for every expansion. His one indulgence may have been the fourteen-room mansion he built in Buffalo and named "Ferrilland." Indeed, the name might have been applied to the entire region, his entrepreneurial empire.[6]

Another place where business went on in some semblance of normalcy was at Kyrock in Edmundson County. Kyrock was not only the trademarked name of the product of the Kentucky Rock Asphalt Company but also the name of the town that was occupied by the company's employees. Kyrock was a nationally known product used in the paving of city streets. Deep veins of rock asphalt ran through the company's quarry, 235 feet above the Nolin River. The processing mill was lower down the bank, and at the river's edge barges waited to take the product down the Nolin and the Green to the L&N Railroad near Bowling Green. From there it went all over the U.S. The Depression killed off five of the seven rock asphalt companies in western Kentucky. The Kentucky Rock Asphalt Company was one of the two that survived, and the men were grateful for a good job when they looked around and saw so many who had lost theirs and had to turn to other means.[7]

Most fortunate, perhaps, were the few who made it through the Depression because of the oil wells on their farms. There had been a tentative attempt to find oil in the Nolin Valley right after the turn of the century, and a small quantity was found but it was so expensive to extract that it was unprofitable. However, with oil selling at $1 a barrel in 1930, a new attempt to find oil in Hart County was called for. This time, the wildcatters had greater success. They drilled on the farm of Eli Bradley in March 1931 and, at a depth of 850 feet, they discovered oil. It was a good find, and it encouraged others to drill. Eventually, three hundred holes were drilled to tap into the underground reservoir named the Logsdon Valley Pool. Nadine Hawkins, writing in the July 1992 Hart County Historical Society *Quarterly,* explained, "Landowners were paid a flat price per acre for the oil and mineral rights to their property, with the promise of one-eighth interest in whatever oil was sold." It was a fortuitous turn of the wheel and it helped a good many families make it through the Depression, but not every farm sat upon a pool of oil.[8]

The widespread hardships of the Great Depression could not be overcome by individual good fortune or by individual efforts. A collective effort was needed to correct the underlying conditions and give the people relief. President Franklin D. Roosevelt later explained what he understood government's role to be in fighting the Depression, saying, "as new conditions and problems arise beyond the power of men and women to meet as individuals, it becomes the duty of government itself to find new remedies with which to meet them."[9]

One problem that held back the rural people of the Nolin Valley in the 1930s was no electricity. No lights in the barn, no lights to study by. No electricity for the washing machine, no electricity for the stove. No power for pumps to bring water into the house, no power to bring the news and entertainment of radio into the home. Thomas Edison had invented the light bulb in 1879, but the urban plutocrats of private interest saw no profit in building power generating plants and stringing lines to the farm house and the general store, so for sixty years the people had lived without—held back and then ridiculed for being backward. By 1938 electric power was still not available to over ninety-five percent of Kentucky's farms. It was time for the "government itself to find new remedies" to this disgraceful inequity. In May 1935, President Roosevelt signed the executive order that created the Rural Electrification Administration whose job it was to furnish loans for the electrification of America's rural areas.

Once the REA made federal dollars available, a temporary board of directors met in Elizabethtown to draw up incorporation papers for the Nolin Rural Electric Cooperative Corporation, serving Hardin and LaRue Counties. The Nolin RECC charter was granted on July 20, 1938. A door-to-door drive for subscribers at $5 apiece was undertaken to get the required 588 customers. The $5 fee to sign up was pretty stiff for the Depression farmers who got only four cents a pound for hogs and seven cents a dozen for eggs, but the farm families signed up. They knew what electricity could do for them and they wanted it. For those who remained not quite convinced, a vigorous ad campaign was launched in the local papers. Articles extolled the benefits of electric power on the farm and cartoon strips illustrated the ease with which traditional chores could be performed once electric power was available. The Hardin County *Enterprise* ran a chart in its June 29, 1939, issue showing how many kilowatt hours were required to do various jobs: the tired farm wife learned that one hundred pounds of butter could be churned at the cost of one kilowatt hour, and the overworked farmer read that three kilowatt hours was more than enough to thresh one hundred pounds of grain. The public relations efforts of the government were very persuasive. In the first month alone, over five hundred Hardin Countians signed up with Nolin RECC.[10]

They showed their support in other ways, too. Did the linemen want to put a pole in some man's tobacco patch? He agreed to it. Was it close to dinnertime? The farm wives cooked the linemen a hot meal and just stretched their kitchen supplies a little farther. After the survey-ors drove stakes to mark an easement, they often came back to find the trees already cut and the right of way cleared. Farmers loaned out their mules and tractors to get the electrification project done. Everyone was eager to retire the old kerosene lamps. Electricity was coming!

On December 10, 1938, REA provided $328,000 to string 301 miles of line. Customers would pay $3, minimum, for forty kilowatt hours with a charge of five cents for each extra kilowatt hour. The lines were energized on July 1, 1939. On that day, the rural people of the upper Nolin were freed from the tyranny of darkness. One remembered, "It was just like a big new world the day they turned the lights on."[11]

The New Deal was felt strongly in the Nolin Valley. Most trans-formative was the Nolin RECC, but that was not the only benefi-cial government program. Much of the 1930s landscaping at Lincoln's Birthplace was done by the PWA, for instance, and the WPA built new schools. Another was the Civilian Conservation Corps. This program was proposed by FDR only five days after his inauguration on March 4, 1933; he signed the bill creating it on March 31. By the end of July, 1,300 camps dotted the U.S. They employed an estimated 275,000 enrollees. In Kentucky, the final tally of young men in the program was more than 89,000.[12]

The CCC was intended to employ young men between the ages of eighteen and twenty-five to work primarily, as the name indicated, at conservation: reforestation, planting ground cover and terracing to pre-vent erosion, clearing fire breaks, and so on. The government paid the enrollees $30 per month, of which $25 was sent home, or if they had no families, put into a savings account, where it was held until the man left the CCC. A handbook warned them that CCC life was different "than most boys have known.... He lives with 200 other men of his own barracks. They work, play and eat together. Learning to get along with 199 other men without hurt feelings or broken noses is one thing every enrollee must learn while in camp." The camps were run army style. There was one at Elizabethtown, one at Leitchfield, and four at Mam-moth Cave (one for black youths and three for whites). Their mission was "the massive job of creating trails, both above- and underground; building park structures and roads; clearing landscape; planting trees; and installing modern utilities in the park."[13]

The Mammoth Cave companies performed their mission admira-bly. Superintendent R. Taylor Hoskins reported that in twelve thousand man-days of work, the Mammoth Cave CCCs made twenty-four miles

CCC Workers at Mammoth Cave Park (photograph courtesy Mammoth Cave National Park's Museum Collection, Mammoth Cave, Kentucky).

of walking trails, made fifty-three miles of gravel road, and planted 750,000 trees, in addition to laying untold lengths of sewer line and stringing miles of telephone wires. The Kentucky boys who served in the CCC worked not only in the national parks, but also created the commonwealth's impressive system of state parks, including Cumberland Falls, Natural Bridge, Pine Mountain, and Columbus-Belmont. Equally important, historians Lowell Harrison and James Klotter say that the CCC "helped awaken the people of Kentucky to environmental matters."[14]

There were detractors, naturally, who claimed the corps was just another example of governmental overreach, a boondoggle and a waste. The term "socialism" was bandied about. However, the critics' arguments appear short-sighted and shallow when one reflects that there were three to four applicants for every opening, and that the fortunate chosen ones gained an average of three to four pounds and grew nearly an inch in height in the camps. These were boys whose growth had been stunted by malnutrition during the earlier years of government nonchalance; three square meals a day remade them.[15]

Those who served in the CCC talked of their experiences in the corps with pleasure until the end of their lives. Many attributed their very survival during the Depression to their service and credited the CCC with being the seed ground of their later successes. They never forgot, and neither should the many visitors to Kentucky's state and national parks forget these young New Deal warriors and what they did for the commonwealth.[16]

The 1920s and 1930s were hard years for the people of the Nolin River Valley, but by the late thirties, conditions began to improve. Life became easier in some important ways, but in some other ways the Nolin Valley had paid a high price for its survival. The general store was gone; the bank was gone. The train depots had closed. Automobiles and improved roads meant that families could travel farther on their summer vacation, and quaint resort hotels like those at White Mills began going out of business. The locally made flour and cornmeal gave way to the regional and national brands. The valley's many gristmills fell quiet for the first time since pioneer days and their grindstones were carted away to become decorations for flowerbeds and driveway entrances. The young people moved to town for jobs. The subscription schools with their advanced curriculums failed when no one could afford to pay tuitions. Free public education took their place.

The Nolin River Valley had survived. But much of the charm was gone, never to be reclaimed.

TWENTY

The Nolin Today

When Dr. John Croghan died of tuberculosis in 1849, he bequeathed his Mammoth Cave property to his nieces and nephews. They maintained it as a tourist attraction. The guides during these years included Mat and Nick Bransford, who were contemporaries of the great Stephen Bishop. Beginning while they were still teenagers, the Bransfords learned not only the underground routes from Bishop, but also his confident demeanor, and they were popular with the tourists.[1]

Mat Bransford was the first of four generations of cave guides in his family. Mat had a son named Henry who was a guide between 1872 and 1891. Henry had two sons, Matt and Lewis, who became guides and their cousin Arthur (the son of John Henry Bransford, who was a cook at the Mammoth Cave Hotel) was a guide also. These men had sons who carried on the tradition.[2]

Dr. Croghan's last surviving heir, Serena Croghan, died in 1927. By that time, plans for a national park at the cave were already underway. Backed by the L&N Railroad, a Mammoth Cave National Park Association had been formed in 1924 and began buying up land, some of which was legally condemned by permission of the Kentucky General Assembly. The Association bought many of the lesser caves in the area, too, so that Mammoth Cave would be the primary attraction, but visitors would not enjoy the pleasure of being led through the cavern by those experienced and knowledgeable guides, the Bransfords. In 1937, they were made to give up their family's longtime vocation for a reason that is not good to think about—they were black, and African Americans were not then allowed to work for the U.S. government.[3]

The government officially took charge of the property in 1941, by which time the Association had displaced seven hundred families and acquired 48,000 acres. The park is larger than that today. Within the boundaries of its almost 53,000 acres, in addition to the phenomenal cave itself, hikers may see more than 1300 varieties of the plant life that so fascinated John Muir and may enjoy nature in the manner he did by camping in one of twelve primitive sites. One may experience the land almost as the Indians saw it. There are foxes and deer, blue heron and hawks, and even flocks of wild turkeys, birds that the Indians knew but which had disappeared until the government reintroduced them to the area.[4]

The cave remains a boon to the economy of the lower Nolin River Valley. Annual visitors number 600,000. In 2018, they spent $62 million on lodging, meals, and gasoline and helped maintain employment for six hundred locals. Ironically, the tourists who come to Mammoth Cave to enjoy a day in a protected natural setting may not realize that they are seeing a park in distress. "Code Red," an environmental study released in 2004, named Mammoth Cave as the second most air-polluted national park in the U.S. (only Smoky Mountain National Park was worse). From the park's hill tops, early explorers were able to see for a distance of up to 116 miles; now the air had become so thick with filth that visitors could see only fourteen miles during the hazy summer months.[5]

The Kentucky Department of Environmental Protection developed a plan to cure the air pollution in the park, but it anticipated a fight with the short-sighted, profit-above-all-else crowd in implementing it. By 2017, it appeared the for-profits side was winning. That year the N.P.S. gave Mammoth Cave National Park a "D for 'healthy air' and an F for 'seeing clearly.'" The park that contains one of the rarest of the earth's treasures continues to suffer in the name of the ready dollar. What would Stephen Bishop say?[6]

Man's interest in manipulating the Nolin River for his own uses dates back to 1811 when the state legislature funded improvements that resulted in a declaration seven years later that the Nolin was navigable in high water. In 1890, the U.S. Congress created Lock and Dam Numbers Five and Six on Green River, making slack water navigation on the Nolin possible. From 1906 until 1951, river traffic was heavy. After that, the business of transporting cargoes by river began to decline.[7]

In 1938, the year after the great flood, construction of a Nolin River reservoir was recommended and that same year the impoundment was "authorized by the Flood Control Act." A site was selected in Edmondson County. There were outcries that the region's best farm land would be flooded, but the *Courier-Journal* editorialized that flood control and the subsequent development of industries would offset the destruction of lower Nolin cropland and pastures. Construction began in 1959.[8]

The earthen dam, a short distance upstream from Dismal Rock, was completed in 1963 at a cost of almost $15 million. The impounded water behind the dam covers 14,000 acres (though the summer pool is smaller) where corn and clover once grew. The lake is thirty-nine miles long and has 172 miles of shoreline. Its watery fingers reach deep into Grayson and Hart Counties. The project has paid for itself many times over, saving "over $115 million in flood damages through 2014." Today, however, the historic mandate of flood protection is secondary to recreation in most people's minds. The roads approaching the lake are dotted with bait stores and gravel lots gleaming with neon signs and the newest model motorboats and trailers. Nearly 1.5 million boaters, skiers, campers, and fishermen come to Nolin Lake each year. What would Jacob Van Meter and Bambo say about the view from Dismal Rock now?[9]

When the Christians built a sanctuary in the shadows of the sycamores at White Mills in 1907, they felt they had found the perfect place to worship. In 1938, they decided to establish a summer camp in White Mills where young people could enjoy the river and study the Bible. The invitation went out. The first campers arrived on June 10, 1940, and stayed for five days. It was a success. The Christians continued their summer camp in White Mills through 1944. There was a five-year interruption when the campers went instead to the campus of Lindsey Wilson College, but they returned to White Mills in 1949 to the newly incorporated White Mills Christian Assembly. Twenty-five churches bought the Richardson Hotel and six acres of ground for $19,000. They removed the top story of the hotel, reducing the grand old lodge to two. Because they feared accidents, they tore down the old mill in 1954–55. The mill was the last one left standing in Hardin County, and it was so sturdy that the man who was hired to dismantle it was astonished at how difficult a task he had undertaken. The mill had withstood a hundred years of flood, Civil War, and hard times. It had gone through a succession of owners since Dan Wortham built it in 1855, and it was still strong, but the distant board in charge of the summer camp did it in. The efforts of locals to save it were of no use. The mill came down. Longtime resident Scott Morrison said, "It was a sad day when they tore it down. It was part of this community." Now it existed only in brown photographs and in the memories of those who had loved it.[10]

In the 1990s and early 2000s, the Christian Camp at White Mills continued to expand, buying up the old properties facing the river. The expansion included the traditional canoe launch site across River Road at the water's edge. In the memory of the oldest residents, the river bank had never been restricted at this point. Now, a chain was stretched across the entrance, and anyone who wanted access to the river and the small beach across the road from the Christian campus was required to register at the camp office. Another boat landing—more remote and with more difficult access to the river—was developed by the community downstream.

Camp expansion proved to be an inconvenience to some of White Mills' citizens, but the young campers enjoyed the new dormitories and the multi-purpose gymnasium and the open air pavilions where they took Bible classes and performed. White Mills echoed again with the laughter and shouts of young people having fun like it had in 1914. Fourteen hundred young people came from all over the state to worship and learn at the camp every summer. Fourteen hundred people at once—undoubtedly more than Benjamin Lynn had preached to in his entire life. What would he say now about the number of people coming down to the river to study the Bible?[11]

There was another expansion project on the Nolin at White Mills, this one secular. In 1990, just above Scott's Spring, Hardin County built a water plant that drew two million gallons out of the Nolin each day (out of the 130 million gallons that flowed past) and treated it to make it potable. The treatment plant cost nearly $4 million. It was named the Mary Ann Baron Treatment Plant in honor of the Farmers Home Administration director who obtained a federal grant to build the stately masonry and glass building with the purification equipment inside. An expansion of the treatment plant in 1998–99 increased its daily water-cleaning capacity to over eight million gallons of water, so much clean water that two million treated gallons of the Nolin River were sold to the Elizabethtown Water District daily. The expansion included a one million gallon water storage tank and a laboratory to analyze the purity of the water. As with the power lines of the 1930s, local citizens allowed an easement across their land for the water lines. For $325, county water could be brought to a person's property, and, as was the case with the Depression-era electricity, the water rates were reasonable: $12.58 a month for two thousand gallons or under and $2.49 for every additional thousand gallons. As of 2003, the White Mills treatment plant served thirteen thousand customers.[12]

Treating the water requires five steps: (1) River water is drawn into the plant where "activated carbon is added to kill unpleasant tastes." (2) The water is circulated through "claricones," each thirty-three feet tall and able to hold "up to 238,000 gallons," where the dirt in the water settles to the bottom. The sludge is pumped out from time to time and spread out on the property to level the rolling ground. (3) Clean water from the claricones is sent through filters of sand and anthracite coal. (4) The filtered water passes into "a closed system where chlorine and fluoride are added." (5) The water is sent to "clear wells behind the treatment plant." From the wells, which hold seven million gallons, the water goes out to the water district's storage tanks. To guarantee that these steps are adequate to the purpose of providing people with clean water, the plant tests almost "100 samples each month."[13]

Such exertions to make water pure enough to drink and people needing to pay money for it would have been a ludicrous mystery to the Indians who once lived in a Nolin Valley so pristine that *it* is a mystery to *us*. What would the Indians say to us about the way we have treated the river that was once theirs?

For fifteen thousand years the Nolin River Valley has been the hospitable home to a small but lucky population of people. We understand them and are connected to them through time by the one constant that never failed: the river itself. We feel a kinship with the Indians who loved the clean, quiet river for what it was and with the settlers whose muscles ached and twitched at night from the work of clearing the valley, loving it for what it could be. We can almost share the frustrated, bitter tears of those who watched marauders of both the Northern and the Southern armies ride away with their livestock and crops. We have all felt the easy peace of mind that comes with a gracious, mannerly way of life. Citizens of the Nolin Valley knew this feeling between the Civil War and World War I, and later they felt the relentless worry of not enough money and no sign of any and no choice but to pick up and try again tomorrow. We understand that, too. Who has not failed, no matter how hard the effort? They felt a pride of place that we had, too, as we came to a late understanding of the struggle to protect the river and the land. As usual, John Muir expressed it best. His words are both a challenge and a benediction for anyone who loves a land and the river that shapes it.

"Let the children walk with nature," Muir said, "let them see the beautiful blendings and communions of death and life, their joyous inseparable unity, as taught in woods and meadows, plains and mountains, and streams of our blessed star.... All is divine harmony."[14]

Part Three
Rough River

The Rough River Valley

Elizabethtown

Meeting Creek

Tules Creek

Rough River Lake

Hardinsburg

Leitchfield

Caney Creek

Rough River

Hartford

Muddy Creek

Livermore

Green River

Map by Sasha Jovanovic.

Introduction

"Don't write about it," was what the canoeist advised. "If you write about it, everybody will want to come."

He knew that Rough River is a hidden treasure. Except for a few places like the state park where the government impounded the waters of the Rough River to make a lake in 1961, the river is not easily seen. It runs through such rough country that the roads do not follow it closely. You can drive along the Nolin or the Rolling Fork for long distances, but not the Rough. If you want to see the play of sun on flowing water, the delicate rafts of floating sycamore leaves in fall, want to hear the splash of jumping fish and the barking of squirrels in the trees that overhang Rough River, you have to make an effort, for the river hides. In some places, the road is miles away.

The broken land that keeps the road at a distance is also what gives the river a beauty so rich that the canoeist wants to preserve all 136 miles of it as a state park. Until that happens, it would be better for the well-being of the river and its rugged valley if the people just kept away. "Don't write about it," he pleaded.

But it deserves to be written about. The shy river was the stage for as colorful a cast of characters as any in frontier Kentucky, for one of the most cold-blooded incidents of Civil War killing, and for a twentieth-century musician whose creative genius gave the world a whole new genre of music. There's something else. History, that most democratic of disciplines, belongs to all the people and it is the special birthright of the people who descend from the pioneers who fought for a land and river that they loved. It is their story and it ought to be told.

"Don't write about it," urged the canoeist.

"I have to," said the writer.

TWENTY-ONE

The Legend of Spanish Fort

From the very beginning, whites who wandered west called the river "Rough," a name of considerable accuracy but little poetry. As early as the spring of 1787, surveyors were using the name "Rough Creek," and six years later, it was used in the description of a grant of 75,000 acres made by Governor Isaac Shelby to a speculator named William Bell. The surveyors and speculators found the river very early by the white man's reckoning, but what of the people who began calling this valley home thirteen thousand years before Christ? By what name did they teach their children to call this river and its tributaries, the hollows and lookouts and the other features of the land? For that matter, what did they call themselves?[1]

The whites called them Indians and would have taken their land without a thought had they still lived there. But they had left. A century and a half before the whites came, the Indians had moved away, leaving behind only a smattering of clues as to how they lived and no clues at all to explain why they had gone. From out of the ground have come the treasures they left behind, the elegant Clovis and Folsom spear points, which the Ice Age hunters used to kill the woolly mammoth and the giant buffalo. The more commonly found smaller points, scholars explain, are from a later time and prove the passing of the Ice Age and the extinction of the large animals. Now the hunt was for deer and elk, supplemented by whatever nuts and berries might be found.

These gatherers and small game hunters often camped in the mouths of caves and in rock shelters when they were on the move. Their projectile points have been found in them, along with pestles, occasional fragments of pottery, and the scribbled images they left on the rock walls. Near Big Clifty in Grayson County, some forgotten hunter's petroglyphs are preserved. Incised on two sections of a boulder are "clear carvings reasonably identifiable as rabbit tracks between more northwesterly and centrally located paw tracks defined as raccoon. The more southerly section bears a clear bird track." Another display of pre–Columbian art is found in a rock shelter that overlooks the Rough River Reservoir in Breckinridge County. On a sandstone slab that fell from the roof, there are found "at least 14 bird tracks and a human hand print." What was the purpose of these petroglyphs? Was a hunter trying to summon animals to within range of his spear, or was he celebrating his prowess as a hunter? No one knows.[2]

These rock shelters were convenient stopovers for travelers, but the Indians became less migratory as time passed. They began to settle down in small villages near the rivers and their tributaries and to cultivate garden plots of goosefoot, little barley, and other indigenous plants. Shell mounds show that the river was another source of food. The natives gathered mussels by the thousands, and they made bone hooks to snag fish. Living in a more restricted area also meant dying in a more restricted area and disposal of the dead became a matter of concern. Often the dead were buried in shell mounds. Indian Knoll, a huge shell mound in Ohio County, contained 298 burials. Richard W. Jefferies says that some of the thousands of excavated Archaic graves in the Green River Valley contained grave goods such as shell or stone beads, tools indicative of gender, projectile points, turtle shell cups, "lumps of red ochre, bone hair pins, and conch shell cups." Some objects in late Archaic graves were made of copper. Over time it became more common to bury the dead in earthen mounds that contained multiple and successive burials. Sometimes graves were prepared with great care, lined with logs or with limestone slabs.[3]

The Rough River Valley is studded with Indian mounds. At places there are clusters of them arranged in patterns. Pre-Columbian remains that have been recovered intact have taught scholars that the people suffered from arthritis "and its effects are readily seen in the degenerations of joints," and that their teeth were badly worn from the stone grit that was in their meal. Skeletons from the later years of Indian occupation show a high percentage of wounds inflicted by the arrow, the club, and the stone-bladed knife. War came to the Indians in the end.[4]

From the graves, the village sites, and the mounds, scholars have developed an idea of how the first Kentuckians lived. They were pre-iron, pre-horse, and pre-literary—but not really prehistoric, though that term is frequently used. The objects the Indians left behind *are* history and inarguably the purest history, for they contain no hidden agenda and are not filtered through a pre-conceived point of view. The mounds and the simple relics of daily existence tell the unbiased truth and if they are sometimes misunderstood, it is the fault of the interpreter, not of the objects themselves.

And they have sometimes been wrongly explained. Overlooking

the Rough River four miles below Hartford is found the "Old Spanish Fort," a hill with nearly perpendicular sides crowned by eight flat-topped mounds, giving the appearance of a battlement complete with merlons and crenels. A 1902 item in the Hartford *Herald* said that no one knew who built it or how long ago, "all is mere tradition," but it was a "plain reminder of *the work of master hands*" (emphasis added).[5]

The prejudices of the time made it obvious that those "master hands" could not have been Indian hands, yet there it stood. To explain it, the legend of "Spanish Fort" was contrived: in the 1750s, a thousand Spanish explorers entered Green River from the Ohio and camped at the site of present day Livermore. A scouting party of three hundred men pushed ahead, up the Rough River, and built the "fort" to defend themselves against Indians. From it, "fifty men could effectively resist an army of 500." Despite the heavy labor involved in building the eight mounds, the Spaniards did not stay but a few days before moving out to rendezvous with the larger party which had continued up Green River. The three hundred got as far as the present site of Cromwell when they were attacked by Indians. The whole party was massacred. "Nothing was ever heard of the Spanish band after that day," the *Herald* said. All that was left was the fort itself, "a grim and mystic sentinel of the past."[6]

Today, no student of the period before white settlement takes seriously the claim that conquistadors explored so far north, much less that they traveled up the Ohio, the Green, and then the Rough to build a fort on an isolated hilltop, only to turn around and abandon it for a fight with the Indians. The colorful, racially biased explanation of the eight mounds of "Spanish Fort" was once accepted because it could *not* be accepted that the Indians were able to build such a thing. Never mind the fact that they did build such impressive works elsewhere, and never mind the lack of buttons, gun parts, or steel blades from the 1750s to support the claim of an army Spaniards tramping around in the valley of the Rough.

The Indians left Kentucky about 1600 CE for reasons that remain a mystery. There is only speculation about why they abandoned the land where they and their ancestors had lived. There were occasional hunting parties and war parties in the valley of the Rough for the next century and a half, but no one made his home along the Rough until the settlers began to arrive in the 1780s. The first and longest period of human history in the valley of the Rough was done.

TWENTY-TWO

Settlers and Speculators

The first explorers of European descent came to the Rough River Valley in the 1770s. The earliest record of a white man may be the tree in Ohio County on which was carved the name Leonard Helm and the date 1776. It is undoubtedly authentic. There are many phony Daniel Boone trees ("D. Boon cilled a bar"), but Helm was not famous like Boone. Why would anyone carve a fake Leonard Helm tree? This is not to defame Helm. He was a true frontiersman, an early resident of Harrod's Fort who later made a name for himself in the Northwest Campaign of 1778–79 during which George Rogers Clark wrested away from the British all the land between the Ohio River and the Great Lakes. This was after his visit to the Rough River country. If Helm had stayed, he would have been the founding settler and might have become a notable leader, but he returned to the settlements east of the valley. He was killed in Jefferson County in 1782.[1]

Others wandered through the valley of the Rough, but the name of the earliest settler there is disputed. There are two claimants to the honor. The first is a man named Blackford who built a cabin on Muddy Creek in 1780. The second is William Hardin, and whether or not he was first, he is the one who counted, for his settlement grew into the most important town in the region. Some say Hardin came to Kentucky in 1779, some say he arrived in 1780. Big Bill Hardin was described by Lewis Collins as a man "perfectly skilled in all the wile and arts of border warfare," one who was "cool, calm, and self-possessed in the midst of the most appalling dangers." The Hardins were a mighty tribe, and they made a distinguished name for themselves in Kentucky. Colonel John Hardin, the soldier and Indian commissioner for whom Hardin County was named, is said by some to have been Big Bill's brother, but he actually seems to have been a cousin. One of John Hardin's sisters, Sarah, married her cousin Ben Hardin and became the mother of the famous lawyer and politician, who was also called Ben Hardin. Another sister, Lydia, married Charles Wickliffe and became the mother of Charles A.

Wickliffe, governor of Kentucky, and the grandmother of Robert Wick-liffe, governor of Louisiana. Soldiers, diplomats, politicians, and plant-ers—his was the family that produced Big Bill Hardin.[2]

Hardin was a veteran of the Revolution when, in 1779 or '80, he led a small party down the Ohio River to settle in Kentucky. The land around the Falls (today's Louisville) looked too swampy, so they floated on down to near present Stephensport and this was where the group landed. They had moved inland about seven miles when they became aware of Indians close by. It was true that no Indians lived in Kentucky, but in these years the British north of the Ohio River were arming the tribesmen with muskets and hiring them to make raids into Kentucky and kill settlers. Hardin and his few men were not yet ready for a fight; they had just arrived. They decided to retire to Andrew Hynes' new fort in Severns Valley. About halfway there, at Big Spring, the Shawnee came swirling through the trees and attacked them. Hardin's men killed three of the Indians and lost one of their own. The other whites made their way to Hynes's where they wintered.[3]

At Hynes's Fort, Big Bill Hardin and his men were out of the val-ley of the Rough. Severns Valley is in the Nolin River basin. It was an area that attracted many settlers—there would soon be four major forts there, along with scattered homesteads—and Hardin and his men might have stayed there and made a success of it, but they did not. In the spring, they returned to the flat ridge that divides the waters of the Ohio River from the waters of the Rough. There, William Hardin, Christo-pher Bush, and Michael Leonard erected a log fort with two-story blockhouses on each corner and loopholes in the walls; they would be ready for the Indians next time. The Indians were a constant threat, but not enough of one to make the whites hunker down and live inside the fort. It was not long before Hardin's stockade was surrounded by cab-ins. A town was laid out only two years later. It was incorporated in 1800 and was officially named Hardinsburg with the creation of the post office in 1803.[4]

In the 1780s the question of whether the Indians or the settlers would prevail was far from settled. Individual settlers were ambushed; sometimes whole communities were taken captive. Canniness and luck were needed to survive. Hardin had both, and he became a leg-end among his red enemies. He was rumored so many times to have been killed that the Indians thought he was surely a ghost when he kept showing up. Hardin's medicine was big. His mere appearance in a fight could spook the Indians into flight or confusion. An Indian once sprang from his hiding place to kill the white man coming down the trail. He pointed his musket and suddenly recognized the man. It was Hardin!

The stunned Indian cried, "Hooh! Big Bill!" His hesitation cost him his life; Big Bill swung his flintlock and clubbed the Indian dead.[5]

Hardin did suffer his share of wounds, the expected peril of such an adventurous life. He once came upon a party of five Indians who instantly fired on him, killing his horse and wounding him in the thigh. Hardin took cover behind the dead animal and held his attackers off, swinging his gun in a threatening manner but not firing, "knowing he would be instantly killed ere he could reload." When men arrived to help, they drove the Indians back, and, it is said, returned to the fort with the Indians' horses as spoils of the little fight.[6]

The contest for horses was part of the deadly game Indians and whites played in these years. The Indians often lingered outside Hardin's Fort, watching for their chance. The settlers could not keep their horses inside the fort; the animals had to graze, so despite the risk, they staked out or hobbled the horses on the prairies nearby and let them eat. The necessity of it cost seventeen-year-old James Jolly his life. When he went out one evening to bring the horses in, waiting Indians fell upon him. A search party later found Jolly's mutilated body. All of the horses were gone, of course.[7]

Defying the danger, settlers continued to pour in. William McDaniels and John Bruner came to Breckinridge County from the Great Kanawha by flatboat. Once they landed, the men set out for Hardin's Fort to borrow wagons. While they were gone, the Indians attacked their wives and children. Scuffling with one brave, Mrs. McDaniels fell into the Ohio and was drowned. Mrs. Bruner, her child, and a slave were captured by the Indians and carried off toward the villages in Illinois. Angered that Mrs. Bruner and her baby were slowing them down, they took the child, suspended it from its wrists by a split in a tree limb, and shot it full of arrows. When the mother fought to save her baby, the Indians stabbed her in the leg and were about to kill her, too, when a warrior intervened, saying he wanted to marry her. The Indians killed the slave instead and took Mrs. Bruner north. The Indian did take her into his lodge, and she had a child by him, but after several years she made her escape with the help of some white men who ran a trading post near the native village. When the Indians came to trade, the whites "concealed her in a room and turned the key upon her, sending a messenger to her husband at Hardin's Fort with intelligence of her whereabouts." John Bruner came for his wife and returned with her to the fort. Bruner was luckier than the other leader of the colony, McDaniels. He lost his wife and, shortly after, his life. McDaniels and Samuel Spencer went out from the fort to bring in the cattle for the night. Indians were waiting in the woods. McDaniels was killed at first fire, but Spencer grabbed the dead man's gun and with it and his own killed two of the Indians. He made for the fort, reloading and firing as he ran. He killed three more of the war party and got safely inside the walls. As in the case of Jolly, searchers later found McDaniels' body, but the animals were gone.[8]

Such incidents fueled the constant warfare between the races, and the races took turns being the aggressor. Big Bill Hardin once led an expedition of eighty men across the Ohio River for a preemptive attack on a Native village that was judged too close to his fort. Arriving, the white men found the village to be nearly empty; the warriors had gone hunting and left only three guards behind. Hardin's men quickly killed the three, then deployed for the battle that would come when the hunters returned. They soon did, a party of eighty to one hundred men. The odds were even, maybe even slightly favoring the Indians, but Hardin's men had surprise on their side. The long rifles of the Kentuckians crackled and the war whoops of both red men and white mingled as the battle was joined. Near the beginning of the fight, Big Bill Hardin was shot through both thighs. He pulled himself onto a fallen tree and sat there astraddle, directing the fight. In the end, thirty of the village defenders were killed, many of them in hand-to-hand combat. The whites suffered eighteen killed and twenty-seven wounded. Lewis Collins said that this costly victory of Hardin's men was "unquestionably one of the most fiercely contested battles ever fought in the west." This was the kind of fight Bill Hardin understood, but like Daniel Boone and Samuel Goodin and a good many other "buckskins," it was in the entangling thicket of deeds, warrants, subpoenas, and depositions that Hardin lost his way.[9]

Hardin had been there first, and he claimed thousands of acres, but his land titles were never properly recorded, and he lost what papers he had when his cabin burned. What importance did such papers have, anyway? He had redeemed his land with his rifle and had signed for it in blood. Everyone knew his story. But he was caught up in the court system as survival gave way to civilization, and his taming of an untracked wilderness did not count for much. The first Breckinridge County Deed Book shows that, in trying to straighten out his growing financial complications, Hardin was in continual deals involving both land and slaves between 1801 and 1808. He bought some land, but he was selling more, and it was becoming known that land bought from Hardin may never have been Hardin's to sell. A revealing notice in Deed Book A for May 18, 1802, reads: "William Hardin bound himself that in case Balser Claycomb should be evicted from any of the within mentioned land, that other land would be conveyed, equal in quantity and quality." Hardin was sinking in debt and what he believed to be his greatest resource, his land titles, were increasingly considered as worthless by others. His setbacks left him bitter in his later years. He died in 1821. As if in a cruel symbolism of his life, his grave was poorly marked and today his exact resting place is lost.[10]

One of the men who was with Hardin at first and helped him build his fort did not stay to commiserate over his late-life troubles. Christopher "Christy" Bush had a Treasury Warrant in hand for two hundred acres, which he claimed on Hardin's Creek. He soon added hundreds of acres more to his holdings. But Christy and Big Bill had a falling out that eventually turned violent, a fight so injurious to each that a twin lawsuit was brought with both pioneers seeking a settlement from the other for damages suffered. About 1802, Bush sold or traded most of his Hardin's Creek property and moved to the Severn's Valley settlements. A new generation took up the feud in 1804 when Christy's son Isaac and Big Bill's son Elijah fought in Hardinsburg. Elijah shot Isaac in the back. Bush was taken to a doctor and clamped his teeth on a rifle ball while the bullet was carved from him. He survived both the gunshot and the surgery. Elijah Hardin was a minor, so Christy Bush brought suit against Big Bill once again and was awarded $1,500 in damages. Big Bill had no money; he paid Bush in land, a transfer recorded in Deed Book A "as settlement of a dispute between Isaac Bush and Elijah Hardin."[11]

Elijah Hardin's cantankerous nature was not cured by this legal remedy. He was later shot dead by a man with the unlikely name of Friend McMahon. Isaac Bush returned to Hardin County. In 1805, he and the Elizabethtown carpenter Thomas Lincoln took a flatboat of goods down to New Orleans, and in 1808 Lincoln bought from Bush the Sinking Spring Farm near Robert Hodgen's mill. Bush had built a one-room cabin on the farm and Lincoln moved his little girl and his pregnant wife into it. Six weeks later, Nancy Lincoln had her baby in that cabin, a little boy, whom was named Abraham.[12]

Thomas Lincoln later took his little family to Indiana, but he returned alone in 1819. His wife had died and he came back to Hardin County looking for Sarah Bush, Isaac's sister and Christy's daughter. She had lost her spouse, too, and Lincoln wanted to marry her. She agreed to his proposal, so he paid the debts she owed, stood up with her before a preacher, and returned to Indiana with her and her children. Sarah Bush Lincoln proved to be a good wife to Thomas and a nurturing stepmother to his two motherless children.

Samuel Haycraft, Jr., wrote of Christy Bush and his son, "There was no back-out in them; never shunned a fight when they considered it necessary ... and nobody ever heard one cry, 'enough.'" But, if Christopher Bush had not cried "enough" and left Hardinsburg for Elizabethtown, how much different might have been the life of Thomas Lincoln—and that of the nation.[13]

Thomas Lincoln knew the headwaters of Rough River well, for he worked near there at times, but it was not an area of burgeoning population. It was farther downstream, at Hardin's settlement, in the middle stretch of the valley of the Rough, and land still farther down, closer to the mouth of the river, that attracted settlers. Two brothers from Virginia, Joseph and Alexander Barnett, were the leading spirits there. Joseph Barnett was the older brother. He was a veteran of the French and Indian War, and both he and his younger brother fought in the Revolution, but they were in Kentucky by 1780, for in that year Alexander Barnett built Fort Hartford.[14]

Joseph Barnett was not with his brother at Hartford. He had lingered in what would later become Hardin County, and on June 18, 1781, helped John Gerrard and William Taylor organize Severns Valley Baptist Church. Sixteen days later, Barnett and Gerrard were among those who started Cedar Creek Baptist Church in Nelson County and Barnett stayed on as preacher there. Two years passed before Joseph Barnett moved west to rejoin his brother. He probably lived at Fort Hartford for the next three years, devoting his Sundays to preaching and the rest of the week to claiming land that would eventually amount to 9,800 acres on Rough River. He was a surveyor and had an eye for good land. In 1786, he established his own fort, Barnett's Station, two miles or so above his brother's fort.[15]

There, as at Hardin's Fort, the Indian threat was real. Martin Vanada learned this. He was caught unawares by the Indians near the mouth of Rough River. The tribesmen took their captive north and, to make sure he did not escape when they camped, they took the double precaution of tying his hands around a tree and slipping a noose around his neck and tying it to a limb. One day while the Indians were otherwise occupied, Vanada tore one of the metal buttons off his coat, bit it in half, and used one jagged edge to cut himself free. Nine days later, he came walking in to Fort Hartford. Not everyone was so resourceful or so lucky.[16]

The Indians attacked John Anderson's family, perhaps at their cabin or maybe it was when they were returning home from church—the accounts are not clear. Two of the Anderson children were quickly killed, and another brave attacked Mrs. Anderson with a sword. He was scalping her when Mr. Anderson turned his rifle on the Indian and pulled the trigger. The powder in the pan flashed; that was all. The rifle had misfired. The Indian finished scalping Mrs. Anderson before he ran away, but he dropped his sword as he did. Mrs. Anderson recovered and lived for another decade or so.[17]

The Barnett brothers lived long enough to see the days of such troubles end and see the settlement they had founded flourish. Alexander Barnett died in February 1819 and was buried in the Alexander Cemetery. His brother had preceded him. Joseph was one of the justices of the Hardin County Court of Quarter Sessions and had to travel 150 miles roundtrip each time the court met. It was during one such trip that he died in 1797. He was buried near Elizabethtown. His estate inventory covered thirty-seven pages of Hardin County Will Book A and was litigated in the Kentucky Courts for years afterward. Among those who acted as arbitrators between the heirs of Barnett's estate were some of Kentucky's finest solicitors: John Rowan of Bardstown; Ninian Edwards, future governor of Illinois; and Felix Grundy, future senator from Tennessee. Finally, even the state legislature became involved.[18]

The year after Joseph Barnett died, Ohio County was formed from Hardin. It originally contained 1,500 square miles, an area greater than Rhode Island. Gabriel Madison donated a tract out of his 4,000 acre Virginia patent for a county seat. The first court met in July 1799 in the residence of Robert Moseley, whose log home resembled a blockhouse, with the upper story overhanging the lower. The county jail was established on the lower floor and the courtroom was in the upper story, and there, Judge Henry P. Broadenax, a man "high-toned, honorable, and sensible, but petulant, irascible, and imperious," dispensed justice.[19]

Hartford was the southwestern point on the base of a large obtuse triangle. About thirty-five miles northeast of Hartford in straight-line miles was Hardinsburg, and about thirty-five miles southeast of Hardinsburg in straight-line miles was Elizabethtown. The line from there back to Hartford made the long, tilted base of the triangle. The trails connecting the points were long and lonely and it was natural that some pioneer visionaries soon understood the advantages of settling between the three. Well-situated, they could prosper by attending to the needs of the peddler, the itinerant preacher, the mail coaches, and any restless wanderer who found himself caught at nightfall between towns.

Rounding a corner of the trail in the slanting light of late day, the traveler would see a small spot of open ground that had been cleared of the overarching trees, and there would be a little cabin, maybe a dogtrot cabin with rooms on either side of a covered walkway, sort of an open-air room. The traveler could roll out his bedding and spend the night there when the weather was clear, or at least not windy. The open sides of the dogtrot offered little protection in a blowing rain.

Smoke from the cook fire rose in a blue curl from the log chimney and, sticking his head in the cabin door, our wanderer might smell cornbread baking and pork frying, maybe even coffee brewing. Behind the cabin, he would notice a single-pen barn. If our pilgrim was riding, he might stable his horse inside. If the weather was raw, he might sleep in the barn, too.

The business-minded settler was within his rights to expect pay of some sort for room, board, and the grain he provided for the traveler's horse. If the pay was in specie, it was likely to be a Spanish or French coin, brought home from New Orleans and put into circulation by some returning flatboatman. The settler or his son might eventually set up a forge and begin shoeing travelers' horses or resetting the loose rims on stagecoach wheels. They might add an ordinary and sell drams of fiery Kentucky whiskey from behind a wooden-caged counter. Since it was convenient to hold the mail for travelers, the government would establish a post office and people would come to pick up their mail, so the peddlers would stop and set up a stand and sell general merchandise to the crowd—calico and cast iron skillets, needles and thimbles, pewter buttons and earthen crockery. Maybe a ferryman would come and put an end to all that splashing across the river. Another man would come along and suggest a gristmill on the river to grind the corn and wheat of the surrounding farmers. It would be easy enough to add a water powered saw to make lumber from logs. There would be carpenters and stonemasons and a preacher to tell them on the Sabbath that they should not swear so much in their work. After a while, there would be a little cemetery beside the church where the old buckskin-and-homespun generation was laid to rest, and a second generation would take over with new ideas to make its settlement grow.

This was how a new town was born between the towns that started as stockades when the Indians lurked and Kentucky was still part of Virginia. Fordsville between Hardinsburg and Hartford was one such town. It was settled by the Huff family and named for Elisha Ford, Revolutionary War veteran and frontier preacher. Another of the connecting settlements between the points of the Rough River triangle was found in Howe Valley on the road that connected the Severns Valley settlements with Hardinsburg. Howe Valley is oriented east to west. It is bordered by high hills and sandstone outcroppings and watered by three springs: Roaring Spring, Pirtle Spring, and Stiles Spring. This wide valley was an attractive place to the pre–Columbian Indians (many stone relics have been found there), and it was attractive, too, to the settlers who came to live there in the first decade of the nineteenth century. John Howe and his family were the first settlers. Howe came out of the Revolutionary War with the rank of sergeant and a ruined arm, but he was a hardy man and lived long enough to make a good start in his new home. About the same time that Howe was settling in, George Klinglesmith arrived.

He built the first brick house in the valley. He hewed the logs for joists and rafters, made the nails by hand, forged the tie rods, and molded and fired enough bricks to make walls sixteen inches thick. The typical pioneer floor plan was used, a central hall with two rooms up and two rooms down, and the third story attic room was used as a hidey hole from the Indians. The outside buildings—"dependencies"—were used for cooking, laundry, and spinning. Thomas Lincoln is said to have done the cabinet work for Klinglesmith. He also made the mantles and some of the furniture, including one of his signature pieces, a corner cupboard. Lincoln was acquainted with other families who lived in Howe Valley, too, the Shipleys and the Geohegans among them.[20]

Klinglesmith's house was used through the years as a stagecoach stop and also as a meeting house for the Methodists when the circuit riders came by. It was certainly the most elegant house on the Hardinsburg Road and it still stands today, one of the finest old rural homes to be found in the valley of the Rough.[21]

Fordsville and Howe Valley were only two of the little communities that sprouted up along the trails between the larger towns, or near them. There were others like Vertrees and Beaver Dam; Dyer and Dundee; McQuady, McDaniels, Meeting Creek, and No Creek. Leitchfield in Grayson County was another. It was the largest of the connecting towns by far, but it got off to a slow start. The site was not on, but rather between Rough River on the north and Nolin River on the south, yet not very close to either. Without a navigable river nearby, there was little hope of economic development.

Benam Shaw built his station at the future site of Leitchfield. The year Shaw came to settle is not certain; even the modern historic marker about Shaw's Station does not specify a date. That uncertainty is typical of Shaw's story. Very little is known about him, less than about the founder of any of the other stations that grew into Rough River Valley towns. Even the preferred spelling of his unusual first name is disputed. What is known is that Shaw was in Severns Valley by 1779, and a creek there was named for him. He later sold his Hardin County holdings and bought land farther west, on Beaver Dam Creek. The fort that Shaw built there was the beginning of a town and of a county, but the people were slow to come.[22]

The problem was not entirely geographic. Partly, it was because the land belonged to absentee owners who had bought or bartered for acres there, or had received land grants for Revolutionary War service. Many of these men had no desire to move to the wilds between Elizabethtown and Hartford, but they did not want to sell it to settlers, either. The land was often believed to contain mineral wealth, and it would not do to sell the Rough River land before the extent of its hidden resources could be determined. Much wiser, they thought, just to hold on to the land and see what it might become in the future.

One such absentee owner was Henry "Light-Horse Harry" Lee. Lee was an aristocratic Virginian whose family had earned a lustrous reputation for its patriotism during the Revolution. They included members of the Continental Congress, signers of the Declaration of Independence, and foreign diplomats. Henry Lee's service during the war was of a more vigorous type. He was a cavalryman, and one of the few men for whom a grateful Congress had commissioned a special gold medal. Lee was a great soldier, but he was a wastrel, and when his finances pinched too tightly, he was not above taking drastic measures.

Lee had gotten his Rough River land as a bequest in the will of Lieutenant Alexander Skinner, who had been the paymaster in Lee's Legion during the war. Skinner had been granted the land by Governor Patrick Henry and now it was Lee's, but it would not be his for long. In 1788, Light-Horse Harry was experiencing one of his frequent monetary emergencies so he disposed of five thousand acres of his Kentucky land to his friend and idol, General George Washington. The price was a stallion named Magnolio, an animal Lee valued at £500. Washington wrote to Lee on November 30, 1788, that he was willing to part with Magnolio "because it is my intention to breed Mules only and for that reason wish to avoid expence of keeping Magnolio," and he noted the conclusion of the deal in his personal journal entry for December 9, 1788.[23]

Lee knew he never would remove to Kentucky, and for Washington, too, it was unthinkable that he would ever leave his beloved Mt. Vernon. Why then, this interest in obtaining from Lee this distant tract of land? Washington had an inscribed copy of *The Discovery, Settlement and Present State of Kentucke* by John Filson, presented by the author himself. In his book, Filson included a map that showed the very area of Lee's Rough River acreage, and a notation that the region contained "an abundance of iron ore." It was not such a far-fetched notion. On their land, Joseph and Alexander Barnett had a secret lead deposit from which they made bullets, and in the twentieth century, coal and oil resources would be profitably developed in the valley of the Rough. Even gold and silver were found in small quantities, but it was the promise of iron that attracted Washington.[24]

Washington's land looked sloppy and unattractive on the plat map. It lay south of a deep bend in the Rough, which gave the property the appearance of a scribbled letter "Y" turned backwards and tilted to the left. The river bounded it on the north for a distance of almost eight miles. The two tracts came together to form the bottom leg of the "Y." Washington was optimistic about the fortune to be made from his Kentucky land. All he needed now was the deed. Washington asked Light Horse Harry for the title to his land, but Lee delayed. Washington insisted. Lee hemmed and hawed some more. Maybe it was not altogether his fault. Maybe he himself had not gotten a clear title from Lieutenant Skinner's estate. It would not be the only example of an easterner who became tangled up in Kentucky's nightmarish system of land claims. In any case, while Lee delayed and Washington fumed, the cavalryman hit another financial rough patch. Desperate for funds, he sold seven thousand acres of Grayson County land to General Alexander Spotswood. It was in three tracts. Two of the tracts were the ones that Lee had already sold to Washington. It was a reckless, short-sighted plan. The swindle was sure to come out.[25]

Spotswood was thinking of relocating to Kentucky, and that spring of 1795, he went to view his purchase. While there, he fell in with Major George Lewis, whom Washington had sent to Kentucky, also to examine the Rough River land. Both Spotswood and Lewis had plat maps, and it was not long before they discovered a scandalous fact: Lee had sold the same land twice. When Lewis returned to Virginia, he reported to Washington what he had learned. At first, Washington refused to believe it was true. He wrote, "To suspect Genl. Lee of fraud in this transaction, I cannot ... the two sales cannot be for the same land."[26]

Spotswood insisted, "That he [Lee] Sold you these lands is certain, that he Sold them to me and got pd. is as certain, and as land is a thing never to be forgotten when once sold, I leave it to you to determine, what could be his motives for this double Sale."[27]

A court battle threatened before a resolution came in January 1797. On the 24th of that month, Spotswood wrote Washington, "General Lee and myself have cancelled our bargain for the ... land in Kentucky." Spotswood was out of it. Lee gave Washington the title he legally deserved in 1799. The land was Washington's at last.[28]

Before he was through, Light Horse Harry Lee ran through the fortunes of two wives, spent time in a debtor's prison, abandoned his family, and deceived so many of his friends that his reputation was gone along with his money. Only one thing rebounds to his honor, his undeniably great service in the War for Independence, but that is not what he is remembered for today. His name lives on because he was the father of Robert E. Lee.

TWENTY-THREE

Murder at Pine Knob

About a decade after George Washington obtained clear title to his Rough River land, Kentucky decided to take a portion of Ohio County and the western half of Hardin County and create from them a new county to be called Grayson, named after Colonel William Grayson, Washington's aide-de-camp during the war. A road had been "viewed" between Severns Valley and Hartford and stagecoaches found a convenient place to stop at a spring about halfway in between. It was here that they decided to place the county seat, Leitchfield, named after Major David Leitch. Really, Millerstown on the Nolin had a better claim to be named the county seat. Millerstown had more people. But from Leitchfield mule riders could get to and back from all parts of the county in one day, so Leitchfield it was. The year was 1810.[1]

The first court met around a wooden table set among the trees above the big spring where the stagecoaches stopped. Henry Broadenax was circuit judge, Ben Hardin was the commonwealth attorney, and Jack Thomas was the county clerk and the circuit court clerk simultaneously. Jack Thomas was only twenty, too young to legally serve, but he had been deputy circuit court clerk in his native Hardin County at age eighteen and had continued in that capacity ever since. Ben Hardin argued that new county government could get around the difficulty if Judge Broadenax appointed Thomas clerk *pro tem*. This Broadenax did. Thomas was officially appointed circuit court clerk a short time later when he reached the legal age and remained so for the next forty-one years. It is believed that Wash Bozarth was the first county judge—that fact, strangely, is not definitely known, but the first courthouse burned along with all the original county records, so there are some uncertainties about the early history.[2]

By the mid–1840s, Leitchfield had official buildings all around the public square. It had grown to a population of 130, about one-fourth that of Hartford and one-tenth that of Elizabethtown, but the population and the coach travelers passing through supported a considerable community of shopkeepers. Collins lists "three stores, one grocery, two taverns, two doctors, two lawyers, one saddler, one gunsmith, one blacksmith, one shoemaker [and] one tannery."[3]

However, it was not a likely center of commerce. Trade was difficult for the early settlers of the Leitchfield area. Since the rivers were not very near, many were compelled to take their surplus up the road to the nearest market, Louisville. It was a time-consuming trip, and if the men were driving livestock, one that required constant effort. The Muldraugh Hill trail was especially difficult. It was steep and many animals slipped and fell to their deaths. When the drovers arrived in Louisville with their herds, the animals had lost so much weight that they did not bring even a fair price, much less a profitable one. Knowing they were being cheated, yet unwilling to drive the worn-out cattle or hogs back home, the Grayson County men gritted their teeth and took what money was offered. Undoubtedly, they spent most of it before they ever left the city.[4]

Such economic setbacks tested severely the Christian virtues of the settlers of the Rough, but they remained a devoutly religious people. The Baptists, usually the first ones on the scene, had constituted Beaver Dam Baptist Church in 1798 and Rock Creek Baptist Church in the future Grayson County as early as 1802. They dominated the religious life of the region, but they had to wait a while longer for their most charismatic and successful preacher to appear. J.S. Coleman held the pulpit at Beaver Dam Baptist in Ohio County. He had forsaken his youthful ambitions for a political career to answer the Lord's call. Beginning his ministry in the 1850s, Coleman helped constitute eleven other churches and in the ordination of twenty other preachers, and during his career at Beaver Dam, he baptized upwards of 3,500 converts, many of them from other denominations. Spencer said they were "mostly from Methodists, next to Baptists, most numerous in his part of the state." The Methodists had organized Goshen, two miles south of Hartford, in 1804. Two more Methodist churches were organized shortly after, Bethel and No Creek. These early churches, said Methodist historian A.H. Redford, "were a nucleus, from which went out a fine religious influence into all the surrounding country." The "first and leading local preacher" was Thomas Taylor, who traveled constantly through the region, preaching, as it was said, "with words that burn."[5]

The Catholics also made their appearance in the county in the early years of the 1800s. In 1810, Father Charles Nerinckx came west from the Kentucky "Holy Land" of Washington, Marion, and Nelson counties to make a "missionary tour" of the Rough River region. He found ten Catholic families at St. Anthony's and decided to make his

"resident station" there. The next month, Nerinckx continued his journey, measuring the devotion of the Catholics he found, raising funds
through subscriptions, and inspecting different locations along the
Rough for mission churches. When he returned, he wrote a letter to
Father Badin in which he identified these places in the valley of the
Rough where Catholic churches could be built: Adams Creek, where
a Captain John Hanley had pledged four hundred acres to the church;
Panther Creek, six miles from Adams Creek; Clifty, where another five
hundred acres had been promised; Hardinsburg, where the church
had three hundred acres; and Hartford, where there were three acres
in town. Now the job was to build the churches, and that meant more
travel. Going from mission to mission, Nerinckx faced every kind of
danger. He nearly drowned once when a swollen river swept his horse
off its feet, and one winter night in Grayson County, when he had
become lost and was looking for shelter, "famished wolves scented him,
and came in hundreds, fiercely howling around him." He remained in
the saddle all through the harrowing night, shouting to keep the wolves
at bay. They vanished into the trees at dawn, and Nerinckx continued
on his way. Camillus Maes wrote that Nerinckx's "courage and vigor
seemed to increase with the labors and privations he had to endure.
As his courage, so neither did his cheerfulness, ever abandon him." He
worked constantly to attend to the needs of the faithful in a wide circle of wilderness that he had chosen as his vineyard. Father Nerinckx
gave Breckinridge County Catholics a proper place to worship in 1810
when St. Romuald Catholic Church was built at Hardinsburg, and he
founded Grayson County's first Catholic church, St. Augustine near
Grayson Springs, in 1815.[6]

The different denominations were a bit suspicious of each other,
especially the Protestant churches and the Catholics, and at first glance
seemed to have little in common, but there were found to be some
areas of agreement. If there was one thing in the life of Leitchfield that
united the strictly devout of all faiths, it may have been in their dis-
approval of the fiddle music that floated across the evening air into
their God-fearing homes. Many considered the fiddle to be a sacrilege,
the Devil's instrument. The music came from the combined cobbler/
cabinet-maker shop of Mordecai Lincoln, Jr. His father, Mordecai, Sr.,
was the older brother of Thomas Lincoln. Mordecai, Jr., was "skilled in
the use of tools," and he worked hard when he was in the mood, but he
was not always in the mood. He sometimes "drank rather too much."
William E. Barton wrote there were days at a time when Mordecai "for-
sook his work and loafed and told stories, or engaged in acrimonious
controversy." He despised Catholics—though his mother was one—and

liked to argue religion. He lived above his shop in a two-story cabin on the public square in Leitchfield. It was from the porch of his living quarters that he made fiddle music on summer evenings. Mordecai's fiddle was said to have been carved out of maple wood with a shoe knife in the hands of an old Revolutionary War soldier who lived over on Clay Lick Creek. Lincoln sat on his porch at night and played, "and would sometimes call forth responsive wild-wolf howls in the neighboring wood."[7]

It is remembered that Mordecai Lincoln was a dedicated bachelor, but it may have been more a case of disappointment than of disinterest. Barton asserts that Lincoln was involved with a Grayson County girl named Patsy, but one night he went straight from her house and left for Illinois, where his sisters and brothers and widowed mother lived. He left everything he owned in Leitchfield, and he never owned a fiddle again. Leitchfield had lost its eccentric cobbler, and his music was heard no more.[8]

It is also remembered Mordecai Lincoln was sometimes hauled into court for swearing in public, and that is fairly indicative of the nature of the crimes committed in the valley of the Rough. There was a little moonshining out in the hollows and, predictably, occasional arrests for drunkenness, but serious offenses were rare. The people were mostly good-natured and law-abiding. They were satisfied to tend to their own business and happy to let others do the same.

The first instance of a criminal fugitive running loose in the valley of the Rough seems to have been that of a slave named Jacob. In 1796 he killed his Hardin County master, John Crow, with an axe. Crow had accused Jacob of laziness. Jacob fled down the Rough River toward its junction with the Green. He was captured and taken back to Hardin County and hanged.[9]

Another case of killing that occurred elsewhere but ended up in the valley of the Rough was one involving William Smothers, the same man who won his freedom in a wrestling contest with Deputy Edward Rawlings, who had apprehended and arrested him. But that was another time. In this instance, an Ohio River flatboat had pulled ashore at Smothers' shack near Owensboro. Some of the crew went up to enjoy Smothers' hospitality. During their visit, a difficulty arose, and Smothers killed one of them. He escaped the dead man's crew mates, and went to Hartford where he surrendered. Joseph Hamilton Daviess volunteered to defend him in Judge Broadenax's court. The day came for Ohio County's first murder trial to be heard. Harrison D. Taylor writes, "Perhaps no trial in the county had ever before collected so great a crowd." Smothers was eventually acquitted, a judgment "generally approved throughout the community.... It was looked upon as no more criminal than to slay a drunken, lawless flatboatman of those days than to shoot a wolf or panther." Such men, says Taylor, were considered "a nuisance to the river border."[10]

Killing a fellow citizen was a different matter, as Francis Irvin found after he murdered William Maxwell over a legal dispute. Irvin was arrested, tried, convicted, and sentenced to be hanged on May 13, 1826. The great crowd that had gathered to witness the execution saw Irvin, dressed in a new suit of white linen, brought to the gallows in a cart. Standing up, he took "an enormous chew of tobacco," and buttoned up the rest of the plug in a coat pocket while the sheriff adjusted the noose. As he pulled the cap over Irvin's head, the condemned man lost his nerve and "clung to him like a drowning man, and the sheriff had to pull from him." The cart was driven away and Irvin fell. He gave a "few convulsive struggles," and Ohio County's first execution was done.[11]

Grayson County never had an execution during these years (and never had but one, and it was because of a change of venue); an irony because one of its citizens was the most worthy candidate for the gallows of anyone in the valley of the Rough, a murderous criminal whose record for homicide would match that of any other maniac in any other time or place. His den was about fifteen miles west of Leitchfield on the Old Hartford Road, in a narrow hollow between knobs two hundred feet high, shadowy with hickory, sycamore, and beech trees. In the autumn, the staghorn sumac turns blood red, a living reminder of the evils that once occurred there. This is Pine Knob and in the 1840s this was the realm of Dock Brown.

Dock Brown's real name was Guilliam Hopper, but he had good reason to travel under an alias. He was one of a wandering criminal clan that had left behind it a trail of larceny and murder in Tennessee, West Virginia, and Kentucky. When Hopper arrived in Grayson County in 1842, he introduced himself as Doctor G. Brown. His informal neighbors soon took to calling him "Doc," usually rendered in writing as "Dock." The year he arrived, he was joined by his brother Pinckney, who was on the run after cheating a man out of $7,000 in a livestock deal. Pinckney began calling himself P.H. Brown. They bought a farm at Pine Knob and built a two-room log cabin with a trap door fitted in the floor of the smaller room. A large cavern called Big Mouth Cave was on the property. It was a perfect criminal lair.[12]

Their first victim was a man named Frank Pugh. As was mentioned earlier, travelers on these lonesome roads were in the habit of stopping at the closest cabin when dusk caught them. At Pine Knob, darkness fell too early for Pugh, an innocent wanderer who stopped for the evening and foolishly bragged to the Browns that he was carrying $1,000. They invited him to go on a hunt that night. When the three stopped to rest at Big Mouth Cave, the brothers stabbed Pugh to death; stuffed his body in a crevice in the cavern; and returned to their cabin with blood on their hands, $1,000 in their pockets, and a new horse for their pasture. The murdered man's horse became a well-known racehorse in Grayson County until someone recognized her as Pugh's. After that, Dock took her to Indiana and sold her. At Hardinsburg, he stole a horse to ride home.[13]

Over the next six years, Dock committed a series of gruesome murders at his "welcoming house." Grayson County historians say that Brown's "methods were sweet and sinister. His invitations to rest and good talk were accepted by several settlers, who, after trust was established, went 'hunting' with Brown," never to return. But he did not confine his murders to passing strangers; killings included his partner in that first crime, brother Pinckney; another brother named James and James's little boy; and their father, the founder of their murderous clan. Dock was questioned about his father's death, but the authorities released him. Then, to show that his heart was in the right place, the grieving son bought headstones from Louisville to be placed over the graves of his father and Pinckney. (James and the little boy were unknown in the community and a public display of mourning was not necessary to keep up the ruse; their bodies were stuffed in some hole in Big Mouth Cave, presumably.) The headstones were an unwelcome drain on Dock's ill-gotten gains, but it further satisfied the law so that he remained free to continue his nefarious, lucrative career. One must spend money to make money.[14]

Thirty years after these events, the tales told about Dock Brown attracted the attention of a Leitchfield lawyer named William R. Haynes. Haynes decided to document the story as best he could and produce a narrative. He began to write in 1875. He planned to serialize his account in the *Grayson Journal*. People up and down the Rough River valley were interested in the subject and proud that a writer had appeared among them. One edition after another, the tale unfolded of Dock Brown's swindles, thefts, and murders. The end of the tale was coming, but not quickly enough for the Hartford *Herald*, which wished on March 15, 1876, that "Mr. Haynes would hurry up and kill that interminable fraud, 'Dock Brown.'"[15]

Haynes had more to tell. Dock's lies began to unravel and he was jailed for perjury. When a friend posted his bail to set him free, Dock took a mule-selling trip to Alabama. Upon his return, he attempted the murder of another brother, Moses, who had appeared in Grayson

County to claim his share of the deceased father's and brother Pinck-ney's estate. Jailed again, he was released on bail again. The charges against him were continued from one court term to the next, but they were never dismissed. More allegations came to light and the charges continued piling up. So did the weekly installments of the Dock Brown story. The Hartford *Herald* complained, "Heaven only knows where Mr. Haynes will stop," and feared he might continue "twenty or thirty years longer leading his readers into horse stealing, murders, arson, amours, courts of justice, lawyers offices, etc., along with the hero of his never ending romance."[16]

The end came for Dock in the fall of 1851. He had left Grayson County with some stolen slaves for Mississippi, where he sold the blacks for $1500. One, Letitia, he stole back and sold again in Memphis for another $800. From Memphis, he traveled to Gibson County, Tennessee, hoping to find and murder a brother named Absalom, who was going to testify against him in Kentucky. Absalom was of a different sort than the rest of his clan. An Athens, Tennessee, newspaper later called him "one of our most industrious, estimable, and good citizens."[17]

When warned by one of his fellow Masonic Lodge members that Dock had been seen in the area, Absalom got his shotgun and went with his son and some neighbors to find his brother and "drive him from his lurking place." As soon as Dock saw Absalom coming, he fired his rifle. Absalom was hit, but he raised his shotgun and emptied both barrels in Dock's direction. Both brothers were wounded, but neither was down. They "closed on each other—A. C. Hopper breaking his gun over the head of the other, cutting with knives, etc." Bleeding from many wounds, Dock finally fell dead. Absalom died a few hours later at his home. The newspaper said, "If accounts be true, society lost nothing by the death of the one from Kentucky." Gibson County sold Dock's horse, saddle, guns, and other smaller items to pay for his burial.[18]

Dock was finished and so was Haynes's serial. But he had other plans. The Hartford *Herald* announced on April 28, 1880, "The story of Dock Brown, written by the Hon. W.R. Haynes, will soon appear in book form." The book was published in an initial run of one thousand and sold for 75¢ each. It was a success, and even the *Herald*, which had once complained of the tedious detail and length of Haynes's articles, wrote in a short review that the book was "written in a very interesting style and is, in the main, entirely reliable." Since then, the book has been reprinted many times, the standard source for Dock Brown's story.[19]

In later years, it became a popular amusement to drive out to Pine Knob and dig in the floor of Big Mouth Cave for Dock's hidden loot. Numerous skeletons turned up, but no money ever did. And for years on Friday and Saturday nights, June through July, the Pine Knob Theater presented a drama called "Dock Brown—Legend of an Outlaw." Tourists from all over the country came to see the play. They bought souvenirs and meals, and rented motel rooms in the area, so, in the end, the community got some good at last out of bad Dock Brown.

TWENTY-FOUR

Falls of Rough

Studying the architecture of a region can, in itself, be a history lesson. Driving around the country roads in the Bluegrass region of Kentucky, a picture of the past begins to form by the large number of Georgian and Greek Revival mansions built before the Civil War. Further west, in the valleys of the Nolin and Rolling Fork Rivers, houses of that style and vintage are not so numerous, though they are not uncommon. But, continuing west to the valley of the Rough, one would think the land was hardly populated at all before the twentieth century because that is when almost all of the houses that can be seen were built. Why is this? It is because the people who settled in the Rough River Valley were not part of that powerful two percent at the top of the social pyramid, the planters. They had no abundant wealth to build fine houses that could withstand a century and a half of wear and weather. They were log cabin people, and their homes have rotted away or burned, taking with them the architectural record and all that it implies.

An exception to this architectural rule in the valley of the Rough was and is the mansion of the Green family. Their mercantile, industrial, and farming empire sprawled over three counties, and their home at Falls of Rough was its jewel.

The original Green property in Grayson County was near George Washington's two tracts. The family bought it from one of the great scoundrels in Kentucky history, Benjamin Sebastian. He was a veteran of the War of Independence, but his first allegiance was always to himself. It was his weak sense of loyalty and exaggerated sense of self that led him into an adventure called the Spanish Conspiracy.[1]

Looking only at the present, it sometimes appears that what *is* was inevitable; that Kentucky being part of the United States is what *had* to be. It is not so. There was a pivot point in the late 1700s when Kentucky might have willingly delivered itself into the hands of the Spanish King. Kentucky was part of Virginia at the time and unhappily so. The capital at Richmond was far away across the rugged Appalachians and was of

182

little practical use to Kentuckians. Likewise, relations with the United States were not satisfactory. Kentucky had been trying since 1784 to join the U.S. as the fourteenth state, but the central government kept rejecting her. The weak Articles of Confederation government seemed to be dying and had a difficult enough time trying to hold together the thirteen existing states—it made no sense to add another. One does not graft a shoot onto a dying tree.

Worse, the government seemed to have no interest in protecting the interests of its province across the mountains. Word had filtered into Kentucky that John Jay, who was Secretary of Foreign Affairs for the Articles of Confederation, was negotiating a treaty with the Spanish government in which the United States agreed to give up all rights to navigation on the Mississippi River for twenty-five years. What an insult! Kentuckians needed the Mississippi; it was the only sensible route for getting their goods to market. The Spanish controlled the Mississippi.

Enter James Wilkinson, a Marylander who had moved to Kentucky in 1784. He kept a store in Lexington that did not nearly support the elegant lifestyle he enjoyed. Money was in constant short supply. When he was elected as a delegate to one of the conventions to determine Kentucky's near future (particularly regarding the question of statehood), he quickly sensed the unhappy mood of the delegates and he hatched a nefarious scheme. Wilkinson took a boatload of bacon, flour, and tobacco down the Mississippi to New Orleans and met there with Spanish Governor Esteban Rodríguez Miró. Wilkinson offered to deliver Kentucky into Spanish control in return for certain considerations, including a monopoly on the trade between Kentucky and New Orleans. That would make him a very rich man someday. In the meantime, he intimated that he would gladly accept a salary from Miró.

Wilkinson's was an all-encompassing vision, and he talked with persuasive ardor to both sides. Spain would benefit in several ways by adding Kentucky to her American empire. To begin with, there were the rich natural resources of the area. In addition, by holding Kentucky, Spain would be able to block the westward expansion of the Americans who, it was feared, threatened her northern colonies in Mexico. Kentucky, also, would benefit. She would have unrestricted use of the Mississippi; she would be able to sell her goods in a market that paid top dollar; and she would be part of one of the world's superpowers, which could reduce the Indian threat by controlling the tribes in the South. With all of these advantages waiting, it would be foolish for Kentucky not to attach herself to the Spanish Empire. It was clear that the Articles of Confederation government did not want her as a state and was ready to sacrifice her economic well-being.[2]

These were Wilkinson's talking points. Already, he had assembled a clutch of allies, Benjamin Sebastian among them. Wilkinson's friends also got a Spanish salary for their support of the conspiracy. In Sebastian's case, it was $2,000 a year. Money only increased their zeal. One of Wilkinson's fellow conspirators expressed the cabal's point of view in plain terms the average Kentuckian could understand: "The direction of the current of the rivers which run in front of their dwellings points clearly to the power to which they ought to ally themselves," he said.[3]

Though the Spanish conspirators' arguments sounded convincing, Kentuckians hesitated. Blood and history bound them to the East and there was a large reservoir of loyalty among the people. Then came the news that the Jay-Gardoqui Treaty had been rejected by the Confederation Congress—the United States was not going to surrender the right of Kentuckians to use the Mississippi. The Spanish Conspiracy quickly lost its momentum. Kentucky would stand with the U.S. and wait for the time when statehood was possible.

Wilkinson and his friends continued to milk their secret relationship with Spain for the next few years. They tried again to bring Kentucky into the Spanish sphere in 1789, but failed. Sebastian and the others petitioned Spain for a grant of sixty thousand acres bordered by the Yazoo and Mississippi Rivers as additional reward "for their efforts on behalf of Spain," but, since the men had not really accomplished anything, Spain refused. Knowing that his chance had passed, Wilkinson accepted a commission in the Army in 1791 and left Kentucky.[4]

Statehood came to Kentucky in 1792. Benjamin Sebastian served on the drafting committee for the Kentucky Constitution and was appointed by Governor Isaac Shelby to be one of the first three justices on the Kentucky Court of Appeals. At the same time, he continued to buy and sell large tracts of land. That he was a land speculator handing down decisions on land law smacked of a conflict of interest. Complaints were raised. An effort to remove Sebastian from the high bench was unsuccessful, but the outcome would have surely been different if the people had known of the judge's clandestine life.

At the same time he served on the Court of Appeals, Sebastian quietly remained in the pay of Spain. In 1795 he met with the Spanish Governor to try to develop a new plan by which Kentucky would become Spanish property. The two men actually drafted the outline of a treaty, but again the plan fell through. Gradually, Sebastian's intrigues began to be suspected. He grew careless. In 1800 he returned to Louisville from a trip to New Orleans. At the wharf, he paid four men to unload what he said was a barrel of flour. It was enormously heavy and for good reason. The barrel was actually filled, according to one of the wharf hands, with "Spanish milled dollars, newly coined [and] all of one date."[5]

It was not until 1806 that Sebastian's role in the Spanish Conspiracy and his pension from the Spanish government were fully revealed. Immediately, impeachment proceedings were begun against him. He hired Ben Hardin as his lawyer, but the evidence was undeniable. Witnesses for the prosecution, including some of his fellow plotters, wove an inescapable web of guilt around him. In the course of the investigation Sebastian was proven to be a Spanish pensioner. He was declared guilty of engaging in "an illicit, unjustifiable, and highly criminal intercourse, subversive of every duty he owed to the constituted authorities of our country." The House voted to impeach him and the Senate was poised to act when Hardin proposed that Sebastian be allowed to resign. This was done.[6]

His political career ruined, Sebastian bought two hundred acres from Isaac Hite at Falls of Rough. There he erected a dam, a gristmill, a saw mill, a distillery, and a general store. In 1824, he moved to the Meade County home of his son Charles and left behind son William to oversee his concerns at Falls of Rough. In 1829, on behalf of his father, William sold Falls of Rough and all of its improvements to Willis Green for $1,000. The hitch was that William Sebastian did not have in hand a deed to the property and could not get one because his father had sold the same property to Nathan Anderson for the same price and at the same time that William and Willis had concluded their deal. Green sued Anderson. Green won the suit and was awarded the land. Benjamin Sebastian still would not produce a deed. The court intervened and turned the property over to Green anyway.[7]

Willis Green was a veteran of the War of 1812, living with his wife Ann and practicing law in Hardinsburg when he caught the land-buying fever. He began to accumulate land at $5 to $10 an acre. It was $5 per acre that he paid William Sebastian for Falls of Rough. To the operations already there, Green added a blacksmith shop and a carding machine, and he expanded the store. Ever the capitalist, he plowed his profits back into the business. He rebuilt the dam and the mills, installed new machinery, and either built a new house or remodeled an existing one for his wife and himself. From his window, he could see the mills and the store and hear the sleepy drone of water spilling over the dam.[8]

It is hard to separate financial power from political power; one always enhances the other, a fact that Green knew. As a slave owner and an industrialist, it was natural that he was first a National Republican and then a member of Henry Clay's Whig Party. Green had first become a Kentucky senator in 1827, representing Ohio, Breckinridge, and Daviess Counties. Re-elected in 1829, he spoke for a district that had grown to include Hancock County. It was typical; every business Green touched grew, even in politics. Green briefly left public life in 1831, but returned in 1836, when he was elected to his one and only term in the Kentucky House of Representatives, representing Grayson County. In 1839, Green won a seat in the U.S. House of Representatives. When Congress was in session, Green lived in the same boarding house where Henry Clay rented rooms. Not everyone could get along with Clay. John Quincy Adams had soured on him, Andrew Jackson hated him, and John Randolph tried to kill him in a duel. But Green and Clay became good friends.[9]

Green was re-elected in 1841 and in 1843, but he did not receive the Whig nomination in 1845. Perhaps it was because he had devoted so much time to Henry Clay's presidential campaign. The Richmond *Enquirer* called him the "chief manager of the Clay committee in Washington." One speech Green made before the Clay Club in Alexandria, Virginia, revealed his disdain for Clay's opponents and his admiration for the Whig candidate. Of the Democrats, whom he accused of being in thrall to "the Southern chivalry of South Carolina and her nullifiers and disunionists," he said, "Self-aggrandizement, and the power and spoils of office, are the sum total of their Democracy, the measure of their patriotism and purity." The Whigs, in contrast, stood for "a sound national currency—protection to American industry—the distribution of the proceeds of the public lands—one Presidential term—and an economical administration of the Government." He praised the party's standard bearer, his friend Clay, as "greatest among the great in this Republic," and said, "the history of his long and eventful career as a public man is so interwoven with that of his country, that to know one is to understand the other." So it went through the campaign. The Louisville *Daily Journal* editorialized, "He [Green] always prefers the good of the Whig cause to the one of his own individual interest." Green never held elective office again, but it was not his first love, anyway. He could not have been too disappointed to return to his businesses at Falls of Rough.[10]

Besides, now there were children in the Green house. Willis and Ann Green never produced any children of their own, but they took in his dead brother Morgan's children in the early 1840s, probably 1842. One of them, Lafayette, would grow up to be his uncle's heir and successor. He began clerking in the Falls of Rough store and from there his responsibilities grew. He sold his uncle's goods in Louisville and other river towns; managed slaves; and even made flatboat trips to New Orleans, delivering loads of lumber and returning safely with stories to tell and the money in hand. By the late 1850s, the precocious Lafayette, "Lafe," was ready to assume management of the wide-ranging Green interests.[11]

About 1858 or 1859, Willis and Ann Green moved to Corpus Christi, Texas, leaving Lafe to look after the family businesses. His uncle had always encouraged Lafe to be a "first rate man." Now the world was going to see that Lafe had become that man, a regular empire-builder. Hugh Ridenour, in his excellent study of the Green family, enumerated the many and expanding activities Lafe supervised: "farming, grain and lumber milling, retail merchandising, railroad building, gas and oil speculating, and banking; in addition, [he] practiced law and participated in the politics of his state." The *Breckinridge News* later said of Lafayette Green, "He believes in making money out of everything," and described him as "one of the few feudal barons left in Kentucky." Thomas D. Clark echoes that, calling Green's domain an "isolated barony" and his efforts "imperial."[12]

With his world at Falls of Rough well-ordered and running smoothly and generating money like he had his own mint, Lafe Green decided to enter politics. He was first elected as a Democrat to the Grayson County seat in the Kentucky House of Representatives in 1859. It was a short apprenticeship that did not prepare him for the epic problems he would have to try to help solve at the acrimonious Democratic National Convention in April 1860.

The convention convened in Charleston, South Carolina, to nominate a candidate for that year's presidential election, but first, a platform had to be approved. Delegates from the Deep South insisted on language that promoted slavery as a positive good and supported its extension into the western territories. Northern Democrats proposed a platform that was more moderate in its tone. This milder platform was the one that the convention narrowly adopted. The fire-eaters from the South stormed out. The remaining delegates tried to nominate a candidate, but after two days and fifty-seven ballots, it was plain that the Democrats were deadlocked. They adjourned, but planned to try again in two months in Baltimore. Before they met again, the solidly united Republicans met in Chicago and nominated Abraham Lincoln as their candidate.

Lafe Green was again with the Democrats when they came together in June. Almost immediately a fight erupted over what to do with those Southerners who had walked away in April, many of whom wanted to come back. It was agreed that some would be allowed in the new convention, but some others would have to be excluded. Now, a second walkout occurred; Green went out with the protestors. At their own convention, the Southern Democrats nominated John C. Breckinridge, the Kentuckian who was the sitting vice president. The Northern Democrats nominated Stephen A. Douglas. There were two Democrats plus the candidate of the Constitutional Union Party to face Lincoln in the November election. A four-way race was a guarantee that Lincoln would win and that the South would live up to its promise to leave the Union. The country would divide and only the most delusional optimist could doubt that war would follow.[13]

Returning home over the long miles to Falls of Rough, Lafayette Green had to have realized how small his family fortune really was in the middle of such events and how fragile were the varied interests of his "barony." His slaves; his thousands of acres of timber, fields, and pastures; his livestock; the mills; and the store were all at risk. He must have wondered how he could protect what two generations of his family had worked to build.

TWENTY-FIVE

The Price of War

Since it was incorporated in 1808, Hartford's population had quadrupled. Its four hundred citizens enjoyed life in a location that was pronounced by Lewis Collins to be "remarkable for its fine waters." There was a practically new courthouse. The first one had collapsed and the townspeople burned the rubble in a memorable bonfire to celebrate Oliver Hazard Perry's victory on Lake Erie in 1813. It was a custom that dated from early in the war. Harrison D. Taylor said, "During the War of 1812 the citizens were so patriotic they had to burn a vacant house—there were quite a few in Hartford then—whenever they heard of a victory." The first bonfire took what remained of the Nathaniel Wickliffe house. The walls had crumbled so that the frame of the roof, an "A-shaped garrett"—rested on the ground. When news of the victory arrived, "this old roof was selected for a bonfire," and, Taylor said, "was soon covered with flames." The crowd was all liquored up, and somehow decided that someone should run through the burning frame as a sign of patriotic courage. Major James Johnson, who was filled with "pure essence of corn," made the run. He fell several times, but he picked up and kept going and finally emerged on the other side, "terribly exhausted and singed."[1]

The community took a personal interest in the progress of the war. Three companies of native sons had marched off to do battle with the British and the Indians on the Wabash, at the River Thames, and finally at New Orleans. So, celebratory fires were lit every time the Americans scored a victory over the British. Taylor mentioned that, beside Wickliffe house and the old courthouse/jail, two more vacant homes were burned, but the last and most important bonfire was the abandoned and decrepit Crowe Tavern, burned to celebrate Jackson's victory at New Orleans. Taylor says, "The torch was applied to the vast pile, and the country was illuminated for miles around."[2]

Hartford was a growing trade center. The state legislature had declared the Rough to be navigable in 1810 and riverboats were making their way up from the Green, and the lawmakers accommodated land travelers as well when they authorized the building of a bridge at Hartford, the first ever to span the Rough. In addition to its county government buildings, Hartford was home to fifteen stores and groceries, and ten mechanics' shops. There was a cotton gin in Hartford and there was a good mill, dating from 1833, whose wheel powered machinery to saw lumber, card wool, and grind grain. Despite the stiff bond of $500 to operate a tavern, there were two. There were six lawyers and six doctors in town. People still remembered the operation performed by Doctor Charles McCreery in 1813. McCreery had come to Hartford in the first decade of the new century. He was a young man then, "and frequently original in his ideas and notions." McCreery "enjoyed a very high reputation, not only as a physician, but also as a fine surgeon, as well, having performed several bold—and then considered hazardous—operations many years ahead of the surgical science of the times." The experimental surgery for which he was most renowned was the successful removal of an entire collarbone from a fourteen-year-old boy. It was "the first known successful operation of its kind," a procedure so remarkable that people compared Doctor McCreery to the great Danville surgeon Doctor Ephraim McDowell.[3]

Out in the country there were still herds of deer and many bee trees. Even now, the timber was described as superior. The land was once so heavily forested that it was "the greatest obstruction to the farmers' progress," and Taylor described it as a "herculean task" for the first settlers to clear fields for crops and grazing. They belted the trees to kill them and then plowed around the tall stumps, which dropped "widow maker" limbs for months and years afterward until the dead trunk itself tumbled down. Dead trees remained for a long time as a hazard to man, beast, and growing crops.[4]

Where the trees had been cleared, farmers grew corn, some wheat and oats, and tobacco, which "yielded the most ready money." It was primarily of the variety called dark leaf. The pungent leaf was ideal for plug tobacco and snuff. Breckinridge County shipped out more than four thousand hogsheads of tobacco each year; Ohio County's crop, going out at Hartford, would not have been much different. The barreled tobacco was sold in New Orleans or, now that the paddle wheelers had made upstream travel possible, in Louisville. There were hopes at one time for a silk industry in the valley of the Rough, and a small quantity of silk was produced, but it never flourished. The effort was eventually abandoned.[5]

Corn, wheat, oats, and tobacco were not crops to sustain the institution of slavery. Tobacco came closest to it, but take notice of what was missing—cotton, sugarcane, rice, indigo. There was some slavery, of course; there had been since pioneer times. Modern researchers find the names of slaves on the charters of the early churches that Joseph Barnett helped plant, and they read the names of slaves in the annals of pioneer adventure. Slavery was a fact of life. However, big slave owners such as one saw down South were not found in the region. On the eve of the Civil War, even the lordly Lafayette Green held only thirty-two slaves, a number that made him major owner by the standards of the Rough River Valley, but not in the same class as the planters in Dixie. For those who held on to their slaves, there was a certain amount of pressure from the pulpit to set things right by manumission. The Baptists had argued about it for years, and the Methodists tended to be strongly anti-slavery. Still, human bondage persisted, and some people left for new homes north of the Ohio because of it. Andrew Isenberg speculates that it was the presence of slavery that drove out one particular family about this time. The Earps had lived near Hartford since 1825. They were Methodists and farmers, and the father, Walter, taught school as a sideline. Walter Earp was a wandering man, but there was something in Ohio County that suited him. He settled in to stay there longer than any other place he had lived, and his family seemed satisfied. His children married there. Son Nicholas married twice, both times in Hartford, both times to Ohio County natives. His first wife, Abigail Storm, died young. His second wife, Virginia Ann Cooksey, became a stepmother to his first wife's orphaned son, Newton, and gave Nicholas several more children, as well. A son, James, was born in Ohio County in 1841; he was followed by Virgil in 1842. They seemed a stable family and prosperous enough, but there was slavery, and after twenty years the Earps moved to Monmouth, Warren County, Illinois, where they became activists "in the antislavery cause." More sons, including Wyatt, Morgan, and Warren, were born to Nicholas and Virginia Earp. Nicholas tried a variety of occupations in the years that followed and kept moving west until finally reaching California. His sons shared his wandering spirit, but, unlike him, they found an occupation at which they earned fame. They went into law enforcement. The world remembers them, the Earp brothers of Tombstone.[6]

If neither economic reality nor religion could persuade the slave owner to give up the practice, the slaves might take direct action of their own by escaping. Their hope was to get north of the Ohio River. The Ohio River was not the legal boundary it once was, however. The Compromise of 1850 gave slave owners the right to cross the river to retrieve their runaways. Kentuckians who were chasing their runaways could also cross the Ohio and there enlist the help of Hoosiers, some of whom made a profitable sideline of catching fugitive slaves. Slave owners who could not personally give pursuit to the runaways sometimes ran newspaper ads asking for assistance. Asa Belt, who lived near the northern end of Rough River in Hardin County, was one who lost a slave. He ran a notice in the *Kentucky Standard,* June 3, 1830, soliciting help in retrieving John, a slave "about 22 to 23 years old, rather yellow complected, 5 feet 10–11 inches tall, his fore teeth are far apart, uncommon long foot and big toe. Has a wife at James Stark's 6–7 miles south of Elizabethtown in the Nolinn area."[7]

This was Hartford, then; a pleasant community with a rambunctious patriotism, a forward-looking and prosperous community for the most part, but disturbed by the question of slavery. In 1860, Ohio County, the heart of the Rough River country, had almost 1,300 slaves out of a population of slightly over twelve thousand. That made the controversy one of some weight but one whose resolution people were willing to approach with a wait-and-see attitude. Other places, the question was being discussed with much more urgency. Passions were flaring up on both sides, opinions were hardening, and the country was being pushed toward the day when a decision would have to be made whether or not the nation would continue, in the words of a familiar phrase, "half slave and half free." The result was war.[8]

The first months of the war, in Kentucky, at least, had little to do with slavery—Lincoln had promised to take no action against slavery where it existed—and everything to do with the dissolution of the Union. On this issue, feelings ran high. Soon after Fort Sumter was fired upon, enlistment for both the Union Army and the Confederate Army began in Hartford which, along with Calhoun, Owensboro, and Paducah, was one of the main recruiting towns in western Kentucky. The Federal camp at Hartford, Camp Calloway, was set up at the Ohio County Fairgrounds on the road between Hartford and Beaver Dam. Colonel John H. McHenry was forming two companies there for the 17th Kentucky Infantry. McHenry later said, "Great difficulty and even danger was experience by recruiting officers in Western Kentucky in filling up their ranks. In many counties were numerous persons who desired to volunteer in the regiments then being formed for the Union army. They had no opportunity for doing so without fleeing to the north side of Green river. Leaving their homes and families unprotected, they would band together in squads, and with such arms as could be procured, cross the river at night and come hastily to the Union camps."[9]

The regiment was still forming when it had its initial encounter with troops who favored the Southern insurgents. McHenry said, "One of the first acts of the new recruits of the 17th was the disarming of the

State Guard company at Hartford, which was done by Col. McHenry on the first demonstration of its purpose to side with the Confederacy. A conflict between the 17th and the State Guard in the streets was narrowly averted." It was fortunate for the 17th that the State Guard did not dig in, for even with their poor militia training, they were better prepared than the new recruits from Camp Calloway. They were not yet ready for action, a realization that was brought home to them in September when Simon Bolivar Buckner occupied Bowling Green. McHenry said, "The camp at Hartford was particularly exposed by its advanced position. It was in no condition to cope with the enemy's troops." Luckily, Buckner did not challenge them. They remained in camp, living in a state of heightened vigilance, learning their business. They went out in small details to patrol the surrounding countryside and even engaged in a minor action against the enemy near Morgantown. In November, they were ordered to proceed to Callhoun and rendezvous with other Kentucky regiments under the command of Brigadier General Thomas L. Crittenden.[10]

The 17th Kentucky went on to fight at Fort Donelson, Shiloh, Corinth, Chickamauga, Missionary Ridge, the battles of the Atlanta Campaign, and at Franklin, Tennessee, before being mustered out in January 1865. But that was not the only regiment made up in whole or in part from the valley of the Rough. Another Federal unit was Colonel Quintus Cincinnatus Shanks's 12th Kentucky Cavalry, who campaigned against John Hunt Morgan before going south to Georgia. After Atlanta fell, the 12th joined with General George Stoneman in his raid against western Virginia. At Saltville, they fought and whipped their fellow Kentuckian, the former vice-president and 1860 presidential candidate John C. Breckinridge. Afterwards, they went to Hardin County, Kentucky, and operated against guerrillas who were threatening the L&N Railroad. The 12th ended the war with patrol duty in East Tennessee and western North Carolina. The men were mustered out in August 1865, months after the war ended.[11]

Boys from the valley of the Rough served in other regiments, singly or in companies, as well. Two companies of the 26th Kentucky Infantry were formed in the Rough River Valley. Company A began as a Home Guard unit at Livermore in McLean County. John W. Belt was its captain. Company B was recruited in Hartford and was led by Captain Gabriel Netter, a French-born businessman who had settled in Ohio County. The organizing officer of the 26th was Colonel Stephen G. Burbridge. He would later become notorious as "Burbridge the Butcher" for the brutal methods he used as commander of the District of Kentucky, but at the beginning of his military service he enjoyed a good reputation as an aggressive defender of the Union, a man eager to get at the Rebels. The 26th spent much of the war guarding railroads and suppressing guerrilla activity in Kentucky, but the regiment saw its share of battlefield action. The regiment fought at Shiloh, Perryville, Saltville, Nashville, and joined General William T. Sherman for the last phase of his Campaign of the Carolinas.[12]

On the Confederate side, men from up and down the Rough River Valley joined Doctor John Pendleton's company of the 9th Kentucky Infantry. Pendleton suspended work on his English style mansion in Hartford to raise his company, and it was not his last sacrifice for the Southern cause. When the men of the 9th were sworn in, Doctor Pendleton gave up field command to become the regimental surgeon. He served through the war in positions of ever-greater responsibility, ending his service as a divisional surgeon in General Joseph Wheeler's cavalry. Pendleton was remembered admiringly by Ed Porter Thompson, historian of the Orphan Brigade, who said, "A discreet and experienced physician, a bold yet prudent and skillful surgeon, a brave and courteous gentleman, he filled the several stations to which he was called with honor to himself, satisfaction to his superior officers, and benefit to those under his care."[13]

The 9th maneuvered and skirmished in western Kentucky all through the fall of 1861, but they saw their first real battle at Shiloh. The survivors went on to fight at Stones River and Chickamauga, where they lost one-half of their remaining men. The 9th fought at Missionary Ridge and in the battles to defend Atlanta. Mounted in September 1864, the 9th maneuvered unsuccessfully against Sherman on his March to the Sea, and, after Richmond fell, it was the 9th that escorted President Jefferson Davis as he fled south and west. What remained of the regiment surrendered at Washington, Georgia, in May 1865.[14]

These were the units from the valley of the Rough who fought on battlefields far from home. Books have been written about the battles of the Western Theatre, detailed studies that are beyond our scope, but there is a quicker lesson to be learned. Compare the list of battles above. Notice the number of them in which local boys in blue fought against local boys in gray—friends from school and church and even relatives—and you will get some notion of the high price of the war in the Rough River country.

For those who stayed home, the war was mostly something they read about in the newspapers or in letters embossed with patriotic motifs. They saw soldiers, but no fighting, at first. The pace of military activity picked up considerably in the valley in the late summer of 1862, when Confederate General Braxton Bragg led a major invasion of

Kentucky. He was miles ahead of Union General Don Carlos Buell and seemed to be driving toward Louisville. The men blamed Buell for their sluggish pursuit of the Confederates and even questioned his loyalty to the Union. Buell, however, felt that he was doing the best he could. He lamented, "I moved my army sixty-five miles while he [Bragg] was moving fifty and I was still thirty miles in rear of him."[15]

It was not the supply train that was slowing the Federals down. At Bowling Green, Buell had detached his supply wagons from the rest of his army and sent it toward Louisville by a different route. While the infantry marched up the western branch of the Louisville and Nashville Turnpike (today's 31-W), the wagons and their cavalry escort moved through Brownsville toward Leitchfield. From there, the wagons followed the Salt River Road. Their way was difficult, crooked and steep. Many of them broke down under the strain. Farmers for years afterward found wheels, boards, and hardware of the government wagons that jarred to pieces on the Salt River Road.

The wagon train moved in three sections, and the cavalry escort under Colonel Lewis Zahm was "properly distributed." Zahm wrote in his report that after the column crossed the Nolin at Brownsville, "We continued our march without any interruption worth mentioning ... over very rough, some places rocky and hilly, roads." The drivers traveled an average of twenty-five miles each day, balancing the need for speed with the well-being of the mules and stopping for the day where the cavalry scouts found, even in this drought crippled land, adequate grazing and water for the stock.[16]

The army supply wagons had a gross weight of 1,850 pounds. Each one carried six hundred pounds of fodder for its draft animals (five days' worth), six barrels of salt pork, four barrels of coffee, and ten pounds of sugar. The people who lived along the Salt River Road pointed out for decades to come the ruts and damaged tree roots caused by the steel-rimmed wheels of the heavy wagons that passed by in September of 1862. Zahm said, "I have never heard of a train moving of this large proportion. At 50 feet to the team, which is a small space for them to travel, it made a column of over seventeen miles in length, besides the brigade of cavalry occupying nearly another mile."[17]

Each section of the wagon train consisted of five hundred wagons, and each section was accompanied by approximately two thousand men, including the drivers, their helpers, and their cavalry escorts. It seems that groups of foragers spread out along parallel roads, looking for rations and forage and fresh horses. One of these groups drifted into Breckinridge County, where it ran into trouble. Two Tennessee slaves, Sandy and George, had escaped their masters to join the

Federals. Originally, they served in General James S. Negley's division as drovers, but when Negley's division was left behind in Nashville to help guard Middle Tennessee, the two contrabands came north with Buell's army pursuing Bragg. Now they were with the wagons and Zahm's column.[18]

In a report made the following spring, Judge Advocate General Joseph Holt wrote to Secretary of War Edwin M. Stanton about what had happened to Sandy and George: "While en route they were seized as fugitive slaves by the civil authorities at Hardinsburg ... where they have remained in jail until the present time, and as stated by the jailer of the county are advertised to be sold as slaves under the local laws of Kentucky on the third Monday in May." Holt argued that the two men were not liable to seizure, since they were at the time in the service of the Federal army, and furthermore, "They have a more decided character assigned to them by the ninth section of the act of 17th July, 1862, ch. 195. Having been the property of men known to be in open rebellion against the Government of the United States, and taking refuge within the lines of our army, which was their status at the time of their arrest, they are declared by the section of the act referred to be 'captives of war and forever free of their servitude.' This act is a part of the supreme law of the land to which the local legislation of the States must give way. The civil authorities have no more right to seize and detain in prison negroes falling within the purview of the section quoted than they have to seize and imprison other captives of war taken by the armies of the United States."[19]

Holt continued that the practice of kidnapping black people who had the legal status of Sandy and George was "disgraceful" and "should be suppressed with a vigorous and decided hand." If necessary, the whole power of the United States government should be brought to bear. Holt concluded, "The claim of $250 for expenses set up against each of these negroes should not be recognized nor regarded. Those who have incurred these expenses, if indeed they have been incurred to the amount named, have done so in their own wrong and in violation of law and they have no right to look either to the Government or to their victims, the negroes, for redress."[20]

Presumably, the case of Sandy and George was eventually settled to Holt's satisfaction, but they were still in the Hardinsburg jail as Zahm moved on toward the Salt River. These were the first bluecoats that some of the more isolated people in the valley of the Rough had seen since the Rebellion started. The citizens of the Rough River were predominantly Unionist, but they could not have welcomed the cavalrymen of their own government who fanned out over the countryside foraging for provisions. The people at Howe Valley surely saw these troopers, and so did the people at Hardin Springs, and at Vertrees, and at all the other small towns near the supply train's route.

The wagons kept pushing toward West Point, and arrived on the morning of October 3, 1862. Zahm reported from there, "We had not lost a dollar's worth of property, with the exception of a few broken down wagons, which we had to abandon." He did not mention Sandy and George. The column crossed Salt River, and proceeded to Louisville, where Buell's infantry waited.[21]

They had only a short time to rest and re-provision before the order came to move out. The time was approaching for their rendezvous with Bragg's Confederates. The two armies met and fought Kentucky's climactic battle at Perryville, far to the east of Rough River. But if the people of the valley thought they had seen the last of soldiers they were disappointed. Shortly after the great battle, Colonel John Hunt Morgan and his raiders came galloping in. As Bragg retreated from Perryville, Morgan received permission to swing back toward the west to attack the L&N. He was still stinging from an early morning skirmish with some Federals on the railroad at Elizabethtown when, on the evening of October 21, 1862, he arrived in Leitchfield. He captured some Home Guards there, and, as it was late in the day, he placed them under guard in the courthouse while implying that they might be executed in the morning. It was just a bit of fooling on Colonel Morgan's part; the next morning he extracted a promise from the prisoners that they would neither make war on the Confederates nor pester the local citizens and then paroled them.[22]

After 1862, Kentucky was wiped clean of Confederate soldiers, but their absence gave rise to another menace—Rebel guerrillas. The guerrillas had little discipline in their ranks and even less mercy toward the populace. They took what they wanted, killed when they felt like it, and the people lived in fear of them. Men like Sue Mundy, "One-Armed" Berry, and Henry Magruder led the most famous guerrilla bands, but many lesser-known gangs terrorized the countryside. In the valley of the Rough, "Old Reverend" Jim Cundiff had a gang that hid out in the hollows along Linder Creek, and W.H. Davison led a bloodthirsty group called "Davison's Hyenas." Thomas Hines led another band of irregulars. In June 1863, Hines' gang moved through Grayson County, killing and robbing before thundering off toward Elizabethtown, looting every post office along the way.

A correspondent from the Louisville *Daily Journal* left the best account of Hines's raid. In a lengthy dispatch dated June 18, 1863, he wrote,

About sunset last evening the peaceful denizens of Litchfield were thrown into a considerable flurry by some fourteen rebel soldiers well mounted and equipped dashing at full speed into their town. They went some distance past the court-house, then wheeled, came back to the public square, hitched their horses, put out guards, and commenced their usual thieving propensities of robbing the stores. About dark some eighty or ninety others came in and participated with them in that operation, which amounted to upwards of three hundred dollars; for some of which they paid their worthless Southern scrip. They had stolen at least five good horses in the vicinity of town previous to their arrival, and made their boast that they had killed two men, one of whom was ascertained to be Mr. John Dearing. The other was thought to be Allen Decker. The former was shot while on his horse, and after he had fallen to the ground they showed their chivalry by shooting him twice again through the body. One rode to the house of Captain Ship Mercer, Captain of the Home Guards, and presented his pistol to shoot him, but the Captain was too quick for him, and seized his double barreled shot-gun, which had in it a suitable load for such a rascal. As he was about to let him have it, the rebel cried out, "Don't shoot a friend!" The Captain replied, "If you are a friend, put down that pistol." The hero from Dixie concluded that prudence was the better part of valor, and retreated for reinforcements; Mercer thought so too, and retired to the woods. After a short time, some twelve or fourteen rode up, used insulting language to the family, and made an attempt to burn the buildings, but were foiled in this by the heroic conduct of the Captain's wife and daughters. The rebels were under the command of Captain Hines, son of Warren Hines, of Warren County, Joe Gray, Whitaker Cunningham, of Elizabethtown, and John Miller of Hardin county, were among the leading spirits of the party.[23]

A Home Guard unit from Grayson County could not catch the guerrillas as they escaped into Hardin County. The Home Guard was a citizens' militia of lightly trained men, not as well-armed as the guerrillas and unaccustomed to blood-letting. Nevertheless, with the added help of Federal patrols, the Home Guards kept to their duties, learned more about their business, and did enjoy some successes. On August 21, 1864, a guerrilla gang appeared at the Falls of Rough, where they "engaged in robbing and plundering the citizens." Thirteen men of the Grayson County Home Guard set out. Reinforced en route, the Guards chased the bushwhackers all the way to Green River. The guerrillas crossed at Borah's Ferry, and, thinking they were safe, stopped at an abandoned house five miles beyond to rest for the night. The Home Guards soon found the guerrillas' hiding place and surrounded it. At daybreak, when the Guards called out for the Confederates to defend themselves, they replied with gunfire. As the Louisville *Daily Journal* reported it, "The guards charged down upon the building, discharged telling volleys into the guerrillas. The fire was too severe and the robbers held up their hands, asking for mercy, and agreeing to surrender." The militiamen delivered their prisoners and their armaments to the authorities at Munfordville. The *Daily Journal* article concluded, "The Grayson Guard have been engaged in hunting down guerrilla bands for some time, and have met with astonishing success."[24]

Neither were the Hardinsburg Home Guards to be looked down upon. In the days of Big Bill Hardin, their grandfathers had defended the settlement against Indians, and these wandering bands of bushwhackers did not seem all that different; at times they even painted their faces and took scalps. In October 1864, the citizens' militia drove off a band of twenty-five guerrillas who came into Hardinsburg and ignored warnings to behave peaceably. The Nashville *Daily Times and True Union* reported, "The citizens told them that if they would pass through the town quietly ... none of them should be molested, but this did not satisfy them, and commenced firing in all directions. The citizens soon rallied and commenced firing on them, when they galloped out of the town faster than they came into it.... The citizens of Breckinridge [County] are determined to defend themselves."[25]

On December 28 there was a bigger fight at Hardinsburg. A band of twenty marauders came into town, raided the courthouse, and set the building ablaze. The men of the town rushed to the courthouse square and opened fire. The raiders galloped out of town, their strength reduced by four, and the citizens put out the flames in the courthouse. The next afternoon a consolidated gang of eighty bushwhackers approached the town and demanded its surrender. The townsmen answered that they would fight to the death before they would lay down their weapons. Properly impressed, the guerrillas replied that private property, including weapons, would be respected, and on those terms they were allowed to enter Hardinsburg. They spent a peaceful night in town and rode out quietly the next morning. Without a doubt, the story would have ended differently in this time of domestic terror, had Hardinsburg been without its "well-regulated militia."[26]

TWENTY-SIX

Confederates

Captain Jacob Bennett was one guerrilla leader against whom the Yankees did not have "astonishing success." He ranged over a wide territory whose corners were Owensboro, Taylorsville, Burkesville, and Rocky Hill, near Bowling Green. His rides often took him through the Rough River country. It was an area Bennett knew well, for he was a native, born in Livermore in 1840.

Bennett was one of those who was captured with Morgan near West Point, Ohio, at the end of the Great Raid in July 1863. Morgan and his officers were sent to the Ohio State Penitentiary and held as common thieves. The Thunderbolt and a few others managed to escape from the prison the following November. Bennett was with them. He made his way to west central Kentucky where he put together a gang of men like himself, Confederate soldiers who had been shaken loose from their regiments. Henceforth, they would fight as irregulars. Bennett's gang is identified by Daniel E. Sutherland in his authoritative study *A Savage Conflict* as one of the three "most prominent bands" of guerrillas in Kentucky. At times the gang numbered two hundred men.[1]

In April 1864, Bennett's gang hit the Lebanon Branch of the L&N Railroad in Nelson County, then doubled back through Hardinsburg, Leitchfield, and Hartford, robbing citizens and taking their horses all along the way. Witnesses specifically remarked upon the surprising fact that one of Bennett's raiders was a heavily armed black man. At Hartford, on April 12, Bennett's men "surrounded the town and collected the main portion of the citizenry on the public square. Here a strong guard was placed over them, and they were forced to stand quietly by and see the town sacked." The bushwhackers took their loot and rode toward Madisonville.[2]

Bennett and his gang spent the next couple of weeks attacking shipping on the Green River. Forcing water craft to stand and deliver was an interesting variation on the theme—the plunder was coming to them for a change. By late April, well rested and ready to ride again, they headed east to the vicinity of Big Spring at the juncture of Hardin, Meade, and Breckinridge counties. There they continued what the Louisville *Daily Journal* called their "nefarious war of plunder."[3]

By the first of May, Bennett's gang was back in the region of the lower Rough River Valley, robbing at will and being ineffectually pursued until May 7, when the 37th Kentucky Mounted Infantry caught up with them in Union County and forced them into a skirmish. Nine of Bennett's men were killed or captured. It was a setback for Bennett, but far from a fatal one. He led his men south and east toward Burkesville on the Cumberland River. They spent the summer raiding south of the valley of the Rough (their raid on Brownsville was described earlier), but in late August they showed up in Hartford again. They took $1,500 from the bank and headed for Owensboro. By this time, Bennett's gang, augmented by some smaller groups of bushwhackers, was at peak strength.[4]

The year 1864 was a good one for Jake Bennett, if not for the Confederacy. By the late fall of that year, the Confederacy in the West was nearly finished. Nashville had been in Federal hands since 1862, so had New Orleans. Memphis was gone as well as Paducah, Baton Rouge, Vicksburg, and Chattanooga, and each city lost was another gush of heart's blood drawn from the weakening South. Now Atlanta was gone, too. CSA General Joseph E. Johnston had retreated steadily through Georgia until he was practically at the northern edge of the city. President Jefferson Davis removed him from command, replacing him with John Bell Hood. Hood was more brave than brilliant. He dashed his army to pieces in three ill-considered attacks against Sherman's Federals, and then he developed a reckless plan: to take what remained of the Confederate Army of Tennessee, swing around Atlanta, and move quickly toward Nashville. Sherman would not be able to tolerate a Rebel army of this size in his rear, cutting his supply lines and gobbling up all the territory that the Yankees had won since 1862. Sherman would have to abandon Atlanta to stop Hood.

For his plan to succeed, Hood had to destroy Federal communications behind the lines. To accomplish the task, Hood turned to a Kentuckian, General Hylan B. Lyon. Hood ordered Lyon to cross the Tennessee and Cumberland Rivers into Kentucky and "tear up and destroy the railroad and telegraph lines running into Nashville, and to put all the mills in running order throughout the entire section for use by the government."[5]

Lyon's two brigades set out from Paris, Tennessee, on December 6, 1864. They crossed the Cumberland River on December 10 and made for Hopkinsville, Kentucky. The garrison of United States Colored Troops withdrew as Lyon approached. On December 12,

Hopkinsville diarist Ellen Kenton McGaughey wrote, "To day at 1 o'clock the southern troops two thousand strong with four pieces of cannon took possession of the town. Oh how our hearts leaped for joy at the sight.... I could not refrain from weeping as I saw the brave heroes, half clad and half frozen pass, with a song of defiance on their lips, to their northern foes, who well fed and well clad had fled on their approach with their black hords."[6]

Lyon's raiders did not remain "half clad and half frozen" for long. They looted the stores for clothes and boots. Then they robbed the bank and burned the courthouse, an act of arson Lyon justified by saying it had housed Hopkinsville's black garrison. Satisfied that the town was secure, Lyon decided to divide his command. He would go with Colonel J.J. Turner's 1st Brigade on a looping ride through Cadiz, Princeton, and Eddyville, while Colonel J.Q. Chenoweth and the 2nd Brigade held Hopkinsville. Two days later, Lyon was returning to Hopkinsville with the freshly provisioned 1st Brigade when he met some of Colonel Chenoweth's men on the road, retreating from a fight with General Edward M. McCook and two brigades of Federal Cavalry. Lyon stopped all the fleeing men he could, added them to the 1st Brigade, and led them back toward Hopkinsville. They fought their way past McCook's surprised Federals and made for Madisonville. En route, they caught up with the rest of the 2nd Brigade. Back at full strength, they galloped into Madisonville, burned the courthouse, and hurried toward the Green River. They crossed the river at Ashbyburg while skirmishing with more of McCook's men, and rode hard for Hartford, burning every bridge behind them. They rode into Hartford on December 20. Lyon peppered the courthouse with small arms fire until the garrison of forty-eight officers and enlisted men (52nd Kentucky Infantry), surrendered. Lyon paroled them and prepared to fire the courthouse.[7]

The citizens admitted that, though he had given them an hour of mayhem and real terror, Lyon's control over his men was excellent. One resident recalled, "They took everything they wanted out of the stores and destroyed a great deal they could not take," but also added, "they did not molest us in any way while they were in Hartford." The Confederates paid for everything they took except for horses. Colonel Chenoweth, writing about the raid later, said that the owners of desirable saddle mounts got nothing in return for their requisitioned stock but "good will." As the raiders prepared to burn the courthouse, Doctor Samuel O. Peyton went to General Lyon and asked him to spare the county clerk's office from the torch, which Lyon did. The county records were saved, even as the flames consumed Ohio County's second courthouse.[8]

As Lyon led his men out of Hartford on December 21 the raid was nearing its climax. He had kept his men safe from serious entanglements with the enemy while he sowed confusion and burned courthouses, and he was primed to inflict multiple breaks in the L&N Railroad. His column was now well-mounted and provisioned, and his success was drawing volunteers by the score. The W.P.A.'s *Military History of Kentucky* estimates that 578 men from Hardin, Breckinridge, and Meade Counties left home to join Lyon in this middle phase of the raid.[9]

The volunteers soon learned for themselves what the veterans could have told them: raiding was serious work and death could come at any time. Between Hartford and Leitchfield, bushwhackers attacked. One of Lyon's men was killed. The rest searched the area and soon captured the leader of the attackers and his wife and placed them under guard on an ammunition wagon. They rode as prisoners, no doubt dreading their fate, while the Rebel column continued into Grayson County. Later, when Lyon called a halt and the men fell out to relax and smoke their pipes, the bushwhacker asked for a light. One of his guards passed him a coal. The man took the ember and dropped it through the stopper hole of a powder keg. The resulting explosion killed the wagon driver and his mules and the prisoner's wife. The accommodating guard was badly hurt, as was the would-be suicide bomber. He was lying wounded in the roadbed when one of Lyon's men came forward and shot him through the head.[10]

Lyon's men rode into Leitchfield unchallenged. Another commander might have turned his face while his outraged men punished the defenseless town for what had happened a few miles back—towns had been destroyed for less—but Lyon kept his men to the job at hand. They burned the courthouse and collected supplies and horses. On this one occasion, at least, they left a horse behind. Bettie Conklin Killick in later years recalled that she confronted the Rebels who appeared at her father's stable. She begged them to leave "Kit," the family's one and only horse. Lieutenant Henry Metcalf ordered his men to leave Kit alone, but informed Bettie that some of his men would bivouac in her house for a few hours. When the Rebels took their leave of the Conklins, Kit was still in his stall, and he had a new stable-mate, a tired old cavalry mount named Dolly. Bettie appreciated the Rebel lieutenant's generosity to her family, but the Conklins' increase in horseflesh was only temporary. When the Yankees came through town a bit later, they took both horses.[11]

Lyon men left Leitchfield in high spirits. It was sublime to have such power, to be able to destroy at will, to burn and steal and ride away with little to fear from the Yankees lagging far behind them. The raiders passed out of the valley of the Rough en route to Elizabethtown. They divided into squads and hit the L&N Railroad at Elizabethtown,

Glendale, and Nolin simultaneously before beginning their return trip south. The raiders left Kentucky by the most direct route Federal patrols permitted and rode through Tennessee to rejoin the Confederates in Alabama.[12]

When they looked at their burned-out courthouses, the people had reason to feel that they had been hard hit by the war, but the courthouses were just buildings and Lyon's raiders had taken nothing but material goods. The war was not finished with the valley of the Rough, however. On Saturday, January 21, 1865, Captain George Clarke, 4th Missouri Cavalry, and forty of his men rode into Hartford. They stopped and spent the rest of the afternoon and night in town. One man later recalled, "Their uniform[s] and good behavior whilst in this place and the conversation we had with said Clarke sufficiently satisfied us that he and his company were Federal."[13]

The next day was Sunday, but the Missourians did not honor the Sabbath with rest, churchgoing, and psalm singing. They spent the day "drinking, fiddling, and dancing, and making merry as only soldiers can." During the gaiety Clarke's mind returned to the business of war. He told his hosts that he and his patrol planned to go out scouting for guerrillas the next day, and being unfamiliar with the roads, they needed a guide.[14]

It happened that Lieutenant Andrew Barnett, 26th Kentucky Infantry, was home "on recruiting duty, helping to enlist African-Americans for the 125th Colored Infantry." Someone suggested him as a guide, and Clarke sent a man to the house of Barnett's father to find the tall young soldier and ask if he would help the strangers. Barnett agreed. Early the next morning, Barnett appeared with two others who had chosen to join them. One was Barnett's comrade in the 26th, Isaac Axton, and the other was Watt Lawton of Evansville, who had come to visit kinfolk in Hartford and lingered with them because he feared "the numerous gangs of guerrillas" in the area. Now, Lawton had a safe way home; he could travel with peace of mind in the company of forty cavalrymen. The party set out on the Hawesville Road. After a short distance, Isaac Axton complained that his horse was not able to keep up. He asked if he could drop out of the column to go home and get a better mount and weapons. Captain Clarke agreed to let Axton go, and he turned back toward Hartford.[15]

Axton's story was a ploy. Something about the strangers alarmed him. He believed they were not the Federals they pretended to be, but disguised guerrillas, and he knew he must warn Mr. Joseph Barnett that Andrew was in danger. Mr. Barnett was convinced by Axton's story, and he went to William Townsley, his hired man, and asked him to go save his son and bring him home.[16]

The approach of the stranger Townsley (when they were expecting Axton) made the Missourians decide their cover was blown, for Axton's intuition had been sound. These men were guerrillas, and their leader was William C. Quantrill. If Axton had spread the alarm, as he evidently had, they would soon have more to deal with than this one hired man. They quickly subdued Townsley and hanged him. They shot and killed Watt Lawton, and, a few miles beyond, they killed Andrew Barnett. Some say the guerrillas shot him in the head, others that they beat him to death. They took his clothes and his horse and turned east toward Leitchfield. The bushwhackers were in a holiday mood. When they went into a country store along the way, one of them broke out laughing. He pointed and said, "We just killed a man as long as that counter."[17]

While the guerrillas were enjoying the joke, Mr. Joseph Barnett was growing more anxious. Townsley and his son had not returned. Finally, Barnett and another man went searching. They found two bodies, Townsley and Lawton, that afternoon, but they had to search for another day before they came across Andrew Barnett. They carried him home, and Mr. Barnett took up the unnatural duty that so many other fathers had since 1861, the planning of his own son's funeral.[18]

Quantrill and his men passed near Hardinsburg and Elizabethtown without chalking up any more known murders. They ended up in the Nelson-Marion County area. From there, they resumed their old Missouri habits of wide-ranging raids. On May 10, 1865, in a surprise attack on their hiding place, Captain Edwin Terrell scattered the Missouri gang and brought down Quantrill with a paralyzing wound. He died at the military prison hospital in Louisville on June 6, 1865. His men were paroled a few weeks later to go back to Missouri.[19]

William C. Quantrill (Library of Congress).

Quantrill's last six months in Kentucky are usually forgotten, over-shadowed by his bloody years in Missouri and Kansas. And it is true that Hartford was no Lawrence, but the memory of Quantrill's visit never faded. The people remembered the needless murders of Townsley, Lawton, and Barnett, and they remembered their disguised killers, too. They called them the Sunday Bluecoats. Their visit was the tragic conclusion to the war in the valley of the Rough.

After the war, people began to commemorate all that had happened. In Hartford, the Union veterans started a GAR post and named it after Preston Morton, a young officer of the 17th Kentucky Infantry who had died at Shiloh. Fordsville had the Remus Whittinghall Post of the GAR. At Meeting Creek, it was the J.H. Meyers Post; at Leitchfield, the J. Wess Grosnell Post; at Caneyville, the Perry Campbell Post. Every town had its post of veterans who wanted to relive the days when they had saved the Union and to honor those who had died in that cause. In Big Clifty, Grayson County, in 1895, the John H. Langley Post of the GAR hosted a grand reunion and, as a gracious gesture, invited all the old Confederates from the area to attend. They wanted to visit with their former enemies in a generous and forgiving spirit.[20]

Among others, forgiveness was not so easy in coming. Mattie Chinn, an Ohio County woman of unreconstructed Southern sympathies said, "I wish I had the key to Hell and all the Union soldiers were in it."[21]

TWENTY-SEVEN

Sinews of Steel

Violence becomes a habit. The more violence there is, the more acceptable it becomes, which leads to more violence. The young men of the country had plenty of chances to become addicted to violence between 1861 and 1865. Bloodletting was the answer then and some came home to the Rough River Valley believing it was the quickest and best solution to post-war problems, too. The war unleashed something ugly in the valley, which suffered through a spell of sudden, sporadic killing such as it had not seen since the days of the Indian raids. One finds in the old newspapers frequent accounts of patricide, lynching, and murders over money, revenge, and alienated affections.

The behavior of some of the people was so alarming that groups of night riders eventually organized to regulate the conduct of the community. One such group, the Possum Hunters, numbered at least fifty men and rode as late as 1915 in the lower Rough River Valley. They began in the Western Coalfield to terrorize mine operators and foremen into better treatment of their workers, but the group spread into other counties and became the morality police, enforcing its own views of right and wrong. Many men were said to have joined the vigilantes under coercion or merely to avoid suspicion, caught up in the eternally popular "you're either for us or against us" mentality. A newspaper called it a "sad commentary on the lack of manhood and honor that exists in some places." Once in, the recruits were forced to participate in the disciplining of targeted victims, men and women alike, "all because some member of a secret, oath-bound association decided that they should be beaten." Mr. and Mrs. Rube Howard were two such victims of the Possum Hunters. The Howards lived out of Hartford on the road to Rosine. They were dragged from their home at night and "most brutally beaten" with switches "eight or ten feet long." The reason for their beating was never made public. It is odd that men who were interested in law and order and moral conduct should themselves become terrorists-by-night whose crimes of assault were as bad or worse than the behavior of the people they condemned as immoral.[1]

It took real law-and-order men to put an end to the violence. In the summer of 1915 Judge T.F. Birkhead convened a special grand jury at the request of the victims of the vigilantes, and with the help of Commonwealth Attorney Ben Ringo, began sending Possum Hunters to the penitentiary. After five of the night riders' leaders were convicted and put away, the judge said that the message had been sent that Ohio County would not tolerate lawlessness, and that the Possum Hunters were a thing of the past. The newspapers said that Birkhead and Ringo deserved "a great deal of credit for breaking up this lawless band."[2]

Men like Birkhead and Ringo helped bring the widespread acts of individual and organized violence under control in the Rough River Valley, but such lawlessness never made up the entire picture, of course. The thirty years following the Civil War were really a time of transition. Some people did cling to the habits of the past, but others pulled just as hard toward the future.

Without a doubt, the greatest single change in the valley of the Rough was the introduction of the region's first railroad, the Elizabethtown & Paducah Railroad. A railroad was certainly needed. The original dirt roads were dreadful at any time of year, but practically impassable in winter. Some of the roads in western Hardin County ranked among the worst in Kentucky, explaining why mail out of the Vertrees post office had to be delivered from horseback through the late 1920s. In addition, those other highways, the rivers, were in danger of becoming the property of private trusts that would monopolize traffic on the Green, Barren, Rough, and other rivers for their own personal profits. The Green and Barren Navigation Company was one; it convinced the state legislature in 1868 to grant it an exclusive thirty-year lease of the Green River. Votes in return for stock in the company was the charge that was leveled against the legislators. The company's monopoly of the Green naturally had a direct effect on all of its tributaries, as well. A railroad to compete with the river trusts would be good for independent business men and consumers of transportation services. A final motivation for bringing railroads into the region was the wealth of natural resources in the valley of the Rough that, for lack of good transportation, had never been fully developed. With a good overland transportation network in place, these could be exploited to the greater benefit of the local economies.[3]

One of these resources was coal. The iron production upon which George Washington had pinned so much hope never came to pass, but further west, south of the Rough River in the last miles of its winding journey, there were large coal deposits close to the surface. There had been a little bit of mining in the Western Coalfield as early as the 1820s. During the Civil War, production had increased to keep up with the demands of a nation at war. Now, in the "Gilded Age," coal was more necessary as a fuel than it had ever been before, and yet there it lay, virtually in the grass roots, mostly untouched.

General Don Carlos Buell, who had struggled against Braxton Bragg in Kentucky in 1862, had retired from the army in 1864 and had come to Kentucky to live and to earn his fortune in coal. He bought one thousand acres and had "just begun his mining operation when the Navigation Company leased the rivers, frustrating his plans to barge coal cheaply." He fought the river monopolists for twenty years from his home at Airdrie in Muhlenberg County. There was something for him in the defeat of the "monarchs of Green River," but Buell was a public minded man—he was on the board of directors of the state's agricultural and mechanical college, today's University of Kentucky, and he was also the state pension agent beginning in 1885—and he undoubtedly saw a greater good to be realized by the railroad project that was going to bring modern transportation into Western Kentucky.[4]

Another man who saw the larger economic and geographic picture was Samuel B. Thomas. Thomas had made a fortune in transportation. He owned a stagecoach line and it might seem that he would have fought the railroad as an unwelcome competitor; the iron road would have to follow the route of his stage line, at least partially. It was the only practical route. To the contrary, Thomas became the moving force behind construction of an east-west railroad. He obtained a charter from the General Assembly in March 1867; construction on the E&P RR began at Elizabethtown in 1869. The length of the completed railroad was expected to be 185 miles and the total cost was projected at $5,700,000.[5]

West by southwest, the railroad was laid down. New towns sprouted up all along its length, just as the old towns had once taken root beside the connecting foot trails between settlements. In Hardin County, there were East View and Summit (so named because it was the highest point on the railroad). In Grayson County, the stations were: Big Clifty, Grayson Springs Station (later renamed Clarkson), Millwood, Caneyville, and Spring Lick. In Ohio County, Horton and Rosine were new towns. The railroad bypassed Hartford, which had little interest in it, and proceeded instead to Beaver Dam.

Beaver Dam was first settled by the family of Martin Kohlman about 1795. Kohlman, noticing a large beaver dam nearby, gave the future community its name. Beaver Dam Baptist Church was begun in

1798 and a village grew up around it. The church experienced a small boom in 1811–12 because of the New Madrid earthquakes. Numerous "missions" of the Baptist Church had to be started to accommodate the suddenly large number of shaky converts. With the growth of the church, the town began growing as well. Now, with the arrival of the railroad, Beaver Dam was incorporated.[6]

Beyond Beaver Dam, the railroad continued west into the valleys of other rivers which do not concern us here. The Elizabethtown & Paducah Railroad was plagued by money problems from the start. Louisville pledged $1,000,000 toward its construction in 1868; and at the western terminus McCracken County approved a subscription of $500,000. Other towns and counties along its length subscribed lesser sums, but Ohio County voted against committing any taxpayer dollars at all to the project, and at one point the railroad company had to mortgage every piece of equipment and all of its property in order to keep building. Difficult terrain, many river crossings, and accidents were the story of the E&P during its construction, but the railroad finally opened in September 1872. Samuel B. Thomas lived to see the first trains run, and to Don Carlos Buell the sound of the first train whistle must have sounded sweet. The Elizabethtown & Paducah Railroad became the Navigation Company's "main competitor for east-west trade."[7]

The economic benefit to the region began even before the first train rolled. The railroad company bought materials from the local farmers as the track was laid. Big Clifty did a profitable trade in selling crossties to the E&P RR. Some days, farmers' wagons loaded with crossties for delivery were lined up for over a mile. Big Clifty was a well named, though oddly spelled, community dating from 1850. It presented special problems for the construction engineers. Clifty Creek flowed at the bottom of a deep, steep-sided, and shadowy dark ravine that lay athwart the route of the E&P RR. Colonel William R. Haynes described Clifty Creek, saying, "Its name is quite suggestive of the character of the stream it is. Save subterranean passages, it is doubtless the darkest watercourse in the state ... a miniature Lethe." It took builders two months in the summer of 1870 to piece together the iron bridge that crossed the ravine. It was finally finished on July 15, 250 feet long and 125 feet above Clifty Creek below, and the first train crossed that afternoon.[8]

East View was one of the new towns that grew up along the railroad. Concurrent with the arrival of the E&P, East View had its first school, a hotel, a liquor dealer, a Baptist church, a shoemaker, and a saw mill. In the years to come, joining the usual dry goods and general stores, it could boast: a stockyard, a sand and clay exporter (the sand for glass and enamel, the clay for bricks and terra cotta tiles), a rock quarry and stone crusher, a sumac factory, an axe handle factory, an undertaker with a glass sided hearse, a baseball team, and in 1887, the railroad bought from the firm of Birtle and Akers seven hundred telegraph poles. The railroad was economic nourishment to a newborn town.[9]

Established towns benefited, as well. Clarkson, formerly called Grayson Springs for the popular mineral waters nearby, saw an increase in business and tourism after the Elizabethtown & Paducah came through, and a few miles down the line Leitchfield profited, too, from its "connection to coalfields in the western part of the state and to Louisville markets." Mark E. Nevils says, "The railroad's arrival on September 6, 1872, sparked a boom in the growth of business and industry," especially in clothing manufacturing and in lumber. Nevils points in particular to the lumber firm of R. Dinwiddie and Company, "which manufactured staves, heading, and lumber and annually shipped over 1,000 boxcar loads of products." Benam Shaw's old village that had experienced such difficulty in growing found its footing at last with the coming of the railroad. It was an interconnected economy that had just been waiting for the railroad to bring the pieces all together.[10]

It was not just in the ledgers of the Rough River businesses that the effect of the railroad was seen. In their little homes, the people now enjoyed those things that brought pleasure and culture into life, carried in by the railroad and paid for with the better wages the railroad made possible. Good medical care was closer. Pleasure trips became possible. The railroad connected the most remote corners of the valley of the Rough to the outside world. Except for rural electrification, it would be hard to think of a more life-changing event that ever benefited the people of Rough River.

One place the railroad was late to reach, despite Lafe Green's best efforts, was Falls of Rough. The Civil War had not been much of a factor at the Falls. That is a mystery, for, with its resources, one would think that the Falls would have been repeatedly looted by the soldiers of both armies, North and South, but an occasional visit by guerrillas was almost the entire story. Likewise is the mystery of what Lafe Green was doing in the war years. He does not seem to have gone to war for either side; perhaps he hired a substitute. He could not have pleaded exemption as a family man, for he did not marry until 1866. Rebecca Eleanor "Ella" Scott of Frankfort was his wife. The couple had met while Green was a state legislator. Ella was a dark-eyed and sprightly young woman, but it may have been her father who first caught Lafe's attention. Robert W. Scott and the gentleman from Grayson County shared many interests. Scott's plantation, Locust Hill, contained a thousand acres or so, and before the war it had been worked by thirty-three slaves. Like

Green, Scott was a hands-on manager (he employed no overseer), and, like him, he was interested in the improvement of livestock through selective breeding. Also, Scott was "an ardent disciple of diversification," which was practically the Green family motto. Under Scott's care, Locust Hill became a model of large scale agrarian life, and Green could not have helped but to be impressed. Then he noticed the daughter.[11]

Ella and Lafe married at her father's mansion, but he did not intend that they stay in Frankfort. He rebuilt the manor house at Falls of Rough for his aristocratic bride. The Hartford *Republican* made reference to it in his obituary, saying that he "built one of the finest mansions in the state. All of the material used in the building was obtained on the farm. A quarry was opened and a brick kiln made for this purpose. All of the lumber used was sawed at Col. Green's mill." The future home of Mr. and Mrs. Green was no hovel—Clark says it was an "oasis in the wilderness"—but it did not compare to the home that Ella was leaving.[12]

From all evidence, Ella Green was a loving wife and genuinely admired her husband, but the seat of his business world was as offensive to her as he feared it would be. Her neighbors she found to be "distressingly ignorant," and she was scared when Lafe was away on business trips. There were "blue devils … hiding in every corner," she wrote in one of her frequent letters home to Frankfort. Before bedtime, Ella checked every lock and bolt and searched the whole of her bedroom, even, as a child might do, under the bed. Should all of her pre-bedtime precautions fail, she had two pistols ready. Sometimes, she kept a lamp burning all night.[13]

Isolation was a torment to Ella, and the nights terrified her, but daytime brought some relief. Clark says that her "dining table was seldom without guests who came either to transact business with her husband or to make extended family visits." Yet, this only led to another source of dissatisfaction. She complained that she could not find good servants, especially a cook. Furthermore, she was "completely hemmed in … by impassable dirt roads." She called the cloistered site along the Rough River where her mansion stood and which so many have admired for its verdant beauty, "this sinkhole."[14]

As late as 1877, Ella wrote her family that she doubted she would ever feel content at the Falls of Rough, but not because she was dissatisfied with her husband, whom she described as "the next best husband in the world" (presumably, her father was the first best). Rather, Ella missed her genteel life in the upper level of Bluegrass society.[15]

However, Ella's life does not seem to have been the barren desert of which she so often complained. The newspapers were full of items about her travels, and she often had visitors. Consider the "Grand Barbeque" held at the Falls of Rough in July of 1882. The ad in the *Breckinridge News* promised "plenty of everything to eat and drink. Good Music, Dancing, etc. for the young people. Candidate from Grayson and Breckinridge will be there and speak. Refreshments of all kinds will be on the grounds." And she hosted elaborate parties like the masquerade ball she threw in August 1893 in honor of her guests the McCracken sisters. The *Breckinridge News* said, "Never in the history of the Falls was there a more enjoyable evening." One McCracken girl costumed herself as a "long-faced pious minister," and the other "decorated herself in a garb of cabbage leaves from head to foot." Mrs. Green was "a large, fat landlady of a third-class boarding house." Lafe Green dressed as a Confederate soldier in a tight shell jacket and "pants that were evidently cut by some fashionable jew tailor." He carried an old musket "nine feet long." Some guests played on the bigoted ethnic humor of the time. Miss Margaret Goodloe of Louisville, "got herself up as an old-time backwoods negroes [sic], with that delicate, greasy complection that vasoline and burnt cork by a skilled artist can only make." The only flaw in her depiction was her "graceful manner." Jennie Green dressed in the costume of a mincing Japanese girl and mimicked the speech of one with a "perfect" accent. One guest dressed up as an Irishman, complete with a black eye. Mr. John Dean represented a baby and carried a bottle to suck. They danced and sang and the paper declared, "As a hostess Mrs. Green has no equal, generous as the day is long and as lively as a young girl." Lafayette Green indulged his wife, but she was not happy in her rural home; she was lonely, she said, and she could not get good help.[16]

In Ohio County during these years was an old woman named Bell Townsley. She was said to be a Cherokee, born north of her tribe's homeland on the Wabash River about 1811. She moved with her family to Graves County in 1815, when it was still Chickasaw country. A fur trader from Jefferson County named Trodgen met Bell, and with her father's consent, took her home with him. She was only ten. What happened to Trodgen is unclear, but in 1832, Bell married a man named Daniel and had by him a son whom she named Anderson. Bell's husband was killed in a sawmill accident just before the child was born. Bell moved to Ohio County then and homesteaded a piece of land by herself, her baby on her back. She acquired six hundred acres and built five houses all before her son was old enough to help. In 1845, she married Ted Townsley, a widower with thirteen children. When the Civil War began, Ted joined the Confederate Army. He was killed, and Bell was left to raise his many children. Her own son, Anderson, was a Rebel soldier, too, but he survived. In 1890, Bell divided her land equally among the children, except for Anderson, whom she gave one hundred acres. He had ten children.

Bell wanted to make sure that each of her grandchildren got his or her legacy, so she planted cedar trees around ten, ten-acre squares to subdivide it for them. Bell Townsley, a resolute woman who had endured many hardships, died in 1904 at the age of 93.[17]

And Ella Green cried because she could not find a cook good enough for her mansion.

Still, Ella always came back to the Falls. The Greens' marriage was not perfect, but there was true affection, and both husband and wife found a way to accept the other's passions and quirks; she, his all-consuming business interests, and he, her complaining and spoiled-girl sensibilities. However, the long-suffering Ella's burdens were soon to be lightened. In 1889, Lafayette Green became president of a new railroad company called the Louisville, Hardinsburg, & Western. Work on the LH&W RR began in late February 1889, and completed the track to McQuady to Dempster to the Falls before the first of October. Since there was no turnaround, the train backed from the "Y" at Dempster to the tiny depot at the Falls on the Breckinridge County side. Then, passengers and freight loaded, it returned, with the locomotive now in front, to the main track. At long last, Ella Green could escape her dirt-road "sinkhole" in easy comfort.[18]

The decade spanning the mid–1880s to the mid–1890s was the apex of the history of Falls of Rough. By 1895, there was a population of 250 citizens. The train station and the Western Union telegraph office had joined the hotel as the new businesses in town. There was a new mill-dam whose tumbling water powered the various mills. The store and the farming operations were thriving. The logging operations could hardly have been pushed harder. The standing timber near Falls of Rough was judged "perhaps, as fine as any in the United States." What gave it added value was that there were two ways to get it out, the railroad and the river. The Hartford *Herald* noted in 1889, "There are 200 miles of stream above the falls navigable for logs, and last year it is estimated that over 40,000,000 feet of lumber in logs passed over the falls and were carried to Evansville." David and Lalie Dick say, "For the white establishment, it [Falls of Rough] was Camelot." Of course, every kingdom must have its vassals and serfs. There were thirty-five houses in town where the Green employees lived. The family paid their wages with "'Green's money,' a coinage especially struck off for them, which passes current at their general store."[19]

The time was coming for Lafayette Green to begin slowing down. For more than thirty years, he had directed most of his energies to running and improving the business empire begun by his uncle back in 1829. Four of his seven children had survived: Willis, Preston, Jennie, and Robert. He loved them, but particularly Robert. Ella remarked that, "Lafayette would even put down the *Courier-Journal* to pick up the baby."[20]

About the turn of the century, Lafayette's children were ready to start assuming control over the different parts of the family's varied interests. Willis, the oldest, took charge of the money-making aspects of the empire. The *Breckinridge News* called him "a splendid type of the Kentucky gentleman." He possessed "the culture and erudition of the scholar, and the executive ability and managerial talent of the high class businessman." Though his business interests were extensive, he "possessed of a wealth of energy and ability and is equal to every demand made upon him." Preston Green managed the saw mill and the gristmill. Robert Green became manager of the family farm. At eight thousand acres, it was the largest farm in the state, and Robert rode "from morning until night in attending his duties." Grain and tobacco cultivation were ubiquitous in the valley of the Rough, but on the Green family's farm, animal husbandry was a profitable specialty. One money-maker for the farm was the famous stallion Beau Chief. Provided with a promising mare, Beau Chief was guaranteed to sire "a living colt," and the price for his stud services was just $12.[21]

Jennie Green, the only daughter, took charge of the mansion. Hugh Ridenour describes Miss Green as "demanding, headstrong, high tempered, and opinionated ... also extremely racist." She seemed to live for travel and entertaining, and she was fascinated by the occult. She had but slight interest in business.[22]

In 1911, Jennie Green sold her share of the family enterprises to her brothers. She used a large part of the proceeds for a luxurious European holiday. She headed home aboard an ocean liner in April 1912. Icy conditions in the North Atlantic made it a perilous month and year to voyage home. Luckily, Jennie's ship escaped accident in the dangerous waters and arrived safely in New York. It was there the passengers learned that the fine new ship steaming behind them had not been so fortunate. The *Titanic* had plowed into an iceberg and had sunk with a terrific loss of life. The *Breckinridge News* made no mention of that in its item about Miss Green's return, reporting merely that her trip had been one of "stirring experiences and incessant activity," and that she returned home in time to "put in [a] garden."[23]

By the time of Jennie Green's close call, the parents were dead. Ella Green died in 1896 and Lafayette died in 1907. The Frankfort *Roundabout* eulogized Lafayette as "an upright and honorable gentleman.... His death will cause sadness to many friends here, of whom we are one." Closer to his home, the board of trustees of the Bank of Hardinsburg passed a resolution that said his family had lost a "loving, kind and affectionate father, advisor and guide; that the people with whom he lived daily, one of their most valued friends and neighbors; that his county and state, one who loved the people and who earnestly endeavored to advance their interest and welfare, and Kentucky one of her best citizens." Lafayette sleeps beside Ella Green in the Frankfort cemetery, a hundred miles away from the valley he loved. After his death, the family enterprises at Falls of Rough continued to flourish, but fault lines ran through the family that threatened everything. Most ominous was the fact that none of the Green sons nor Jennie had married, and, unless one of them became the late-life parent of a fourth generation to take over someday, the long reign of the Green family at Falls of Rough would certainly come to an end.[24]

While the leading family of the valley began to falter and relinquish its leadership role, others (many from outside the area) took advantage of the opportunities. Railroad magnates extended their lines into new areas. Hartford got its railroad in January 1910, when the L&N completed a short branch called the Madisonville, Hartford, & Eastern. Only fifty-five miles long, it was intended to create "a shorter route between Louisville, Kentucky, and the coal fields and agricultural regions of Western Kentucky."[25]

For Hartford, however, it was not the railroad but Rough River that continued to be the most important source of commercial revenue. Ferry operators paid $2,000 for a bond, but far more important than the bank-to-bank trade was the downriver trade that linked Hartford with her traditional out-of-state trading partner, Evansville, Indiana. The trade had been limited before 1896 because the Rough River was too shallow and narrow for larger boats to make it as far as the Ohio County seat. The new lock and dam at Livermore completed in December of that year provided nearly ten feet of lift in Rough River and allowed modern steamboats to come farther upstream than ever before. Profits increased accordingly. The boats included paddle wheelers like the *Lena Archer* and the *City of Hartford*.[26]

These two steamers were the very ones that gave Hartford one of the most memorable events in its century-long history. A Hartford newspaper article from December 23, 1896, described how exciting an event it was the day that not one but *two* steamboats arrived in town. "The people of Hartford were more than delighted to see two steamers in sight at once," it said. "Whistles blew, guns fired, and the people turned out en masse to witness the scene." Such a horde of citizens crowded the Rough River bridge that some feared its collapse, but nothing like that happened to spoil the happy arrival of the two boats. To celebrate, the people of the town gave the boat crews and passengers a roast turkey supper with all the trimmings.[27]

Let other towns rely on the screeching, dirty, and dangerous locomotives of the railroads. Maybe they would last; maybe not. Hartford loved the Rough, the eternal river that had made possible its past and, now, its future.

TWENTY-EIGHT

Dying Time

Humankind's efforts to shape the valley of the Rough had dramatic results. The mills that harnessed the river's power, the locks and dams that contained it, the clearing of the forests and the creation of pastures and cropland, not to mention the web of improved roads and railroads that connected the towns—all of these had transformed the land that the Barnett brothers, Big Bill Hardin, and John Howe had known. The work required to accomplish it is almost unimaginable. But even the most impressive accomplishments of man could not stand against the ancient forces of water, fire, and wind. The Rough had its floods, a bad one in 1840, followed by another in 1854, and still another in 1884. For the most part, the population lived back from the river and were not too badly hurt by the high waters, though the mills suffered. Fires devastated East View in 1889 and Caneyville in 1891, and Leitchfield had two fires that gutted the town; the first in 1891 was followed by one even worse in 1898. Leitchfield had no fire department, and at least eight buildings and the Methodist Episcopal Church burned. Most shocking, perhaps, to a people who were only trying to mind their business and make a living was the tornado of March 27, 1890, which descended without warning and destroyed lives and property all the way from western Kentucky to Louisville. These were the vagaries of life, and no community of people was forever safe from them.[1]

In those things in which the people could make improvements, they did. But progress is always a trade-off. New ways come, the old ways die, and sometimes the people are left wondering if the trade-off was worth it. Take the coming of the automobile as an example. That was progress, but its price was high. One cost was the Rough River resort towns that dotted the valley in the early 1900s. Hardin Springs was such a town. There, the Louisville entrepreneurs Ollie Whallen and James Moore owned a twenty-nine room hotel that was so crowded between Memorial Day and Labor Day each year that people rented open-air sleeping space on the verandas. Whallen and Moore were only the most recent owners of the hotel. It was built by Elijah Hansborough in about 1870. It cost him $7,000 and the furniture and fixtures cost him another $10,000. The building of the hotel set off a small boom in this remote settlement on the Rough. In the decade that followed, Hardin Springs got a new wooden bridge, a post office; a new school, its first blacksmith, and a physician, Dr. Zack Carnes. After Hansborough, four others owned the hotel until Whallen and Moore bought it for $800 in 1899.[2]

Vacationers from the city arrived by train in Big Clifty or in East View on the E&P RR. From East View they chose either a surrey to White Mills on the Nolin or a four-horse stagecoach to Hardin Springs on the Rough. White Mills was closer, but Hardin Springs offered something that White Mills did not—three mineral springs whose waters were said to have marvelous healing powers for a variety of ailments.[3]

Those who chose Hardin Springs descended a long, steep hill into the valley; passed through the village; and then, coming to the river, saw the 1866 mill and mill dam and finally the white L-shaped hotel. The hotel served three hot meals a day. Between meals, all kinds of amusements awaited the guests: horseshoes, hiking, swimming, excursions to Gibraltar Blowing Cave, trail riding, tennis, and dancing, even bowling. Guests at the Hardin Springs Hotel thirsting for a drink could get one if they knew the right people, for the surrounding hills were a haven for moonshiners. An item in the Elizabethtown *News* from 1903 said that the nearby hills and ravines "are almost inaccessible to revenue officers. So well adapted are the cliffs and ravines in this locality, it is said that no United States Marshal has ever been able to locate a still unaided and that all the distilleries which have been captured were accomplished through a connivance of the natives, who through spite, or for a promise of a reward have led the officers to the distilleries."[4]

Local citizens who disapproved of the illegal brew being produced in their hollows continued their "connivance" with the authorities for years, and sometimes it cost them dearly. John Whitworth lost his barn to arsonists in supposed retaliation for informing on moonshiners, and a few months later, in June of 1922, S.H. "Boat" Pierce, owner of Pierce's Mill, lost his garage and Ford automobile in the same way. The Elizabethtown *News* reported, "Pierce has been connected with John and Felix Whitworth in reporting illicit stills." Nine months after that, arsonists burned two unoccupied tenant houses on Pierce's farm. The newspaper noted, "Mr. Pierce has been active in turning up moonshiners in his community, and the fire is believed to have been the work of incendiaries."[5]

Such strife between neighbors did not involve vacationers. Year after year, families returned on the East View train for the stagecoach ride to the resort on the Rough and a two-week respite from the heat and headaches of city life. Then came the automobile. The period 1900 to 1925 was one of relative prosperity and people earning disposable income began to spend it on cars. It was an odd phenomenon. There were so few decent roads that the automobiles had to arrive by train. Then, once the car arrived, there was no easy place to drive it and no gas stations, either. Gasoline had to be delivered in drums by freight train. The new technology and the money to buy it had outraced the support system of highways, fueling stations, and trained mechanics necessary to make it work. Yet people wanted the cars and, gradually, they became an unremarkable sight on the roads in the Rough River Valley.

At first, though, they were such a curiosity that people did not even know what to call them. They just knew that the bumping, backfiring thing spooked the horses and mules and chickens. It was an adventure in both travel and public relations to be an early motorist, but no hardship dissuaded the people and the number of cars increased. Since they plainly were not going away, cars and their drivers had to be accommodated. The dirt roads were macadamized and then paved. Better bridges were erected across the river. The improvements made it possible for vacationers to go in new directions to see new things, so the old resort towns on the Rough began to perish for lack of business. All through the twenties the slide continued, and by the mid-thirties, the quaint resorts at the river's edge had almost entirely passed away into memory.

The automobile was progress, but the blacksmiths and the owners of the summer resorts recalled the sound of horses' hooves and the whisper of surrey wheels. And didn't the sky used to be bluer?

As some towns found themselves bypassed and dying, others thrived. Livermore, at the mouth of Rough River, was a regional center for the timber trade, for shipping and small manufacturing, and it was bustling. Tied up at the Livermore landing were rafts of logs with tents on them where the loggers lived until their timber sold. Livermore shipped other products of the area, too, but timber was king. Some of it went down to Evansville, but two local chair factories bought a great deal of the timber. The WPA *Guide to Kentucky* noted that chair making at Livermore "exists also on a home production basis, and new rattan-bottom chairs are displayed on porches and in the yards of many dwellings." The timber was not used only for chairs. The craftsmen in Livermore had a different product for almost every variety of tree that grew in the valley. Hickory was for spokes for buggy wheels, ash was for the rims, poplar and chestnut made good shingles, and oak made the best barrels. Livermore was prospering, "another New South boomtown," and the home to about 1,220 citizens, 188 of whom were black. As a rule, people got along.[6]

Then, on April 20, 1911, there occurred an event that destroyed Livermore's image of Southern comfort and Christian congeniality, a murder that made international news and harkened back to another era in its brutality. That spring afternoon, two white men, Clarence Mitchell and his friend Clifton Schroeter, stopped by one of Livermore's two poolrooms. This one was operated for blacks to enjoy in segregated Livermore. It was managed by a young black man named Will Potter. It is hard to escape the conclusion that Clarence Mitchell was spoiling for trouble. He was later described by the Owensboro *Daily Inquirer* as "a negro hater [who] had a special dislike for Potter," and yet the bigoted Mitchell chose to go to a pool room frequented by blacks and managed by the very man for whom he harbored "a special dislike." Mitchell and his sidekick Schroeter shot a game of pool and then refused to pay for the use of the table. An argument ensued. Hot words became a scuffle. When Mitchell and Schroeter finally left, Potter followed them as far as the door and fired two shots in their direction. Mitchell was hit and wounded.[7]

Potter hurriedly made his way to his employer, J.D. Whitaker, who was at the other pool room he owned, this one for the exclusive use of white patrons. It was located in the back of the opera house, and that is where Livermore Marshal V.P. Stateler arrested Potter. Stateler also deputized some men to make a protective cordon around the prisoner. Everyone knew what often happened in small southern towns when a black man assaulted a white.[8]

It happened in Livermore, too. A crowd of angry whites gathered outside the opera house. Mayor V.B. Morton, who was one of Potter's protectors, made a telephone call to McLean County Sheriff C.E. Beeler with news of what had happened. He asked him to come at once with a posse to help move Potter to the jail. Until then, they would hold him in the opera house. They bolted the doors, turned out the lights, and waited for the sheriff to come. The mob continued to grow outside. About 7:30, they broke in. What happened next is not entirely certain, except for the outcome. In Mayor Morton's telling, fifteen men rushed the officers; found Potter; and shot him twice, killing him almost instantly. "Two or three more random shots were fired and being assured the negro was dead, the mob dispersed," said the mayor.[9]

The more commonly believed account is the one that appeared in the New York *Times*, which ran an item about the killing the next day. It said that the mob broke in, and "a search was then made for the negro, who was finally dragged from underneath the stage, shivering with terror. After a short consultation he was dragged before the footlights and tied. His captors then ranged themselves in the orchestra pit, and at a given signal began to shoot. For a minute or more the auditorium reverberated with the roar of the pistols and rifles, and then all was still. Leaving the negro where he lay, a limp and bloody bundle, the mob filed out into the streets, and in a few minutes, had disappeared." William Quantrill and his Sunday Bluecoats would have felt right at home in Livermore on this day. It was later said that tickets were sold to the public to come and watch the execution, and that the higher priced tickets permitted the holder to join in the shooting. All proceeds were intended to be a charitable contribution to the Mitchell family.[10]

Potter's bullet-riddled body was claimed by mortician John Hughart. A coroner's jury was convened to determine the cause of Potter's death (verdict: death by gunshot), and arrangements for burial began—and almost as soon fell apart. Hughart offered a black man $5 to help bury Potter, but the man turned him down. None of the black citizens wanted to be associated in any way with Potter, whom they described as "a strange negro [who] had not behaved himself since coming to Livermore." Furthermore, the leaders of the African American community refused to allow Potter to be buried in the Negro Cemetery. Potter was finally buried in the pauper graveyard on April 24.[11]

Meanwhile, news of the murder was reaching far beyond the city limits of Livermore. The New York *Times* covered the story, as did, among others, the Chicago *Tribune*, the Indianapolis *Freeman*, and the Louisville *Courier-Journal*. The NAACP became involved. Perhaps because of the unflattering attention, or perhaps because of the innate decency of some of the citizens, events were about to take an unusual turn in McLean County. Circuit Court Judge T.F. Birkhead convened a grand jury in Calhoun. Birkhead's instructions to the jury left no doubt of what he expected of them, and they indicted eighteen of the participants in the event at Livermore. Lawrence Mitchell (Clarence Mitchell's brother), Clifton Schroeter, and his cousin Jesse Schroeter were indicted separately and charged with murder. The other fifteen were charged with being accessories. The Hartford *Herald* said, "The news of the action of the grand jury came like a thunderbolt out of a clear sky."[12]

County Attorney R.W. Alexander "declared that he would use all the means within his power to erase the blot on the fair name of McLean County." This was one of the few times in Kentucky or anywhere in the South—that members of a lynch mob were indicted for their crime. Before the trial came up, the eighteen accused posted bail and were all released from custody. Clifton and Jesse Schroeter were soon arrested again, accused of running a counterfeiting operation from a floating photography studio which was anchored in the river at Hartford, and they went straight back to jail. During that same interim period, Clarence Mitchell recovered from his wound and in June married Miss Ruth English of Livermore.[13]

Judge Birkhead presided at the trial when court convened on August 21 in Calhoun. Commonwealth Attorney Ben Ringo and County Attorney R.W. Alexander chaired the prosecution, and Joseph Miller and Lawrence Turner appeared for the defense. Defense made the usual motions for a continuance—denied—and to dismiss the case—denied—and a request for separate trials. To this last motion, the judge agreed. Lawrence Mitchell's case was up first. The prosecution called numerous witnesses who swore he was at the scene of the murder, armed with a shotgun, and that he fired one of the first shots at Potter. Mitchell took the stand to say that he was not even in Livermore at the time of the lynching; he was at his mother's house and knew nothing of it until afterward. Several family members corroborated the story. A rebuttal witness, the Livermore telephone operator, testified that Mitchell had come into her office to use the phone just minutes after the crime. Her testimony placed him in town at the hour of the murder. Nevertheless, after a short deliberation, the jury found Mitchell not guilty.[14]

The prosecutors decided to try next John W. Taylor, one of those accused of being an accessory. Testimony was heard through the afternoon of Thursday, August 24, and the case was turned over to the jury. Early Friday morning, it found Taylor not guilty.[15]

The two acquittals made it clear to Judge Birkhead and attorneys Ringo and Alexander that no matter how strong the evidence none of the defendants in Potter's murder was going to be found guilty. Judge Birkhead announced that the trials of the other sixteen defendants would be heard during the October session of the circuit court, but before then, the prosecution quietly dropped the remaining cases.[16]

In the newspapers of America, Livermore was convicted for being the kind of town where a lynching could not only occur but also become a paid event. It was the second decade of the twentieth century. Automobiles were becoming common and men had flown. There were phonographs and motion pictures. America had a kind of genius for making progress, but progress in the dark soul of man was harder to achieve.

The Livermore Opera House stood until 1940 when it was torn down. The salvaged materials were used to build three small dwelling houses on the site where the murder was committed. The event was allowed to quietly die in the community's memory, or perhaps it was forcibly ejected from memory. David and Lalie Dick relate that, in 2001, when they were researching their book *Rivers of Kentucky*, they went to Livermore and spoke to the ladies working in the library. The ladies said they had never heard of the lynching that shamed Kentucky and for a time made their town the symbol of Southern racism.[17]

TWENTY-NINE

That High, Lonesome Sound

It's been accurately noted that there was an increase in violent acts in the valley of the Rough after the war and sometimes they took on horrible aspects. It cannot be ignored, but neither should it be exaggerated. Bloody deeds overshadow the fact that daily life went on and, as a rule, the people found more acceptable outlets for their energies. The Northern boys had spread baseball all across the country during the Civil War. Most, if not all, of the towns in the valley of the Rough had a baseball team. The Rosine team was called the Red Legs, and the players might have had a particular swagger when they walked to the plate, for the Louisville Slugger bats they carried were most likely made from hardwoods that came from the forests around their town. The Falls of Rough team was known as a "pleasant, mannerly team," and the Hardinsburg squad was practically unbeatable, but the McDaniels Beer Kegs had the best team name.[1]

Bicycles became a rage around the turn of the twentieth century. There were bicycle parties, bicycle teas, bicycle races; it seemed that anything young people found to be fun was enhanced if it could be prefixed with the adjective "bicycle." Bikes even affected fashion. The Hartford *Republican* said, "The bicycle girl, her needs and her fads, is a positive influence in the various departments of commercial enterprise. The 'bicycle skirt' is an industry all by itself.... The 'bicycle boudoir' has appeared, and now on every hand we are confronted with the very latest novelty—bicycle jewelry," such as "various colored enameled 'bikes' which are worn as miniature scarf pins." The bicycle was at first dismissed as a "evanescent toy," but the newspaper was forced to admit in July 1898 that the bike "has long ago established itself as one of the most practical and useful facts of our nineteenth century civilization."[2]

Homegrown musicians gave informal musicales down at the crossroads store, and there were dances. Barn dances were popular and so were the more stylish "hops," where the young collegians from Hartford College and elsewhere performed waltzes, polkas, and quadrilles.

There were amateur theatrics and there were house parties like taffy pulls and the apron parties where the men brought the needles, thimble, and thread. Arriving, the men were randomly paired with a young lady whose name was on a piece of cloth in the bundle of apron-material the men were given at the door. Together, the couple was supposed to sew an apron in thirty minutes. Each apron was judged by a panel of female judges. A prize, and also a booby prize, were awarded. Refreshments and more games followed. Quilting parties were popular, too.

Telephones were becoming common by now, a modern source of news and gossip and of help in emergencies. People had read about telephones in Bowling Green and Owensboro for some months before the first notice of telephone service coming to Hartford appeared in the *Herald* in November 1879: "The Hartford Telephone Company has been organized and will proceed at once to construct a telephone [line] from Hartford to Beaver Dam.... The work will begin at once. Mr. [H. D.] McHenry will erect another line from Beaver Dam to McHenry." Telephone service was not established between Hartford and Leitchfield until the spring of 1900. The *Republican* announced that the Commercial Telephone and Telegraph Company was going to string lines "in a short time" from Hartford through Rosine to Leitchfield.[3]

The people looked forward with great eagerness to the arrival of traveling circuses and troupes of performers. Medicine shows like "Dr. Emmerson's Health Giver" were a related entertainment. Sometimes attendance was so good the shows stayed over for an extra week. Moving pictures arrived soon after the new century began and audiences came to expect more excitement than entertainers like Dr. Emmerson could provide, but horse racing continued as a spectacle for which there was no substitute. Betting on the horses was an honored tradition, though not strictly legal.

And of course, there was always the river. Skating parties in the winter and, in summer, swimming parties at the millpond, swinging on the grapevine or the rope suspended from the tall limb of some sycamore tree, drying slowly in the shade while enjoying a picnic lunch with some special boy or girl—these were memories to be treasured.

With such a knack for pleasure, it was natural for people from the valley of the Rough to carry their talents into the larger world. One was Lazy Jim Day from Short Creek in Grayson County. He was a Grand Ole Opry comedian in the 1940s and drew on Rough River memories for his routine. However, it was not Lazy Jim with his homey stories and songs that represented in the brightest light the talents of the Rough River Valley. That honor falls to Bill Monroe. He was a son of the Rough River, too, and he developed an entirely new musical genre: Bluegrass.

Monroe was born on September 13, 1911, in Rosine, a railroad town begun by Henry D. McHenry on the E&P RR between Leitchfield and Beaver Dam in 1872. When the post office was established that year, the town was called Pigeon Roost for the nearby stream (a tributary of Muddy Creek, which is a tributary of Rough River) where pioneers had observed passenger pigeons roosting in such numbers that they broke the limbs out of the cedar trees. The town was rechristened Rosine in 1873. The new name was given in honor of the founder's wife who wrote poetry under the *nom de plume* "Rosine." Lumber and farming were the major industries. It was a hardscrabble country town where the work was tough and entertainment was homemade.[4]

One of those homemade pastimes was music. Bill Monroe came from a family with a musical strain. His mother, Malissa, played harmonica, fiddle, and accordion. She sang the old English and Scottish ballads and taught her eight sons and daughters to love music like she did. They all played instruments. One reason Bill Monroe played mandolin was that, by the time he came along, it was the only instrument left—there were seven kids ahead of him. Hubert Stringfield, one of his father's farmhands, played the mandolin and "gave the boy his first pointers on the instrument."[5]

Monroe was surrounded by music. His Uncle Pendleton Vandiver played the fiddle at dances all around the county. The shaped-note singers sang their hymns on Sunday. He heard the records of Jimmie Rogers and Charley Poole. And then there was Arnold Shultz, a black guitarist and fiddle player in Rosine, who made friends with the white boy and invited him to play alongside him at local dances. "There's things in my music, you know, that come from Arnold Shultz," Monroe said. "In following a fiddle piece or a breakdown, he used a pick and he could run from one chord to another the prettiest you ever heard." Music was more than just a pleasure to Monroe; it was his sanctuary. He was born cross-eyed and was so shy that he hid in the barn when company came. There was something in the music, though, that brought Bill out of his introspection, and he enjoyed backing up Arnold Shultz or Uncle Pen when they had a dance to play.[6]

Monroe's mother died when he was ten and his father six years later. He went to live with his Uncle Pen until, at age seventeen, he followed his brothers to East Chicago to find work. Birch and Charlie Monroe had jobs at a refinery, but on the side, they continued to play their Kentucky brand of music. Birch was a fiddler, Charlie a guitarist, and now Bill was in town to add his galloping mandolin rhythms to the act. They played at house parties and earned such a reputation that, in 1934, station WLS offered them a radio show. WLS performer Karl

Davis said of Monroe, "He took this mandolin and I've never heard any-body play as fast in my life."[7]

Birch decided that music was an uncertain way to make a living in the midst of the Great Depression, and he finally left the act in favor of dependable work at the northern Indiana refineries. Bill and Charlie, reorganized into The Monroe Brothers, worked full time at their music over the next four years. In 1936, they recorded "What Would You Give in Exchange for Your Soul?" for Bluebird Records, but in 1938, they split up. Like the Everly Brothers (who came from Central City, just over the ridge from Rosine), they could not get along.[8]

What was bad for the act was good for Bill. There was a sound in his head that he wanted to develop. What was this new music that no one could yet hear but Bill? The themes were the familiar ones of love, loneliness, and childhood. It came out of the rural tradition and com-bined elements of both Uncle Pen's ballads and hoedowns and Arnold Shultz's blues. Thrown into the mix was the energy and improvisation of jazz, which Monroe was hearing over Chicago radio. Instrumentally, Monroe depended on the fiddle, guitar, and his own mandolin. Later came the banjo and the bass fiddle and even an accordion. His mother had played accordion and it was a rare sentimental gesture on his part to have one in his band, but it was not really a part of the sound he was hearing and soon the accordion was out. Vocally, Monroe was imagin-ing tight harmonies with the lead singer—often himself—soaring high above the others in a loud, tense style that came to be known to all as the "high, lonesome sound."[9]

That's what the new music was. What it was *not* was mountain music. Bill Monroe was not from the mountains and his music was not of the mountain tradition. If you want to hear the difference, listen to the old 78s of the Carter Family and of the original Coon Creek Girls. Their music is an old music, not polished, but worn smooth by repeti-tion over the long flow of time. You'll hear vestiges of the Renaissance melodies and the drone of the Highland pipes replicated in the guitar, and the old, sad lyrics warning: Daughter, don't go out walking with a boy alone and get yourself killed like that Pretty Polly did. It is true that you'll hear many of the same instruments in both Bluegrass and in these mountain songs, but you can also hear a piano in both the Moon-light Sonata and "Whole Lotta Shakin' Goin' On." They are not the same music.

The new music, Monroe's music, was also not folk music. Folk music is composed of anonymous tunes passed down orally and played by untrained amateurs. The composers of Monroe's tunes were known and the performers learned by instruction. This was a business. Monroe's players had to be smooth and professional if they expected to earn any money. This new music was aimed at a more urban audience, not to the rural crowd that used to pay the musicians fifteen cents a set.

The music Bill Monroe was imagining harkened back to soft memories of country life without celebrating the hard *reality* of country life. Audiences seeing Monroe's band noticed the lack of overalls and flannel shirts. His boys came onstage in dress shirts and neckties, and often in dignified business suits. Only their white cattlemen's hats might be considered novel.

This was a revolutionary music that Monroe was fine tuning and it took work. He and his band practiced for a month before their first performance and then, needing a name, Monroe christened them "The Blue Grass Boys." Why he made two words out of it for the band's name is not known but his inspiration is. Monroe said, "I'd already decided on using the name 'blue grass' because that's what they call Kentucky, the Bluegrass State. So I just used 'Bill Monroe and the Blue Grass Boys' and that let people throughout the country know I was from Kentucky."[10]

Some say that this was the moment when Bluegrass music was born. Others say that it was the next year, 1939, when George D. Hay, the "Solemn Old Judge" of the Grand Ole Opry, hired the Blue Grass Boys after hearing them in a radio broadcast from Atlanta. Hay said, "Bill Monroe is one of the most authentic representatives of homespun music—more properly known as American Folk Music—that I have met in a quarter of a century. He sings straight from the heart." But even at the time of their Opry debut, the sound was not quite perfected. Monroe's banjo player was another Kentuckian, Dave "Stringbean" Akeman. Akeman's talent often goes overlooked because of the corny stage costume he wore when he went off on his own, but Stringbean was a gifted interpreter of traditional songs. He played his banjo clawhammer style. Dave Akeman was good, and Monroe liked him, but his contribution to the group did not result in the sound sought by Monroe.[11]

Then, in 1945, he hired Earl Scruggs as one of the Blue Grass Boys. Scruggs was a North Carolinian who had been performing since age six. He had invented a banjo method called the three-finger roll, a driving style distinguished by a blizzard of perfectly distinct notes and no strumming. Also in Monroe's band that year were Chubby Wise on fiddle, Lester Flatt on guitar, and Howard Watts on bass. *This* was the sound Monroe had been trying to capture, the sound recognized everywhere today as Bluegrass music. Over the years, there was a constantly rotating cast of musicians, but the sound remained the same. In 1949, Bill Monroe and the Blue Grass Boys signed a recording contract with Decca Records. With Jimmy Martin on board as a guitar player and vocalist, Monroe now entered a period of writing that produced a string of classics, including the song that many consider to be his masterpiece, "Uncle Pen."[12]

Monroe's mandolin was a Gibson F-5 that he had bought for $150 after seeing it in a barbershop window in Miami, Florida. He strung it with bronze Gibsons and he chopped at them with a tortoise-shell flat-pick with the point shaved off. Inside his mandolin, Monroe kept a rattlesnake rattle. It was an old fiddler's trick meant to keep insects out. Aside from this bit of whimsy, Monroe was all business. He was a man of little humor and did not joke. Mark Hambree, who was one of the Blue Grass Boys from 1979 to 1984, said, "Almost everyone I knew was scared of Bill Monroe." He did not take real or imagined slights gracefully. He was a long time forgiving Flatt and Scruggs for leaving him in '48.[13]

The same flinty attitude helped hold back the very music he had created. The advent of rock and roll in the middle fifties and the popularity of Elvis Presley shifted attention away from Bluegrass music. Monroe refused to adapt his music to make it more palatable to the ears of rock fans, though he did enjoy the royalties from Elvis's cover of "Blue Moon of Kentucky" and did re-record the song to reflect Elvis's more energetic version. That exception notwithstanding, the revolutionary musician had become the most intractable conservative. Play dates began to diminish.[14]

Monroe biographer Richard D. Smith writes that Monroe was forced to play "a patchwork of jobs. There was always WSM's *Friday Night Frolic* and the *Grand Ole Opry* on Saturday night for union scale and a few moments of prestige. Otherwise, the Blue Grass Boys performed at the little country music parks as well as in a pre-dusk act at drive-in theaters and in high school auditoriums, courthouses, and American Legion Halls. They even played for square dances if someone would hire them." One night in Georgia, the band played for a man and his wife, the only two people in town who were interested enough to come to the high school gym to hear an American original who now had grown *passé*.[15]

The turning point came in 1963, when Monroe got a new manager, Ralph Rinzler, the author of a story for the February–March *Sing Out!* It was entitled "Bill Monroe—The Daddy of Blue Grass Music," and Monroe's picture was on the cover. That same year Monroe and the Blue Grass Boys played the University of Chicago Folk Festival and the Newport Folk Festival; they also played in New York for the first time. Musicians in the burgeoning Greenwich Village folk revival began to discover Bluegrass music and Monroe's style of playing. Mike Seeger became one of his best friends. The young folkies helped keep a spark of interest alive in Bluegrass. Two years later, in 1965, the first major Blue Grass festival was held in Roanoke, Virginia, and the next year Bill Monroe began hosting an annual festival at his farm in Bean Blossom, Indiana. About the same time, two popular television shows, *The Andy Griffith Show* and *The Beverly Hillbillies*, were airing episodes that featured Bluegrass music, introducing it to millions who had never heard the records. "The Ballad of Jed Clampett" by Flatt and Scruggs was the first #1 Bluegrass hit on the Billboard charts. Flatt and Scruggs also had bit parts in a few episodes of *The Beverly Hillbillies*. They charted another hit in 1967 when their song "Foggy Mountain Breakdown" was used as the getaway theme in *Bonnie and Clyde*. The song was seventeen years old, but it was fresh to the moviegoers. After this, to many listeners, Flatt and Scruggs were *the* face of Bluegrass music and "Foggy Mountain Breakdown" its most representative tune.[16]

Slowly, Bluegrass was coming back, but it was changing. Monroe could not control the new direction his music was taking, no matter how much he balked. In 1966 Jim and Jesse included electric guitar, drums, and pedal steel on their song "Diesel on My Tail." The Osborne Brothers amplified their banjo and mandolin in 1969 and, in shades of Bob Dylan at Newport, were booed off the stage, but they also became the first Bluegrass act to perform at the White House (1973). The New Grass Revival recorded the songs of hippie icon Leon Russell and employed Jerry Lee Lewis as a sideman on its first LP. Women were getting in on the act, too. Ronnie Stoneman, daughter of traditional musician Ernest "Pop" Stoneman, was a mistress of the banjo in the manner of Earl Scruggs (and, like him, tried her hand at acting, on the television series *Hee Haw* and also in the movie *W.W. and the Dixie Dancekings*). Dolly Parton recorded a Bluegrass album and Patty Loveless took her career in a direction that was almost entirely Bluegrass. Alison Krauss was another gifted and innovative Bluegrass performer. Many of these acts, called Progressive Bluegrass or New Acoustic, changed not only the sound but also the appearance of Bluegrass. They did not wear suits.[17]

Bluegrass was breaking out of the narrow confines of the Grand Ole Opry and country music radio, growing in ways that Monroe could never have foreseen. Still, he did not approve of many of the musicians performing it, although they loved his music and were bringing along a new generation of younger fans. When the Nitty Gritty Dirt Band recorded a three-LP set of acoustical music in the early seventies, the band invited Bill Monroe to play on the sessions. Earl Scruggs performed on *Will the Circle be Unbroken.* So did Jimmy Martin, Vassar Clements, Doc Watson, Mother Maybelle Carter, and Merle Travis from

Muhlenberg County. Even Roy Acuff, an East Tennessee reactionary who was clearly disapproving of the long-haired, denim-wearing musicians, agreed to perform when he heard the respect they had for the music and the talent they brought into the studio. Of all the important old-timers, only Bill Monroe would not play. In the first month alone, *Will the Circle be Unbroken* sold a phenomenal 25,000 copies, but without Monroe's help.[18]

Ever so slowly, another change of direction was occurring—not in the music, however, but in the man. He was elected to the Country Music Hall of Fame in 1970. In 1986, the U.S. Senate passed a resolution that called him a "cultural figure and force of signal importance." Somewhere along the line, his crossed eyes had been surgically corrected and the hair, which he was wearing longer, was a dignified gray. His posture was still erect. He looked like a statesman, like a legend.

And he could still play. He won a Grammy in 1989 for the album *Southern Flavor.* Ricky Skaggs recorded his songs and even got him to appear in music videos and to do a little clog dance for the camera. His attitude and demeanor were loosening up. He danced with the lovely Emmylou Harris on the stage of Ryman Auditorium and sometimes the audience even saw him smile. Monroe seemed to enjoy performing now more than ever before, and he continued until he could play no more.[19]

Bill Monroe had a stroke in 1995 and died at the Springfield Nursing Home outside of Nashville on September 9, 1996. At his funeral at

Bill Monroe (photograph by Rick Gardner and used with his permission).

the Ryman, there was an open casket viewing, but the casket was closed for the funeral, his white Stetson hat resting on top. Vince Gill, Ricky Skaggs, and Marty Stuart played "Working on a Building." Emmylou Harris joined them on stage for "Poor Wayfaring Stranger." After the first eulogy, Ralph Stanley sang "Rank Stranger" and "Angel Band" with Alison Krauss singing harmony. Connie Smith performed and, after a second eulogy, Patty Loveless sang "Go Rest High on that Mountain." As the funeral procession left the Mother Church, three bagpipers played "Amazing Grace."[20]

Ricky Skaggs picked it up the next day when they brought Bill Monroe home to Rosine, a day before what would have been his birthday. The circle of Monroe's life was almost perfectly closed. A crowd of nearly 1,200 mourners heard Skaggs begin the favorite hymn of many: "Amazing Grace, how sweet the sound...." Ralph Stanley performed again and a local African American woman named Alma Randolph sang "Take My Hand, Precious Lord." Several former Blue Grass Boys and other Opry performers attended. When the service in the little Methodist Church was finished, they took Bill Monroe to the cemetery and buried him not far from Uncle Pen.[21]

The music Bill Monroe invented has grown to encompass the globe, but he made sure the world knew where the first seeds were planted. Now, that same place, the valley of the Rough, honors Monroe. The road between Hartford and Rosine might officially be U.S. 62, but road signs proclaim it to be the "Blue Moon of Kentucky Highway." The famous mandolin might be in the collection of the Country Music Hall of Fame, but Rosine has his boyhood home and also the cabin of Uncle Pen, both of which have been restored. In October, the little town hosts the Jerusalem Ridge Festival and Bluegrass Celebration. Local groups and Bluegrass music associations keep the music alive in the valley that inspired it. It is not only practitioners of the music that are fascinated by Bluegrass. Academics, too, have begun to look at the music as an American art form as diverse as jazz. Western Kentucky University in Bowling Green has hosted a symposium of scholars to dissect the music and to trace its many sources.

It does not end there. The 2000 movie *O Brother, Where Art Thou?* gave Bluegrass a definite boost among the listening public. It spawned the 2001 concert series of acoustical music "Down from the Mountain" and the imitation *O Mickey, Where Art Thou?* (a film from Disney Studios aimed at youngsters—Bluegrass fans of the future, no doubt).[22]

There is no telling what new direction Bluegrass might take or how long its popularity may last. The founding father himself deserves the last word on that. In 1983, Mr. Monroe observed, "Bluegrass is growing every day; it's still growing."[23]

THIRTY

Rough River Today

Kentucky coal production boomed during World War I and so did the market for farm products, but in the 1920s and '30s, the foundation stones of the local economy crumbled. Western Kentucky coal producers could not compete because of the too-narrow locks on the rivers. Worse, the tobacco market collapsed and corn production fell by twenty percent. Out of forty-eight states, Kentucky ranked forty-seventh in farm income. In *A New History of Kentucky*, Lowell Harrison and James Klotter draw a statistical sketch of the lives of Kentucky's farmers: by 1930 "only 2.8 percent of farms had tractors (one-fifth of the American average), only 4.3 percent were lighted by electricity (one-third the national mean), and only one-fourth had telephones (versus one-third of U.S. farm homes)."[1]

The depression became widespread with the lingering effects of the stock market crash in 1929, but there was no relief from the misery just because there was more company. Then there was more company still. In 1930 a devastating drought settled over the land. "In some counties, 85% of an already decreased corn crop withered and died." State-wide, "crop losses exceeded one hundred million dollars."[2]

Relief did not come to the Rough River Valley until the election of President Franklin Roosevelt and the initiation of the New Deal. WPA workers built new roads and bridges in addition to the schools and courthouses. Both Hardin County and Grayson County got a new courthouse in the 1930s. The CCC offered boys the chance to leave their impoverished families, which reduced the number of mouths to feed and at the same time provided a small monthly income taken from the boys' earnings. Their work helped restore an exhausted land by reforestation and erosion control. The AAA attacked farm poverty from an economic standpoint. Its idea was to increase prices by reducing crop production. Tobacco farmers, for instance, benefited by the Tobacco Control Act of 1934. Like the cotton farmers down South, Kentucky's tobacco growers had grown their crops to excess, but now they were encouraged to accept "mandatory quotas for a minimum price ... guaranteed by federal policy." By the end of the second growing season after the act, farmers had "reduced their harvest by 28 percent while increasing overall income by several million dollars."[3]

Then there was the REA, which brought low-cost electricity to corners of the Rough River Valley where the private power companies had refused to string lines. The Green River Electric Corporation first began to be discussed in Daviess County in March 1937. It appeared there was popular support. When twenty-five local farmers were invited to a March 20 meeting with the county extension agent Jack McClure, fifty showed up. The uninvited attendees "had learned of the proposed project and were interested."[4]

Ten days later, "a total of 1,056 signed survey/membership sheets were on McClure's desk," and when it was learned that "about three hundred" farmers in Ohio and McLean counties wanted to be included, the project's boundaries were extended east. The federal loans began in May of 1937, and the next month Green River Electric was incorporated. Then the project began to run into difficulty. Unlike the case of the Nolin RECC, the early numbers were deceiving as to "membership recruitment." A history of Green River Electric says, "There was a lot of skepticism, doubt, and superstition.... Then, too, jealousy and dislike for neighbors entered into it. Some farmers would not agree to a line running across their farm that would also serve a neighbor they did not like." It was "rough going." Nevertheless, the officials and the crews did keep going, and the lines were electrified in May 1938.[5]

One New Deal initiative that is not so well known was a widespread program of archaeological excavation across the Southeast. The creation of the Tennessee Valley Authority in 1933 was a spur to archaeological surveys and excavations because hundreds of pre–Columbian sites would soon be flooded. William S. Webb, chair of the University of Kentucky's Department of Anthropology and Archaeology, became the head of the TVA archaeological project. In the twenties, Webb and William D. Funkhouser, a zoologist, had located and excavated a number of Indian sites in Kentucky and had published their findings in *Ancient Life in Kentucky* (1928) and *Archaeological Survey of Kentucky* (1932). Though some of their interpretations were later challenged and their field techniques criticized, their work was groundbreaking and well regarded in its time. Working for the TVA, Webb had the chance to indulge his interest across a much wider area. Webb's crews excavated sites in nine of the ten TVA reservoirs that were created between 1933 and 1945, a region stretching across seven states. There was a lack of skilled archaeologists at first, but Webb was sure that that problem was not insurmountable. He said, "I recall when this country went to war [in 1917], it called 4.5 million men into the army, and gave every man a job. Many of these men knew nothing about their new jobs, but they had to do them and they did." Now, in Depression-era America, he said, "There are not enough archaeologists to do the work, men with common sense enough to handle laborers have to be chosen and trained to know a little about archaeology." Webb's faith was justified. Over time, his workforce grew to nineteen field supervisors and more than a thousand workers. The northern-born field supervisors and the southern work crews made an unlikely team, but they worked well together, and, on the whole, the supervisors reported favorably on the work ethic of their workers and the quickness with which they mastered the exacting techniques of excavation.[6]

In the summer of 1937, Webb organized his first major WPA archaeological excavations in Kentucky. The lower Tennessee River Valley, where the impounded waters would soon cover the land to create Kentucky Lake, was of great importance, of course, but Webb did not limit his attention solely to that locality. Several sites along Green River and its tributaries were excavated under the supervision of John B. Elliott of Chicago. He came to Calhoun, the McLean County seat, rented quarters, and immediately bumped up against the local attitude when his landlady eyed him carefully and asked, "Doesn't the WPA have better things to spend the government's money on?" One wonders if the local people took a suspicious and resentful attitude toward outsiders because of the negative national attention paid to their county during the ugly racial events of 1911.[7]

Unintimidated, Elliott began his work in 1938 at the Ward Site on Cypress Creek, a short distance from where Rough River enters the Green. He had a crew of twenty-five men (who "impressed him from the beginning"), and the settlement they excavated turned out to be one of the most rewarding of the late Archaic sites.[8]

The site was dated to 2184 BCE, plus or minus sixty years. Four scalping victims were found buried there, suggesting that occasional warfare existed in Kentucky even before the Woodland era, and there were grave goods of seashells, a clear indication of trade. There were sixty-three dog burials. The workers found 481 projectile points, 705 scrapers, 201 drills, and 216 pestles. Curiously, there were few mortars. About this, Sara E. Pedde and Olaf H. Prufer say, "Perhaps the excavators in the 1930s did not recognize such informal objects unless they were obvious; also, such objects may have been made of wood."[9]

There were 1,036 bone and antler tools uncovered at the Ward Site, including fish hooks, bone pins, a turtle shell rattle, and shuttles that were used in rudimentary weaving. The food remains included deer bones, hickory nuts, acorns, squash, sunflowers, goosefoot, and little barley. Victor D. Thompson writes, "The Ward Site and its surrounding area stands out above all others in the Cypress Creek landscape," and concludes that "during the late Middle Archaic continuing into the Late Archaic, it became important for groups to claim specific areas of the landscape.... I suggest that, collectively, intensely occupied sites in the Cypress Creek area served to define territories of Archaic hunter-gatherer groups."[10]

When work ended at the Ward Site, only nineteen percent had been excavated. Who knows what information the Ward Site might have yielded up if Elliott and his crew had been allowed to continue? Certainly, there was much more to be found. It is estimated that the 465 burials excavated at Ward represented only one-fifth of the total. Yet, perhaps ending the work was not a bad thing. The quality of Elliott's work has been criticized in recent times, and eighty-one percent of the site remains undisturbed, waiting for later scholars with more advanced techniques to continue where Elliott left off. It is well to leave something for the future.[11]

As World War II loomed, the personnel and money of the New Deal archaeology program were siphoned away for other purposes. In its brief life, the program had given work to nearly three hundred Kentuckians during the dark days of economic collapse, and it had connected the distant past and the future in a meaningful way. Scholar Lynne P. Sullivan and her colleagues say in a paper that was presented to the Southern Archaeology Society that the number of artifacts recovered by New Deal archaeologists led to the creation of museums and the start of anthropology departments in state universities, and also "to the creation of a regional archaeology conference. The Southeastern Archaeological Conference (SEAC) was created in 1938 as a platform for archaeologists to report on New Deal excavations, discuss findings, synthesize broad trends, and coordinate regional efforts." And so, in Kentucky and across the South, New Deal archaeology had thrown impoverished men and women an economic lifeline, had laid the groundwork for good and substantive work that continues to this day, and had led to the creation of museums that attract tourists—and tourist dollars—by the thousands.[12]

A fantasy of permanence seems to be part of human nature. The people of the Ward Site lived there a very long time, long enough to inter 2,300 dead. The people must have developed an emotional connection to the setting, must have passed on traditions and stories of life in their Cypress Creek village to the younger generations over a span of hundreds of years. Nothing much ever changed. They had reason to consider their situation to be permanent. Yet, today nothing remains but ruins, and, more than that, the earth has buried the site so deeply that this once vibrant community has to be *excavated* to reveal its mysteries.

People's attitudes are no different in modern times. We feel confident that our works will endure, even when the evidence of the past proves otherwise. Nearly one hundred years ago, the Depression saw the decline and disappearance of communities that had once hummed with industry. Falls of Rough was one. It was only about one hundred years old—the blink of an eye—when, in the 1920s, it began losing ground. A sign of the coming trouble may have been detected in April 1920, when the Green brothers had to advertise for weeks in the *Breckinridge News* for a farmhand to drive a tractor. In autumn of the same year, Falls of Rough lost its blacksmith. Once again, the brothers had to place ads in the *News*, promising applicants a "Good Shop with Good Trade."[13]

The Depression accelerated the slide. Farm prices dropped. Money was tight and business suffered. Falls of Rough had not recovered before another blow came. Rail service to Falls of Rough ended in 1941. Hugh Ridenour says, "because much of the Green business had in some way been connected with the railroad, profits suffered severely." Time, too, had turned against the Green family and its domain. The brothers were growing old. Between 1943 and 1945, all three died. They had never married and left no heirs. Their sister Jennie was the survivor. She, too, had never married. She remained at the family mansion, living on the bequests of her brothers until she died in 1965. The village, in decline for the last forty years and in steep decline for the last thirty, barely survived her.[14]

The debacle of the 1930s taught people how precariously balanced is the economy built by man. Systemic reforms were made in hopes of preventing another such disaster, and out of the floods and the droughts of that decade progress was made in people's understanding of how fragile the earth is, also, and how better to protect its resources. The farmers came to see their responsibility to conserve the land while using it and also their responsibility to their neighbors downstream.

Rough River begins in Hardin County and the creeks and the springs on the western side of the county nourish it as it bends toward Grayson and Breckinridge. Pirtle Spring in Howe Valley provides drinking water for people living in Hardin County Water District Number One; Rough River Lake supplies Grayson County and Leitchfield; and Hardinsburg's drinking water comes from Tules Creek. The land is pockmarked with sinkholes, and the run-off from farms, factories, and homes is of concern to almost everyone in the valley, for it will surely show up again. "This whole area is one of the most sensitive karst areas in the state," explains Rob Grusy, the Hardin County Extension Agent.[15]

So it was that a group of fifty farmers met one night in March 2005, concerned about water tests at the Pirtle Springs water treatment plant that had shown more than twice the permitted amount of the herbicide atrazine. To prevent soil erosion, the once-common method of plowing to control weeds had mostly been abandoned. Richard Preston, who farmed 2,400 acres, explained in a *News-Enterprise* article that tilling for weed control would greatly accelerate soil erosion. "All the (best part of the land) would wash away and Nolin Lake (or Rough River Lake) would fill up and become a delta. And pretty soon the land would become desolate ... because top soil is the key resource."[16]

Since plowing was out, farmers turned to chemicals like atrazine, an effective and inexpensive weed killer. At low levels, it is safe, even in drinking water, but heavy rains in 2005 had caused excessive runoff and now it was measured at dangerous levels. When the alarm was raised, eighty-five percent of the farmers who lived near the headwaters of the Rough came to learn what they could do to help. Farmers are among the most independent-minded of citizens, but this response showed that now as never before they understood their role as the first line in the conservation of the land and water.[17]

At the meeting, government men encouraged the farmers to plant filter strips between crops and creeks and around sinkholes. A federal cost-sharing program would help to make up for the loss of cropland. Cutting the amount of atrazine to smaller applications was shown to be both cost effective and still lethal to weeds and was urgently recommended. Simple solutions, accomplished by the cooperation of farmers and federal officials. That *is* progress.[18]

In the enduring fight to protect the land and the water of the Rough River Valley, the farmers are allied with a powerful collection of government agencies, including the Kentucky Department of Agriculture, the Kentucky Department of Natural Resources (Division of Water), the University of Kentucky College of Agriculture Co-operative Extension Service, the U.S. Department of Agriculture Natural Resource Conservation Service, the U.S. Environmental Protection Agency, the Kentucky Department of Fish and Wildlife (which also administers the L.B. Davison Wildlife Management Area south of Fordsville), and the Kentucky Rural Water Association. Another one is the U.S. Army Corps of Engineers. In 1955, the Corps undertook one of the largest and most beneficial of all Rough River projects, the completion of Rough River Dam and Lake.[19]

Authorized by the Flood Control Act of 1938, the project was begun in 1959 and finished in 1961. The end result was an earth and rock dam, 130 feet high and 1,590 feet long, impounding enough of Rough River to create a lake of 5,100 acres. That equals 303,650 acre feet of water, from which Leitchfield draws its drinking water. The cost was $10.5 million, a sum to make some people cry humbug and throw their hands up in dismay at this waste of the taxpayer's money.[20]

Was it worth it? The numbers do not lie. Since the dam was finished, flood damage reduction has averaged $4.4 million yearly. As of 2022, that equals almost $270 million in total. But that is not all. The lake was intended to bring the pleasures of Rough River to the people and it has done that. There is overnight lodging in the lodge itself, in the detached cottages, and in the campground. There is a golf course; the main attractions of boating, skiing, and fishing; and in recent years the pleasure of bald eagle watching—all in a beautiful setting of water, woods and hills. Johnson says, "When the Louisville District planned Rough River Lake in the 1950s, it estimated 60,000 visitation days during the first year, rising ultimately to 100,000 a year; with 1.8 million visitation days in 1982, Rough River Lake was tops among the six lakes in the District." Tourist spending amounts to more than $40 million every year.[21]

The fight to intelligently use and regulate the land, water, and forests of the Rough River Valley and to pass them on to the children is not the kind of bloody fight that the people of Rough River have always won in their long written history. It is not like the fight against the Shawnee with their British flintlocks or the fight against skulking outlaws like Dock Brown. It is not like fighting the marauding guerrilla band of 1864 or the racist lynch mob of 1911.

The fight to protect the shy river, this hidden treasure of Kentucky, is a different kind of fight. It requires new tactics that are sometimes hard to understand. It requires a deeper level of cooperation because it does not involve only one county or one community. And yet the fight must be made, for both the present and the future. Kentucky's own Wendell Berry harkens back to an ancient wisdom to remind us of our very modern responsibilities. He says: "Do unto those downstream as you would have those upstream do unto you."[22]

Chapter Notes

Chapter One

1. National Park Service, "Convergent Plate Boundaries—Collisional Mountain Ranges," nps.gov/subjects/geology/plate-tectonics-collisional-mountain-ranges. htm. Accessed June 18, 2022.
2. Ronald L. Jones, *Plant Life of Kentucky: An Illustrated Guide to Vascular Flora* (Lexington: University Press of Kentucky, 2005), 57, 59, 149; Kenneth B. Tankersley, "Ice Age Hunters and Gatherers," in *Kentucky Archaeology—Perceptions in Kentucky's Past: Architecture, Archaeology, and Landscape*, ed. R. Barry Lewis (Lexington: University Press of Kentucky, 2014), 21.
3. Greg J. Maggard and Kary L. Stackelbeck, "Paleoindian Period," in *The Archaeology of Kentucky: An Update, Volume One*, ed. David Pollack (Kentucky Heritage Council, 2008), 145.
4. Philip DiBlasi, "Prehistoric Inhabitants," in *The Encyclopedia of Louisville*, ed. John E. Kleber (Lexington: University of Kentucky Press, 2001), 720–721; R. Berle Clay, "Prehistoric Peoples," in *The Kentucky Encyclopedia*, ed. John E. Kleber (Lexington: University Press of Kentucky, 1992), 734.
5. A. Gwynn Henderson and Eric J. Schlarb, *Adena: Woodland Period Moundbuilders of the Bluegrass* (Lexington: Kentucky Archaeological Survey, 2007), 1–2, 15.
6. *Ibid.*, 20.
7. John H. Blitz, "Adoption of the Bow and Arrow in Prehistoric North America," in *North American Archaeologist*, Vol. 9, No. 2, 1998, 131.

8. Bennett H. Young, *The Prehistoric Men of Kentucky* (Louisville: John P. Morton & Co., 1910), 59.
9. *Ibid.*, 96.
10. *Ibid.*, 97–98.

Chapter Two

1. Samuel Haycraft, *A History of Elizabethtown, Ky. and Its Surroundings* (Elizabethtown: Hardin County Historical Society, 1975), 23.
2. *Ibid.*
3. *Ibid.*, 13–14; Lewis Collins, *History of Kentucky* (Lexington: Henry Clay Press, 1968), 336–337 (hereafter cited as Collins, 1968 ed.); Ruth Bruner Sims, unpublished family history in author's collection and letter to the author, Nov. 10, 1979.
4. Nelson County, Kentucky, Will Book A.
5. Francis D. Cogliano, *Revolutionary America, 1763–1815: A Political History* (New York: Routledge, 2000), 90. Cogliano offers the following statistic to show just how fierce the Indian wars were in Kentucky: During the Revolution, "there was one war-related death for every thousand people. In Kentucky (which of course had a much smaller population) there was one death for every seventy inhabitants" (p. 90).
6. Otis Mather, "Explorers and Early Settlers South of Muldraugh Hill," *Register of the Kentucky Historical Society*, Jan. 1924.
7. Evelyn Crady Adams, "Goodin's Fort (1780) in Nelson County, Ky.," *Filson Club History Quarterly*, Jan. 1953, 5;

"DAR-SAR mark Capt. Samuel Pottinger, Revolutionary War Soldier," *Kentucky Standard* [Bardstown] Nov. 5, 2015; Nancy O'Malley, "Pottinger's Station," *The Kentucky Encyclopedia*, 731.

8. O'Malley, *Kentucky Encyclopedia*, 731; David Hall, "Pottinger's Home was Finest in State," Pottinger-Pottenger and Kin, pottinger-pottenger.com/pictures/pottingers-home-was-finest-in-state-published-in-ky-standard-newspaper-1985-2099249. Accessed Apr. 19, 2021.

9. Adams, 3–6.

10. Adams, 6; Collins, 1968 ed., 335–336.

11. Adams, 8–10; Sarah B. Smith, *Historic Nelson County* (Bardstown: Gateway Press, 1971), 29.

12. Dixie Hibbs, "Bardstown," *The Kentucky Encyclopedia*, 51; Robert M. Rennick, *Kentucky Place Names* (Lexington: University Press of Kentucky, 1984), 34.

13. Jerry Long, "Rogers Station, Nelson County, Kentucky," *West Central Kentucky Family Research Association Bulletin*, Summer 1996, 2–3, 22; J. H. Spencer, *History of Kentucky Baptists from 1769 to 1885, Volume I* (Cincinnati: by the author, 1886), 134.

14. Long, 4; Spencer, 134, 484.

15. M.L. Coomes, "Benjamin Lynn, John Ritchie, John Gilkey and a Story of an Early Distillery in Kentucky," Filson Club Paper, Jan. 7, 1895.

16. Bob Sehlinger and Johnny Molloy, *A Canoeing and Kayaking Guide to Kentucky* (Manasha Ridge Press, 2001), 175.

17. "The Ritchies," Nelson County *Record*, Mar. 16, 1897.

Chapter Three

1. "National Historic Landmarks," *The Kentucky Encyclopedia*, 672.

2. Daniel McClure, *Two Centuries in Elizabethtown and Hardin County, Kentucky* (Elizabethtown: Hardin County Historical Society, 1979), 6 (cited hereafter as McClure, *Two Centuries*).

3. Robert E. McDowell, "Bullitt's Lick: The Related Saltworks and Settlement,"

Filson Club History Quarterly, July 1956, 252.

4. Collins, 1968 ed., 219. The woman who was abandoned on the flatboat was taken by the Indians to Canada. A trader redeemed her and delivered her to General Anthony Wayne's camp in Ohio in 1794. She told him her story. In the Battle of Pitts Point, she said, there had been 120 Indians at the start, but the flatboatmen had killed thirty of them.

5. Collins, 1968 ed., 219.

6. *Ibid.*, 220.

7. *Ibid.*; McClure, *Two Centuries*, 43.

8. Thomas W. Riley, "Autobiography of Gen Henry Crist of Kentucky," *Wilderness Road: Quarterly of the Bullitt County Genealogical Society*, Sept. 1990.

9. Hardin County, Kentucky, Marriage Book A, 9; Joshua D. Farrington, "Braddock, General," in *The Kentucky African American Encyclopedia*, eds. Gerald K. Smith, Karen Cotton McDaniel, and John A. Hardin (Lexington: University Press of Kentucky, 2015), 61–62; Ruth Bruner Sims, letter to the author, Jan. 1, 1980.

10. Ben J. Webb, *The Centenary of Catholicity in Kentucky* (Louisville: J.C. Webb & Co., 1884), 102.

Chapter Four

1. L.F. Johnson, *Famous Kentucky Trials and Tragedies* (Lexington: Henry Clay Press, 1972), 20.

2. "Springfield Presbyterian Church celebrates history with 220th anniversary," The Springfield *Sun*, Nov. 24, 2008; William E. Arnold, *A History of Methodism in Kentucky, Volume I* (Louisville: The Herald Press, 1935), 71; Kentucky Historical Marker 1066.

3. McClure, *Two Centuries*, 36–37.

4. M. J. Spalding and Stephen T. Badin, *Sketches of the Early Catholic Missions of Kentucky* (Louisville: B.J. Webb & Brother, 1844), 43–48.

5. Webb, 33.

6. *Ibid.*, 161.

7. Collins, 1968 ed., 140; Webb, 460.

8. Webb, 179.

9. Clyde F. Crews, "Badin, Stephen Theodore," in *The Kentucky Encyclopedia*, 43.

10. Collins, 1968 ed., 141.

11. Webb, 144; 188–89.

12. Works Progress Administration, *The WPA Guide to Kentucky,* ed. F. Kevin Simon (Lexington: University Press of Kentucky, 1996), 291–292; Florence Wolff, "Sisters of Loretto," in *The Kentucky Encyclopedia*, 824–825.

13. Hannah O'Daniel, "Southern Veils: The Sisters of Loretto in Early National Kentucky" (Master's Thesis, University of Louisville, 2014), 1, 69, 101, https://doi.org/10.18297/etd/2859. Accessed June 25, 2022. Susanna Pyatt, "Federal Census for Loretto Slaveholding, 1820–1860." lorettocommunity. org/federal-census-evidence-for-loretto-slaveholding-1820–1860/. Accessed June 24, 2022. "We Repent," lorettocommunity.org. Accessed June 24, 2022. Calling the holding of slaves Loretto's "original sin," the order set up a slave memorial at the motherhouse in 2000. It lists the names of the known Loretto slaves and bears the legend "Pray for us."

14. Martin J. Spalding, *Sketches of the Life and Times and Character of the Right Reverend Benedict Joseph Flaget* (Louisville: Webb & Levering, 1852), 114.

15. J. Herman Schauinger, *Cathedrals in the Widlerness.* (Milwaukee: The Bruce Publishing Co., 1952), 61.

16. Spalding, *Flaget*, 102–104.

17. Schauinger, 70.

18. *Ibid.*, 176.

19. Schauinger, 222–224.

20. Crews, *Kentucky Encyclopedia*, 323; Spalding, *Flaget*, 355.

21. Smith, *Historic Nelson County*, 67.

22. Ibid.

Chapter Five

1. William E. Baringer, *Lincoln Day by Day, Volume I* (Washington: Lincoln Sesquicentennial Commission, 1960), 6; Louis-Philippe, King of France, *Diary of My Travels in America*, translated from the French by Stephen Becker (New York: Delacorte Press, 1977), 117.

2. "Zachariah Riney," Elizabethtown *News*, Oct. 1, 1940.

3. John Wade Thompson, "Account of Sarah Mitchell by her son John Wade Thompson Papers found at his death," Mitchell Family File, Kentucky Historical Society, Frankfort, Kentucky; Louis A. Warren, "The Romance of Thomas Lincoln and Nancy Hanks," *Indiana Magazine of History*, Sept. 1934, 215–216.

4. Harry H. Smith, *Lincoln and the Lincolns* (New York: Pioneer Publications, 1931), 231–232; Louis A. Warren, "Abraham Lincoln, Sr., Grandfather of the President," *Filson Club History Quarterly*, Oct. 1935.

5. Warren, "Romance of Thomas Lincoln and Nancy Hanks," 221; Ida M. Tarbell, *The Early Life of Abraham Lincoln* (New York: S. S. McClure, Limited, 1896), 40, 228–229.

6. Mitchell Family File, Kentucky Historical Society, Frankfort, Kentucky.

7. Francis Marion Van Natter, "Little Grave on Knob Creek," *National Republic*, Feb. 1934, 3.

8. Richard N. Current, *The Lincoln Nobody Knows* (New York: Hill & Wang, 1958), 27.

9. *Ibid.*, 24; Stefan Lorant, *Lincoln: A Picture Story of His Life* (New York: Norton, 1969), 14–15.

10. "He Played with Lincoln," *Elizabethtown News*, Mar. 23, 1894.

11. *Ibid.*

12. *Ibid.*

13. Ida Tarbell, *In the Footsteps of the Lincolns* (New York: Harper & Bros., 1924), 105.

14. *Ibid.*, 20, 27; Tarbell, Early *Life of Lincoln*, 109–112.

15. Lowell H. Harrison, *Lincoln of Kentucky* (Lexington: University Press of Kentucky, 2010), 23; Sandburg, 30; National Park Service, *Lincoln's Boyhood Home at Knob Creek*, 12.

16. Van Natter, 3; Sandburg, 30–31.

17. "Zachariah Riney," Elizabethtown *News*, Oct. 1, 1940.

18. Carolyn Wimp, compiler, *Hardin County, Kentucky Newspaper Abstracts, 1905–1907* (Vine Grove: Ancestral Trails Historical Society, 2002), 265; Lincoln Boyhood Home Brochure ,n.d., collection of the author; James R. Carroll, "Farm where Lincoln lived may become park," *Courier Journal*, Nov. 9, 1998. Caleb Hazel was the Lincoln children's second teacher at Knob Creek.

Chapter Six

1. WPA, *Guide to Kentucky*, 291.
2. *Ibid.*
3. Collins, 1968 ed., 216, 334, 397, 426, 474.
4. Nancy O'Malley, *A Documentary History of Pitts Point: A River Town in Bullitt County, Ky.* (Lexington: Program for Cultural Resources Assessment, Department of Anthropology, University of Kentucky, 1996), 4, 8, 15, 50. George W. Hawes, *Kentucky State Gazetteer and Business Directory for 1859 and 1860* (Vine Grove: Ancestral Trails Historical Society, 2006).
5. Rennick, *Kentucky Place Names*, 145–146; Hay, Melba Porter, et al., *Roadside History: A Guide to Kentucky Highway Markers* (Lexington: University Press of Kentucky, 2002), 106.
6. "Our Tennessee Correspondence," New York *Times*, Mar. 28, 1862.
7. Tom Pack, "Bullitt County," in *The Kentucky Encyclopedia*, 140.
8. Carolyn Wimp, compiler, *Newspaper Abstracts, Hardin County, Kentucky, 1829–1893* (Vine Grove: Ancestral Trails Historical Society, 1999), 15.
9. Carolyn Wimp, complier, *Newspaper Abstracts, 1905 to 1907*, 286.
10. *Ibid.*, 287.

Chapter Seven

1. U.S. War Department, *The War of the Rebellion: A Compilation of the Official Records of the Union and Confederate Armies*, 129 vols. (Washington, D.C.: Government Printing Office, 1880–1901), Series I, Vol. 4, 278 (hereafter cited as *OR*).
2. *Ibid.*, 297.
3. "Absalom Harrison's Civil War Letters, Number 3." www.civilwarhome.com/letter3.htm.
4. *OR*, Series I, Vol. 16, Part I, 738.
5. Kenneth A. Hafendorfer, "Perryville, Battle of." *The Kentucky Encyclopedia*, 717–718.
6. James A. Ramage, *Rebel Raider: The Life of General John Hunt Morgan* (Lexington: University of Kentucky Press, 1986), 124–125.
7. *Ibid.*, 135, 142–143.

8. Basil Duke, *A History of Morgan's Cavalry* (Cincinnati: Miami Printing and Publishing Company, 1867), 341.
9. Child's chant, Kentucky folk tradition.
10. Henry C. Magruder, *Three Years in the Saddle: The Life and Confession of Henry C. Magruder* (Utica, KY: McDowell Publications, no date), 21; "A Fond Recollection of Ben F. Bowman," Lebanon *Enterprise*, 27 June 1963.
11. Ramage, 164–165.
12. *OR*, Series I, Vol. 23, Part I, 652.
13. *Ibid.*, 653.
14. Ramage, 166, 170, 180–182, 194.
15. Steven L. Wright, compiler, *Kentucky Soldiers and Their Regiments in the Civil War, Volume III: 1863* (Utica, KY: McDowell Publications, 2009), 210.
16. *Ibid.*, 222.
17. *Ibid.*, 211.
18. *Ibid.*, 263.
19. Edward Benningfield, *Lincoln's Birth County (LaRue County) in the Civil War* (Utica, KY: McDowell Publications, 1990), 47–48; Sergeant E. [Eastham] Tarrant, *The Wild Riders of the 1st Kentucky Cavalry* (Lexington: Henry Clay Press, 1969), 113–115.
20. Benningfield, 47; Thomas Speed, *The Union Regiments of Kentucky* (Louisville: The Courier-Journal Job Printing Co., 1897), 588–590.
21. Edward E. Leslie, *The Devil Knows How to Ride: The True Story of William Clarke Quantrill and His Confederate Raiders* (New York: Da Capo, 1998), 347, 351–355; Henry C. Magruder, *Three Years in the Saddle* (Louisville, 1865), 54.
22. Leslie, 357–358; Magruder, 58–59.
23. Steven L. Wright, compiler, *On Trial for Their Lives: Kentucky's Guerrillas and Military Justice in the Civil War*, Vol. I (by the author, 2012), 3, 4.
24. Steven L. Wright, *On Trial*, 1–16.
25. John M. Palmer, *Personal Recollections of John M. Palmer: The Story of an Earnest Life* (Cincinnati: R. Clarke & Co., 1901), 260.
26. O.S. Barton, *Three Years With Quantrill: A True Story Told by His Scout John McCorkle* (Norman: University of Oklahoma Press, 1992), 200; Steven L. Wright, compiler, *Kentucky Soldiers and Their Regiments in the Civil War:*

Abstracted from the Pages of Contemporary Newspapers, Vol. V (Utica, KY: McDowell Publications, 2009), 110.
27. Leslie, 364.
28. *Ibid.*, 364–369.
29. Gerald W. Fischer, *Guerrilla Warfare in Civil War Kentucky* (Morely, MO: Acclaim Press, 2014), 171–172.
30. "Execution of Henry C. Magruder," New York *Times*, Oct. 25, 1865; "The Execution of Magruder," Chicago *Times*, Oct. 24, 1865.
31. "A Man's Terrible Oath," Hartford [KY] *Herald*, June 28, 1899.
32. *Ibid.*; Todd Haydon, conversation with the author, Oct. 27, 2004.

Chapter Eight

1. Carl Howell and Don Waters, *Hardin and LaRue Counties, 1880–1930* (Charleston, SC: Arcadia, 1998), 11; Roscoe, Rebecca and Linda Ireland, "New Haven; Athertonville's roots: Distilleries and Watie Boone," LaRue County *Herald News*, July 9, 2013.
2. David A. Holt, "Fort Knox," in *The Kentucky Encyclopedia*, 345.
3. "Block Signals and Disaster," Washington, D.C., *Evening Star*, Dec. 21, 1917.
4. Dixie Hibbs and Carl Howell, *Central Kentucky: Bullitt, Marion, Nelson, Spencer, and Washington Counties* (Charleston, SC: Arcadia, 2000), 49.
5. "Kentucky Negress Lynched," New York *Times*, June 16, 1904.
6. "Killing in Nelson County: Wm. Hill Shot by Lige Hazel," *LaRue County Herald*, Aug. 15, 1901; "Nelson County," *LaRue County Herald*, Feb. 27, 1902; "Nelson County, *LaRue County Herald*, July 2, 1903.
7. "A Street Duel," Maysville *Evening Bulletin*, Apr. 14, 1904. "Locals," Stanford *Semi-Weekly Interior Journal*, May 24, 1904.
8. Untitled, Nelson County *Record*, Oct. 15, 1897.

Chapter Nine

1. Joseph Earl Dabney, *Mountain Spirits* (New York: Copple House Books, 1978), 7–8.
2. Dabney, 8–9; Eliot Wigginton, ed., *The Foxfire Book* (New York: Anchor, 1972), 318.
3. Dabney, 15–16.
4. Flaget M. Nally, "Bourbon," *The Kentucky Encyclopedia*, 103.
5. Laurel Shackelford and Bill Weinberg, *Our Appalachia* (Lexington: University Press of Kentucky, 1988), 107.
6. Dabney, 118–120.
7. *Ibid.*, 168; David Lewis, "Tales of Archie the fabulous bootlegger," Hardin County *Independent*, Aug. 12, 2004; Esther Kellner, *Moonshine: Its History and Folklore* (New York: Weathervane, 1971), 217.
8. Kellner, 92–94, 188; Wigginton, 310.
9. Dabney, 151–152, 156, 158.
10. Joe Creason, *Crossroads and Coffee Trees* (Louisville: The Courier-Journal and the Louisville Times, 1975), 225.
11. Rick Bell, *The Great Flood of 1937* (Louisville: Butler Books, 2007), 13; Jack Godbey, "1937 Flood in Kentucky," *The Kentucky Explorer*, Feb. 2018, 16.
12. Sallie Pope, "Flood District," *Pioneer News*, Feb. 18, 1937.
13. Robert Louis Moser, "Memories of My Big Brother William Thomas (Bill) Moser." http://www.bullitcountyhistory.com/bchistory/flood1937moser.html. Accessed June 26, 2022.
14. Bell, 56, 79; "1937 Flood reported by Sallie Pope." http://www.bullitcounty history.com/bchistory/flood1937moser.html. Accessed June 26, 2022.
15. Bell, 74. "'37 Flood: Human Spirit Was Never Dampened," *News-Enterprise*, Feb. 4, 1987.
16. "'37 Flood," *News-Enterprise*.
17. *Ibid.*
18. "Water...Death...Disease...Mud." http://www.bullitcountyhistory.com/bchistory/flood1937fifty.html. Accessed Jan. 23, 2014.
19. "A Letter from the Flood of 1937." http://www.bullitcountyhistory.com/bchistory/flood1937moser.html. Accessed June 26, 2022.
20. "Flood Damage," Kentucky *Standard*, Feb. 18, 1937.
21. "REA," Kentucky *Standard*, Feb. 11, 1937.

Chapter Ten

1. McClure, *Two Centuries*, 404–405, 552; "Fort Knox Scrapbook," *Turret News*, Jan. 20, 2005.

2. McClure, *Two Centuries*, 405; "Fort Knox Scrapbook," *Turret News*, Jan. 10, 2006; Charles A. Lindbergh, *The Spirit of St. Louis* (New York: Charles Scribner's Sons, 1953), 347.

3. Jerianne Strange, "To honor thy Father," *New-Enterprise*, Dec. 25, 2003; David Holt, "Fort Knox," in *The Kentucky Encyclopedia*, 345.

4. Connie M. Huddleston, *Kentucky's Civilian Conservation Corps* (Charleston, SC: The History Press, 2009), 18–19.

5. "Golden Age: Knox's History Intertwined with Hardin County's," *News-Enterprise*, Sept. 2004; Holt, "Fort Knox," *The Kentucky Encyclopedia*, 346; McClure, *Two Centuries*, 404.

6. "Fort Knox Scrapbook," *Turret News*, Jan. 25, 2007; John A. Campbell, "U.S. Bullion Depository," in *The Kentucky Encyclopedia*, 910–911.

7. "Golden Age," *News-Enterprise*, Sept. 2004; Campbell, "U.S. Bullion Depository," 910.

8. "Fort Knox Scrapbook," *Turret News*, July 20, 2006; Holt, "Fort Knox," *The Kentucky Encyclopedia*, 346.

9. "Knox Gunnery renders nearby waterways unsafe, off-limits." *Inside the Turret*, Sept. 2, 2004.

10. Frank H. Bunce, "Dreams from a Pack: Isaac Wolfe Bernheim and Bernheim Forest," *Filson Club History Quarterly*, Oct. 1973, 328; Herman Landau and Lee Shai Weissbach, "Bernheim, Isaac Wolfe," in *The Encyclopedia of Louisville*, edited by John E. Kleber (Lexington: University Press of Kentucky, 2001), 86.

11. Bunce, 328; Landau and Weissbach, 86.

12. "Bernheim Arboretum and Research Forest," www.bernheim.org; "Forest Building Beckons," *The Courier-Journal*, Oct. 6, 2004; "New center enhances experiences at Bernheim," *The Courier-Journal*, Apr. 10, 2005.

13. Michael A. Lindenberger, "Monks' vow of poverty only goes so far," *The Courier-Journal*, Jan. 16, 2006.

14. "Fabulous Farm Cheeses," *Kentucky Living*, Nov. 2004.

15. Thomas Merton, *The Seven Storey Mountain* (San Diego: Harcourt Brace, 1998), 346.

16. Robert Giroux, Introduction, in Thomas Merton, *The Seven Storey Mountain* (New York: Harcourt Brace, 1998), xvi.

17. Giroux, xviii; "Institute expands Merton's work," *The Courier-Journal*, Sept. 23, 2006.

18. Van Natter, 4.

19. *Ibid.*

20. Greg Kocher, "Owner of Abraham Lincoln's boyhood home decides to auction it off," *News-Enterprise*, Jan. 8, 1986; "Lincoln's boyhood home sells for $120, 500," *News-Enterprise*, Jan. 12, 1986; James R. Carroll, "Farm where Lincoln lived my become park," *The Courier-Journal*, Nov. 9, 1998.

21. J.S. Newton, "Ford moves to expand Lincoln Historic Site to include farm," *News-Enterprise*, Feb. 16, 1997; Forrest Berkshire, "Lincoln's birthday marked with wreath ceremony, deed transfer," *News-Enterprise*, Feb. 13, 2002.

Chapter Eleven

1. Lowell H. Harrison and James C. Klotter, *A New History of Kentucky* (Lexington: University of Kentucky Press, 1997), 6; DiBlasi, 720; National Park Service, *Lincoln Boyhood Home at Knob Creek Cultural Landscape Report* (Atlanta: Cultural Resources Division, Southeast Regional Office, NPS, 2013), 1.

2. DiBlasi, 720–721; Clay, 734; Roger W. Brucker and Richard A. Watson, *The Longest Cave* (Carbondale: SIU Press, 1976), 259.

3. Fred E. Coy, Jr., Thomas C. Fuller, Larry G. Meadows, and James F. Swauger, *Rock Art of Kentucky* (Lexington: University Press of Kentucky, 1997), 142.

4. *Ibid.*, 13 16.

5. Henderson and Schlarb, 1–2, 20.

6. *Ibid.*

7. Blitz, 131; Robert P. Mansfort, "Human Trophy Taking in Eastern North America During the Archaic Period: The Relationship to Warfare and Social

Complexity," in Richard J. Chacon and David H. Dye, eds., *The Taking and Displaying of Human Body Parts as Trophies by Amerindians* (New York: Springer Science and Business Media, 2007), 175.

8. R. Barry Lewis, "Mississippian Farmers," in *Kentucky Archaeology—Perceptions in Kentucky's Past: Architecture, Archaeology, and Landscape*, ed. R. Barry Lewis (Lexington: University Press of Kentucky, 2014), 141–142.

9. Charles Stout and R. Barry Lewis, "Mississippian Towns in Kentucky," in R. Barry Lewis, Charles Stout, Jon Muller, Gerald F. Schroedl, Hypatia Kelly, and John F. Scarry, *Mississippian Towns and Sacred Spaces: Searching for an Architectural Grammar* (Tuscaloosa: University of Alabama Press, 1998), 155–156.

10. Collins, 1968 ed., 397–398.

11. Blitz, 136.

12. Young, *Prehistoric Men of Kentucky*, 258.

Chapter Twelve

1. Otis Mather, "Benjamin Lynn," Elizabethtown *News*, Feb. 20, 1940.

2. "Ben Linn sought adventure in the new West," *Kentucky Standard*, May 29, 1985; Mather, "Explorers and Early Settlers South of Muldraugh Hill," 30; George William Bettie and Helen Pruitt Beattie, "Pioneer Lynns of Kentucky, Part II," *Filson Club History Quarterly*, Apr. 1946, 141–146.

3. "Ben Linn," *Kentucky Standard*, May 29, 1985; Mather, "Benjamin Lynn"; James Alton James, ed., *George Rogers Clark Papers, 1775–1781* (Danville: Illinois State Historical Library, 1912), 21.

4. James, *Clark Papers*, 22, 218; Lowell Harrison, *George Rogers Clark and the War in the West* (Lexington: University Press of Kentucky, 1976), 15; Hugh F. Rankin, *George Rogers Clark and The Winning of the West* (Richmond: Virginia Independence Bicentennial Commission, 1976), 8.

5. Mather, "Benjamin Lynn"; "Explorers and Early Settlers South of Muldraugh Hill," 25–26.

6. "Ben Linn," *Kentucky Standard*, May 29, 1985; James, *Clark Papers*, 28.

7. Harrison, *George Rogers Clark*, 22–31, 32–35, 44–60, 66–67.

8. Kunigunde Duncan and D.F. Nickols, *Mentor Graham* (Chicago: University of Chicago Press, 1944), Prologue, xxiii.

9. Mather, "Explorers and Early Settlers South of Muldraugh Hill," 25; McClure, *Two Centuries*, 39–40, 139.

10. Bessie Miller Elliott, *History of LaRue County, Kentucky* (Vine Grove: Ancestral Trails Historical Society, 2000), 4.

11. McClure, *Two Centuries*, 35, 38–39, 190–193.

12. *Ibid.*, 569–571; Elliott, 4.

13. McClure, *Two Centuries*, 194, 234; Mather, *Mather Papers*, 4; Paul McClure, *Millerstown and Its People* (Elizabethtown: Hardin County Historical Society, 1992), 36.

14. Mather, *Mather Papers*, 36.

Chapter Thirteen

1. James Thomas Flexner, *George Washington: Anguish and Farewell, 1793–1795* (Boston: Little, Brown, 1969), 52.

2. Thomas D. Clark, *A History of Kentucky* (Lexington: The Bradford Press, 1950), 102.

3. Clark, 103.

4. Louis-Philippe, 117; 116.

5. *Ibid.*, 116.

6. *Ibid.*

7. Mather, "Benjamin Lynn"; Hay, et al., *Roadside History*, 106; Spencer, 17; Duncan and Nickols, 6–8, 69.

8. Spencer, 18; Duncan and Nickols, 22–23.

9. "Ben Linn sought adventure," *Kentucky Standard*; Duncan and Nickols, 25.

10. McClure, *Two Centuries*, 28–29, 214, 236.

11. *Ibid.*, 144–145, 146; Nellie B. Hoke, "Warren Cash," Elizabethtown *News*, Aug. 26, 1941.

12. Hoke, "Warren Cash," Elizabethtown *News*; McClure, *Two Centuries*, 145.

13. Duncan and Nickols, 24, 66–67; R. Gerald McMurtry, *A Series of Monographs Concerning the Lincolns and Hardin County, Kentucky* (Elizabethtown: The Enterprise Press, 1999), 70.

14. *Minutes*, Gilead Baptist Church (Glendale, KY), May 10, 1828; McClure, *Two Centuries*, 194, 198, 226.

15. U.S. Census, 1790, Kentucky; J. Edward Murr, *Abraham Lincoln's Wilderness Years: Collected Works of J. Edward Murr*, ed. Joshua Claybourn (Bloomington: Indiana University Press, 2023), 31; Duncan and Nickols, 9, 19, 27.

16. McMurtry, *Monographs*, 85–86.

Chapter Fourteen

1. McMurtry, *Monographs*, 1.

2. Smith, *Lincoln and the Lincolns*, 231–232.

3. *Ibid.*

4. Carl Sandburg, *Abraham Lincoln: The Prairie Years*, Vol. I (New York: Scribners, 1948), 7.

5. McMurtry, *Monographs*, 2; *Lincoln Lore*, "The Helm-Haycraft Collection of Kentucky Manscripts," May 1970, 1; Duncan and Nickols, 25.

6. McMurtry, *Monographs*, 2–3, 11–12.

7. Louis A. Warren, *Lincoln's Parentage and Childhood* (New York: The Century Co., 1926), 102–103.

8. Lynwood Montell, ed., *Folk Medicine of the Mammoth Cave Area*, booklet, n.d., 10, 17, 20, 23, 29.

9. NPS, *Lincoln Boyhood Home at Knob Creek*, 1, 10, 12; McMurtry, *Monographs*, 4.

10. *Ibid.*, 1.

11. Harrison, *Lincoln of Kentucky*, 26–27.

12. Abraham Lincoln, "Autobiographical Sketch," 1860 Presidential Campaign; *Lincoln Lore*, "Widower Lincoln Marries Widow Johnston," Dec. 6, 1943.

13. Current, 24.

14. Harrison, *Lincoln of Kentucky*, 31–32.

15. McMurtry, *Monographs*, 34.

16. *Ibid.*, 96–97.

17. *Ibid.*, 100–101.

18. Untitled, The *Centre Democrat* [Bellefonte, PA], Nov. 7, 1861.

19. McMurtry, *Monographs*, 96.

Chapter Fifteen

1. Burton Faust, "The History of Saltpeter Mining in Mammoth Cave, Kentucky, Part II," *Filson Club History Quarterly*, Apr. 1967, 135; Angelo I. George and Gary A. O'Dell, "The Saltpeter Works at Mammoth Cave and the New Madrid Earthquake," *Filson Club History Quarterly*, Jan. 1992, 6–10, 20, 21; Robert K. Murray and Roger K. Bruker, *Trapped! The Story of Floyd Collins* (Lexington: University Press of Kentucky, 1979), 28–30; National Park Service, "A Short Legal History of Mammoth Cave," npshistory.com/brochures/maca/history-2.pdf. Accessed June 28, 2022.

2. Nathaniel Parker Willis, *Health Trip to the Tropics* (New York: Charles Scribner, 1853), 199–204.

3. Young, 258.

4. Murray and Brucker, 28.

5. *Ibid.*; Marianne Finch, *An Englishwoman's Experience in America* (London: Richard Bentley, Publisher in Ordinary to Her Majesty, 1853), 350.

6. Willis, 152; Finch, 350.

7. Brucker and Watson, 266, 273; Lawrence Muhammed, "Slave left his mark on history and cave," *Courier-Journal*, Feb. 32, 1996.

8. Brucker and Watson, 266; Willis, 152–153; Ralph Seymour Thompson, *The Sucker's Visit to the Mammoth Cave* (Springfield, OH: by the author, 1879), 75.

9. Willis, 159; Taylor, 205; Jeanne C. Schmitzer, "The Sable Guides of Mammoth Cave," *Filson Club History Quarterly*, Apr. 1993, 247.

10. Willis, 157; Muhammed, "Slave left his mark."

11. Schmitzer, 249; Willis, 178.

12. Willis, 182.

13. *Ibid.*, 204–205; Taylor, 193.

14. Willis, 154; Muhammed, "Slave left his mark."

15. Muhammed, "Slave left his mark."

16. Samuel W. Thomas, Eugene H. Connor, and Harold Meloy, "A History of Mammoth Cave, Emphasizing Tourist Development and Medical Experimentation Under Dr. John Croghan," *Register of the Kentucky Historical Society*, Oct. 1970, 326.

17. *Ibid.*, 326, 385, 339.

18. *Ibid.*, 328; Taylor, 199.

19. Nitsan Shorer, "The Unlikely Guide Who Mapped Mammoth Cave," *National Geographic*, May 1995, 8; Taylor, 206; Gwynne Tuell Potts and Samuel W. Thomas, *George Rogers Clark and Locust Grove* (Louisville: Historic Locust Grove, Inc., 2006), 106; John A. Alexander, "Stephen Bishop: Freedom's Darker Face," http://faculty.virginia.edu/jalexander/Alexander.StephenBishop.doc. Accessed June 28, 2016.

20. Maury and Brucker, 39; Muhammed, "Slave left his mark."

21. Collins, 1968 ed., 327, 334, 344, 353, 397.

22. John Lay, *Mills Along the Nolin* (Elizabethtown; by the author, 2007), 18, 23, 28, 32; Rennick, 40.

23. McClure, *Millerstown*, 36.

24. *Ibid.*, 50–51.

Chapter Sixteen

1. Grayson County Historical Society, *Historical Sketches and Family Histories—Grayson County, Kentucky* (Utica, KY: McDowell Publications, 2002), 120.

2. *Ibid.*

3. Richard Collins, "Civil War Annals of Kentucky," ed. Hambleton Tapp, *Filson Club History Quarterly*, July 1961, 224–225, 226–227; Dan Lee, *The L&N Railroad in the Civil War* (Jefferson, NC: McFarland, 2011), 28–30.

4. Lee, *L&N Railroad*, 33–34.

5. Josie Underwood, *Josie Underwood's Civil War Diary*, ed. Nancy Disher Baird (Lexington: University Press of Kentucky, 2009), 167–168.

6. Dan Lee, *Kentuckian In Blue: A Biography of Major General Lovell Harrison Rousseau* (Jefferson, NC: McFarland, 2010), 47–49; *OR*, Series I, Vol. 4, 308; Alexander McDowell McCook, letter to William Dennison, Nov. 15, 1861, Collection of the Ohio Historical Society, Columbus, OH; Alpheus Bloomfield, letter to parents, Oct. 30, 1861, "Bloomfield Letters," ohiostatehouse.org/museum/battery-a/bloomfield-letters. Accessed Feb. 5, 2020.

7. *OR*, Series I, Vol. 4, 337.

8. *Ibid.*, 347.

9. "Redstick," letter to the Fremont (OH) *Journal*, Nov. 22, 1861. Collection of Bowling Green State University, Bowling Green, Ohio.

10. "The Rebellion in Kentucky," New York *Times*, Oct. 21, 1861.

11. Milton T. Jay, ed., *History of Jay County, Indiana: Including Its War Record and Incorporating the Montgomery History*, Vol. I (Indianapolis: Historical Publishing Co., 1922), 129–130.

12. "Cecil," letter to the Belmont *Chronicle* (St. Clairsville, OH), November 28, 1861; Alexis Cope, *The Fifteenth Ohio Volunteers and Its Campaigns: War of 1861–5* (Columbus: by the author, 1916), 39.

13. *Minutes*, Gilead Baptist Church, Dec. 28, 1861; "Redstick," letter to the Fremont (OH) *Journal*, Dec. 13, 1861.

14. "Redstick," letter to the Fremont (OH) *Journal*, Nov. 22, 1861. Collection of Bowling Green State University, Bowling Green, Ohio; "Redstick," letter to the Fremont (OH) *Journal*, Nov. 29, 1861. Collection of Bowling Green State University, Bowling Green, Ohio; "One of the Boys," letter to the Portage (OH) *Sentinel*, Dec. 7, 1861.

15. Lyman S. Widney, *Campaigning With Uncle Billy*, ed. Robert I. Girandi (Victoria, B.C.: Trafford, 2008), 21–22.

16. Duke, *Morgan's Cavalry*, 94.

17. "L," letter to the Hancock (OH) *Courier*, Dec. 27, 1861. Collection of Bowling Green State University, Bowling Green, Ohio.

18. Kim Cook and Brad Quinlin, *On the Line of Bacon Creek* (Bonnieville, KY: Bacon Creek Historical Society, n.d.), 49.

19. *Ibid.*, 50–51.

20. *OR*, Series I, Vol. 7, 556.

21. Cook and Quinlin, 55.

22. *OR*, Series I, Vol. 16, Part I, 968–971; Vol. 16, Part II, 843.

23. *OR*, Series I, Vol. 16, Part I, 895.

24. Collins, "Civil War Annals of Kentucky," 257–260.

25. Mary Josephine Jones, *The Civil War in Hardin County, Kentucky* (Vine Grove: Ancestral Trails Historical Society, 1995), 22.

26. Duke, 331–332.

27. *Ibid.*, 332.

28. *Ibid.*, 332–335; Ramage, 139–140.
29. Duke, 335.
30. Henry Magruder, 35; *Three Years in the Saddle* (Utica, KY: McDowell Publications, n.d.), 35; Wright IV, 47.
31. Wright, IV, 201.
32. Dan Lee, *Hylan B. Lyon: A Kentucky Confederate and the War in the West* (Knoxville: University of Tennessee Press, 2019) 174; *OR*, Series I, Vol. 45, Part I, 805 (hereafter cited as Lyon's Report).
33. Lee, *Lyon*, 175; Lyon's Report, 805.
34. Lee, *Lyon*, 175; Lyon's Report, 805.
35. Jones, 55.

Chapter Seventeen

1. William Frederic Badè, Introduction to John Muir, *A Thousand-Mile Walk to the Gulf* (Boston: Mariner, 1998), xv; Muir, 2; Millis Stanley, "John Muir and the Civil War," *John Muir Newsletter*, Fall 2002, 8; "John Muir (1838–1914): A Brief Biography," *Journal of the Sierra College Natural History Museum*, Winter 2008, seirracollege.edu/ejournals/jsc-nhm/v1n2/muir.html.
2. Muir, 4.
3. *Ibid.*, 5–6
4. *Ibid.*, 6.
5. McClure, *Two Centuries*, 231, 577–578; Guy Winstead, "History of Glendale, Part 6," *Hardin County Independent*, Aug. 5, 1993.
6. McClure, *Two Centuries*, 210, 230, 261.
7. John Lay, *Mills Along the Nolin*, 23.
8. *Ibid.*, 28–23; *The Lynnlander*, Nov. 1928, 3–5.
9. Muir, 14.
10. "From Kunkle's Cleveland Battery," The Cleveland *Morning Leader*, Mar. 6, 1862.
11. Muir, 11.
12. *Ibid.*
13. A.D. Binkerd, *Mammoth Cave and Its Denizens: A Complete Descriptive Guide* (Cincinnati: Robert Clarke & Co., 1869), 61–62.
14. Greg Kocher, "Boom Town Buffalo," *News-Enterprise*, June 29 July 1, 1984.
15. *Ibid.*

16. "Swedish Immigrants Pleased in Rugged Kentucky Hill Country," *Echoes from Edmonson County*, Jan., Feb., Mar. 1955.
17. Lafayette Wilson, Affidavit, undated. Photocopy from the Abraham Lincoln Birthplace National Historic Site, Hodgenville, KY (original on file at Mammoth Cave National Park). Zerelda Jane Goff, Affidavit, May 30, 1906. Photocopy, John Lay Collection (original on file at Abraham Lincoln Birthplace National Historic Site).
18. Robert W. Blythe, Maureen Carroll, and Steven H. Moffson, *Abraham Lincoln Birthplace National Historic Site, Historic Resource Study*, revised and updated by Brian F. Coffey (Atlanta: Cultural Resources Stewardship, Southeast Regional Office, National Park Service, Department of the Interior, 2001), 27–28.
19. *Ibid.*, 29–30.
20. *Ibid.*, 30, 32.
21. *Ibid.*, 33; Greg Kocher, "Teddy Roosevelt and ex-slave praised Lincoln," *News-Enterprise*, Feb. 11–13, 1983.
22. Kocher, "Teddy Roosevelt and ex-slave."
23. Blythe, Carroll, and Moffson, 33–34.
24. Warren, *Lincoln's Parentage and Childhood*, 89–90; Harrison, *Lincoln of Kentucky*, 14–15.
25. McClure, *Two Centuries*, 243.

Chapter Eighteen

1. Tom Stephens, "White Mills was popular summer resort," *News-Enterprise*, Jan. 5, 1994; postcard from Katherine and Dora to Miss Katherine Michael, Aug. 13, 1919, photocopy in the collection of the author.
2. Josie D. Richardson, "The Story of White Mills As I Remember," *Hardin County Enterprise*, Jan. 1, 1970.
3. McClure, *Two Centuries*, 418.
4. Brian T. Kehl, "Religious Roots," *News-Enterprise*, Aug. 27–28, 2007.
5. McClure, *Two Centuries*, 419; Tom Wallace, "An Early Auto Adventure to the Nolin River Area." *Kentucky Explorer*, May 1988 (reprint of a *Courier-Journal* article from August 20, 1916).

6. Helen Bartter Crocker, *The Green River of Kentucky* (Lexington: University Press of Kentucky, 1976), 55.

7. Mark Nevils, "Millerstown Settled Before 1800 by Jacob Miller," Grayson County *News Gazette*, Nov. 3, 1998.

8. McMurtry, *Monographs*, 119–120; Stephen E. Ambrose, *Crazy Horse and Custer* (Garden City: Doubleday, 1975), 311, 319.

9. "Court House Steps a Gallows," New York *Times*, Nov. 1, 1901.

10. McClure, *Two Centuries*, 379.

11. *Ibid.*, 363; "Letter from the Past," *Bits and Pieces: A Quarterly Publication of the Hardin County Historical Society*, Fall 2010, 3; Hubert Lee, conversation with the author, May 11, 1983.

12. "Thos. Tillery Brutally Murdered by Negroes," Hardin County *Enterprise*, Apr. 9, 1931; McClure, *Two Centuries*, 633–34; Hubert Lee, conversation with the author, May 11, 1983.

13. "Letter from the Past," *Bits and Pieces*, 3–4; "Guards Subdue One of Three Executed," Washington [D.C.] *Times*, Apr. 29, 1932; Daniel Allen Hearn, *Legal Executions in Illinois, Indiana, Iowa, Kentucky, and Missouri: A Comprehensive Registry, 1866–1965* (Jefferson, NC: McFarland, 2016), 110.

Chapter Nineteen

1. McClure, *Two Centuries*, 393, 578; Paul McClure, *Millerstown*, 93–94.

2. Paul McClure, *Millerstown*, 96.

3. *Ibid.*, 95.

4. Melissa Muscovalley, "'37 Flood: Hardin becomes a waterway," *News-Enterprise*, Feb. 4, 1987.

5. *Ibid.*

6. Kocher, "Boom Town Buffalo."

7. J. Richard Bowersox, *Rocks to Roads to Ruin: A Brief History of Western Kentucky's Rock Asphalt Industry, 1888–1957* (Lexington: Kentucky Geological Survey, 2016), 5, 13, 16.

8. Nadine Hawkins, "Black Gold in the Green Hills," *Hart County Historical Society Quarterly*, July 1992.

9. Franklin D. Roosevelt, *The Public Papers and Addresses of Franklin D. Roosevelt, 1938 Volume: the Continuing Struggle for Liberalism* (New York: Macmillan, 1941), Introduction, xxix.

10. "Let There Be Light," Nolin RECC Special Publication, June 1988, 4–5; John M. Ramsey, "Rural Electrification," in *The Kentucky Encyclopedia*, 788; Greg Kocher, "Recounting 'the day they turned the lights on," *News-Enterprise*, June 22, 1988.

11. "The Case of The Fly-Filled Dairy," "The Case of The Tired Farm Wife," "Cost of Operating Farm Appliances," and Pauline Duff, "History of Organizing Nolin Cooperative in Two Counties," Hardin County *Enterprise*, June 29, 1939; Pauline Duff, "Nolin Cooperative provided electricity to rural areas," Elizabethtown *News*, Bicentennial Edition, May 1974.

12. Duff, "Nolin Cooperative provided electricity."

13. Blythe, Carroll, and Moffson, 47; Huddleston, 13, 120.

14. *Ibid.*, 17–18, 125–126; Ray Hoyt, *Your CCC: A Handbook for Enrollees, Third Edition* (Washington, D.C.: Happy Days, n.d.), 5

15. Huddleston, 125–126; Harrison & Klotter, 364.

16. Huddleston, 19.

Chapter Twenty

1. Jacob Bennett, "A Light in the Tunnel," *News-Enterprise*, Feb. 9, 2004; Bayard Taylor, 205.

2. Bennett, "A Light in the Tunnel."

3. *Ibid.*; Brucker and Watson, 285–286.

4. Murray and Brucker, 238–239; NPS, "Foundation Document Overview, Mammoth Cave National Park," npshistory.com/publications/foundation-documents/maca-fd-overview.pdf.; nps.gov/maca/index.htm. Both accessed June 29, 2022.

5. "Mammoth Cave National Park," UNESCO, whc.unesco.org/en/list/150/. Accessed June 30, 2022. "Mammoth Cave added $62 million to local economy." *New-Enterprise*, May 31–June 1, 2019. Wasson, Matt and Harvard Ayers, "And the Winner Is..." *The Appalachian Voice*, appvoices.org/2004/06/01/2731.

Accessed July 14, 2010. Another federally operated economic powerhouse, this one in the upper Nolin valley, is the Abraham Lincoln Birthplace National Historic Site. In 2018, over a quarter million visited the park and poured nearly $21 million into the local economy ("Report: More than 260,000 visited Lincoln Birthplace in 2018," *News-Enterprise*, May 30, 2019).

6. National Park Service, "Natural Resource Condition Assessment: Mammoth Cave National Park," npshistory.com/publications/maca/nrr-2021-2258.pdf. Accessed June 17, 2022.

7. Leland Johnson, *The Falls City Engineers: A History of the Louisville District, Corps of Engineers, U.S. Army* (Louisville: U.S. Army Corps of Engineers, 1974), 145; "Nolin River Lake," U.S. Army Corps of Engineers, lrl.usace.army.mil/Missions/Civil-Works/Recreation/Lakes/Nolin-River-Lake/. Accessed June 30, 2022.

8. "Nolin Lake," U.S. Army Corps of Engineers.

9. *Ibid.*; "Lakes," *The Kentucky Encyclopedia*, 532.

10. Julian Shipp, "Camping out with God," *News-Enterprise*, Aug. 4, 1991; Peggy B. Riley, "White Mills a vacation mecca in its heyday," *News-Enterprise*, Jan. 25, 1988.

11. "Million dollar expansion set for White Mills camp," *Hardin County Independent*, July 11, 1991.

12. Gerald Lush, "New water plant treats 2 million gallons a day," *Hardin County Independent*, Oct. 11, 1990; Forrest Berkshire, "Piping the water," *News-Enterprise*, Oct. 3–4, 2003.

13. Christopher Carpenter, "Water's world," *News-Enterprise*, Aug. 8, 2004.

14. Muir, 70–71.

Chapter Twenty-One

1. McClure, *Two Centuries*, 8, 781 782.

2. Coy, Fuller, Meadows, and Swauger, *Rock Art of Kentucky*, 17, 60–61.

3. DiBlasi, 720–721; Clay, 734; W. S. Webb and W. D. Funkhouser, *Ancient Life in Kentucky* (Berea: Kentucky

Imprints, 1972), 155; Richard W. Jefferies, "Hunters and Gatherers After the Ice Age," in *Kentucky Archaeology—Perceptions in Kentucky's Past: Architecture, Archaeology, and Landscape*, ed. R. Barry Lewis (Lexington: University Press of Kentucky, 2014), 61.

4. Jefferies, 62; Blitz, 136.

5. "Old Spanish Fort," Hartford *Herald*, Nov. 19, 1902.

6. *Ibid.*, "Joyous Fourth," Hartford *Republican*, July 8, 1904.

Chapter Twenty-Two

1. Harrison D. Taylor, *Ohio County, Kentucky, in the Olden Days* (Louisville: John P. Morton & Company, 1926), 3; Rankin, 15; William Hayden English, *Conquest of the Country Northwest of the River Ohio, 1778–1783, and Life of Gen. George Rogers Clark, Vol. I* (Indianapolis: The Bowen-Merrill Company, 1896), 107.

2. Collins, 1968 ed., 213; Harrison D. Taylor, 6; George K. Holbert, "Capt. Thomas Helm," Elizabethtown *News*, Feb. 18, 1941; David C. Hall, "Wickland," in *The Kentucky Encyclopedia*, 950.

3. Josephine L. Holbert, "General William Hardin," Elizabethtown *News*, Aug. 22, 1939.

4. *Ibid.*, Rennick, 130.

5. Lewis Collins and Richard Henry Collins, *Collins' Historical Sketches of Kentucky: History of Kentucky, Volumes I and II* (Covington: Collins & Co., 1882), 308.

6. "Over 100 Years Ago: Some Early History of the Good Old Town of Hardinsburg," *Breckinridge News*, Dec. 8, 1897.

7. "Brave Beginnings," *Breckinridge News*, July 4, 1976.

8. *Ibid.*; Wallace Gruelle, "Mrs. John Bruner," *Breckinridge News*, Nov. 8, 1862.

9. Collins, 1968 ed., 123–214.

10. Michael L. Cook and Bettie Ann Cook, *Breckinridge County, Kentucky, Records, Vol. I* (Evansville: Cook Publications, 1977), 10; Holbert, "General William Hardin."

11. McClure, *Two Centuries*, 140–141; Cook and Cook, 12.

12. McClure, *Two Centuries*, 142;

"Thomas Lincoln Goes to New Orleans," *Lincoln Lore*, May 1950.

13. Samuel Haycraft, Jr., *A History of Elizabethtown, Kentucky and Its Surroundings* (Elizabethtown: Hardin County Historical Society, 1975), 16.

14. George K. Holbert, "Joseph Barnett," Elizabethtown *News*, June 10, 1941.

15. *Ibid.*

16. Harrison D. Taylor, 122–123.

17. *Ibid.*, 122.

18. Holbert, "Joseph Barnett."

19. Harrison D. Taylor, 21.

20. Rennick, 105, 146.

21. McClure, *Two Centuries*, 132–134.

22. Hay, et al., *Roadside History*, 250.

23. Curtis Dewees, *George Washington's Kentucky Land* (by the author, 2005), 47; George Washington, letter to Henry Lee, Nov. 30, 1788, "Founders Online," founders.archives.gov/documents/Washington/05-01-02-0109. Accessed July 2, 2022.

24. Willard Rouse Jillson, "George Washington's Western Kentucky Lands," *Register of the Kentucky Historical Society*, Oct. 1931, 379; Nancy Richey, "George Washington's Kentucky Lands," mountvernon.org/library/digitalhistory/digital-encyclopedia/article/george-washingtons/kentucky-lands/. Accessed July 2, 2022.

25. Dewees, 55.

26. George Washington, letter to George Lewis, July 27, 1795, "Founders Online," founders.archives.gov/documents/Washington/05-18-02-0297. Accessed July 2, 2022.

27. Alexander Spotswood, letter to George Washington, Sept. 21, 1795, "Founders Online," founders.archives.gov/documents/Washington/05-18-02-0468. Accessed July 2, 2022.

28. Dewees, 73; Richey, "George Washington's Kentucky Lands."

Chapter Twenty-Three

1. Hay, et al., *Roadside History*, 69, 210.

2. *Ibid.*; Allen P. Cubbage, "Jack Thomas," Elizabethtown *News*, Apr. 9, 1940.

3. Collins, 1968 ed., 327–328, 335, 486.

4. Grayson County Historical Society, *Historical Sketches and Family Histories*, 35.

5. Spencer, 410–413; A.H. Redford, *The History of Methodism in Kentucky, Vol. I* (Nashville: Southern Methodist Publishing House, 1868), 457.

6. Camillus P. Maes, *The Life of Rev. Charles Nerinckx* (Cincinnati: R. Clarke & Co., 1880), 215–221; 225–226; Hay, et al., *Roadside History*, 54.

7. William E. Barton, "'Mord' Lincoln, the Woman Hater," in *The Open Court* (Chicago: Open Court, 1924), 292–293, 296.

8. *Ibid.*, 291, 294.

9. Winstead, 4.

10. Harrison D. Taylor, 26–27.

11. *Ibid.*, 53–56.

12. William R. Haynes, *Dock Brown: The Outlaw of Grayson County* (Leitchfield: Leitchfield Gazette, 1876), 47–48, 59.

13. *Ibid.*, 63–66, 83.

14. *Ibid.*, 86–89, 91–96, 106; Grayson County Historical Society, *Historical Sketches*, 36; The Hopper Chair," www.rootsweb.com/~tngibson/photos/hopper-chair.htm. Accessed Feb. 12, 2014.

15. Haynes., 107; "Grayson County Items," Hartford *Herald*, Mar. 15, 1876.

16. Haynes, 103–106; "Grayson County Items," Hartford *Herald*, Mar. 22, 1876; "Dock Letter," www.dockbrown.com/html/letter.html.

17. Haynes, 111; "The Gibson Tragedy," Athens [TN] *Post*, Oct. 3, 1851; "The Hopper Chair." Accessed Feb. 12, 2014.

18. "The Gibson Tragedy," Athens *Post*.

19. "Grayson County," Hartford *Herald*, Apr. 28, 1880; untitled, Hartford *Herald*, June 9, 1880.

Chapter Twenty-Four

1. Elaine M. Harrison, "Falls of Rough," in *The Kentucky Encyclopedia*, 305.

2. Lowell H. Harrison, *Kentucky's Road to Statehood* (Lexington: University Press of Kentucky, 1992), 49–50

3. *Ibid.*, 53.

4. *Ibid.*, 72.

5. Elizabeth Warren, "Benjamin Sebastian and the Spanish Conspiracy in Kentucky," *Filson Club History Quarterly*, Apr. 1946, 121.

6. *Ibid.*, 122.

7. Hugh Ridenour, *The Greens of Falls of Rough* (Hanson, KY: Treetops Enterprises, 1997), 9–10.

8. *Ibid.*, 6–11.

9. *Ibid.*, 15–17.

10. *Ibid.*, 21–29; "The Last and Littlest of the Humbugs," Richmond *Enquirer*, Oct. 22, 1844; Willis Green, "Address of the Hon. Willis Green, of Kentucky, Before the Alexandria (D.C.) Clay Club," July 19, 1844, campaign literature.

11. Ridenour, 29–31.

12. *Ibid.*, 30, 33, 89–90; "Col. Lafe Green Has One Hundred and Fifty Head of Cattle," *Breckinridge News*, Aug. 30, 1899; "Lafe Green's Home and Business," *Breckinridge News*, Aug. 24, 1904; Thomas D. Clark, *Footloose in Jacksonian America: Robert W. Scott and His Agrarian* World (Lexington: University Press of Kentucky, 1989), 165, 176.

13. Ridenour, 36–37; William C. Davis, *Breckinridge: Statesman, Soldier, Symbol* (Baton Rouge: Louisiana State University Press, 1974), 217–219.

Chapter Twenty-Five

1. Collins, 1968 ed., 486; Harrison D. Taylor, 31.

2. Harrison D. Taylor, 31–32.

3. *Ibid.*, 76, 78; Helen Crocker, "Rough River," in *The Kentucky Encyclopedia*, 783; Collins, 1968 edition, 486; Ohio County, Kentucky, *Tavern Keepers Bonds, 1857–1880*.

4. Harrison D. Taylor, 50–52.

5. *Ibid.*, 52; Collins, 1968 ed., 486.

6. U.S. Federal Census—Slave Schedules, 1860; Andrew C. Isenberg, *Wyatt Earp: A Vigilant Life* (New York: Hill & Wang, 2013), 14–18.

7. Carolyn Wimp, compiler, *Newspaper Abstracts, 1829–1893*, 3.

8. Harrison D. Taylor, 120.

9. John H. McHenry, "Seventeenth Kentucky Infantry," in *The Union*

Regiments of Kentucky, ed. Thomas Speed (Louisville: Courier-Journal Job Printing Company, 1897), 450.

10. *Ibid.*, 450–451, 456.

11. Speed, ed., *Union Regiments of Kentucky*, 233–236.

12. *Ibid.*, 539–542; Dan Lee, *The 26th Kentucky Infantry*, unpublished manuscript, 10.

13. Ed Porter Thompson, *History of the Orphan Brigade* (Louisville: Lewis H. Thompson, 1898), 298–299.

14. *Ibid.*

15. United States Congress, *Congressional Serial Set* (Washington, D.C.: Government Printing Office, 1872), 61.

16. Thomas Crofts, *History of the Service of the Third Ohio Volunteer Cavalry* (Toledo: The Stoneman Press, 1910), 49.

17. *Ibid.*, 49–50; Display, "Turning Point: The American Civil War," Atlanta History Center, Atlanta, GA.

18. *OR*, Series II, Vol. 5, 510.

19. *Ibid.*, 510–511.

20. *Ibid.*

21. Crofts, 50.

22. Duke, 289; Ramage, 125.

23. "The Guerrilla Raid in Litchfield [sic], Ky.," *Louisville Daily Journal*, June 18, 1863.

24. Steven L. Wright, compiler, *Kentucky Soldiers and Their Regiments, Volume IV: 1864*, 201–202.

25. *Ibid.*, 261.

26. Steven L. Wright, compiler, Kentucky Soldiers and Their Regiments, Volume V: 1865, 1.

Chapter Twenty-Six

1. Daniel E. Sutherland, *A Savage Conflict: The Decisive Role of Guerrillas in the American Civil War* (Chapel Hill: University of North Carolina Press, 2009), 224.

2. Wright, *Volume IV*, 78.

3. *Ibid.*, 86.

4. Wright, *Volume IV*, 90, 92, 126, 201, 206; Beth Chinn Harp, *Torn Asunder* (Georgetown, KY: Kinnersley Press, 2009), 104.

5. *OR*, Series I, Vol. 45, Pt. I, 803 (hereafter cited as Lyon's Report).

6. "Ellen Kenton McGaughey Wallace Diary," Wallace-Starling Family Diaries, Collection of the Kentucky Historical Society, Frankfort, Kentucky.

7. Lyon's Report, 805; Lee, *Lyon*, 164–170, 170–172.

8. Lee, *Lyon*, 172–173; Wright, *On Trial for Their Lives*, 37; James Q. Chenoweth, "The Rangers' Last Campaign," in *The Partisan Rangers of the Confederate States Army*, ed. William J. Davis (Louisville: George G. Fetter Company, 1904), 191; Fogle, 176.

9. Works Progress Administration, *Military History of Kentucky* (Frankfort: The State *Journal*, 1939), 223.

10. Chenoweth, 190.

11. Bettie Conklin Killick, "Memories of Leitchfield," Leitchfield *Gazette*, Feb. 29, 1940.

12. Lee, *Lyon*, 174–175; Lyon's Report, 805.

13. Leslie, 346.

14. "Graphic Account of the Visit of the 'Bluecoats' to Hartford," *Kentucky Explorer*, Feb. 2015, 30. Reprinted from the Hartford *Herald*, June 4, 1902.

15. *Ibid.*; Dan Lee, "The Enemy I Soon May See: William C. Quantrill in Kentucky," *North & South*, Nov. 2011, 53.

16. "Graphic Account of the Visit of the 'Bluecoats.'"

17. McDowell A. Fogle, *Fogle's Papers: A History of Ohio County, Kentucky* (Utica, KY: McDowell Publications, 1981), 79.

18. *Ibid.*; "Graphic Account of the Visit of the 'Bluecoats.'"

19. Leslie, 364–365.

20. Hartford *Herald*, Aug. 16, 1895.

21. Beth Chinn Harp, *Torn Asunder* (Georgetown, KY: Kinnersley Press, 2003), 135.

Chapter Twenty-Seven

1. "State of Terror," Hopkinsville *Kentuckian*, Apr. 7, 1914; "Rank Outrages and What They Amount To," Hartford *Herald*, Sept. 1, 1915; "Possum Hunter Makes Confession," Hartford *Republican*, July 9, 1915.

2. Untitled, Hartford *Herald*, Sept. 8, 1915; "May Not Try Other Possum Hunter Cases," Hartford *Republican*, Oct. 1, 1915.

3. McClure, *Two Centuries*, 132; Helen Bartter Crocker, 31–32.

4. Crocker, 39; "Don Carlos Buell," *The Kentucky Encyclopedia*, 137.

5. McClure, *Two Centuries*, 288–289; "Elizabethtown and Paducah Railroad," Evansville *Journal*, Mar. 30, 1870.

6. Rennick, 17; "Beaver Dam," *The Kentucky Encyclopedia*, 64.

7. Crocker, 37; McClure, *Two Centuries*, 312.

8. Rennick, 24; Haynes, 55; "Louisville: Completion of an Important Railroad Bridge," Memphis *Public Ledger*, July 15, 1870.

9. McClure, *Two Centuries*, 362–363; Carolyn Wimp, compiler, *Hardin County, Kentucky, Newspaper Abstracts: April 1895—December 1901* (Vine Grove: Ancestral Trails Historical Society, 2000), 41, 201; John Lay, *East View* (Elizabethtown: by the author), n.p.

10. Rennick, 59; Mark E. Nevils, "Leitchfield," *The Kentucky Encyclopedia*, 544.

11. Clark, *Footloose in Jacksonian America*, 118.

12. *Ibid.*, 163; "Col. Lafe Green Dies Suddenly," Hartford *Republican*, Feb. 1, 1907.

13. Ridenour, 47, 48.

14. Clark, *Footloose in Jacksonian America*, 105; Hugh Ridenour, "The Greens of Falls of Rough: A Kentucky Family Biography, 1795–1965" (Master's Thesis, Western Kentucky University, 1966), 51, 70. https://digitalcommons.wku.edu/theses/3039. Accessed July 2, 2022 (cited hereafter as Ridenour, "Kentucky Family Biography"). An 1865 visitor to Lafe Green's home left a partial account of his visit. If accurate, it gives a glimpse of Green's affable and undeniably corny sense of humor: "Stopping over Sunday here with hospitable gent, Lafayette Green, present owner of the fine estate of his uncle, Willis P. Green, former M.C. from that district; was shown the tree where an early hunter of Kentucky lost his favorite 'bear dog.' Asked how it occurred. Says G: 'You see that for, forty feet from the ground. Well, the dog seized the bear at the root of the tree,

when Bruin made up the tree to the fork. The hunter then fired and killed the bear.' After a pause, we inquired what that had to do with the dog. 'Why, you see,' rejoined G, 'the dog held on to the bear and when it fell it fell on top'" ("Editor's Drawer," *Harper's New Monthly Magazine*, Jan. 1866).

15. Ridenour, "Kentucky Family Biography," 55, 71.

16. Advertisement, *Breckinridge News*, July 26, 1882; "Fun at the Falls," *Breckinridge News*, Aug. 30, 1893.

17. Fogle, 13.

18. "Kentucky News," Hartford *Herald*, Feb. 20, 1889; "Booked for Completion," Hartford *Herald*, Mar. 13, 1889; Ridenour, "Kentucky Family Biography," 104; John Lay, conversation with the author, July 20, 2022.

19. *R. L. Polk & Company's Kentucky State Gazetteer and Business Directory, 1896, Vol. VII* (Detroit: R. L. Polk & Co., 1896), 260; "Lafe Green's Home and His Business," *Breckinridge* News, August 24, 1904; David and Lalie Dick, *Rivers of Kentucky* (North Middletown, KY: Plum Lick Publishing, 2002), 168; "Booked for Completion," Hartford *Herald*, Mar. 13, 1889.

20. Ridenour, "Kentucky Family Biography," 79.

21. *Ibid.*, 124, 125, 127; "Lafe Green's Home and His Business," *Breckinridge News*, Aug. 24, 1904; "A Typical Kentuckian," *Breckinridge News*, Mar. 30, 1898; Advertisement, *Breckinridge News*, Apr. 5, 1916.

22. Ridenour, "Kentucky Family Biography," 128–129.

23. *Ibid.*, 130, 132–133; "Local Brevities," *Breckinridge News*, Apr. 24, 1912.

24. "Mrs. Green Dead," Hartford *Republican*, Mar. 13, 1896; "Death of Col. Lafayette Green," Frankfort *Roundabout*, Feb. 2, 1907; "Col. Lafe Green Dies Suddenly," Hartford *Republican*, Feb. 1, 1907; "Resolutions of Respect," *Breckinridge News*, Feb. 6, 1907; Ridenour, Kentucky Family Biography," 135.

25. Kincaid A. Herr, *The Louisville and Nashville Railroad, 1850–1963* (Lexington: University of Kentucky Press, 2021), 175.

26. Ohio County, Kentucky, Ferry Keepers Bonds; Johnson, *Falls City Engineers*, 1, 246.

27. "Rough River Now Opened to Navigation to Hartford, Ky.," Hartford *Herald*, Dec. 23, 1896.

Chapter Twenty-Eight

1. Carolyn Wimp, compiler, *Newspaper Abstracts, 1829–1893*, 244, 255; Carolyn Wimp, compiler, *Newspaper Abstracts, April 1895—December 1901*, 195; John Lay, *East View* (Elizabethtown: by the author, no date), n.p.; "Devastation! A Terrible Tornado Tears Its Terrific Way Through Ohio County," Hartford *Herald*, Apr. 2, 1890.

2. John Lay, *Hardin Springs: Quaint Town Along the Rough River* (Elizabethtown: by the author), n.p.

3. *Ibid.*

4. "Moonshiners Held Over," Elizabethtown *News*, Aug. 7, 1903.

5. "Incendiaries Suspected in Pierce Fire," Elizabethtown *News*, June 6, 1922; "Man Active Against Moonshiners Has House Burned," Elizabethtown *News*, Mar. 23, 1923.

6. WPA, *Guide to Kentucky*, 358; Woodrow Wilson Maglinger, "Dark Days in the Ohio Valley: Three Western Kentucky Lynchings, 1884–1911" (Master's Thesis, Western Kentucky University, 2004), 115–116. http://digitalcommons. wku.edu/theses/242. Accessed Jan. 21, 2014.

7. "Mob Lynches Negro Over At Livermore." Owensboro *Daily Inquirer*, Apr. 21, 1911.

8. Maglinger, 118–119.

9. *Ibid.*, 119–120; "A Statement by Livermore Mayor." Hartford *Herald*, Apr. 26, 1911.

10. "Lynched On Stage; Shots Came From Pit." New York *Times*, Apr. 21, 1911.

11. "As Members of Livermore Mob." Hartford *Herald*, May 17, 1911.

12. *Ibid.*, "A Special Term of McLean's Court," Hartford *Herald*, Aug. 23, 1911.

13. "As Members of Livermore Mob," Hartford *Herald*, May 17, 1911.

14. Maglinger, 138, 139; "The Alibi Was Weak," Owensboro *Daily Inquirer*, Aug. 22, 1911.

15. Maglinger, 141–142.

16. *Ibid.*, 142.

17. David and Lalie Dick, *Rivers of Kentucky* (North Middleton, KY: Plum Lick Publishing, 2002), 161.

Chapter Twenty-Nine

1. "McDaniels," Breckinridge News, May 25, 1921; Richard D. Smith, *Can't You Hear Me Callin': The Life of Bill Monroe* (Boston: Little, Brown, 2000), 7.

2. "Girl's Jewelry," Hartford *Republican*, Nov. 20, 1896; "The Modern Flying Machine," Hartford *Republican*, July 13, 1898.

3. "Telephone from Hartford to Beaver Dam," Hartford *Herald*, Nov. 12, 1879; untitled, Hartford *Republican*, Apr. 27, 1900.

4. Grayson County Historical Society, *Historical Sketches*, 105; Rennick, 256.

5. Charles K. Wolfe, *Kentucky Country* (Lexington: University of Kentucky Press, 1982), 98; Richard D. Smith, *Can't You Hear Me Callin'*, 3, 10, 20.

6. Wolfe, 99; Smith, 4, 27.

7. Neil V. Rosenberg, *Bluegrass: A History* (Champaign: University of Illinois Press, 2005), 30.

8. Wolfe, 100.

9. Rosenberg, *Bluegrass*, 7.

10. Wolfe, 101. Bill Monroe's insistence upon making two words out of bluegrass when naming his band, the Blue Grass Boys, has confused the issue of spelling ever since. Strictly speaking, the music is Bluegrass and the band is Blue Grass, but even professional music writers do not abide strictly by the rule.

11. Rosenberg, *Bluegrass*, 56; George D. Hay and Gene Dudley, *Bill Monroe's WSM Grand Ole Opry Song Folio No. 1* (New York: Peer International, 1947), 4.

12. Neil V. Rosenberg and Charles K. Wolfe, *The Music of Bill Monroe* (Champaign: University of Illinois Press, 2007), 56–57; Rosenberg, *Bluegrass*, 88.

13. L. Mayne Smith, "First Bluegrass Festival Honors Bill Monroe," in *The Bill Monroe Reader*, ed. Tom Ewing (Champaign: University of Illinois Press, 2000) 36; Mark Hembree, *On the Bus with Bill Monroe: My Five Year Ride with the*

Father of Bluegrass (Champaign: University of Illinois Press, 2022), 5.

14. Wolfe, 103; Neil V. Rosenberg, "From Sound to Style: The Emergence of Bluegrass," *The Journal of American Folklore*, Apr.–June 1967, 148–149.

15. Smith, *Can't You Hear Me Callin'*, 154.

16. Smith, "First Bluegrass Festival," in *Monroe Reader*, 33; Wolfe, 103, 104.

17. Wolfe, 107–108.

18. Stephanie P. Ledgin, *Homegrown Music: Discovering Bluegrass* (Westport, CT: Praeger, 2004), 81; Chris Varias, "For Nitty Gritty Dirt Band, folk rock a way to escape," Cincinnati *Enquirer*, Mar. 9, 2017; "Music Forms a New Circle," Nashville *Tennessean*, Aug. 15, 1971.

19. U.S. Senate, Congressional Record, "Senate Resolution 463—Recognizing William Smith 'Bill' Monroe on His Seventy-Fifth Birthday," Aug. 9, 1986; Jon Pareles, "Bill Monroe Dies at 84; Fused Musical Roots Into Bluegrass," New York *Times*, Sept. 10, 1996. "Bill Monroe," bluegrasshall.org/inductees/bill-monroe. Accessed July 3, 2022.

20. Jay Orr, "Tears, Music Fill Bluegrass Legend's Final Ryman Show," Nashville *Banner*, Sept. 12, 1996.

21. Smith, *Can't You Hear Me Callin'*, 290–291.

22. Ledgin, Introduction, xvii, xviii; 33, 44, 80

23. Ledgin, 123.

Chapter Thirty

1. Harrison and Klotter, *A New History of Kentucky*, 358.

2. *Ibid.*, 359.

3. *Ibid.*, 297, 364.

4. David Dick, *Let There Be Light: The Story of Rural Electrification in Kentucky* (North Middletown, KY: Plum Lick Publishing, 2009), 100.

5. *Ibid.*, 101. Most of the quotes taken from David Dick first appeared in "A History of Phenomenal Growth," a publication of the Green River Electric Corporation.

6. Edwin A. Lyon, *A New Deal for Southeastern Archaeology* (Tuscaloosa: University of Alabama Press, 1996), 40.

7. Nick Taylor, *American-Made: The Enduring Legacy of the WPA* (New York: Bantam Dell, 2009), 371.

8. *Ibid.*, 372.

9. Sara E. Pedde and Olaf H. Prufer, "The Kentucky Green River Archaic as Seen from the Ward Site," in *Archaic Transitions in Ohio and Kentucky Prehistory*, eds. Olaf H. Prufer, Sara E. Pedde, and Richard S. Meindl (Kent: Kent State University Press, 2001), 69.

10. Victor Dominic Thompson, "Diversity in Hunter-Gatherer Landscapes in the North American Midcontinent" (Master's Thesis, University of Kentucky, 2001), 125, http://uknowledge.uky.edu/gradschool_thesis/186. Accessed Feb. 21, 2015.

11. Richard S. Meindl, Robert P. Mensforth, and Heather P. York, "Mortality, Fertility, and Growth in the Kentucky Late Archaic: The Paleodemography of the Ward Site," in Prufer, Pedde, and Meindl, 63.

12. Lynne P. Sullivan, Bobby R. Braly, Michaelyn S. Harle, and Shannon D. Koerner, "Remembering New Deal Archaeology in the Southeast: A Legacy in Museum Collections," 72, www.lib.utk.edu/newfoundpress/pubs/museums/chp3.pdf. Accessed Feb. 22, 2015.

13. Advertisement, *Breckinridge News*, Nov. 3, 1920.

14. Ridenour, "Kentucky Family Biography," 140, 141, 146.

15. Melinda J. Overstreet, "Bad Mix? Levels of Heavily Used Weed Killer in Area Drinking Water Comes Under Scrutiny," *News-Enterprise*, Apr. 24, 2005.

16. Melinda J. Overstreet, "Farmers on frontline in water quality fight," *News-Enterprise*, Apr. 24, 2005.

17. Melinda J. Overstreet, "Atrazine's threat open to debate." *News-Enterprise*, Apr. 24, 2005.

18. Melinda J. Overstreet, "Best Management Practices," *News-Enterprise*, Apr. 24, 2005.

19. Overstreet, "Bad Mix?"

20. U.S. Army Corps of Engineers, "USACE Dam Safety Facts for Rough River Lake Dam," booklet, June 29, 2017; U.S. Army Corps of Engineers, *Water Resources Development by the U.S. Army Corps of Engineers in Kentucky* (Vicksburg: Department of the Army, Lower Mississippi Valley Division, 1977), 79–80; Johnson, *Falls City Engineers*, 165.

21. Corps of Engineers, "Dam Safety Facts."

22. Wendell Berry, Watershed and Commonwealth," in *Citizenship Papers: Essays* (Berkeley: Counterpoint Press, 2004), 157.

Bibliography
and Note to Readers

The author suggests these books as a general introduction to the Rolling Fork, the Nolin, and the Rough and the people who settled alongside them: Lewis Collins and Richard Henry Collins, *Historical Sketches of Kentucky: History of Kentucky, Volumes I and II*; Works Progress Administration, *The WPA Guide to Kentucky*; John E. Kleber, ed., *The Encyclopedia of Kentucky*; Lowell H. Harrison and James C. Klotter, *A New History of Kentucky*; and Robert M. Rennick, *Kentucky Place Names*. If one wishes to dive deeper, local county and historical society libraries contain county and town histories. Deeper still are the various county court order books, wills, deeds, and old newspapers. After learning more about their history, one will surely wish to see the rivers, and that is encouraged, too.

"Absalom A. Harrison Civil War Letters." www.civilwarhome.com/letter3.htm. Accessed July 7, 2002.

Adams, Evelyn Crady. "The Coxes of Cox's Creek, Kentucky." *Filson Club History Quarterly*, Apr. 1948.

Adams, Evelyn Crady. "Goodin's Fort (1780) in Nelson County, Ky." *Filson Club History Quarterly*, Jan. 1953.

Alford, Warren A., Wayne Alford, and Lafayette Alford. *We All Must Dye Sooner or Later*. Edited by Richard S. Skodmore. Hanover, IN: Nugget, 1995.

Allen, Frederick Lewis. *Since Yesterday*. New York: Bantam, 1965.

Allen, Michael. *Western Rivermen, 1763–1861: Ohio and Mississippi Boatmen and the Myth of the Alligator Horse*. Baton Rouge: Louisiana State University Press, 1994.

Allen, William B. *A History of Kentucky*. Louisville: Bradley & Gilbert, Publishers, 1872.

Allison, Young E. "A Chapter of Trappist History." *Filson Club History Quarterly*, Jan. 1927.

Altsheler, Brent. "The Long Hunters and James Knox, Their Leader." *Filson Club History Quarterly*, Oct. 1931.

Anonymous. Letter from Camp Nevin. November 25, 1861. Collection of the Abraham Lincoln Presidential Library, Springfield, Illinois.

Arnold, William E. *A History of Methodism in Kentucky*, Volume I. Louisville: The Herald Press, 1935.

Atlanta History Center. "Turning Point: The American Civil War." Oct. 29, 2005.

Badè, William Frederic. Introduction to John Muir, *A Thousand-Mile Walk to the Gulf*. Boston: Mariner, 1998.

Bakeless, John. *Daniel Boone*. Harrisburg, PA: Stackpole Books, 1965.

Baringer, William E. *Lincoln Day by Day, Volume 1*. Washington, D.C.: Lincoln Sesquicentennial Commission, 1960.

Barton, O.S. *Three Years With Quantrill: A True Story Told by His Scout*

John McCorkle. Norman: University of Oklahoma Press, 1992.

Barton, William E. "'Mord' Lincoln the Woman Hater." *The Open Court*, May 1924.

Baylor, Orval W., et al. *Pioneer History of Washington County, Ky*. Owensboro, KY, 1980.

Beattie, George W., and Helen P. Beattie. "Pioneer Linns of Kentucky, Part II." *Filson Club History Quarterly*, Apr. 1946.

Bell, Rick. *The Great Flood of 1937*. Louisville: Butler Books, 2007.

Belue, Ted Franklin. *Hunters of Kentucky: A Narrative History of America's First Far West, 1750–1792*. Mechanicsburg, PA: Stackpole Books, 2011.

Benningfield, Edward. *Larue County, Kentucky Marriage Records, 1843–1876*. Utica, KY: McDowell Publications, 1986.

Benningfield, Edward. *Lincoln's Birth County (LaRue County) in the Civil War*. Utica, KY: McDowell Publications, 1990.

Berry, Wendell. "Watershed and Commonwealth." In *Citizenship Papers: Essays*. Berkeley: Counterpoint Press, 2004.

"Bill Monroe." www.bluegrass.org. au/Magazine/monroe/index.cfm. Accessed Mar. 14, 2006.

Binkerd, A.D. *Mammoth Cave and Its Denizens: A Complete Descriptive Guide*. Cincinnati: Robert Clarke & Co., 1869.

Blakey, George T. *Hard Times and New Deal in Kentucky: 1929–1939*. Lexington: University Press of Kentucky, 2015.

Blitz, John H. "Adoption of the Bow and Arrow in Prehistoric North America." *North American Archaeologist*, Vol. 9, No. 2, 1998.

Bloomfield, A.S. "Bloomfield Letters." www.csrab.state.oh.us/images/pdf/ september_1861.pdf. Accessed Feb. 5, 2020.

Blythe, Robert W., Maureen Carroll, and Steven H. Moffson. *Abraham Lincoln Birthplace National Historic Site, Historic Resource Study*. Revised and updated by Brian F. Coffey. Atlanta: Cultural Resources Stewardship,

Southeast Regional Office, National Park Service, Department of the Interior, 2001.

"Bonnieville." File Folder. Hart County, Kentucky Historical Society Library. Munfordville, Kentucky.

Bowersox, J. Richard. *Rocks to Roads to Ruin: A Brief History of Western Kentucky's Rock-Asphalt Industry, 1888–1957*. Lexington: Kentucky Geological Survey, 2016.

Brucker, Roger W., and Richard A. Watson. *The Longest Cave*. Carbondale: SIU Press, 1976.

Bullitt, Alexander Clark. *Rambles in the Mammoth Cave, During the Year 1844*. Louisville: Morton & Griswold, 1845.

Bunce, Frank H. "Dreams from a Pack: Isaac Wolfe Bernheim and Bernheim Forest." *Filson Club History Quarterly*, Oct. 1973.

Calloway, Collin. *The Shawnees and the War for America*. New York: Penguin, 2007.

Campbell, John A. "U.S. Bullion Depository." In *The Kentucky Encyclopedia*. Edited by John E. Kleber. Lexington: University Press of Kentucky, 1992.

"Camps." File Folder. Hart County Kentucky Historical Society Library. Munfordville, Kentucky.

Carmen, Harry J., ed. "Diary of Amos Glover." http://publications.ohiohistory.org/ohstemplate.cfm?action= dated&page=0044258.html&s. Accessed Jan. 29, 2008.

Cawthorn, C.P., and N.L. Warnell. *Pioneer Baptist Church Records of South Central Kentucky and the Upper Cumberland of Tennessee, 1799–1899*. N.p., 1985.

Chacon, Richard J., and David H. Dye, eds. *The Taking and Displaying of Human Body Parts as Trophies by Amerindians*. New York: Springer Science & Business Media, 2007.

Chenoweth, James Q. "The Rangers' Last Campaign." In *The Partisan Rangers of the Confederate States Army*. Edited by William J. Davis. Louisville: George G. Fetter Company, 1904.

"Civilian Accounts." File Folder. Hart County Kentucky Historical Society Library. Munfordville, Kentucky.

Clark, Thomas D. *Footloose in Jacksonian*

America: Robert W. Scott and His Agrarian World. Lexington: University Press of Kentucky, 1989.

Clark, Thomas D. *Historic Maps of Kentucky.* Lexington: University Press of Kentucky, 1979.

Clark, Thomas D. *A History of Kentucky.* Lexington: The John Bradford Press, 1950.

Clark, Thomas D. *The Kentucky.* New York: Farrar and Rinehart, 1942.

Clay, R. Berle. "Prehistoric Peoples." In *The Kentucky Encyclopedia.* Edited by John E. Kleber. Lexington: University of Kentucky Press, 1992.

Cogliano, Francis D. *Revolutionary America, 1763–1815: A Political History.* New York: Routledge, 2000.

Coleman, J. Winston. *200 Years in Kentucky.* Frankfort: America's Historic Records, 1978.

Collins, Lewis. *History of Kentucky.* Lexington: Henry Clay Press, 1968.

Collins, Lewis, and Richard Henry Collins. *Collins' Historical Sketches of Kentucky: History of Kentucky, Volumes I and II.* Covington: Collins & Co., 1882.

Collins, Richard. "Civil War Annals of Kentucky." Edited by Hambleton Tapp. *Filson Club History Quarterly,* July 1961.

Commonwealth of Kentucky Department of Public Information. "It Started at Springfield." Feb. 1, 1967.

Cook, Kim, and Brad Quinlin. *On the Line of Bacon Creek.* Bonnieville, KY: Bacon Creek Historical Society, n.d.

Cook, Michael L., and Bettie Ann Cook. *Breckinridge County, Kentucky Records, Volume I.* Evansville, IN: Cook Publications, 1977.

Coomes, M.L. "Benjamin Lynn, John Ritchie, John Gilkey and a Story of an Early Distillery in Kentucky." Filson Club Paper, January 7, 1895.

Coy, Fred E., Jr., Thomas C. Fuller, Larry G. Meadows, and James F. Swauger. *Rock Art of Kentucky.* Lexington: University Press of Kentucky, 1997.

Creason, Joe. *Crossroads and Coffeetrees.* Louisville: The Courier-Journal & the Louisville Times, 1975.

Creason, Joe. "I, Thomas Lincoln Take Thee, Nancy Hanks..." *Courier-Journal Magazine.* June 7, 1959.

Crews, Clyde F. "Badin, Stephen Theodore." In *The Kentucky Encyclopedia.* Edited by John E. Kleber. Lexington: University Press of Kentucky, 1992.

Crews, Clyde F. *The Faithful Image: Glimpses of the Two Hundred Year History of Kentucky Catholics in the Archdiocese of Louisville.* Louisville: Prairie Lithography, 1986.

Crist Family File. Bullitt County Free Public Library, Shepherdsville, KY.

Crocker, Helen B. "Green River." In *The Kentucky Encyclopedia.* Edited by John E. Kleber. Lexington: University Press of Kentucky, 1992.

Crocker, Helen B. *The Green River of Kentucky.* Lexington: University Press of Kentucky, 1976.

Crofts, Thomas. *History of the Service of The Third Ohio Volunteer Cavalry.* Toledo: The Stoneman Press, 1910.

Cunningham, John W. "Early History of Leitchfield." "Grayson County, Kentucky in the 20th Century, Pictorial Edition." Supplement to the Grayson County *Gazette,* Nov. 1903 (reprint).

Current, Richard N. *The Lincoln Nobody Knows.* New York: Hill & Wang, 1958.

Dabney, Joseph Earl. *Mountain Spirits.* New York: Copple House Books, 1978.

Daniel, Larry J. *Days of Glory: The Army of the Cumberland: 1861–1865.* Baton Rouge: Louisiana State University Press, 2004.

Daniels, Jonathan. *The Devil's Backbone: The Story of the Natchez Trace.* New York: McGraw-Hill, 1962.

Darnell, Betty Rolwing. "Henry Magruder, CSA." *Wilderness Road, Quarterly of the Bullitt County Genealogical Society.* Sept. 2000.

Darnell, Betty Rolwing, ed. *Bullitt County, Ky. Court Order Book A, 1779–1800.* N.p., 2003.

Daughters of the American Revolution. *DAR Patriot Index.* Washington, D.C.: The American Society of the Daughters of the Revolution, 1966.

Davis, William C. *Breckinridge: Statesman, Soldier, Symbol.* Baton Rouge: Louisiana State University Press, 1974.

Davis, William C. *The Orphan Brigade.* New York: Doubleday, 1980.

Dewees, Curtis. *George Washington's*

Kentucky Land. Lake Orion, MI: Lake Orion Books, 2005.

DiBlasi, Philip. "Prehistoric Inhabitants." In *The Encyclopedia of Louisville.* Edited by John E. Kleber. Lexington: University of Kentucky Press, 2001.

Dick, David. *Let There Be Light: The Story of Rural Electrification in Kentucky.* North Middletown, KY: Plum Lick Publishing, 2009.

Dick, David, and Lalie Dick. *Rivers of Kentucky.* North Middletown, KY: Plum Lick Publishing, 2001.

"Dock Letter." www.dockbrown.com/html/letter.html. Accessed Oct. 26, 2006.

Driscoll, David R., Jr. "Stephen Theodore Badin: Priest of Frontier Kentucky." *Filson Club History Quarterly,* July 1957.

Duke, Basil W. *The Civil War Reminiscences of General Basil W. Duke.* New York: Cooper Square Press, 2001.

Duke, Basil W. *A History of Morgan's Cavalry.* Cincinnati: Miami Printing and Publishing Company, 1867.

Duncan, Kunigunde, and D.F. Nickols. *Mentor Graham.* Chicago: University of Chicago Press, 1944.

"Editor's Drawer." *Harper's New Monthly Magazine,* January 1866.

"Edmonson Countians Know They Have More Than Cave, Lakes." *Echoes From Edmonson County,* Apr., May, June, 1999.

"Ellen Kenton McGaughey Wallace Diary." Wallace-Starling Family Diaries. Collection of the Kentucky Historical Society, Frankfort, Kentucky.

Elliott, Bessie Miller Elliott. *History of LaRue County, Kentucky.* Vine Grove: Ancestral Trails Historical Society, 2000.

Emerson, Ralph Waldo. "Illusions." In *The Conduct of Life.* Cambridge: Houghton, Mifflin, 1860.

Emerson, Thomas E., and Dale L. McElrath. *Late Woodland Societies: Tradition and Transformation Across the Midcontinent.* Lincoln: University of Nebraska Press, 2000.

English, William Hayden. *Conquest of the Country Northwest of the River Ohio, 1778–1783, and Life of Gen. George Rogers Clark, Vol. I.* Indianapolis: The Bowen-Merrill Company, 1896.

Farrington, Joshua D. "Braddock, General." In *The Kentucky African American Encyclopedia.* Edited by Gerald K. Smith, Karen Cotton McDaniel, and John A. Hardin. Lexington: University Press of Kentucky, 2015.

Faust, Burton. "The History of Saltpeter Mining in Mammoth Cave." *Filson Club History Quarterly,* four parts, Jan.–Oct. 1967.

Finch, Marianne. *An Englishwoman's Experience in America.* London: Richard Bentley, Publisher in Ordinary to Her Majesty, 1853.

Fischer, Gerald, W. *Guerrilla Warfare in Civil War Kentucky.* Morley, MO: Acclaim Press, 2014.

Flexner, James Thomas. *George Washington: Anguish and Farewell, 1793–1799.* Boston: Little, Brown, 1969.

Flippo, Chet. "Industry Mourns Father of Bluegrass." *Billboard,* Sept. 21, 1996.

Fogle, McDowell A. *Fogle's Papers: A History of Ohio County, Kentucky.* Utica, KY: McDowell Publications, 1981.

Foote, Shelby. *The Civil War: A Narrative, Volumes 1–3.* New York: Vintage, 1986.

Fordyce, Jim. "Fordyce Family Archives: Civil War Correspondence of William J. and Mary Elizabeth (Fordyce) Strieby." www.fordyce.org./genealogy/misc_records/Strieby_CW.html. Accessed Jan. 23, 2003.

Froman Family File. Bullitt County Free Public Library, Shepherdsville, KY.

"Gandertown in Days of Old." The *Lynnlander,* Nov. 1928.

"GAR Posts in the State of Kentucky." www.suvcw.org/garposts/ky.polf#search='GAR%20kentucky. Accessed Nov. 7, 2006.

George, Angelo I. "Saltpeter and Gunpowder Manufacturing in Kentucky." *Filson Club History Quarterly,* Apr. 1986.

George, Angelo I., and Gary A. O'Dell. "The Saltpeter Works at Mammoth Cave and the New Madrid Earthquake." *Filson Club History Quarterly,* Jan. 1992.

"Gethsemani." www.monks.org. Accessed Nov. 1, 2004.

Gilead Baptist Church. *Minutes.*

Giroux, Robert. Introduction to the

fiftieth anniversary edition of *The Seven Storey Mountain.* In Merton, Thomas. *The Seven Storey Mountain.* New York: Harcourt Brace, 1998.

Godbey, Jack. "1937 Flood in Kentucky." *The Kentucky Explorer,* Feb. 2018.

Goff, Zerelda Jane. Affidavit, 30 May 1906. Photocopy, John Lay Collection. Original on file at Abraham Lincoln Birthplace National Historic Site, Hodgenville, KY.

Grayson County Historical Society. *Historical Sketches and Family Histories—Grayson County, Kentucky.* Utica, KY: McDowell Publications, 2002.

Green, Thomas Marshall. *The Spanish Conspiracy.* Cincinnati: Robert Clarke & Co., 1891.

Green, Willis. "Address of the Hon. Willis Green, of Kentucky, Before the Alexandria (D.C.) Clay Club." July 19, 1844.

Hackensmith, C.W. "Lincoln's Family and His Teachers." *Register of the Kentucky Historical Society,* Oct. 1969.

Haggman, Bertil. "Confederate Martyr, Henry Magruder." *Wilderness Road, Quarterly of the Bullitt County Genealogical Society,* Dec. 2000.

Hall, David C. "Wickland." In *The Kentucky Encyclopedia.* Edited by John E. Kleber. Lexington: University Press of Kentucky, 1992.

Hammack, James W. *Kentucky and the Second American Revolution.* Lexington: University Press of Kentucky, 1976.

Hammon, Neal O., ed. *My Father, Daniel Boone: The Draper Interviews with Nathan Boone.* Lexington: University Press of Kentucky, 1999.

Hardin County, Kentucky, Court Order Book B.

Hardin County, Kentucky, Marriage Book A.

Hardin County Planning and Development Commission. *Hardin Heritage: The Historic Architecture of Hardin County, Kentucky.* Elizabethtown: Hardin County Planning and Zoning Commission, 1986.

Harp, Beth Chinn. *Torn Asunder: Civil War in Ohio County and the Green River Country.* Georgetown, KY: Kinnersley Press, 2003.

Harralson, Agnes S. *Steamboats on the Green.* Berea: Kentucky Imprints, 1981.

Harrison, Lowell. *George Rogers Clark and the War in the West.* Lexington: University Press of Kentucky, 1976.

Harrison, Lowell H. *Kentucky's Road to Statehood.* Lexington: University Press of Kentucky, 1992.

Harrison, Lowell H. *Lincoln of Kentucky.* Lexington: University Press of Kentucky, 1999.

Harrison, Lowell H., and James C. Klotter. *A New History of Kentucky.* Lexington: University Press of Kentucky, 1997.

Harville, Bobbie. "Lebanon Junction." www.courier-journal.com/reweb/community/placetime/bullitt/lebanonjunction.html. Accessed Sept. 23, 2004.

Hawes, George W. *Kentucky State Gazetteer and Business Directory of 1859 and 1860.* Vine Grove: Ancestral Trails Historical Society, 2006.

Hawkins, Nadine. "Black Gold in the Green Hills." Hart County Historical Society *Quarterly,* July 1992.

Hay, George D., and Gene Dudley. *Bill Monroe's WSM Grand Ole Opry Song Folio No. 1.* New York: Peer International, 1947.

Haycraft, Samuel. *A History of Elizabethtown, Ky. and Its Surroundings.* Elizabethtown: Hardin County Historical Society, 1975.

Haynes, William R. *Dock Brown: The Outlaw of Grayson County.* Leitchfield, KY: Leitchfield *Gazette,* 1950.

Hearn, Daniel Allen. *Legal Executions in Illinois, Indiana, Iowa, Kentucky, and Missouri: A Comprehensive Registry, 1866–1965.* Jefferson, NC: McFarland, 2016.

Hembree, Mark. *On the Bus with Bill Monroe: My Five-Year Ride with the Father of Bluegrass.* Champaign: University of Illinois Press, 2022.

Henderson, A. Gwynn, and Eric J. Schlarb. *Adena: Woodland Period Moundbuilders of the Bluegrass.* Lexington: Kentucky Archaeological Survey, 2007.

Herndon, William. H. *Herndon's Lincoln.* Indianapolis: Bobbs-Merrill, 1970.

Herr, Kincaid A. *The Louisville and Nashville Railroad, 1850–1963*. Lexington: University of Kentucky Press, 2021.

Hibbs, Dixie. *Nelson County, Kentucky: A Pictorial History*. Norfolk, VA: Donning Co., 1989.

Hibbs, Dixie. *Nelson County: A Portrait of the Civil War*. Charleston, SC: Arcadia, 1999.

Hibbs, Dixie, and Carl Howell. *Central Kentucky*. Charleston, SC: Arcadia, 2000.

Hill, Carol A., and Duane DePaepe. "Saltpeter Mining in Kentucky Caves." *Register of Kentucky Historical Society*, Autumn 1979.

"History of the 34th Illinois Infantry." http://users.cis.net/daver/sboo4a.htm. Accessed Jan. 18, 2003.

Holt, David. "Fort Knox." In *The Kentucky Encyclopedia*. Edited by John E. Kleber. Lexington: University Press of Kentucky, 1992.

"Hopper Chair." www.rootsweb.com/~tngibson/photos/hopper-chair.htm. Accessed Nov. 6, 2006.

"Howardstown." www.cinci.rr.com/odaniel/howardstown%201901.html. Accessed July 24, 2004.

Howell, Carl, and Don Waters. *Hardin and LaRue Counties, 1880–1930*. Charleston, SC: Arcadia, 1998.

Hoyt, Ray. *Your CCC: A Handbook for Enrollees*, Third Edition. Washington, D.C.: Happy Days, n.d.

Huber, Margaret W., ed. *In Museums and Memory: Selected Papers from the Annual Meeting of the Southern Anthropological Society, Staunton, Virginia, March 2008*. Knoxville: Newfound Press, 2001. www.lib.utk.edu/newfoundpress/pubs/museums/chp3.pdf. Accessed Feb. 22, 2015.

Huddleston, Connie M. *Kentucky's Civilian Conservation Corps*. Charleston, SC: The History Press, 2009.

Indiana University–Purdue University Indianapolis. *Indiana's German Sons: A History of the Irst German 32nd Regiment, Indiana Volunteer Infantry*, Volume 15 by Michael Peake. Found on IUPUI Max Kade German American Center, July 11, 2002. http://www.ulib.iupui.edu.kade.peake/p.8.html. Accessed Jan. 18, 2003.

Isenberg, Andrew C. *Wyatt Earp: A Vigilante Life*. New York: Hill & Wang, 2013.

James, James Alton. *The Life of George Rogers Clark*. New York: Greenwood, 1928.

James, James Alton, ed. *George Rogers Clark Papers, 1775–1781*. Danville: Illinois State Historical Library, 1912.

James, James Alton, ed. *George Rogers Clark Papers, 1781–1784*. Springfield: Illinois State Historical Library, 1926.

Jay, Milton T., ed. *History of Jay County, Indiana: Including Its War Record and Incorporating the Montgomery History, Vol. I*. Indianapolis: Historical Publishing Co., 1922.

"Jay County and The War, Company C, 39th Regiment." http://www.countyhistory.com/jay/history21b.htm. Accessed June 8, 2003.

Jefferies, Richard W. "Hunters and Gatherers After the Ice Age." In *Kentucky Archaeology—Perceptions in Kentucky's Past: Architecture, Archaeology, and Landscape*. Edited by R. Barry Lewis. Lexington: University Press of Kentucky, 2014.

Jillson, Willard Rouse. "George Washington's Western Kentucky Lands." *Register of the Kentucky Historical Society*, Oct. 1931.

"John Muir (1838–1914): A Brief Biography." *Journal of the Sierra College Natural History Museum*, Winter 2008. Sierracollege.edu/ejournals/jscnhm/v1n2/muir.html.

Johnson, Leland R. *Falls City Engineers: A History of the Louisville District, Corps of Engineers, United States Army*. Louisville: U.S. Army Corps of Engineers, 1974.

Johnson, L.F. *Famous Kentucky Trials and Tragedies*. Lexington: Henry Clay Press, 1972.

Johnson, Mark W. *That Body of Brave Men*. Cambridge: Da Capo Press, 2003.

Jones, Albert. *The Highbaugh Family*. By the author, 1961.

Jones, Mary Josephine. *The Civil War in Hardin County, Kentucky*. Vine Grove: Ancestral Trails Historical Society, 1995.

Jones, Mary Josephine. *Hardin County, Kentucky Marriages, 1793 to 1829*.

Vine Grove: Ancestral Trails Historical Society, 1996.

Jones, Mary Josephine. *Hardin County, Kentucky Wills, 1793–1866.* Vine Grove: Ancestral Trails Historical Society, 1984.

Jones, Ronald L. *Plant Life of Kentucky: All Illustrated Guide to Vascular Flora.* Lexington: University Press of Kentucky, 2005.

Kellner, Esther. *Moonshine: Its History and Folklore.* New York: Weathervane, 1971.

Kempf, Gary. *The Land Before Fort Knox.* Charleston, SC: Arcadia, 2004.

Kentucky Division of Water, Rivers, and Trails. *Kentucky Rivers Assessment.* Kentucky Division of Water, 1992.

Kentucky Heritage Council. *Hardin Heritage.* Elizabethtown: Hardin County Planning and Zoning Commission, 1986.

Kentucky Kindred Genealogical Research. "2017 Maryland to Kentucky and Beyond Genealogy Conference." kentuckykindredgenealogy. com/2017/06/16/2017-maryland-go-kentucky-and-beyond-genealogy-conference. Accessed May 2, 2022.

"Kentucky State Parks." www.parks. ky.gov/resortparks/rr/index.htm. Accessed Aug. 6, 2005.

Kincaid, Robert L. *The Wilderness Road.* Indianapolis: McGraw- Hill, 1947.

Knott, W.T. *History of Marion County.* N.p., N.d.

Kochman, Marilyn, ed. *The Big Book of Bluegrass.* New York: William Morrow, 1984.

Lake, Stuart. *Wyatt Earp: Frontier Marshall.* New York: Pocket Books, 1994.

Landau, Herman, and Lee Shai Weissbach. "Berheim, Isaac Wolfe." In *The Encyclopedia of Louisville.* Edited by John E. Kleber. Lexington: University Press of Kentucky, 2001.

Lay, John. *East View.* Elizabethtown: by the author, no date.

Lay, John. *Hardin Springs: Quaint Town Along the Rough River.* Elizabethtown: by the author, 2012,

Lay, John. *Mills Along the Nolin.* Elizabethtown: by the author, 2007.

Lay, John. *Nolin.* Elizabethtown,: by the author, 2012.

Lay, John. *An Overview of Abraham Lincoln's Ancestry.* Elizabethtown: by the author, no date.

Lay, John. *White Mills.* Elizabethtown: by the author, 2009.

Ledgin, Stephanie P. *Homegrown Music: Discovering Bluegrass.* Westport, CT: Praeger, 2004.

Lee, Dan. *Camp Nevin: Hardin County's Contribution to Victory in the War of the Rebellion.* Cecilia, KY: by the author, 2008.

Lee, Dan. "The Enemy I Soon May See: William C. Quantrill in Kentucky." *North & South,* Nov. 2011.

Lee, Dan. *Kentuckian in Blue: A Biography of Major General Lovell Harrison Rousseau.* Jefferson, NC: McFarland, 2010.

Lee, Dan. *The L&N Railroad in the Civil War.* Jefferson, NC: McFarland, 2011.

Lee, Dan. *Your Son Until Death: The Boys of the 27th Kentucky Infantry.* Cecilia, KY: by the author, 2007.

Lee, Hubert. "A Short History of White Mills Baptist Church." *Bits and Pieces: A Quarterly Publication of the Hardin County Historical Society,* Winter 1990.

Lee, Jacob. "Electrification and the Transformation of Rural America." Research Paper. University of Louisville, 2003. Collection of the author.

Lee, Lloyd G. *A Brief History of Kentucky and Its Counties.* Berea, KY: Kentucky Imprints, 1981.

Leonard-Boone, Shannon. "Fabulous Farm Cheeses." *Kentucky Living,* Nov. 2004.

Leslie, Edward E. *The Devil Knows How to Ride: The True Story of William Clarke Quantrill and His Confederate Raiders.* New York: Da Capo, 1998.

Lewis, R. Barry. "Mississippian Farmers." In *Kentucky Archaeology—Perceptions in Kentucky's Past: Architecture, Archaeology, and Landscape.* Edited by R. Barry Lewis. Lexington: University Press of Kentucky, 2014.

Lincoln, Abraham. "My Ancestors—A. Lincoln." *Lincoln Lore,* Feb. 10, 1936.

Lincoln Lore. "The Helm-Haycraft Collection of Kentucky Manuscripts." May 1970.

Lindbergh, Charles A. *The Spirit of St.*

Louis. New York: Charles Scribner's Sons, 1953.

Long, Jerry. "Rogers Station, Nelson County, Kentucky," West Central Kentucky Family Research Association *Bulletin,* Summer 1996.

Lorant, Stefan. *Lincoln: A Picture Story of His Life.* New York: Norton, 1969.

Lorant, Stephan. *The Presidency.* New York: Macmillan, 1952.

Louis-Philippe, King of France. *Diary of My Travels in America.* Translated from the French by Stephen Becker. New York: Delacorte Press, 1977.

Lyon, Edwin A. *A New Deal for Southeastern Archaeology.* Tuscaloosa: University of Alabama Press, 1996.

Maes, Camillus P. *The Life of Rev. Charles Nerinckx.* Cincinnati: R. Clarke & Co., 1880.

Magers, Harry. *The Lincoln Book.* Tompkinsville, KY: Monroe County Press, 1971.

Maggard, Greg J., and Kary L. Stackelbeck, "Paleoindian Period." In *The Archaeology of Kentucky: An Update, Volume One.* Edited by David Pollack. N.p.: Kentucky Heritage Council, 2008.

Maglinger, Woodrow Wilson, "Dark Days in the Ohio Valley: Three Western Kentucky Lynchings, 1884–1911." Master's Thesis, Western Kentucky University, 2004. http://digitalcommons.wku.edu/theses/242. Accessed Jan. 21, 2014.

Magruder, Henry C. *Three Years in the Saddle.* Louisville, 1865.

Malone, Dumas. *Jefferson and His Time: Jefferson and the Ordeal of Liberty.* Boston: Little, Brown, 1962.

Mansfort, Robert P. "Human Trophy Taking in Eastern North America During the Archaic Period: The Relationship to Warfare and Social Complexity." In *The Taking and Displaying of Human Body Parts as Trophies by Amerindians.* Edited by Richard J. Chacon and David H. Dye. New York: Springer Science and Business Media, 2007.

Marion County Historical Society. *History of Marion County, Volume I.* New Hope, KY: Marion County Historical Society, 2001.

Mather, Otis M. "Explorers and Early Settlers South of Muldraugh Hill." *Register of the Kentucky Historical Society,* Jan. 1924.

Mather, Otis M. *Six Generations of LaRues and Allied Families.* Hodgenville, KY, 1921.

Matthews, William E. "Guerrillas of the Civil War." In *Kentucky's Civil War, 1861–1865.* Edited by Jerlene Rose. Clay City: Back Home in Kentucky, 2005.

McClure, Daniel E. *Two Centuries in Elizabethtown and Hardin County, Kentucky, 1776–1976.* Elizabethtown: Hardin County Historical Society, 1979.

McClure, Paul. *Millerstown and Its People: A Brief History of Millerstown, KY.* Elizabethtown: Hardin County Historical Society, 1992.

McCook, Alexander McDowell. Letter to Gov. William Dennison, Nov. 15, 1861. Collection of the Ohio Historical Society, Columbus, Ohio.

McDonough, James Lee. *War in Kentucky: From Shiloh to Perryville.* Knoxville: University of Tennessee Press, 1979.

McDowell, Robert E. "Bullitt's Lick: The Related Saltworks and Settlement." *Filson Club History Quarterly,* July 1956.

McHenry, John H. "Seventeenth Kentucky Infantry." In *The Union Regiments of Kentucky.* Edited by Thomas Speed. Louisville: Courier-Journal Job Printing Company, 1897.

McManamon, Francis P., Linda S. Cordell, Kent G. Lightfoot, and George R. Milner, eds. *Archaeology in America.* Four Volumes. Westport, CT: Greenwood Press, 2008.

McMurtry, R. Gerald. *A Series of Monographs Concerning the Lincolns and Hardin County, Ky.* Elizabethtown: The Enterprise Press, 1959.

Meindl, Richard S., Robert P. Mensforth, and Heather P. York, "Mortality, Fertility, and Growth in the Kentucky Late Archaic: The Paleodemography of the Ward Site." In *Archaic Traditions in Ohio and Kentucky Archaeology.* Edited by Olaf H. Prufer, Sara E. Pedde, and Richard J. Meindl. Kent: Kent State University Press, 2001.

Merton, Thomas. *The Seven Storey Mountain.* New York: Harcourt Brace, 1998.

Meyer, Jana. "Courting Miss Nall." *The Filson*, Summer 2015.

Montell, Lynnwood, ed. *Folk Medicine of the Mammoth Cave Area.* Booklet, n.d.

Morrison, Duvall. *A History of Grayson County, Kentucky.* Utica, KY: McDowell Publications, 1979.

Moser, Robert Louis. "Memories of My Big Brother William Thomas (Bill) Moser." http://www.bullitcountyhistory.com/bchistory/flood1937moser.html. Accessed Jan. 23, 2014.

Muir, John. *A Thousand Mile Walk to the Gulf.* Boston: Mariner Books, 1998.

Munson, William O. Letters, loc. 945, Item 16, Item 25. Special Collections, University of Arkansas Libraries, Fayetteville.

Murr, J. Edward. *Abraham Lincoln's Wilderness Years: Collected Works of J. Edward Murr.* Edited by Joshua Claybourn. Bloomington: Indiana University Press, 2023.

Murray, Robert K., and Roger K. Bruker. *Trapped! The Story of Floyd Collins.* Lexington: University of Kentucky Press, 1979.

Nally, Flaget M. "Bourbon." In *The Kentucky Encyclopedia.* Edited by John E. Kleber. Lexington: University Press of Kentucky, 1992.

National Park Service. "Convergent Plate Boundaries—Collisional Mountain Ranges." nps.gov/subjects.geology/plate-tectonics-collisional-mountain-ranges.htm. Accessed June 18, 2022.

National Park Service. "Foundation Document Overview, Mammoth Cave National Park." npshistory.com/publications/foundation documents/maca-fd-overview.pdf. Accessed June 29, 2022.

National Park Service. "Index." nps.gov/maca/index.htm. Accessed June 29, 2022.

National Park Service. *Lincoln Boyhood Home at Knob Creek Cultural Landscape Report.* Atlanta: Cultural Resources Division, Southeast Regional Office, NPS, 2013.

Nelson County, Kentucky, Will Book A.

Nevils, Mark E. "Leitchfield." In *The Kentucky Encyclopedia.* Edited by John E. Kleber. Lexington: University Press of Kentucky, 1992.

Noe, Kenneth W. *Perryville: This Grand Havoc of Battle.* Lexington: University Press of Kentucky, 2001.

O'Daniel, Hannah. "Southern Veils: The Sisters of Loretto in Early National Kentucky." Master's Thesis, University of Louisville, 2014. https://doi.org/10.18297/etd/2859. Accessed June 25, 2022.

Ohio County, Kentucky, *Ferry Keepers Bonds, 1857–1936.*

Ohio County, Kentucky, *Tavern Keepers Bonds, 1857–1880.*

O'Malley, Nancy. *A Documentary History of Pitts Point: A River Town in Bullitt County, Kentucky.* Lexington: Program for Cultural Resource Assessment, Department of Anthropology, University of Kentucky, 1996.

O'Malley, Nancy. *The Historic Milling Industry in the Fort Knox Military Reservation: Bullitt, Hardin, and Meade Counties, Kentucky.* Lexington: Program for Cultural Resource Assessment, 1996.

O'Malley, Nancy. "Pottinger's Station." In *The Kentucky Encyclopedia.* Edited by John E. Kleber. Lexington: University Press of Kentucky, 1992.

"Operations Division, U.S. Army Corps of Engineers." www.lrl.usace.aramy.mil/rrl/htm. Aug. 6, 2005.

Owens, M. Lilliana. "The Origin of the Sister of Loretto at the Foot of the Cross." *Filson Club History Quarterly*, July 1965.

Pack, Tom. "Bullitt County." In *The Kentucky Encyclopedia.* Edited by John E. Kleber. Lexington: University Press of Kentucky, 1992.

Palmer, John M. *Personal Recollections of John M. Palmer: The Story of an Earnest Life* Cincinnati: R. Clarke & Co., 1901.

Pearce, John Ed. "Enchanted Forest." *Courier-Journal Magazine*, May 29, 1983.

Pedde, Sara E., and Olaf H. Prufer. "The Kentucky Green River Archaic as Seen from the Ward Site." In *Archaic Transitions in Ohio and Kentucky Prehistory.* Edited by Olaf H. Prufer, Sara E.

Pedde, and Richard S. Meindl. Kent: Kent State University Press, 2001.

Pilgrim Hall Museum. "Thanksgiving 'Over There': Civil War Voices from the Front." www.pilgrimhall.org/cwar.htm. Accessed Jan. 18, 2003.

Potts, Gwynne Tuell, and Samuel W. Thomas. *George Rogers Clark, Military Leader in the Pioneer West, and Locust Grove, the Croghan Homestead Honoring Him.* Louisville: Historic Locust Grove, , 2006.

Puetz, C.J. *Kentucky County Maps.* Lyndon Station, WI, n.d.

Pyatt, Susanna. "Federal Census for Loretto Slaveholding, 1820–1860." lorettocommunity.org/federal-census-evidence-for-loretto-slaveholding-1820–1860/. Accessed June 24, 2022.

R. L. Polk & Company's Kentucky State Gazetteer and Business Directory, 1896, Vol. VII. Detroit: R.L. Polk & Co. 1896.

Ramage, James A. *Rebel Raider: The Life of General John Hunt Morgan.* Lexington: University Press of Kentucky, 1986.

Ramsey, John M. "Rural Electrification." In *The Kentucky Encyclopedia.* Edited by John E. Kleeber. Lexington: University Press of Kentucky, 1992.

Rankin, Hugh F. *George Rogers Clark and the Winning of the West.* Richmond: Virginia Independence Bicentennial Commission, 1976.

Redford, A.H. *The History of Methodism in Kentucky, Vol. I.* Nashville: Southern Methodist Publishing House, 1868.

"Regiments." www.civilwar.nps.gov/cwss/regiments.cfm. Accessed Oct. 23, 2006.

Rennick, Robert M. *Kentucky Place Names.* Lexington: University Press of Kentucky, 1984.

Richey, Nancy. "George Washington's Kentucky Lands." mountvernon.org/library/digitalhistory/digital encyclopedia/article/george-washingtons/kentucky/lands/. Accessed July 2, 2022.

Ridenour, Hugh. "The Greens of Falls of Rough: A Kentucky Family Biography, 1795–1965." Master's Thesis,

Western Kentucky University, 1966. https://digitalcommons.wku.edu/theses/3039. Accessed July 2, 2022.

Ridenour, Hugh A. *The Greens of Falls of Rough.* Hanson, KY: Treetops Enterprises, 1997.

Riley, Thomas W. "Autobiography of Gen. Henry Crist of Kentucky." *Wilderness Road, Quarterly of the Bullitt County Genealogical Society,* Dec. 1999.

Riley, Thomas W. "General Henry Crist's Remains." *Wilderness Road, Quarterly of the Bullitt County Genealogical Society,* Sept. 1990.

Robertson, John E.L. "Hell on the Ohio." *Kentucky Humanities,* Apr. 2007.

Rone, Wendell H. *A History of the Daviess-McLean Baptist Association in Kentucky, 1844–1943.* Owensboro: Messenger Job Printing Co., 1944.

Roosevelt, Franklin D. *The Public Papers and Addresses of Franklin D. Roosevelt. 1938 Volume: The Continuing Struggle for Liberalism.* Compiled by Samuel I. Rosenman. New York: Macmillan, 1941.

Rose, Anthony H. *Alcoholic Beverages.* London: Academic Press, 1977.

Rosenberg, C.G. *Jenny Lind in America.* New York: Stringer and Townsend, 1851.

Rosenberg, Neil V. *Bluegrass: A History.* Champaign: University of Illinois Press, 2005.

Rosenberg, Neil V. "From Sound to Style: The Emergence of Bluegrass." *The Journal of American Folklore,* Apr.–June 1967.

Rosenberg, Neil. V., and Charles K. Wolfe. *The Music of Bill Monroe.* Champaign: University of Illinois Press, 2007.

St. Clair, Burl. "Falls of Rough." Address by Burl St. Clair to Ancestral Trails Historical Society. *Ancestral News: A Publication of Ancestral Trails Historical Society,* July 1996.

St. Clair, Burl. "Grayson County Gleanings. Mordecai Lincoln of Grayson County." *Ancestral News,* Winter 1996.

Salmond, John A. *The Civilian Conservation Corps, 1933–1942: A New Deal Case Study.* Durham: Duke University Press, 1967.

Sandburg, Carl. *Abraham Lincoln: The*

Prairie Years, Volume I. New York: Scribners, 1948.

Sanders, Faye S. *Washington County, Kentucky Deed Abstracts, 1803–1811,* Volume 2. Louisville: F.S. Sanders, 1992.

Schauinger, J. Herman. *Cathedrals in the Wilderness.* Milwaukee: Bruce, 1952.

Schmitzer, Jeanne C. "The Sable Guides of Mammoth Cave." *Filson Club History Quarterly,* Apr. 1993.

Schneider, Grace. "Pitt's Point." July 4, 2004. www.courier-journal.com/reweb/community/placetime/bullitt-pittspoint.html. Accessed Jan. 19, 2014.

Schroeder, Margaret, and Carl Schroeder. *Residents of Nelson County, Virginia (now Kentucky) Recorded in Tithables and Taxlists, 1785–1791, Volume I.* Bardstown, KY: Schroeder, 1988.

Sehlinger, Bob, and Johnny Molloy *A Canoeing and Kayaking Guide to Kentucky.* Menasha Ridge Press, 2011.

Shackelford, Laurel, and Bill Weinberg. *Our Appalachia.* Lexington: University Press of Kentucky, 1988.

Shorer, Nitsan. "The Unlikely Guide Who Mapped Mammoth Cave." *National Geographic,* May 1995.

Sickles, John. *The Legends of Sue Mundy and One Armed Berry.* Merrillville, IN: Heritage Press, 1999.

Sims, Ruth B. Letters to the author. Nov. 10, 1979, Jan. 28, 1980.

Sims, Ruth B. Unpublished ms. "Jacob Van Meter, 1723–1798." Collection of the author.

Sims, Ruth B. Unpublished ms. "The Story of Elizabeth (Rawlings) Hart Gunterman." Collection of the author.

Sipes, Ann Tyson. *The Ray Book.* Louisville: Historical Research, 1993.

Smith, Harry H. *Lincoln and the Lincolns.* New York: Lacoste Printing Co., 1931.

Smith, L. Mayne. "First Bluegrass Festival Honors Bill Monroe." In *The Bill Monroe Reader.* Edited by Tom Ewing. Champaign: University of Illinois Press, 2000.

Smith, Richard D. *Can't You Hear Me Callin': The Life of Bill Monroe.* Boston: Little, Brown, 2000.

Smith, Sarah B. *Historic Nelson County.* Bardstown, KY: Gateway Press, 1971.

"Soldiers." www.civilwar.nps.gov/cwss/soldiers.cfm. Aug. 5, 2006.

Sommers, H.A. *Elizabethtown & Hardin County, Kentucky, 1869–1921.* Elizabethtown: Hardin County Historical Society, 2001.

Spalding, Martin J. *Sketches of the Life and Times and Character of the Right Reverend Benedict Joseph Flaget.* Louisville, KY: Webb & Levering, 1852.

Spalding, Martin J., and Stephen T. Badin. *Sketches of the Early Catholic Missions of Kentucky.* Louisville: B.J. Webb & Brother, 1844.

Speed, Thomas. *The Union Regiments of Kentucky.* Louisville: The Courier-Journal Job Printing Co., 1897

Spencer, J.H. *A History of Kentucky Baptists from 1769 to 1885, Volume 1.* Cincinnati: by the author, 1886.

Stanley, Millie. "John Muir and the Civil War." *John Muir Newsletter,* Fall 2002.

Stout, Charles, and R. Barry Lewis, "Mississippian Towns in Kentucky." In R. Barry Lewis, Charles Stout, Jon Muller, Gerald F. Schroedl, Hypatia Kelly, and John F. Scarry, eds. *Mississippian Towns and Sacred Spaces: Searching for an Architectural Grammar.* Tuscaloosa: University of Alabama Press, 1998.

Sullivan, Lynne P., Bobby R. Braly, Michaelyn S. Harle, and Shannon D. Koerner. "Remembering New Deal Archaeology in the Southeast: A Legacy in Museum Collections." www.lib.utk.edu/newfoundpress/pubs/museums/chp3.pdf. Accessed Feb. 22, 2015.

Sutherland, Daniel E. *A Savage Conflict: The Decisive Role of Guerrillas in the American Civil War.* Chapel Hill: University of North Carolina Press, 2009.

"Swedish Immigrants Pleased in Rugged Kentucky Hill Country." *Echoes from Edmonson County,* Jan., Feb., Mar. 1995.

Tankersley, Kenneth B. ""Ice Age Hunters and Gatherers." In *Kentucky Archaeology—Perspectives on Kentucky's Past: Architecture, Archaeology, and Landscape.* Edited by R. Barry Lewis.

Lexington: University Press of Kentucky, 2014.

Tarbell, Ida M. *The Early Life of Abraham Lincoln.* New York: S.S. McClure, 1896,

Tarbell, Ida M. *In the Footsteps of the Lincolns.* New York: Harper & Brothers, 1924.

Tarbell, Ida M. *The Life of Abraham Lincoln, Volume I.* New York: Lincoln Memorial Association, 1900.

Tarrant, Sergeant E. [Eastham]. *The Wild Riders of the First Kentucky Cavalry.* Lexington: Henry Clay Press, 1969.

Taylor, Bayard. *At Home and Abroad: A Sketch-Book of Life, Scenery, and Men.* New York: G.P. Putnam's Sons, 1889.

Taylor, Harrison D. *Ohio County, Kentucky, in the Olden Days.* Louisville: John P. Morton & Company, 1926.

Taylor, Nick. *American-Made: The Enduring Legacy of the WPA.* New York: Bantam Dell, 2009.

Thomas, John B., Jr. *It Happened Right Here: A History of the Civil War in Nelson County.* N.p., n.d.

Thomas, Samuel W., Eugene H. Conner, and Harold Meloy. "A History of Mammoth Cave, Emphasizing Tourist Development and Medical Experimentation Under Dr. John Croghan." *Register of the Kentucky Historical Society,* Oct. 1970.

Thompson, Bill. *History and Legend of Breckinridge County, Kentucky.* 1976.

Thompson, Ed Porter. *History of the Orphan Brigade.* Louisville: Lewis H. Thompson, 1898.

Thompson, John Wade. "Account of Sarah Mitchell by her son John Wade Thompson Papers found at his death." Mitchell Family File, Kentucky Historical Society, Frankfort, Kentucky

Thompson, Ralph Seymour. *The Sucker's Visit to the Mammoth Cave.* N.p.: by the author, 1879.

Thompson, Victor Dominic "Diversity in Hunter-Gatherer Landscapes in the North American Midcontinent." Master's Thesis, University of Kentucky, 2001. http://uknowledge.uky.edu/gradschool_thesis/186. Accessed Feb. 19, 2015.

Tinsley, Harry D. *History of No Creek,*

Kentucky. Frankfort, KY: Roberts Printing Co., 1953.

Tinsley, Harry D. *Lineage Lines: Newspaper Articles by Harry D. Tinsley, Vols. I—VI, 1972–1998.* Hartford Times-News. Compiled by Helen McKeown.

Trabue, Daniel. *Westward into Kentucky: The Narrative of Daniel Trabue.* Edited by Chester Raymond Young. Lexington: University Press of Kentucky, 1981.

U. S. War Department. *The War of the Rebellion: A Compilation of the Official Records of the Union and Confederate Armies.* 129 volumes. Washington, D.C.: Government Printing Office, 1880–1901.

Underwood, Josie. *Josie Underwood's Civil War Diary.* Edited by Nancy Disher Baird. Lexington: University Press of Kentucky, 2009.

UNESCO. "Mammoth Cave National Park." whc.unesco.org/en/list.150. Accessed July 1, 2022.

United States National Archives. Jacob Van Meter File, No. W8798.

U.S. Army Corps of Engineers. "Nolin River Lake." lrl.usace.army.mil/Missions/Civil-Works/Recreation/Lakes/Nolin-River-Lake/. Accessed June 30, 2022.

U.S. Army Corps of Engineers. *Water Resources Development by the U.S. Army Corps of Engineers in Kentucky.* Vicksburg: Department of the Army, Lower Mississippi Valley Division, 1977.

U.S. Congress. *Congressional Serial Set.* Washington, D.C.: Government Printing Office, 1872.

Van Natter, Francis Marion. "Little Grave on Knob Creek." *National Republic,* Feb. 1934.

Wallace, Tom. "An Early Auto Adventure to the Nolin River Area." *Kentucky Explorer,* May 1988.

Wallace Starling Family Diaries. Collection of the Kentucky Historical Society. Frankfort, KY.

Warren, Elizabeth. "Benjamin Sebastian and the Spanish Conspiracy in Kentucky." *Filson Club History Quarterly,* Apr. 1946.

Warren, Louis A. "Abraham Lincoln, Sr.,

Grandfather of the President." *Filson Club History Quarterly*, Oct. 1935.

Warren, Louis A. *Lincoln's Parentage and Childhood*. New York: The Century Company, 1926.

Warren, Louis A. "The Romance of Thomas Lincoln and Nancy Hanks." *Indiana Magazine of History*, Sept. 1934.

Washington County, Kentucky, Court Order Book A.

Washington County, Kentucky, Court Order Book C.

Wasson, Matt, and Harvard Ayers. "And the Winner Is..." *The Appalachian Voice*. appvoices.org/2004/06/01/2731. Accessed July 14, 2010.

"Water...Death...Disease...Mud." http://www.bullitcountyhistory.com/bchistory/flood1937fifty.html. Accessed Jan. 23, 2014.

Watkins, Sam. *Company Aytch*. New York: Plume, 1999.

Watson, Thomas Shelby. *The Silent Riders*. Louisville: Beechmont Press, 1971.

Watson, Thomas Shelby, with Perry A. Brantley. *Confederate Guerrilla Sue Mundy: A Biography of Kentucky Soldier Jerome Clark*. Jefferson, NC: McFarland, 2008.

Webb, Ben J. *The Centenary of Catholicity in Kentucky*. Louisville: J.C. Webb and Co., 1884

Webb, W.S., and W.D. Funkhouser. *Ancient Life in Kentucky*. Berea: Kentucky Imprints, 1972.

Wells, Dianne, Melba Porter Hay, Dianne Wells, Thomas H. Appleton, Jr. *Roadside History: A Guide to Kentucky Highway Markers*. Lexington: University Press of Kentucky, 2002.

West, Peter. "Trying the Dark: Mammoth Cave and the Racial Imagination, 1839–1869. http://southernspaces.org/2010/trying-dark-mammoth-cave-and-racial-imagination-1839-1869. Accessed Feb. 22, 2015.

White Mills Civic League. White Mills Day Program. July 2, 1977.

Whittle, Charles E. "The Baker Iron Furnace on Nolin." *Echoes From Edmonson County*, Oct., Nov., Dec. 1998.

Widney, Lyman S. *Campaigning With Uncle Billy*. Edited by Robert I. Girandi. Victoria, B.C.: Trafford, 2008.

Wigginton, Eliot, ed. *The Foxfire Book*. New York: Anchor ooks, 1972.

Willington, Eliot. *The Foxfire Book*. New York: Anchor Press/Doubleday, 1972.

Willis, N. Parker. *Health Trip to the Tropics*. New York: Charles Scribner's, 1853.

Wilson, Lafayette. Affidavit, 5 June 1906. Photocopy of original in the files of the Abraham Lincoln Birthplace National Historic Site, Hodgenville, Kentucky.

Wimp, Carolyn, compiler. *Hardin County, Kentucky Newspaper Abstracts, Apr. 1895—Dec. 1901*. Vine Grove: Ancestral Trails Historical Society, 2000.

Wimp, Carolyn, compiler. *Newspaper Abstracts, Hardin County, Kentucky, 1829–1893*. Vine Grove: Ancestral Trails Historical Society, 1999.

Wimp, Carolyn, compiler. *Hardin County, Kentucky Newspaper Abstracts, 1905 to 1907*. Vine Grove: Ancestral Trails Historical Society, 2002.

Winstead, Mrs. T.D. *Chronicles of Hardin County, Kentucky, 1766–1974*. Elizabethtown: Citizens Bank of Elizabethtown, 1974.

Wolfe, Charles K. *Kentucky Country*. Lexington: University Press of Kentucky, 1982.

Wolff, Florence. "Sisters of Loretto." In *The Kentucky Encyclopedia*. Edited by John E. Kleeber. Lexington: University Press of Kentucky, 1992.

Works Progress Administration. *Military History of Kentucky*. Frankfort: The State *Journal*, 1939.

Works Progress Administration. *The WPA Guide to Kentucky*. Edited by F. Kevin Simon. Lexington: University Press of Kentucky, 1996.

Wright, Steven L., compiler. *Kentucky Soldiers and Their Regiments in the Civil War: Abstracted from the Pages of Contemporary Newspapers*. Five volumes. Utica, KY: McDowell Publications, 2009.

Wright, Steven L., compiler. *On Trial for Their Lives: Kentucky's Guerrillas and Military Justice in the Civil War*. N.p.: by the compiler, 2012.

Young, Bennett H. *The Prehistoric Men of Kentucky*. Louisville: John P. Morton and Co., 1910.

Index

273